SELECTED WRITINGS

MERIDIAN

Crossing Aesthetics

Werner Hamacher

Editor

Edited by Thomas Albrecht,
with Georgia Albert and Elizabeth Rottenberg

Introduction by Jacques Derrida

Stanford
University
Press

Stanford
California
2007

SELECTED WRITINGS

Sarah Kofman

Stanford University Press
Stanford, California

© 2007 by the Board of Trustees of the Leland Stanford Junior University. All rights reserved.

No part of this book may be reproduced or transmitted in any form or by any means, electronic or mechanical, including photocopying and recording, or in any information storage or retrieval system without the prior written permission of Stanford University Press.

Printed in the United States of America on acid-free, archival-quality paper

Library of Congress Cataloging-in-Publication Data

Kofman, Sarah.
   [Selections. English. 2007]
   Selected writings / Sarah Kofman ; edited by Thomas Albrecht, with Georgia Albert and Elizabeth Rottenberg ; introduction by Jacques Derrida.
      p. cm.—(Meridian)
   Includes bibliographical references (p.   ).
   ISBN 978-0-8047-3296-3 (cloth : alk. paper)
   ISBN 978-0-8047-3297-0 (pbk. : alk. paper)
   1. Philosophy, French—20th century   I. Albrecht, Thomas, 1965–   II. Albert, Georgia.   III. Rottenberg, Elizabeth, 1969–   IV. Title.

B2430.K642E6 2007
194—dc22   2007025702

Typeset by Westchester Book Group in 10.9/13 Adobe Garamond

Contents

Acknowledgments	IX
Editor's Preface	XI
Thomas Albrecht	
Introduction	1
Jacques Derrida	

PART 1: READING (WITH) FREUD

§ 1	The Double Reading	37
§ 2	The Impossible Profession	56
§ 3	Ça cloche	71

PART 2: NIETZSCHE AND THE SCENE OF PHILOSOPHY

§ 4	The Evil Eye	99
§ 5	Scorning Jews: Nietzsche, the Jews, Anti-Semitism	123

PART 3: WITH RESPECT TO WOMAN

§ 6	From *The Enigma of Woman: Woman in Freud's Writings*	159

§ 7 The Economy of Respect: Kant and
     Respect for Women   187

PART 4: THE TRUTH IN PAINTING

§ 8 The Melancholy of Art   205

§ 9 The Resemblance of Portraits: Imitation
     According to Diderot   218

§ 10 Conjuring Death: Remarks on *The Anatomy
     Lesson of Doctor Nicolas Tulp* (1632)   237

PART 5: JUDAISM AND ANTI-SEMITISM /
AUTOBIOGRAPHY

§ 11 *Shoah* (or Dis-grace)   245

§ 12 Autobiographical Writings   247
     Damned Food 247   Tomb for a Proper Name 248
     Post-scriptum—1992 249   "My Life" and
     Psychoanalysis 250   Nightmare: At the Margins
     of Medieval Studies 251

     Notes   255

     Contributors   297

Acknowledgments

The editors would like to thank Chris Lewis and Philip Leider, for the inspired idea of putting together an anthology of Sarah Kofman's writings and for their contributions to the early stages of this project; Werner Hamacher, editor of the Meridian Series at Stanford University Press; Elizabeth Constable; all the translators who prepared the translations especially commissioned for this volume (Jennifer Bajorek, Pascale-Anne Brault, Ben Elwood, Patience Moll, Michael Naas, and Ann Smock), for their attentive and thoughtful responses to Kofman's prose and for their patience and understanding during the years it took to compile this collection; Jacques Derrida, for the gift of his untitled eulogy for Sarah Kofman, which serves as the introduction; Alexandre Kyritsos, Sarah Kofman's companion and literary executor, for his stated enthusiasm about this project and for permissions; Megan Holt, M. J. Severson, and Megan M. Haissig at Tulane University, for their work as research assistants; Santhosh Daniel, former editorial assistant at Stanford University Press, for all his help and good humor; production editors Mariana Raykov at Stanford University Press and Deborah Masi; Julie Palmer-Hoffman, for her careful and conscientious copy editing; Emily-Jane Cohen, Assistant Editor at Stanford University Press; and Norris Pope, Director of Scholarly Publishing at Stanford University Press, for helping to bring this project, as Sarah Kofman might have said, to term. Finally and foremost, we thank Helen Tartar, editor during the formative stages of the project, for her guidance and her often expressed belief in the timeliness and relevance of this book.

"The Impossible Profession," "Ça cloche," "The Evil Eye," "Scorning Jews," "The Melancholy of Art," and "The Resemblance of Portraits" are translated from the original French and published by permission of Éditions Galilée. "The Double Reading," from *The Childhood of Art* (Copyright © 1988 by Columbia University Press), is reprinted with the permission of the publisher. The excerpt from *The Enigma of Woman: Woman in Freud's Writings* (translated by Catherine Porter, translation copyright © 1985 by Cornell University) is used by permission of the publisher, Cornell University Press. "The Economy of Respect: Kant and Respect for Women," originally from *Le respect des femmes* (Paris: Galilée, 1982), is reprinted from the English translation by permission of *Social Research* from *Social Research* 49.2 (1982): 383–404. In Chapter 12, the texts entitled "Damned Food," "Tomb for a Proper Name," and "Nightmare: At the Margins of Medieval Studies" originally appeared in *SubStance* 49 (Copyright © 1986) and are reprinted by permission of The University of Wisconsin Press. All previously published translations have been slightly modified to conform to the conventions of style and usage prescribed by Stanford University Press. "Conjuring Death," "*Shoah* (or Dis-grace)," and, in Chapter 12, the texts entitled "Post-scriptum—1992" and " 'My Life' and Psychoanalysis" are translated and published by permission of Alexandre Kyritsos. The volume introduction is translated and published by permission of Jacques Derrida.

Editor's Preface
Thomas Albrecht

The diversity and extensiveness of Sarah Kofman's body of work make choosing essays and book excerpts that would be somehow representative an impossible task, in some ways not unlike the impossible tasks of the art critic and the psychoanalyst Kofman has written about. And as we learn from Kofman herself, to make claims for the exemplarity or special significance of particular texts in an author's oeuvre, over and above other texts, is always a suspect gesture to begin with, and is usually destined in one or another way to fail. It is suspect insofar as it implies on the part of the anthologist the would-be "gesture of mastery" that Kofman so frequently finds in the texts she writes about. And it is destined to fail insofar as it is often the seemingly insignificant or marginal texts and passages in an author's body of work, rather than those texts and passages commonly regarded as paradigmatic or central, that prove to be the most telling about that author, as Kofman repeatedly demonstrates in her readings. So our task as editors of an anthology entitled *Selected Writings of Sarah Kofman*, given everything that such a title conventionally implies, puts us into a double bind: between a demand and a necessary suspicion of that demand, between the demand and the impossibility of being able properly to fulfill it.

In making our selections, what we have done, therefore, is to relinquish any overt claims to exemplarity or comprehensiveness. We have chosen for inclusion in this volume a series of texts that speak in one or more ways to six topics with which Kofman's work has been in particular identified by its readers, and with which her work has in particular identified itself: (1) Freud's writings; (2) Nietzsche's writings; (3) the figure of woman in

Western philosophy and metaphysics; (4) visual art and aesthetic theory; (5) Judaism and Anti-Semitism in European history, literature, and philosophy; and (6) autobiography. We have divided the book into five sections corresponding to these six topics and then assigned several texts to each section. Some of the included texts are taken from existing English-language publications and may thus already be familiar to readers of Kofman in translation. However, most of the materials in this book have been translated into English for the first time.

The book's opening section, entitled "Reading (with) Freud," presents the aspect of Kofman's work that is perhaps most familiar to her English-language readers, given that much of it is available in translation: her engagement with psychoanalysis in general and with Freud's writings in particular. Its first two selections are "The Double Reading" and "The Impossible Profession," the introductory chapters of two monographs on Freud: *L'enfance de l'art: Une interprétation de l'esthétique freudienne* (1970), Kofman's first book; and *Un métier impossible: Lecture de "Constructions en analyse"* (1983).[1] The former is excerpted from *The Childhood of Art: An Interpretation of Freud's Aesthetics*, a 1988 translation of *L'enfance de l'art*, while the latter, the introduction to a book-length study of Freud's metapsychological writings, appears in English for the first time. The third selection in this section, "Ça cloche," a 1981 essay on sexual difference and the undecidable economy of fetishism in texts by Freud and Jacques Derrida, appeared in translation in 1989 and is republished here in a new translation.[2]

The book's second section, "Nietzsche and the Scene of Philosophy," is an obvious choice as companion and follow-up to the first section, given that Kofman returned to Nietzsche's texts as often as she did to Freud's, and far more frequently than to any other topic she wrote about. It contains two previously untranslated works: "The Evil Eye," an essay on Schopenhauer's and Nietzsche's divergent views of tragedy and their far-reaching implications, taken from Kofman's 1979 book, *Nietzsche et la scène philosophique*; and "Scorning Jews: Nietzsche, the Jews, Anti-Semitism," a longer text originally published in 1994 in book form under the title *Le mépris des Juifs: Nietzsche, les Juifs, l'antisémitisme*. The latter is a relevant and timely contribution by Kofman to the ongoing debate about Nietzsche's anti-Semitism and relation to Judaism, and we are especially pleased that this text, long overdue for publication in translation, has now been made available to English-language readers.[3]

The book's third section, "With Respect to Woman," also presents an aspect of Kofman's work that is comparatively well known to English-language readers, especially to readers in the fields of feminist theory and Women's Studies. The first selection is an excerpt from another monograph on Freud, *The Enigma of Woman: Woman in Freud's Writings*, a 1985 translation of *L'énigme de la femme: la femme dans les textes de Freud* (1980). The second piece, entitled "The Economy of Respect: Kant and Respect for Women," an essay on the figure of woman in Kant's texts on sublimity and the moral law, is a previously published translation of a chapter from Kofman's 1982 book, *Le respect des femmes (Kant et Rousseau)*.[4]

The book's fourth section, "The Truth in Painting," introduces work on visual art and portraiture, a particular area of interest for Kofman toward the end of her career. In contrast to the material included in the previous sections, this work is likely to be unfamiliar to most readers of this anthology, as very little of it has thus far been translated. The section includes two chapters from Kofman's 1985 book, *Mélancolie de l'art*, "The Melancholy of Art" and "The Resemblance of Portraits: Imitation According to Diderot," and concludes with Kofman's last text: "Conjuring Death: Remarks on *The Anatomy Lesson of Doctor Nicolas Tulp* (1632)," an incomplete fragment of an essay on Rembrandt on which Kofman had been working at the time of her death in 1994, which also appears in English translation for the first time.[5]

The book's final section, "Judaism and Anti-Semitism / Autobiography," contains a poem by Kofman on needful memory and potential obliteration of the Holocaust as well as a series of five short autobiographical texts, here brought together for the first time, several of which speak specifically to Kofman's childhood experiences during the Holocaust and to her Judaism.[6]

As readers at all familiar with her work are aware, Kofman's way of quoting from the texts she writes about is informal, inconsistent, and idiosyncratic. More than a few quotations are not attributed, or only very generally attributed, to source texts, and some are incorrectly attributed. In addition, Kofman sometimes modifies the lines and passages she quotes, in accordance with her specific purpose or meaning or with her memory of the texts she is discussing. In the translations that were prepared specifically for this volume, the translators and editors have attempted to identify as many of the unattributed quotations as we were able, quoting from and giving reference to existing English translations whenever possible. In some cases, we have modified the quoted translation, in accordance with Kofman's version of the passage in question, or with her meaning. In cases where no English translation exists, we have whenever possible translated from and made reference to an identified foreign-language source. Any attributions by Kofman of quotations to incorrect page, section, or volume numbers in a given source text have been silently corrected; the occasional attributions of quotations to incorrect source texts have been marked as such and corrected. In our translations of Kofman's notes, we have, for reasons of space, limited ourselves to making reference to existing English translations. In the absence of any English translation, we have kept the original foreign-language reference, supplying full publication information and page numbers where possible. The previously published translations included in this volume have been left largely unaltered, except that we have updated their notes so as to identify previously unidentified references, and so as to refer to any English translations of Kofman's sources (including her own texts) that have appeared since the translations' original publication. Any inaccuracies in the notes and references have been silently corrected.

The intentional tentativeness of this book's structure should be noted. The five topical sections to which the individual selections have been assigned are meant to be entirely provisional categories. Although their use is of course a standard convention for organizing an anthology like this one, they are also susceptible to—and symptomatic of—all the limitations inherent in such a convention: the limitations inherent, for example, in the assumption of certain thematic categories (over and above others), in the assumption of categories as such, and in the accompanying reduction of complexities and specificities. We intend them to be taken as similar to what Freud calls *constructions*, or to what Kofman calls *speculations*: fictions whose function and very being is provisional and whose durability and self-identity is always open to question. It will be obvious to readers that most of the selections included in this book could be classified under several of the organizing rubrics, and that all of them speak to more than just a single topic and to more than their most manifest topic. In addition, the selections directly and indirectly speak to and echo one another across the topical lines between them, among other ways through explicitly shared formulations, motifs, themes, metaphors, and references. In making the selections that we did, we have therefore tried to bring out not only the richness and heterogeneity of Sarah Kofman's body of work, but also its surprising coherence. We encourage readers of this book to take as their guide Jacques Derrida's insistence in his introduction that we

> take into account, each time we evoke a theme or motif in the work of Sarah Kofman, the intertwining threads that weave and displace the insistence on a motif in the long series of books, each very different but each bearing in itself the metonymic reference to all the others, in what is a sort of open quasi system, a coherent network that is nonetheless without closure, at once consistent and structurally interminable, an incomplete–incompletable seriality.

SELECTED WRITINGS

Introduction
Jacques Derrida

At first I did not know—and in fact still do not know—what title to give to these words.

What is the gift of a title?

I even had the fleeting suspicion that such a gift would be somewhat indecent: it would imply the violent selection of a perspective, an abusive interpretative framing or narcissistic reappropriation, a conspicuous signature there where it is Sarah Kofman, Sarah Kofman alone, Sarah Kofman herself, *over there* [*là-bas*],[1] beyond here, well beyond me or us here and now, Sarah Kofman who should be spoken about and whom I hear speaking.

Sarah Kofman

would then be the best title, were I not afraid of being unable to measure up to it.

Finally—since the question remains that of the gift and of what it means to give a title—it seemed to me more just to speak, and for just this reason, of the gift in Sarah Kofman, of her gifts: those she gave us, those she left us, and those she, too, perhaps received.

The title would then be

Sarah Kofman's Gifts

And here are a few possible subtitles, to give you some idea of what I would like to say:

Here There
Open Book, Closed Book
Protestations

Here and there, we find the body and we find the book, the open book and the closed book. And protestations. Between the two, between here and there, between the body and the book, between the open book and the closed one, there would be, here and there, the third, the witness, the *terstis*, testimony, attestation, and testament—but in the form of protest or protestation.

I

One wonders what is taking place. One wonders what a place is, the right or just place, and what placement is, or displacement, or replacement. One wonders about such things insofar as a book always comes to take the place of the body, insofar as it has always tended to replace the proper body, and the sexed body, to become its name even, and occupy its place, to serve in place of this occupant, and insofar as we collaborate with this substitution, lending or giving ourselves over to it, for this is all we ever really do, we are this, we like this, and each word speaks volumes for lending itself from the very first moment to this spiriting away of the proper body, as if already at the behest of the proper body in question, following its paradoxical desire, its impossible desire, the desire to interrupt itself, to interrupt itself in sexual difference, interrupt itself as sexual difference.

What is a place, then, a right or just place when everything seems to be ordered, and seems to begin, by the mourning of this replacement?

What is a just place when everything takes place and takes its place as if the dying wish of the so-called proper, or lived, or living body—for when I say "body," I mean the living body as well as the sexed body—as if the supreme affirmation of this headstrong living being were this testament, the oldest and the newest: "this is my body," "keep it in memory of me," and so, "replace it, in memory of me, with a book or discourse to be bound in hide or put into digital memory. Transfigure me into a *corpus*. So that there will no longer be any difference between the place of real presence or of the Eucharist and the great computerized library of knowledge."

This great eucharistic paradigm was first of all, and perhaps will always remain, what is proper to man, I mean to the son or the father. For is this not a scene of men? No doubt, as long, that is, as we keep to the visibility of the scene.

We will perhaps talk later about the veil of a certain Last Supper scene, I mean the Last Supper [*Cène*] of the Holy Table. We will touch upon the veil of modesty that it lays out or barely lifts over sexual difference, from the promise and the gift of the body, the "this is my body and keep it in memory of me," right up to the laying in the tomb and the Resurrection.

Sarah Kofman knew this; she thought it, I believe, and analyzed it—but she protested, yes, she no doubt protested with all the strength of a living irredentist against this movement to which, like all of us, and from the very first day, she had to succumb. It is of this protestation that I would like to speak, Sarah Kofman's protestation, such as I hear it and believe myself, in my own way, to share in it.

I am not sure I have the right to assume you would know this, but you should be aware that Sarah Kofman was for me, in her own way, and for more than twenty years, a great friend. Yes, in her own way, but I was her friend in my own way, too. I will not be able to speak of our own way, which was certainly different, nor of our ways toward one another, whether good or bad. But were we not the only ones, she and I, and am I not the only one today to know, if not to understand, something about this?

What we shared within the public space, for instance in places of publication, had to do first with the exercises and interests, the aims and challenges of philosophy, of thinking, teaching, reading, and writing. These interests and exercises go so far beyond the limits of a short narrative, indeed of a terminable analysis, that I will not even attempt to speak of them. Those interested will find innumerable small signs in our respective publications. These remains are little more than elliptical greetings, sometimes just a wink; they remain to be interpreted by anyone, including myself, for I am not always certain from where I stand today that I am still able to decipher them.

I have spent the past few weeks rereading certain of Sarah's texts with the feeling, the certainty even, that for me everything still remains to come and to be understood.

But there is no longer any doubt: such testimonies survive us, incalculable in their number and meaning.

They survive us. Already they survive us, keeping the last word—and keeping silent.

But the place of a survivor is unlocatable. If such a place were ever located, it would remain untenable, unbearable, I would almost say deadly. And if it appeared tenable, the speech to be held or the word to be kept there would remain impossible. Such speech or such a word is thus also untenable—unbearable.

The word kept untenable, held to be unbearable [*parole dé-tenue intenable*].

In a text that I shall cite later, Sarah speaks of a "secret" that is held (a "secret they would hold," she says, the "they" being "doctors," men of science, appointed physicians), and it is the secret of a life, of life, of what she calls "an opening onto life."²

How does one give an account of the secret of what is held or kept and so refuses itself in this way? The question is all the more formidable insofar as this unlocatable double, the place *to hold* and the speech *to be held* or the word *to be kept*, the experience of what is twice *held untenable*, is at the same time the most common experience of friendship.

There is nothing exceptional about this.

From the first moment, friends become, as a result of their situation, virtual survivors, actually virtual or virtually actual, which amounts to just about the same thing. Friends know this, and friendship breathes this knowledge, breathes it right up to expiration, right up to the last breath. These possible survivors thus see themselves held to the untenable. Held to the impossible as possible impossible survivors, so that some might be tempted to conclude from this that friends are impossible people.

We are that, we were that. I will talk a great deal, here again today, of the impossible. And of the impossible between Sarah and me.

Impossible: that is no doubt what we were for one another, Sarah and I. Perhaps more than others or in some other way, in innumerable ways that I will not be able to recount here, considering all the scenes in which we found ourselves together, all the scenes we made before one another. I sometimes catch myself again making a scene before her, in order to catch up with her, and I smile at this sign of life, of the life in which I am no doubt still obscurely trying to keep her, that is, keep her alive. To "conjure death," as she says in her last text—which implies both conjuring it up and conjuring it away, to summon ghosts and chase them away, always in the name of life, to summon and chase away, and thus to pursue the other as the other dead. As if I were making yet another scene before her in response to hers, just so as to make things last long enough to say to her: you see, life goes on, it is still the same old story. . . .

But because it is all about "being impossible" here, perhaps we must accept this side of things. That is, if we can. We cannot say everything—it would be impossible to say everything about Sarah, what she was, what she thought and wrote, to say everything about a work whose richness, force, and necessity the future will never cease to appreciate. We can only accept this side of things [*en prendre son parti*] and take up sides [*prendre parti*].

I am thus taking up this side of things by taking a side—the side of Sarah.

So here would be another title:

Sarah's Side

Taking a side, then, within this side of things, I finally chose to speak of the art of Sarah. Her art—and this is the side on which I will wager—will have given me the chance to take sides.

I will thus speak of her art but also of her laughter—indissociably. We would thus have two additional subtitles.

Since the death of Sarah—and I owe it to her, as I owe it to the truth, to say this, assuming that I might at last be able to do so—since the death of Sarah—and what a death—it has been impossible for me to speak as I knew I wanted to, impossible to speak *to her*, *to* her, as one does without pretending to friends who have disappeared, impossible also to speak *of* her, as other friends, who are also mine, have known how to do—and have done so well, and were so right to do.

I thus had to try to relearn everything, and I am still at it.

Let us then not hasten to think of mourning, of an impossible mourning. For we would then run the risk of missing, or actually we would not fail to miss, under some clinical category, some general type of mourning—to which a certain guilt is always associated—this incisive, singular, and unappeasable suffering that I simply could not bear, precisely out of friendship, to transfer onto someone else, and even less onto some conceptual generality that would not be Sarah, Sarah Kofman herself.

For me, too, of course, Sarah was unique.

And even if I were still to blame her for my suffering, at least it would be her, and her alone, who would be implicated, and that is my first concern here. There would be nothing very new in this, for over the course of twenty years of a tender, tense, and sometimes stormy friendship, of, dare I say, an impossible friendship, impossible right up to the end, we often blamed one another. She would make fun of me, she in me would once more take me to task, were I to try to deny, transfigure, sublimate, or idealize this long story.

Against such a lie, she would once again be right.

Among all the things we shared (I have already said that I would not be able to count them, and besides, the texts bear witness to them to a certain point), there was this protestation (a word I prefer to accusation), of which I would like to let something be heard through her laughter and her art.

I will thus venture a few words to try to say what I believe I can hear through her art and her laughter, as well as through her interpretation of both art and laughter, which, it seems to me, carries through all her work and, from her body, carries all the books in the great body of work she has left us.

According to the hypothesis I am going to put before you, Sarah interpreted laughter like an artist, she laughed like an artist but also laughed at art, like an artist and in the name of life, not without knowing that neither art nor laughter saves us from pain, anxiety, illness, and death. For she knew these things better than anyone else: pain, anxiety, illness—and death. Art and laughter, when they go together, do not run counter to suffering, they do not ransom or redeem it, but live off it; as for salvation, redemption, and resurrection, the absence of any illusion shines like a ray of living light through all of Sarah's life and work. We will later hear a few of her texts that say this better than I can right now. This ray of living light concerns the absence of salvation, through an art and a laughter that, while promising neither resurrection nor redemption, nonetheless remain necessary. With a necessity to which we must yield. This ray of living light was her lucidity and what I was tempted to call, a moment ago, by analogy, her irredentism, right up to the end, and even through the end.

Her art and her laughter, themselves indissociable, were also indissociably interpretations of art and laughter. Her interpretations were not only readings or theoretical acts but affirmations, themselves art and laughter, and always affirmations of life. When I insist that they were not only readings but also acts and experience itself, my point is not to exclude reading from this. For reading was always on the part of Sarah a firm, unconditional, uncompromising, unrelenting, and implacable demand.

Implacable interpretations, implacable like Nietzsche and Freud, for example, and all those pitiless doctors of arts and of laughter whom she cited and summoned to appear and speak, inexhaustibly, sometimes against themselves, in truth protesting always against themselves, and against one another, while laughing it up.

For she, too, was without pity, if not without mercy, in the end, for both Nietzsche and Freud, whom she knew and whose bodies of work she had read inside and out. Like no one else in this century, I dare say. She loved them pitilessly and was implacable toward them (not to mention a few others) at the very moment when, giving them without mercy all that she could, and all that she had, she was inheriting from them and was keeping watch over what they had—what they still have—to tell us, especially regarding art and laughter.

Art and laughter were also for her, no doubt, readings of art and of laughter, but these readings were also operations, experiences or experiments, journeys. These readings [*lectures*] were *lessons* in the magisterial sense of an exemplary lecturing or teaching (and Sarah was a great professor, as so many students throughout the world can testify); they were lessons of the lesson in the sense of an exemplary teaching, lessons in the course of which, life never being interrupted, the teacher experiments: she unveils in the act, through experimentation and performance, giving the example of what she says through what she does, giving of her person, as we say, with nothing held back, throwing herself into it headlong, body and soul. The truth being in the symptom.

One of these lessons of the lesson given by Sarah is, for example, that this tormented being laughed a lot, as her friends know, like a little girl shaken by the irresistible joy of uncontrollable laughter on the verge of tears, a little girl whose kept secret does not age and whose tragedies have not stifled the freshness and sparkle of her innocent laughter.

Another of these lessons of the lesson given by Sarah is that she not only talked about art, painting, and drawing in others—or interpreted by others, such as Nietzsche or Freud—but painted and drew as well. And among all the things that she gave me, which I keep and keep looking at, there are some of these works.

And then, and those who knew her well know this, Sarah laughed a lot even when she did not laugh, and even when, as was often the case—and others here can also bear witness to this—she did not laugh at all. For she did not laugh everyday, as you know—indeed, it was quite often the opposite—but even then she was still laughing—and right away, both during and after. I want to believe that she laughed right up to the end, right up to the very last second.

She would cry *for laughs*—that is my thesis or hypothesis.

I would thus like to imagine that all the meditation we see at work in her work might resemble a long reverie on everything that might be meant by the expressions "for laughs" and "to cry for laughs," following the

Nietzschean–Freudian interpretation of laughter, on the edge of anxiety, on the edge of the conscious and unconscious ends of laughter, of what is done for laughs, in view of laughing, by virtue of laughing, by virtue of laughter's apotropaic economy or economy of drives (I will come back to this in relation to Freud's *Jokes and Their Relation to the Unconscious* and Sarah's book *Pourquoi rit-on?* [*Why Do We Laugh?*][3]—yes, why do we laugh, and why do we cry?), right up to the post-Platonic or nonmetaphysical structure of fiction or the simulacrum, of what has worth only "for laughs," for example, the simulacrum in art and in literature.

2

In what sense were these great lessons of art and laughter affirmations of life for Sarah?

The affirmation of life is nothing other than a certain thought of death; it is neither opposition nor indifference to death—indeed one would almost say the opposite, if this were not giving in to opposition.

I take as testimony, and as a sign, even before beginning, Sarah's last text, "Conjuring Death," published after her death by Alexandre Kyritsos in *La part de l'oeil*. Like others, perhaps, I am tempted to approach Sarah's last text today so as to take by surprise, in some sense, but also to make linger these last words leaving her lips, to make them resonate with her first words, as I will later do, and to hear in them a final confidence imparted or confided to us—and notice I am not saying a last wish or last word.

Something for which we must be responsible, a confident confidence barely veiled, to which we should also respond or correspond.

This very beautiful text is unfinished. A sketch, then, brought to term—interminably, as if a sign of life. It begins with a sentence of just a couple of words, an *incipit* that fits on one line alone, it alone on the line:

"It is a lesson."

It is a lesson, she says.

She is talking about *The Anatomy Lesson of Doctor Nicolas Tulp* (1632), by Rembrandt. Sarah interprets in this painting the strange historical relationship between the book and the body, between the book and the proper or lived body of the mortal, to be sure, but also between the book and the body of the body or corporation of doctors gathered there, a body whose gaze is completely occupied by the book rather than by the body.

There is too much to say about this text, so I will choose just a few themes, three or four, to let them speak to us today—of Sarah, from Sarah, mixing my words with hers. I read this both posthumous and living—so very living—text as an ironic autobiography of Sarah Kofman, her *autobiogriffure*, her auto-bi-claw-graphy, as she would have said, but also as a painting that has been re-painted and de-picted by her own hand.

It is, in the first place, the story or history of a preference for the book. We can there follow the narrative of a historical fascination with the book when it comes to occupy the place of the dead, of the body cadaver. Actually, I prefer the English word *corpse* here because it incorporates at once the body [*le corps*], the corpus, and the cadaver, and because, when read in French, *la corpse* seems to put the body in the feminine and to become an allusion to sexual difference, if not a respect for it.

Une corpse: here would be the subject; there would be the object.

I say "*historical* fascination" or "*history* of a preference" for the book because all this belongs to a history. It is precisely a reading of this history that this lesson on a lesson offers us.

For what does Sarah Kofman tell us of this corpse in *The Anatomy Lesson*? That this image of the corpse is *replaced* or *displaced*, its *place taken* by the book (as seems to be happening to us at this very instant), replaced–displaced by a "book wide open at the foot of the deceased." This open book organizes: an organ detached from the body, it has an organizing mission. Detached from the body, this quasi organ, this corpus, in turn organizes space. In an at once centripetal and centrifugal fashion. Decentered with regard to the body, as you look at the body, it centers or recenters in turn a new magnetic field; it irradiates it but also capitalizes on it and captures all the forces of the painting. An open book attracts all the gazes.

This book [Translators' Note: *lui*—masculine pronoun] stands up to, and stands in for, the body: a corpse replaced by a corpus, a corpse yielding its place to the bookish thing, the doctors having eyes only for the book facing them, as if, by reading, by observing the signs on the drawn sheet of paper, they were trying to forget, repress, deny, or conjure away death—and the anxiety before death.

Sarah Kofman remarks on this fascinated repression and insists firmly on it—the difference being barely perceptible between a fascinated repression and the repression of a fascination. Perhaps fascination has in fact a privileged relationship with *la corpse*, with the possibility of the cadaver of a sexual difference, of sexual difference as cadaver. One would have to inquire once again, from this point of view, into what Blanchot analyzes under the words "fascination," "remains," "cadaverous presence," and "cadaverous resemblance" in "The Two Versions of the Imaginary" (*The Space of Literature*).[4]

But instead of seeing here a simple negativity of *distraction* (negation, denegation, lie, occultation, dissimulation), Sarah Kofman seems to sense in this repression, in a no doubt very Nietzschean fashion, a cunning affirmation of life, its irrepressible movement to *survive*, to *live on* [*sur-vivre*], to get the better of itself in itself, to lie by telling its truth of life, to affirm this truth of life through the symptom of repression, to express the irrepressible as it is put to the test of repression, to get, in a word, the better of life, that is to say, of death, giving an account of life: to defeat death by affirming a "hold on the truth of life," a "science of life and its mastery."

There would thus be a secret of life. Life would hold the secret of the secret, and all secrets would keep life alive. For the claim over such a secret, even if it is not justified, even if it is merely an allegation of anguished scholars, could still be read as a redoubled affirmation of life.

Lessons given: what this lesson on the *Lesson*, this physiological lesson on a lesson of anatomy, gives us would be not only a diagnosis concerning a repression or a denegation (later on, we will also talk about a "conjuring" and a "conspiracy"), not only a thesis on the historicity of this repression and this denegation, but an at least implicit interpretation of the very concepts of repression and denegation, an interpretation of their ultimate function, of the ultimate meaning of their strategy. Under their negative or oppositional appearance, through their grammatical or strategic negativity, repression, suppression, and denegation would be in the service of an affirmation of life. Repression would be yet another ruse of affirmation, a *trop* [*too much*] and a *trope*, an excess and a figure of the "yes" to life, a number or figure of the *amor fati*. The science of life would itself be an art of living; it would have come from, and would take part in, an art of life. The side or part taken by the artist, the art of the painter (like that of the interpreter), would consist in interpreting the truth of this art of life.

The invincible force of this art of life, a force that is at once irreducible, irredentist, its time literally interminable, even in death, at the moment of death, the élan of an art that is at once all powerful and, in the end, powerless, given to failure, frustrated before what is called death itself, this impotence of the all powerful, this ineffectiveness of an all powerful that refuses to let up even though it is really nothing—that is what invites a good laugh: it is truly comical, is it not, laughable, crazy, off the wall, and we can receive from it, as a lesson, the inheritance of an art of living that knows a thing or two about the art of laughter.

That is at least what I think I hear in the following passage, which mentions *life* three times in this place where *book, cadaver, corpus,* and *corpse* exchange places.

> They have before them not a subject but an object, a purely technical instrument that one of them manipulates in order to get a hold on the truth of *life*. The dead man and the opening of his body are seen only insofar as they provide an opening onto *life*, whose secret they would hold. The fascination is displaced, and with this displacement, the anxiety is repressed, the intolerable made tolerable, from the sight of the cadaver to that of the book wide open at the foot of the deceased, who might now serve as a lectern.
>
> This opening of the book in all its light points back to the opening of the body. For the book alone allows the body to be deciphered and invites the passage from the exterior to the interior. It is this book (and the opening it provides onto the science of *life* and its mastery) that attracts the gazes, much more even than does the point of the scissors that has begun to peel away the skin from the body stretched out there. (My emphases)

Sarah Kofman thus says "displacement" of an "anxiety repressed" and the "intolerable made tolerable." In numerous texts, too numerous to cite and analyze here, Sarah Kofman has thoroughly examined the question of the relationship among laughter, jokes, and the economy of repression, the complicated symptomatology of repressed anxiety. She did so in the wake of a Freud whose work she interpreted without concession or complacency, particularly in *Pourquoi rit-on? Freud et le mot d'esprit*, this magnificent book to which I said I would return shortly and with which I will, in fact, conclude. As for "the intolerable made tolerable," I might be tempted to read this economical formulation, this formulation of economy itself, as, if you will allow me, the anticipated description or prognosis–diagnosis of what we are doing here: to make the intolerable tolerable by looking toward books, toward Sarah's great book in so many volumes, in order to turn away from her. But at the risk of persisting in this guilty turning away and of making the offense even more serious, all the while cultivating memory, I read this formulation of a last text ("the intolerable made tolerable") as a quasi self-citation of Sarah herself: ten years earlier, in *Mélancolie de l'art* [The Melancholy of Art], she used the same formulation in a paragraph that I would also like to cite, as a citation within the citation:

> And what if the beauty that hides the evanescent aspect of all things were itself ephemeral? The decline of what makes the intolerable tolerable [here are the words that echo a decade later in the formulation I just read] would cause vertigo and disarray. This refusal of the mourning of beauty reveals the cathartic function of art, which is as mystifying as that of the speculative, a mirror capturing images that are too devastating, unbearable. To break with everything in art that responds to our desire for eternity is to dislocate the space of representation and meaning; it is to invent a space of indetermination and play—to open up a wholly other space. Thus beauty is never exempt from melancholy: it fails to get over philosophy, to get over mourning it, it cries over the collapse of meaning, the loss of reference and discourse, the "sacrifice" of the subject and the object. (back cover, signed S. K.)[5]

The "logic" of this argument is twisted. Its spiral frustrates every attempt at getting a grasp on it.

In the first place, there is a demystification. It cruelly lays bare a cathartic function, the sublimation at work in art or in the experience of beauty. It dissects everything that makes the *intolerable tolerable*. This cathartic function of the fine arts [*beaux-arts*] is "as mystifying as that of the speculative," and thus of philosophy, or at least of a certain knowledge on the subject of philosophy. This insistence on associating the speculative and art, on seeing in them the same mystification to be demystified, the same cathartic function, the same purifying denegation, the same occultation to be undone, can be found once again ten years later, in Sarah's last text, the one with which we began, "Conjuring Death: Remarks on *The Anatomy Lesson of Dr. Nicolas Tulp* (1632)." We find there, for example, this sentence, which I will read again later, but differently: "The lesson of this *Anatomy Lesson* is thus not that of a *memento mori*; it is not that of a triumph of death but of a triumph over death; and this is due not to the life of an illusion, but to that of the speculative, whose function, too, is one of occultation."

In the second place, the same demystification targets the melancholy of art or of beauty: an inability to get over or be done with mourning, the very failure of mourning that it nonetheless endures.

But, in the third place, and especially—and this is for me the most important point, the most difficult argument—the consequence that Sarah Kofman draws from this double demystification is not the injunction to get over mourning this impossible mourning, not to abandon art, beauty, or the speculative. Quite the contrary. In breaking with the "desire for eternity" that engenders at once mourning and the impossibility of mourning, mourning and melancholy, *it is necessary*—and here is the injunction or, at least, the necessity, in the most enigmatic, most fatalistic, sense of this term—*it is necessary "to invent."*

It is necessary to invent, but what? Something with which to play and over which to laugh as an artist. *It is necessary* here implies at once lack or mourning *and* joyous necessity: "to invent" "a space of indetermination and play," "to open up a wholly other space"—there where place is lacking, where the place is already taken, where there is only replacement.

A space of indetermination and play, a wholly other space. This is what she tells us, what she asks us, as what remains, but remains "to be invented." This other space would not be deserted by the beautiful; it would not be a desert of art and beauty. It would open the way to another affirmation, other but older, more ancient; and since it, too, remains to come, this affirmation is also younger than everything it endures, through, and thus beyond, if this is possible, the experience of an impossible mourning become possible.

A mourning of mourning or a mourning without mourning, therefore. An affirmation that no doubt passes through a denegation of denegation, with all its symptomatology, but a laughing affirmation of life that does not let itself be overcome by the negative logic—the doubly negative or dialectical logic—of this double denegation.

Here is, I think, were I to risk formalizing it in such a dry, cold, abstract form, Sarah Kofman's logic, the one that is insistently working through and over her entire oeuvre: a laughing affirmation as an art of life that does not let itself be overcome by the denegation of denegation but endures it right up to the end. No matter how much you try to deny, and to deny denegation, the negative of denegation never wins out, and neither does dialectic, only an invincible affirmation whose desire can never be denied [*se dément*].

Or if you prefer, here is what happens to what we assume can be called desire: *desire denies, like crazy* [*le désir dément*].

It denies negation through or beyond denegation. That is its madness, but also the only chance of living desire. A denial of negativity—that is the signature: a "not to deny" that in the very end *denies* negativity. This energy gives to the signature that concerns us here its singular form.

It is not a question of an end of melancholy, not necessarily, not only, but of another relationship, this time affirmative, to the melancholy that is endured, traversed, analyzed, thought through, set to work, set up for failure or frustrated in the setting to work. Forgive me for citing the dedication that Sarah wrote to me in 1985 in my copy of *Mélancolie de l'art*; I will do it quickly, for it consists of just one word, a playful and lightly ironical adverb: "For Jacques, melancholically."

3

Before the diagnosis, after the diagnosis of the diagnosis, before and after the lesson on the *Lesson*, before and after Sarah Kofman's diagnosis of the diagnosing attitude of the doctors, of the anatomical gaze and medical knowledge, the little word *là* comes up, meaning at once *here* [*ici*] and *over there* [*là-bas*], right there, between here and over there, between *da* and *fort*. It comes up, *right there* [*là*], three times. Three times to speak of the presence of the dead person or of the corpse stretched out *right there*, of the *corpse* of man's body [*corps*], of a man's body—and not a woman's.

Three times *right there* [*là*]: the same number of times as the word *life*.

And the whole lesson on the *Lesson* questions and teaches this here [*cela*], this *right there* [*ce là*], this being-right-there of the body [*corps*] or of *la corpse* in the corpus of the work of art.

It is often said (but we do not have the time to reopen or dissect this question here) that what risks being left out or unthematized in *Sein und Zeit*, and in Heidegger more generally—and it is perhaps in light of this sign that we might ask why Sarah Kofman never really shared so many of her closest friends' interest in Heidegger—what seems to be lacking, so the hypothesis goes, on the surface of *Sein und Zeit* and in the analysis of being-there [*être-là*], would be an attention to the original being of the *corpse*, which is neither a living *Dasein* nor a *Vorhandensein* nor a *Zuhandensein*. Beyond the original responsibility that obligates us before the dead, and first of all before the *corpse*, the original being-there of the body of the other who has died (this strange responsibility that is perhaps the first and the ultimate, the extreme responsibility, the source of every other) seems to require, like the animal, and then like the living in general, an other, a fourth (categorical or existential) concept. And then there would be that other possible evasion in Heidegger, the one having to do in fact with art, with fictionality or the simulacrum, with the "for laughs" in the work of art, and singularly so in painting, and in particular in its relationship to the unconscious—yet a third reason, perhaps, why Heidegger appears to have had so little appeal for Sarah Kofman, not to mention sexual difference, which, like the *corpse*, is consigned to a certain silence in *Sein und Zeit*—and not to mention, especially, the rest, a more than suffocating rest, the worst, what took place over there [*là-bas*], in 1942, near Rue Ordener. Between Rue Ordener and Rue Labat.

What is at stake here is indeed the being-right-there (here and over there) of the *corpse*. Three times the adverb *là* [Translators' Note: like the musical note "la"] comes to set the tone. Three times it comes to localize both the body of death and its taking-place in the work, the work of art, its representation, as we say, in a painting, although it is already, as dead, framed or displayed in the anatomical exhibition, which is also a work or operation between the eye and the hand: gaze, surgery, dissection.

So here are the three *là*s, and then *voilà*, there it is, a gift of modesty, only a veil there [*un voile est là*] to veil the sex, the *being-right-there* of (the) sex, that is to say, sexual difference:

> And with this dissimulation of the body, its fragility, its mortality, comes to be forgotten, even though it is exhibited in full light by the pale cadaver *that is right there* [*là*], purely and simply lying there, naked (only the sex is modestly veiled), in the most absolute anonymity. (My emphasis)

What is most remarkable here is the insistence on anonymity, on the loss of the name in the being-right-there of the corpse; it is as if death cut the name off in the midst of life, severed the name from the living one who bore it, and this would be precisely its work as death, the operation proper to it; as if death separated the name and the body, as if it tore the name away from the body, as if, as a result, everywhere the name were detached from the body—and this happens to us all the time, especially when we speak, write, and publish—we were attesting, right there, to death, as if we were witnessing to it, all the while protesting against it:

> Those around him seem to be unmoved by any feelings for him, for someone who, just a short time ago, was still full of life, had a name [and Sarah takes

> pleasure in recalling in a note the child, the little boy, under the name of this corpse: "According to the account, the cadaver is that of a recently hanged man, identified by name and nickname as Abrian Adriaenz, called the kid, *Het Kind*"], was a man just like them. Their gazes display neither pity, nor terror, nor fright. They do not seem to identify with the cadaver stretched out *there*. They do not see in it the image of what they themselves will one day be, of what, *unbeknownst* to themselves, they are in the process of becoming. (My emphases)

In other words, this *there*, this *right there*, which they hold at a distance to disrupt an identification that they unconsciously fear, is also, right here, the place of their *unbeknowing*, to wit, that which they are here and now unwittingly in the process of becoming—according to the process of life and the process of art, two processes to which they are, in all the senses of this word, *exposed*, *three times* exposed without knowing it: exposed to gazes or looks when they believe themselves to be looking; exposed as mortals, as living beings destined to die; and exposed in the painting as a work of art and by the work of art.

> They do not see in it the image of what they themselves will one day be, of what, unbeknownst to themselves, they are in the process of becoming. They are not fascinated by the cadaver, which they do not seem to see as such.

They are thus seen not seeing, and, visible as nonseeing, visible as blinded, they are being diverted, distracted from the fascination for that thing there, diverted by the distracting distance of this *right there*; and this distraction is their very position of objective knowing or learning, their very gaze, their point of view, and their doctoral objectivization:

> ... and their solemnity is not the sort that can be awakened by the mystery of death.
> They have before them not a subject but an object, a purely technical instrument that one of them manipulates in order to get a hold on the truth of life. The dead man and the opening of his body are seen only insofar as they provide an opening onto life, whose secret they would hold. The fascination is displaced. . . .

A moment ago, we were told that they are not fascinated, not fascinated by the cadaver, but that did not mean that they are not fascinated at all: they have simply turned from one fascination to another, the fascination simply being displaced:

> ... and with this displacement, the anxiety is repressed, the intolerable made tolerable, from the sight of the cadaver to that of the book wide open at the foot of the deceased, who might now serve as a lectern.
> This opening of the book in all its light points back to the opening of the body. For the book alone allows the body to be deciphered and invites the passage from the exterior to the interior. It is this book (and the opening it provides onto the science of life and its mastery) that attracts the gazes, much more even than does the point of the scissors that has begun to peel away the skin from the body *stretched out there*. (My emphasis)

"The fascination is displaced." I suggested earlier that the statement "they are not fascinated" still implies fascination. The repression of fascination is a repression fascinated by what it represses, and which it simply submits to a topical translation, to a change of place, in a play between the here and the over there. In the text by Blanchot that I mentioned a moment ago, which also ends with an analysis of "fascination," the place of the cadaver is not simply situated "over there." It makes of the *here* an *over there*, so that the cadaver becomes in the first place a cadaver of the *here*, thus reminding us of a "distance" "in the heart of the thing." The distance does not happen to the thing, as if it could also sometimes, by accident, not happen to it. No, "*here* the distance is in the heart of the thing" (my emphasis).[6]

> The cadaverous presence establishes a relation between here and nowhere. The quiet that must be preserved in the room where someone dies and around the deathbed gives a first indication of how fragile the position par excellence is. The cadaver is here, but here in its turn becomes a cadaver: it becomes "here below" in absolute terms, for there is not yet any "there above" to be exalted.

(It would be necessary to follow the consequences of this discourse on the "aid of the remote" that brings to idealization, to the "idealism" of art, "no guarantee other than a cadaver"—and on "the cadaverous resemblance" as wandering and haunting: not the "unreal visitation of the ideal," but the spectrality of the deceased, his wandering over there, restless, beyond any sojourn, far from any dwelling.)

This would be another way of saying that the science of life, along with the book, along with the corpus and the corporation, do indeed fascinate, and let themselves be fascinated, and so displace attention, and replace, repress, deny, and divert, distracting one from death as much as from life, to be sure, but always *in the name of life*. These are at once symptoms and affirmations of a life that, in the end, as the unconscious that it is, does not know and does not want to know death, wants not to know it, actively wanting this before reactively doing so.

Here is a lesson, then, concerning what we do, in place of death, when we write or read books, when we talk about one book in lieu of another. Sarah points a finger at these doctors, denouncing them to some extent, for having suddenly become indifferent, all taken up by the book, apparently "unmoved by any feelings for him, for someone who, just a short time ago, was still full of life, had a name, was a man just like them"—and whom the book of science, just like the effect of the corpse, returns to anonymity.

When she writes "had a name, was a man just like them," I do not know if in naming this link between *name* and *man* [*homme*], she names in man *homo* or *vir*. One and the other, one or the other, the slash between *and* and *or*, and/or between *or* or *and*.

Sarah is not content simply to situate the singular *occurrence* [instance] *of the book* in this *Anatomy Lesson*. She sketches out a history of the book in the work of art, particularly in the pictorial corpus of Rembrandt. Each book has, in some sense, a pictorial genealogy. It is not enough just to decipher, in the thematic content of a painting, the role or meaning an element like the book wide open at the foot of the deceased has *there*, with respect, that is, to the other spectators or gazes in the painting ("the anxiety repressed," "the intolerable made tolerable," and so forth). One must also inscribe this power of the book, like a metonymy, in the series of books that haunt the corpus of Rembrandt, the whole artistic oeuvre of Rembrandt. (I insist, all too briefly of course, on this necessity, in order to recall what should here be our law: to take into account, each time we evoke a theme or motif in the work of Sarah Kofman, the intertwining threads that weave and displace the insistence on a motif in the long series of books, each very different but each bearing in itself the metonymic reference to all the others, in what is a sort of open quasi system, a coherent network that is nonetheless without closure, at once consistent and structurally interminable, an incomplete–incompletable seriality.)

Sarah Kofman submits to this law, this law of respect for the work and the art of Rembrandt, when she relates this book to all of Rembrandt's painted books and then to a history of the book in the West. It is a matter of clarifying the link between the internal analysis of this work, in its singularity, and what in this work "communicates" (this is her word) with the interpicturality of the works of Rembrandt with regard to the book, so as to evoke all the painted books, which are also paintings to be read, written about, and deciphered:

> The book of this *Lesson*, which, on its own, balances out the rest of the painting, communicates with the many other books found in Rembrandt's paintings: for example [only one example, for lack of time, just as we here can cite only one or another example among all her works and books], with that held open by Jan Six (in *Jan Six Standing at the Window* [1647]), who is depicted leaning against the opening of a window, his back turned to it, *there*by suggesting that only the book provides a true opening onto the world and access to knowledge. (My emphasis)

This library or gallery of books *within* Rembrandt's art gallery is itself reinscribed, as we come to see, in a larger library. Without getting lost in it, Sarah in some sense depicts, by giving it to be read, this library *en abyme*, which includes the Book, the Bible, within the book of science, but also the book of science within the Bible, as all the former did was supplement or supplant the latter, coming *in its place*, occupying its space, serving in place of a Bible for which it is still the substitute or metonymy:

> It [the book of Rembrandt, the whole book of Rembrandt] can also be compared with the one found in the *Minerva* at the Hague Museum; there, too, the book is open and luminous, supported by a closed book (the equivalent of the feet of the cadaver), while a draping droops downward, symbolizing the dispelling of darkness through knowledge.

And just as she is about to draw a double lesson, what she calls the "lesson of this *Anatomy Lesson*," her own lesson, Sarah Kofman makes a gesture that I would regard as a sort of initialing. It is like the short stroke, the economic signature that was always hers, the logic of a testimonial idiom: her affirmation, her protestation in the name of life. She ends up affirming the triumph of life, as Shelley would have said, not the triumph of death but the triumph over death—not through a denegation regarding an anxiety over death (Sarah knew what that could be), not through the relinquishing of a knowledge of death, but, on the contrary, through an active interpretation that renounces neither knowledge nor the knowledge of knowledge, that is to say, the knowledge of the role that occultation or repression might still play in certain forms of knowledge. Whence the deployment of so many types of knowledge, the rigorous analysis of an intersemiotic and intertextual imbrication of speech, writing, and the silence of the body, of the sacred book and the book of science, of book and painting, in more than one corpus, and first of all within Rembrandt's corpus, especially in the two *Anatomy Lessons* painted by Rembrandt some twenty years apart.

Twenty years apart, and there is always another anatomy lesson, yet one more lesson.

Here is the conclusion, where you will be able to admire along with me the precision of an analytical scalpel that does not forego any knowledge but that also does not fail to reaffirm life—operating in fact so as to reaffirm life, but without resurrection or redemption, without any glorious body:

> The doctors of *The Anatomy Lesson* are gazing down at the book of science with the same attentive fervor as that found in other paintings in which the evangelists are poring over the sacred books from which they draw the confirmation of their message (see, for example, Jordaens's *The Four Evangelists*, mentioned by Claudel).
>
> In *The Anatomy Lesson*, the book of science takes the place of the Bible; for one truth another has been substituted, a truth that is no longer simply confined to books, since it finds its experimental confirmation in the opening of a cadaver. The cadaver of Christ (for example, the one by Mantegna in the Brera Art Gallery in Milan, alluded to by the second *Anatomy Lesson*, that of Amsterdam) has been replaced by that of a man recently hanged, a purely passive object, manipulated, displaying no emotion, signaling no Resurrection, Redemption, or nobility. The cut into the flayed body thus also cuts into the religious illusion of a glorious body.
>
> The lesson of this *Anatomy Lesson* is thus not that of a *memento mori*; it is not that of a triumph of death but of a triumph over death; and this is due not to the life of an illusion, but to that of the speculative, whose function, too, is one of occultation.

Though uncompromising in her analysis of a speculation, this ruse of the speculative whose economy remains in the service of occultation and repression, indeed of sublimation or denegation, Sarah Kofman nonetheless detects in it the work of art, that is to say, art's work. She does so in order both to have some fun with it and to subscribe to it, to laugh at it but also to approve in it, to love, affirm, and repeat in it, the affirmation of art. She deciphers in it, or once again sees in it, the invincible triumph of life. This becomes clear when the word *life* gets drawn into a strange syntax: not illusory life or, as she says, "life of an illusion," the "religious illusion of a glorious body," which she had just mentioned, but life again, the life of the speculative, insofar as it remains, even in its function of occultation or illusion, the *nonillusory life of an illusion*, manifesting, affirming, and still holding on to life, carrying it living right to its limit.

The subject *denies* [*dément*]—denegation, and that is perhaps the logic of protestation, of a protestation that says *no(t) without illusion*, that says, not without illusion, no without illusion to the illusion and the denegation of death, no to a death conspired or conjured away. ("Conjuring Death" is the title of this last text on the *Anatomy Lessons*, which shows, in short, the body or corporation of doctors as the gathering of a conspiring or a *conspiracy* [*conjuration*]: the body of the corporation is the body of a conspiracy, the oath, intrigue, and plot of a social body that will do anything to conjure away death.) But this no to conjuring death is not spoken in the name of death; it speaks still in the name of life, of the work of art and of the book of life. It is inscribed in the book of life, in the book of the living, there where, *it is crazy to deny it, it denies like crazy* [*ça dément*]—in the name of a life that knows that the name of life, as we have said, is not life. Yes, no(t) without any illusion.

Some might consider my granting such a privilege to this last text, to the reaffirmation of the work of life as work of art, to be a stratagem on my part, a ruse to conjure away death in my turn, and, through this ruse, which I do not deny, a sort of protestation against her death: a protestation, which is to say a sort of testimony so as to attest to what was in her a constant protestation. A lesson in protestation. In nonnegative protestation. But also a lesson in the fact that "protestation" will have been, I now realize as I listen to all the resonances of this word, the privileged mode, the most constant and most common tonality of our face-to-face encounters.

Throughout our entire friendship, during decades of work and shared concerns, we protested, sometimes even against one another, right up until the end, and I catch myself still protesting. I catch myself still making scenes before her, as I said earlier, and I smile over this, while smiling to her, as if over a sign of life in reconciliation. And when it comes to scenes, I have to say that I will never be able to make as many as she; I will never catch up.

I began with the end; I would now like to end with the beginning.

"Some twenty years apart," as I emphasized and repeated earlier when quoting her on the two works of Rembrandt that bear the title *The Anatomy Lesson*.

Some twenty years apart.

Had I the time, I would tell you how I reread today what worked, for more than twenty years, as this protestation of life devoted to art and laughter. More than twenty years ago, Sarah came to see me for the first time, already in order to tell me, among other things, that she protested or objected to something I had ventured in "Plato's Pharmacy." Everything thus began with this scene. When, after becoming friends, we chose together, or so I thought, the title of her first book, *The Childhood of Art*,[7] I did not understand or recognize what I understand better today, after having read *Smothered Words*[8] (between Blanchot and Antelme, in the wake of Auschwitz), and *Rue Ordener, Rue Labat*,[9] namely, that this first book—so rich, so sharp, so perfectly lucid in its reading of Freud—was also the childhood of the art, the child's play, of Sarah Kofman. An autobiographical anamnesis, an *autobiogriffure*. All the places—of the father, of the mothers, of the substitution of mothers, of laughter and life as works of art—were there already acknowledged, rigorously assigned.

Because I do not want to keep you too long, and because it is impossible for me to develop here all the necessary analyses, I will cite just a couple of passages. They will at least give you some indication of the direction in which I would have gone, the sides I would have taken. I select these quotes while underscoring at the same time a thematics of the gift, but of the gift of life, a gift that seems to run throughout all of Sarah's work, the gift of a life that is, in truth, *given again, given back* [*redonnée*].

I would like, in conclusion, to pause in the vicinity of this gift *given back*, not far from a joke and from *Pourquoi rit-on?*, published midway, about ten years ago.

But what does it mean "to give back" when we are talking about life? In what way might a giving imply a giving back, as if *giving back* came before *giving*, in a reaffirmation of the gift that does not amount to returning the gift but to giving it once more? Perhaps also to accepting, by affirming, by reaffirming, the given gift: yes, yes to the gift received. And perhaps to forgiveness as well. And what if this question held that of art in reserve? What would art have to do—what would it have in view or give to be viewed, give to live or give to laugh—with protestation? And with the gift of the gift? With the gift given back? Perhaps with forgiveness?

Already in the introduction to *The Childhood of Art*, Sarah asks the question of the gift and announces that she will develop it further in the final chapter. She asks the question of the gift for art as a gift bestowed by life, where psychoanalysis at once admits its limits and introduces "a radically new conception" (*CA*, 5):

> [Freud] acknowledges just as openly the limits of psychoanalysis, which are repeated in all his works. Completely outside its province are the "aesthetic appreciation of a work of art" or of the artist's formal procedures on the one hand, which properly belong to aestheticians, and on the other, the explanation of the artistic "gift," genius, and the possibility of creation. . . . What lies this side of it—the gift, genius—remains a mysterious enigma that absolutely escapes all scientific knowledge. By virtue of this gift, the artist is an inexplicable being, exceptional and favored by the gods. Does Freud accept this theological and ideological conception of the artist? That is the question. But does the claim that the "gift" cannot be explained by psychoanalysis amount to an affirmation that it is, by its very nature, mysterious? For Freud, it is biological science that should take up the problem where psychoanalysis leaves off, for it is life that bestows "gifts." . . . But does this substitution of life for God repeat differently the same ideological conception of art, or does it introduce a radically new conception? (*CA*, 4–5)

While providing an elaborate answer to this question of the gift, and of the gift as the gift of life, the gift of life given by life, *The Childhood of Art* underscores in passing that *Jokes* (to which I will turn in a moment to conclude) "leads to the second moment in Freud's procedure, which is begun in the truly pivotal essay on *Gradiva*" (*CA*, 24).

In the course of lifting one mask after another (the word *unmasking* coming up with great frequency), and of treating the question of the mask and of the veil between Nietzsche and Freud, especially around sexual difference, modesty, and its veilings–unveilings, this book recalls the gift at each moment, the reaffirmation of the gift in the act of *giving back*. The reaffirmation of the gift, no less or earlier than the restitution of the gift.

I shall select just a single example of this. The scene of the gift also opens up the scene of laughter [*rire*] or of the smile [*sourire*], of the smile of the mother. Can we not reread these pages here and there, between here and there, between, so to speak, Rue Ordener and Rue Labat? Would we not see a little girl laughing and smiling through all these disasters, disasters one does not survive, that one can at the very most only survive? (Need I specify, as I am about to smile at this smile, that no feeling of familiarity can ever come to interrupt an abyssal vertigo? Those close to us remain absolutely unknown to us, unreachable, farther away even for being "close": right up until the end, up until the end beyond all knowledge.)

When Freud, talking about the smile of the Mona Lisa, speaks of what led Leonardo da Vinci to "a glorification of motherhood" that consists in "giving back (*wiederzugeben*) to his mother the smile that he had found in the noble lady,"[10] Sarah comments, distinguishing the giving back from the restitution of a first giving out:

> The term to "give back" is obviously very ambiguous here, and seems to imply that the mother initially possessed the smile. However, the context [attention to the context and to the order of reasons in the text is always taken into consideration with an impeccable sense for the law of the text] makes it clear that "to give back" means to give for the second time in a work of art, the *St. Anne*. For St. Anne is but another symbolic substitute for the mother. The "gift" is as unconscious as the memory of his mother sparked by the sight of Mona Lisa. What must be understood is that the production of the first work was the occasion for a return of the repressed, which allowed Leonardo to express clearly the fantasies of his childhood history. That is why the second painting [here again there is a second painting] was necessary: it repeats the smile of the first, but with a difference that is symptomatic of the lifting of repression performed by the *Mona Lisa*. "But although the smile that plays on the lips of the two women is unmistakably the same as that in the picture of Mona Lisa, it has lost its uncanny (*unheimliche*) and enigmatic (*rätselhaften*) character; what it expresses is inward feeling and quiet blissfulness." (*CA*, 80–81)

A page later, the following remark might resemble, in the eyes of some, though more than twenty years in advance, a sort of ironic note at the bottom of a page of *Rue Ordener, Rue Labat*: "St. Anne's 'blissful smile' is the product of repression, because it marks the artist's denial of his mother's suffering and masks the jealousy she felt when she was forced to give up her son [or one might say her daughter] to her rival" (*CA*, 82).

The analysis of the gift will continue to be developed everywhere, especially in *Don Juan ou le refus de la dette*, which calculates precisely an "unpayable debt" with regard to the "gift of life."[11] This analysis is closely linked, even if the link is not made explicit, to the analysis of laughter, of the smile and the comical. One would almost be tempted to conclude, with all the ambiguity of this joke, that the gift is always a gift for laughs, a gift for laughter.

I would have so much liked to linger a while on a page that cites Freud on poetic irony ("A great imaginative writer may permit himself to give expression—jokingly, at all events—to psychological truths that are severely proscribed" [*CA*, 96]), and that multiplies examples of what Freud calls "comical" treatment, in particular of the taboo surrounding virginity. Once again, the following page (*CA*, 97) seems, more than twenty years in advance, already to be roaming about *Rue Ordener, Rue Labat*. For we there read this about one of the great figures for Sarah Kofman—herself a great reader of "The Sandman"—the figure of her almost homonym Hoffmann: "When he [Hoffmann] was three years old, his father left the family and never came back to it [*auprès d'elle*: the feminine pronoun *elle* refers to the family here, though], so the storyteller's relation to his father was always one of the painful aspects of his affective life" (*CA*, 97, translation modified).

And we could continue with the first words of *Rue Ordener, Rue Labat*: "Of him all I have left is the fountain pen. . . . As it turned out, we never did see my father again."[12]

Rather than multiplying conjectures and conjunctions of this type from the final chapter of *The Childhood of Art* concerning "the artistic 'gift' " (*CA*, 149) (this is a subtitle and the word "gift" is in quotation marks), I will simply situate what is repeatedly underscored about this "gift" of the artist attributed by Freud to a "kindly nature" (*CA*, 150). This economy of the gift reckons always with a figure of nature, one of the three figures of woman (the mother, the companion, and the corruptor or death). Nature is here called "the earth, characterized as a nurturing mother" (*CA*, 152). We could reread and relate this entire analysis to that found in "Damned Food" (published in *Manger*, 1980), "Damned food! And twice damned!"[13]: little Sarah finds herself caught, and for life, between the excesses of the "you must eat" of the mother and the "you must not eat everything" of the father.

Indeed, you must eat. I have already taken up too much of your time.

Instead of spending the time we really ought to around the final pages of *The Childhood of Art* (around what is said there about laughter, about the enigma of art as life, about artistic life, about what Nietzsche calls "laughing at oneself" [*CA*, 224 n. 14], about the phrase "one can either cry or laugh" on the next-to-last page [*CA*, 173], about the world that, for Nietzsche as for Freud, plays "an innocent 'child's game' guided by chance and necessity," when "the true art is the art of life" [*CA*, 174]), I rush toward a scene at the table, and toward laughter, as is often done in the most difficult moments of mourning.

Sarah dedicated a copy of her text "Damned Food" to me in 1980 by circling the title of the volume, *Manger* [Eating], in order to write the words "in the hopes of *Eating* together."

Six years later, on New Year's Day 1986, the dedication to *Pourquoi rit-on? Freud et le mot d'esprit* still spoke of the table. It read: "For Jacques and Marguerite, recalling the good Jewish jokes we once peddled at table, and hoping we can do it again one day."

Now, what is the last word of this great book that says both everything and the rest about laughter, as well as about the apotropaic economy of laughter according to Freud? It is, precisely, the "last word." The book ends in this way: "By way of conclusion, let's give laughter the last word" (*PR*, 198).

But right before this last word on the last word comes a Jewish joke, a sort of postscriptum. It is a joke we had once told each other. Here is the postscriptum:

> Finishing this book today, September 25, the day of Yom Kippur, I cannot resist peddling [this word was already used, recall, in the dedication, which was itself alluding to a subsection of the book entitled *Peddling*, whose subtitle is *The Economic Necessity of the Third*; and I recall that my last conversation with Sarah must have more or less directly concerned, at the time it was interrupted, a story about the peddling of history and the economic necessity of the third] this Jewish joke told by Theodor Reik [who has written much on the Great Atonement and the song of Kol Nidre]: "Two Jews, long-standing enemies, meet at the synagogue on the day of the Great Atonement. One says to the other [by way of forgiveness]: 'I wish you what you wish me.' And the other replies, giving tit for tat: 'See, you're doing it again!'" (*PR*, 198)

An unfathomable story, a story that seems to stop in its tracks, whose movement consists in interrupting itself, in paralyzing itself in order to refuse any future, an absolute story of the unsolvable, a vertiginous depthlessness, an irresistible whirlwind that draws forgiveness, the gift, and the giving back of forgiveness right to the abyss of the impossible.

How does one acquit oneself of forgiving? Must not forgiveness exclude all acquittal, all acquittal of oneself, of the other? To forgive is certainly not to discharge a debt. Neither one's own, nor the other's. That would be to repeat the evil, to countersign or consecrate it, to let it be what it is, unalterable and identical to itself. No adequation is here appropriate or tolerable. So what then?

As I said, we must have told this Jewish joke to each other, and probably while eating. And we must have agreed that it was not only funny but memorable, unforgettable, precisely insofar as it treats this treatment of memory called forgiveness. There is no forgiveness without memory, surely, but neither is there any forgiveness that can be reduced to an act of memory. And forgiving does not amount to forgetting, especially not. A joke "for laughs," no doubt, but what about it makes us laugh, laugh and cry, and laugh through our tears or our anxiety?

It is no doubt first a matter of its economy, an economy powerfully analyzed by Freud, and then by Sarah Kofman questioning Freud. In fact, in the chapter "The Three Thieves," in the subsection "Peddling: The Economic Necessity of the Third," a note also speaks of forgiveness. It speaks of the economy of "pleasure given by the superego, the *forgiveness* that it in some sense grants, bringing humor close to the maniacal phase, since, thanks to these '*gifts*,' the diminished 'I' finds itself if not euphoric, at least lifted back up" (*PR*, 104, my emphasis).

Without venturing any further in this direction, let me keep for the moment to a rough analysis of this Jewish joke: two enemies make the gesture to forgive one another, they feign to do so "for laughs," but by inwardly reopening or pursuing the hostilities. In the process, they admit to this inexpiable war and blame one another for it reciprocally, as if in a mirror. That the admission should be made by way of a symptom rather than a declaration changes nothing as far as the truth is concerned: they have not disarmed; they continue to wish one another ill.

I will thus venture to say this, to address to you something that once again concerns laughter, art "for laughs" and the art of laughter, and to address this to you as if to Sarah, to Sarah in me. Allegorically, what these two Jews come to experience and what makes us laugh is indeed the radical impossibility of forgiveness.

A Jew, a Jew from time immemorial, and especially in this century, Sarah knew this and lived it better than any of us here, better in the worst of ways, for she was also someone who was put to the test of the impossibility of forgiveness, its radical impossibility.

Who, in fact, could give us the right to forgive? Who could give whom the right to forgive on behalf of the dead, and to forgive the infinite violence that was done to them, depriving them of both a grave and a name, everywhere in the world and not only at Auschwitz? And thus everywhere that the unforgivable would have taken place?

But the impossibility of forgiveness—let us not hide this from ourselves—must still be thought differently, right down to the most radical root of its paradox, in the very formation of a concept of forgiveness. What a strange concept! Because it does not resist the impossibility of what one would wish to conceive in it, because it explodes or implodes upon contact with it, a whole chain of concepts goes down with it, even the concept of the concept, which is now put to the test of its own essential precariousness and finitude, its own deconstructability.

The impossibility of forgiveness gives itself to be thought as, in truth, its only possibility. Why is forgiveness impossible? Not just difficult for innumerable psychological reasons, but absolutely impossible? Simply because what is to be forgiven must be and must remain unforgivable. If forgiveness is possible, if there is forgiveness, it must be a forgiveness of the unforgivable—that is the logical aporia. If we had to forgive only what is forgivable, even excusable, *venial*, as we say, or insignificant, we would not really be forgiving. We would be excusing, forgetting, or erasing, but we would not be giving our forgiveness. If, through some transformation, the fault, the evil deed, the crime, were attenuated or extenuated to the point of venality, if the effects of the wound were to hurt less, or were perhaps even to come with a certain pleasure attached, then the very thing that becomes forgivable is exonerated and can do without any forgiveness. Forgiving the forgivable thus forgives nothing; it is not a forgiving.

In order to forgive, then, one must forgive the unforgivable, an unforgivable that remains unforgivable, the worst of the worst: an unforgivable that resists every transformation of the I or of the other, every alteration, every historical reconciliation that might come to change the conditions or circumstances of the judgment. Whether as remorse or repentance, the eventual purification of the guilty party has no place here. In fact, it is not a question of forgiving a guilty party, a subject subject to transforming himself above and beyond the fault, but of forgiving the fault itself—which must remain unforgivable so that there can even be a question of appealing on its behalf for some forgiveness. But isn't forgiving the unforgivable impossible in all good logic? If forgiveness must thus remain impossible, then it must do the impossible; it must be put to the test of its own impossibility by forgiving the unforgivable—and thus be put to the test, indeed become one with the test, of this aporia or this paradox: the possibility—if it is possible, if there is any—of the impossible. And the impossibility of the possible.

Here is perhaps a condition that forgiveness shares with the gift. Beyond the formal analogy, this might also mean that the condition of impossibility of the one is fixed on the other, the gift on forgiveness, or forgiveness on the gift. Not to mention the fact that one must also be forgiven for the gift (which cannot but risk doing harm, doing evil, for example, in giving death) and that a gift perhaps remains the most unforgivable thing in the world. Doesn't the question that one day became imperative to me ("What does it mean to give in or to the name of the other [*au nom de l'autre*]?"; "Who knows what we are doing when we give in or to the name of the other?")[14]—in order to suggest that this is perhaps the only chance for the gift—doesn't this question let itself be translated into forgiveness? If I forgive in my name, my forgiveness expresses something of which I myself am capable, and this decision (which is then no longer a decision) is but the deployment of my potential, my power, the potential energy of my aptitudes, predicates, characteristics, and so on. Just as I cannot decide—decide, as we say, in my own name—so I cannot forgive in my own name, but only in the name of the other, there where I alone am capable of neither deciding nor forgiving. I must thus forgive what I do not have to forgive, what I do not have the power to give or to forgive: I must forgive beyond myself. That this is done in the name of the other in no way exonerates my freedom or my responsibility—quite the contrary.

The impossibility of the possible, the possibility of the impossible—that is a definition that resembles the one often given to death, particularly since Heidegger. And there is nothing fortuitous in this. We must think this affinity between this impossibility called death and the one called forgiveness, between the gift of death and the gift of forgiveness as the possibility of the impossible. The impossible for me, for a "me," for what is "mine" or proper to me in general.

For where is forgiveness more impossible, and thus possible *as* impossible, than beyond the border between the living and the dead? How can the living forgive the dead? What meaning and what gift would there be in a forgiveness that can no longer hope to reach its destination, except within oneself, the other being welcomed or taken in as a narcissistic ghost within the self? And reciprocally, how can the living hope to be forgiven by the dead or by a specter within them? The consequences of this logic can be followed out ad infinitum.

And you know, I bet that this insurmountable limit—surmounted, nonetheless, as insurmountable, in the setting free of what is insuperable in the unsurmounted—is indeed the line that our two Jews have crossed—with or within the confession, though without repentance, of their reciprocal accusation. To admit to, to share, to entrust to one another this insurmountable test of the unforgivable, to deem oneself unforgivable for not forgiving, is perhaps not to forgive—since forgiveness appears impossible, even when it takes place—but to sympathize with the other in this test of the impossible.

Here it is, then—the ultimate compassion.

It is to tell the other, or to hear oneself tell the other, and to hear the other tell you: you see, you're doing it again, you do not want to forgive me, even on the day of the Great Atonement, but me too, me neither, a "me" neither, we are in agreement, we forgive ourselves for nothing, for that is impossible, so let's not forgive one another, all right? And then you burst into complicit, uncontrollable laughter, laughing like crazy, with a laughter gone crazy. For isn't this paradoxical agreement peace? Yes, that's peace, that's life: that, in the end, is the great atonement. And what is more comical than the great atonement or forgiveness as the test of the unforgivable? What could be more alive? What better reconciliation could there be? What an art of living! How to do otherwise, in fact, how to do better, as soon as we live, or live on? Without having chosen to do so? This reconciliation in the impossible is the definition of today, of a today, of life's reprieve.

But I want to imagine that these two Jews in their infinite compassion for one another, at the very moment when they conclude that they do not know how to conclude, at the very moment when they recognize that they cannot disarm, just as life itself never disarms, I want to believe that these two Jews have forgiven one another, but without telling one another. At least they have spoken to one another, even if they haven't said that they forgive one another. They have said to one another, in silence, a silence made up of tacit understanding, where misunderstanding can always find a place, that the forgiveness granted implies neither "reconciliation" (Hegel) nor "the work itself," "the profound work" of discontinuous time, a time that is delivered or that delivers us from continuity through the interruption of the other, with a view to the "messianic triumph" "secured against the revenge of evil" (Levinas).[15]

For here is the last aporia of forgiveness, the most artistic perhaps, the most gifted to make us laugh like crazy, and I confide it to you, as well as to Sarah, to Sarah in me, to Sarah between you and me, in order to end today.

On the one hand, when you forgive someone (for the worst possible wound, for example, or, more simply still—something that can redouble or compound it to the point of perversity—for the evocation or recollection of a wound), well, above all you must not tell them; the other must not hear, and you must not say, that you forgive—not only so as not to recall the (double) fault but so as not to recall or show that something has been given (forgiven, given as forgiveness), given back in return, something that deserves some gratitude or that risks obligating the person forgiven. In the end, nothing is more vulgar and impolite, indeed injurious or wounding, than obligating someone by telling them "I forgive you," which implies "I give you," and so already opens up a scene of recognition or gratefulness, a transaction of gratitude, a commerce of thanks that destroys the gift. One must thus keep quiet, keep forgiveness quiet wherever it takes place, if it takes place. It is this silence, this inaudibility, that is called death or that death allows. As if one could forgive only the dead (or at least make as if the other were dead ["for laughs"], in the situation of never again being there to hear or to receive forgiveness), as if one could forgive only the dead by making as if one were oneself dead (as if one were in fact not forgiving at all, as if one did not let it be known or, even, did not know it oneself). From this point of view, two living beings cannot forgive one another and declare that they forgive one another as living beings. One would have to be dead in order to believe forgiveness possible. The two Jews had the profundity, the rigor, the honesty to acknowledge this. Better yet, to declare it.

But on the other hand, and inversely, what would a silent forgiveness be, a forgiveness that goes unnoticed, unrecognized, that is granted unbeknownst to the one who receives it? What would forgiveness be when the person forgiven knows nothing about it? This would no longer be forgiveness. Such a silence in forgiveness would be just as harmful as that which the silence had meant to avoid. Wouldn't a forgiveness that addresses the other only when dead (once dead, and even if their specter survives "in me") be little more than a theatrical display, a pitiful simulacrum, at most a phantasm aimed at consoling oneself for not having known how to forgive in time? A reconciliation with oneself that would be of no concern to the other? If there is to be forgiveness, then I should forgive when there is still time, before the death of the other. And, of course, before my own: what kind of forgiveness could come from the dead? It is true that this forgiveness of the dead by the dead, from one shore of death to the other, is the one to which we most often have recourse, our lives being made up of this, a spectral and phantasmatic recourse, a process of forgiveness, a historical forgiveness in place of a forgiveness that must remain irreducible to History, a forgiveness that gets lost in forgetting and whose nature is altered through excuse and venality as soon as true forgiveness, from one living being to another, the forgiving of the unforgivable, remains forbidden. A priori and thus forever forbidden.

So what then? To do exactly what is always forbidden, forbidden forever? To forgive there where it is forbidden, where it is possible *because* it is impossible? And even worse, to do what is forbidden on the day of the Great Atonement? There is no worse sin, no more dangerous profanation, so close to the moment when God writes you—or else does not—into the book of the living.

Let us recapitulate this properly scandalous aporia, the one at which we cannot help but stop when we stumble upon it: impossible, possible only *as* impossible, an impossible concept of the impossible that would begin to resemble a *flatus vocis* if this were not what we desire most in the world—indeed just as impossible as forgiving the unforgivable—forgiveness remains impossible in every way: between two living beings, between one dead and one living, or one living and one dead, or between two who are dead. It is possible, in its very impossibility, only at the invisible border between life and death (for as we have seen, one can forgive only there where the one who forgives and the one who is forgiven are not there to know it), but this scandalous border does not let itself be crossed or surmounted: neither by what is living nor by what is dead.

Nor even, though this might be the unlocatable place over which all these questions keep vigil, by *a corpse* [*une corpse*]. At what moment does

Abraham reawaken the memory of his being foreign in a foreign land? For Abraham does indeed recall that he is destined by God to be a guest (*gêr*), an immigrant, a foreign body in a foreign land ("Go from your country and your kindred and your father's house," "your offspring shall be guests in a land that is not theirs"[16]). Presenting himself as a foreigner who has no home, keeping watch over the body of the dead, his dead, Sarah (the woman who laughs when told she is to have a child and then pretends not to have laughed[17]), Abraham requests a place for her. A final dwelling, a final resting place. He wants to be able to give her a burial place worthy of her, but also a place that would separate her from him, like death from life, a place "in front of me," says one translation, or "out of my sight," says another.[18] And for this—you know the scene—he wants to pay, this husband of Sarah, the woman who laughs; he insists on it, he wants at all costs that this not be given to him. In fact, Abraham had himself also laughed upon hearing the same news, the news of the belated birth of Isaac. (*Yiskhak*: he laughs: Isaac, the coming of Isaac, makes them both shake with laughter, one after the other; Isaac is the name of the one who *comes* to make them laugh, to laugh about his coming, at his very coming, as if laughter should greet a birth, the coming of a happy event, a coming of laughter, a coming to laugh: come-laugh-with-me.) The moment having come to laugh was also the moment when Elohim named Sarah. He gave her a new name, deciding that Abraham, who had himself just received another name (changed from Abram to Abraham), would no longer call her Sarai, my princess, but Sarah, princess.[19] So what, then? *Comment s'en sortir* [How to get out of this]?[20] To this question in the form of an aporia, I know of no satisfying answer. Not even crazed laughter. Nothing is given in advance for an act of forgiveness, no rule, no criterion, no norm. It is the chaos at the origin of the world. The abyss of this nonanswer or nonresponse would be the condition of responsibility—decision and forgiveness, the decision to forgive without any concept, if there ever is any. And always (in) the name of the other.

(Last vertigo, last sigh: to forgive (in) the name of the other—is this only to forgive in their place, for the other, in substitution? Or is it to forgive the other their name, to forgive what is in their name, what survives the corpse, to forgive the name of the other as their first wrongdoing?)

The answer must each time be invented, singular, signed, and each time only one time like the gift of a work, a giving of art and of life, unique and, right up until the end of the world, played back.

Given back. To the impossible, I mean right up to the impossible.

This is what Sarah Kofman gives me to think about today, in the overflowing of memory, there where she remains for me unique, and where I want to believe that this reaffirmation of life was hers, right up to when the time came, to when it became time, right up to the end.

TRANSLATED BY PASCALE-ANNE BRAULT AND MICHAEL NAAS

PART I

Reading (with) Freud

§ 1 The Double Reading

The "Application" of Psychoanalysis to Art

Does Freud himself not declare that the interests of psychoanalysis from the point of view of art are very limited indeed?[1] Under these circumstances, the resistance with which attempts to "apply" psychoanalysis to art have met and continue to meet might appear unjustified. And yet this undertaking has encountered vehement opposition that takes the same form as the initial resistance to psychoanalysis: vehement rejection and incomprehension, accusations of pansexualism and degradation of the highest cultural values.[2] Therein lies the explanation for Freud's caution, his care in precisely defining the task of psychoanalysis in the aesthetic realm, the polemical character of most of his writings, and the nuances introduced from one work to the other as resistances are overcome. However, because the resistances are never abolished once and for all, a more or less deliberate self-censorship persists in Freud's discourse.

These few remarks guide my reading of Freud's texts.[3] They enjoin us to distinguish the works in which he sets out the relations between psychoanalysis and art (noting the differences he introduces from one work to the other) from the works where he engages in an "application," and to distinguish what Freud declares in his discourse as a matter of strategy from what he masks more or less consciously. They urge us, therefore, to do a symptomal reading of his text, making it say something more or other than what it says literally, yet basing the reading on the literal sense alone. But once these distinctions are made, do the limits of psychoanalysis in its "application" to art, so often pointed out by Freud, still stand?

Indeed, judging from his discourse, Freud seems fascinated by artists, particularly in his earliest works, and imposes very clear limits on a psychoanalysis of art. But "application" itself exceeds these limits and forces him to curb his admiration. Two texts separated by a ten-year period clearly show the nuances introduced from one work to the other.

In the 1913 essay "The Claims of Psycho-Analysis to Scientific Interest," Freud writes, "Psycho-analysis throws a satisfactory light upon some of the problems concerning art and artists; but others escape it completely." And further on: "The connection between the impressions of the artist's childhood and his life-history on the one hand and his works, as reactions to those impressions (*Anregungen*) on the other is one of the most attractive subjects of analytic examination" (13:187). But in "A Short Account of Psycho-Analysis," written in 1923, Freud says:

> The researches of psycho-analysis have in fact thrown a flood of light on the fields of mythology, the science of literature, and the psychology of artists. . . . We have shown that myths and fairy tales can be interpreted like dreams,[4] we have traced the convoluted paths that lead from the urge of the unconscious wish to its realization in a work of art, we have learnt to understand the emotional effect (*Affectivewirkung*) of a work of art on the observer, and in the case of the artist himself we have made clear his internal kinship with the neurotic as well as his distinction from him, and we have pointed out the connection between his innate disposition (*Anlage*), his chance experiences and his achievements. The aesthetic appreciation of works of art and the elucidation of the artistic gift (*künstlerische Begabung*) are, it is true, not among the tasks set to psycho-analysis. But it seems that psycho-analysis is in a position to speak the decisive word in all questions that touch upon the imaginative life of man.

And further on:

> It must not be forgotten, however, that psycho-analysis alone cannot offer a complete picture of the world. If we accept the distinction which I have recently proposed of dividing the mental apparatus into an ego, turned towards the external world and equipped with consciousness, and an unconscious id, dominated by its instinctual needs, then psycho-analysis is to be described as a psychology of the id (and of its effects on the ego). If these contributions often contain the essence of the facts, this only corresponds to the important part which, it may be claimed, is played in our lives by the mental unconscious that has so long remained unknown. (19:208)

In the first text, it is said that psychoanalysis can provide only a "satisfactory light"; in the second, that it can release a "flood of light." In the one, there is an avowal of total incompetence to resolve certain problems, whereas in the other, though it is acknowledged that certain tasks are not within the province of psychoanalysis and that psychoanalysis can make only "contributions," these contributions reveal the *essence* of the facts, and psychoanalysis speaks the "decisive word" on man's imaginative life. The latter text is a good example of Freud's method of self-censorship. For polemical reasons, it is a compromise between what Freud thinks and what he openly declares; each phrase affirms the opposite of what the previous one asserted and in that very gesture cancels it, or at least alters it in a peculiar fashion. The modesty of Freud's declarations, which is merely apparent, obliges us to read his text carefully. Like all compromises, it must be deciphered.

What happened in the interval between the two texts? Freud discovered close relationships among the various psychic productions: myths, tales, literature, and art can be explained *like* dreams. Freud's method consists essentially in showing the relationship and the distinction between these phenomena. It introduces continuity where there is apparently only a lacuna, a void, a rupture, or a disjunction, establishing a link between the conscious and the unconscious, the normal and the pathological, the child and the adult, the civilized man and the primitive man, the individual and the species, the ordinary and the extraordinary, the human and the divine. It links various cultural and psychic productions, representation and affect, and so forth. In this way, Freud effaces all the oppositions inherited from traditional metaphysics. That is why what he does is not an "application" of psychoanalysis to art; he does not apply to art, from the outside, a method belonging to a supposedly alien sphere. If the method is coherent, it is because each of its objects of study is but a different repetition of the same. For Freud, works of art are like all other psychic productions insofar as they are compromises and constitute "riddles" to be solved. Thus, the interpreter of these productions is a new type of mediator, working on behalf of Eros: to solve the riddles is to reestablish a contact. Moreover, the work of interpretation itself is not cut off from its libidinal roots. In the first text, Freud speaks of an "attractive subject" for analytic examination and elsewhere he speaks in terms of "*disturbance*" and "*fascination*," to express art's powerful effect on him and other men.

To render this effect intelligible is precisely what Freud proposes to do, claiming that speculation, far from suppressing fascination, strengthens it. The opposition between intellect and sensibility is abstract; it arises from a psychology of the faculties of which classical aesthetics is the heir and whose weakness Freud demonstrates. Freud himself could not enjoy without understanding; his lack of taste for music,[5] as well as his taste for literature[6] can be accounted for in this way. It also explains why, except for his work on Leonardo da Vinci and Michelangelo's *Moses*, he limited himself to the psychoanalysis of literary works. To render intelligible the effects of affect; to establish links between dispositions, the vagaries of life, and production, between works of art and other cultural or psychic productions in general, whether dreams or neuroses; to show their resemblance and their difference—such is the sole task that Freud sets himself, or at least it is the only one he openly acknowledges. He acknowledges just as openly the limits of psychoanalysis, which are repeated in all his works. Completely outside the province of psychoanalysis are the "aesthetic appreciation of a work of art" or of the artist's formal procedures, which falls under the purview of aestheticians, and the explanation of the artistic "gift," genius, and the possibility of creation.[7] Psychoanalysis is said to make a mere "contribution" to art, drawing on the psychology of the id and its effects on the ego. Everything that lies outside the sphere of the id is left to others. What lies beyond this sphere—the work of the artist—depends for its analysis on ego psychology and the science of aesthetics. What lies this side of it—the gift, genius—remains a mysterious enigma that absolutely escapes all scientific knowledge. By virtue of this gift, the artist is an inexplicable being, exceptional and favored by the gods.

Does Freud accept this theological and ideological conception of the artist? That is the question. Does the claim that the "gift" cannot be explained by psychoanalysis amount to an affirmation that it is, by its very nature, mysterious? For Freud, it is biological science that should take up the problem where psychoanalysis leaves off, for it is life that bestows "gifts." But does this substitution of life for God repeat differently the same ideological conception of art, or does it introduce a radically new conception? Moreover, if what lies on either side of the id escapes psychoanalysis completely, how could Freud say that its "contribution" sometimes reveals what is most essential about the object of study and that psychoanalysis is "in a position to speak the decisive word in all questions that touch upon the imaginative life of man"? Would this not amount to removing what is essential to the work of art from the field of psychoanalysis? How, then, are we to understand the fact that psychoanalysis encountered resistance and was so often reproached for having a reductive project? Indeed, the distinction Freud establishes in the text cited above between a "psychology of the id" and a "psychology of the ego" is dangerous, for it contradicts other texts in which Freud considers it illegitimate to assimilate the ego to consciousness and the id to the unconscious. The simplistic quality of his exposition offers additional proof of its polemical character and invites a reading of Freud's text that discloses something other and something more than what it literally says.

A Symptomal Reading

Let us refer, then, to two examples of "applied" psychoanalysis in which we can see more clearly the functioning of the opposition between what is openly declared and what is masked in Freud's discourse.

"The 'Uncanny' " begins thus:

> It is only rarely that a psycho-analyst feels impelled to investigate the subject of aesthetics, even when aesthetics is understood to mean not merely the theory of beauty but the theory of the qualities of feeling. He works in other strata of mental life and has little to do with the subdued emotional impulses (*Gefühlsregungen*) which, inhibited in their aims and dependent on a host of concurrent factors, usually furnish the material for the study of aesthetics. But it does occasionally happen that he has to interest himself in some particular province of that subject; and this province usually proves to be a rather remote one, and one which has been neglected in the specialist literature of aesthetics. (17:219)

Freud begins by excluding aesthetics from the sphere of psychoanalysis proper and expressing his indifference toward emotional impulses that result from drives that are either inhibited in their aims or sublimated (although the two expressions do not have exactly the same meaning). However, this statement should perhaps be read as meaning the opposite of what it says—that is, as disclosing something like an indirect response to the vulgar belief that psychoanalysis is interested only in the "demoniacal" in man. In his discourse, Freud repeats the distinction between the "lowly" and the "sublime," the better to denounce it, convinced as he is that psychoanalysis has something to say about the "highest" cultural phenomena. As he shows in the study that follows this introduction to "The 'Uncanny,'" muted emotional impulses cannot be understood if they are seen as cut off from the uninhibited sexual drives of which they are a diversion. What Freud here attempts to put under erasure is the moral and metaphysical opposition between the "high" and the "low," thereby showing that a "pure" aesthetics cut off from psychoanalysis and reserved for specialists can only be a vain science. At the end of "The 'Uncanny,'" Freud states that aestheticians are but fine talkers: the quality of uncanniness, that "remote region" of aesthetics that the discipline generally neglects, and which Freud consequently takes the liberty of studying with no risk of offending it, appears on examination to be the essential quality of the work of art.[8] Here again, Freud establishes links between the disciplines and stands opposed to a psychology of the faculties. The specialist can only fail and keep men in a state of metaphysical illusion. In the preface to *Totem and Taboo* (1913), Freud writes: "[These essays] seek to bridge the gap (*vermitteln*) between students of such subjects as social anthropology, philology and folklore on the one hand, and psycho-analysts on the other." Freud links these disciplines because there exists an unsuspected unity among phenomena heretofore considered distinct, such as the totemic meal and the Christian communion, the divine and the human, as *Totem and Taboo* is devoted to proving. And Freud writes in "On the Teaching of Psycho-Analysis in Universities," published in 1919:

> The application of this method is by no means confined to the field of psychological disorders, but extends also to the solution of problems in art, philosophy and religion.... Thus the general psycho-analytic course should be thrown open to the students of these branches of learning as well. The fertilizing effect of psycho-analytic thought on these other disciplines would certainly contribute greatly towards forging a closer link, in the sense of a *universitas literarum*, between medical science and the branches of learning which lie within the sphere of philosophy and the arts. (17:173)[9]

It is interesting to note that this text dates from the same year as "The 'Uncanny.'" It supports my interpretation of the first lines of that work, as does the rest of "The 'Uncanny'" itself. To cite a single example, the uncanny impression produced by the *Tales of Hoffmann*, especially "The Sandman," cannot be understood without reference to the symbolism of dreams. Only an acknowledgment of the symbolic equivalence between tearing out the eyes and castration can account for this effect. A view that simply accepts the text at face value and looks for no deeper secret "does not account adequately for the substitutive relation between the eye and the male organ which is seen to exist in dreams and myths and phantasies; nor can it dispel the impression that the threat of being castrated in especial excites a peculiarly violent and obscure emotion, and that this emotion is what first gives the idea of losing other organs its intense colouring" (17:231). Similarly, such a view renders incomprehensible the fact that in this tale the fear for the eyes is always tied to the death of the father, and that the Sandman keeps coming back as a disturber of love.[10]

Freud thus establishes a link between disciplines and the phenomena under study on the basis of a common nucleus, the oedipal structure. But only the reaction formations to this structure present themselves, as so many differential variations of an invariant, of a postulated type.[11]

What Freud does in "The 'Uncanny'" makes possible, then, another reading of his initial declarations: above all, they must be seen as the denunciation of an aesthetics reserved for specialists and of an ego psychology cut off from a psychology of the id.

Let us refer now to the first lines of "The Moses of Michelangelo":

> I may say at once that I am no connoisseur in art, but simply a layman (*Laie*). I have often observed that the subject-matter of works of art has a stronger attraction for me than their formal and technical qualities, though to the artist their value lies first and foremost in these latter. I am unable rightly to appreciate many of the methods used and the effects obtained in art. I state this so as to secure the reader's indulgence for the attempt I propose to make here.
>
> Nevertheless, works of art do exercise a powerful effect on me, especially those of literature and sculpture, less often of painting. This has occasioned me, when I have been contemplating such things, to spend a long time before them trying to apprehend them in my own way, i.e., to explain to myself what their effect is due to. Wherever I cannot do this, as for instance with music, I am almost incapable of obtaining any pleasure. Some rationalistic, or perhaps analytic, turn of mind in me rebels against being moved by a thing without knowing why I am thus affected and what it is that affects me.

The paradox is that we can gain only a dim understanding of the most grandiose works of art; they overwhelm us without our being able to comprehend them.

> I am not sufficiently well-read to know whether this fact has already been remarked upon; possibly, indeed, some writer on aesthetics has discovered that

> this state of intellectual bewilderment is a necessary condition when a work of art is to achieve its greatest effects. It would be only with the greatest reluctance that I could bring myself to believe in any such necessity.
>
> I do not mean that connoisseurs and lovers of art find no words with which to praise such objects to us. They are eloquent enough, it seems to me. But usually in the presence of a great work of art each says something different from the other; and none of them says anything that solves the riddle (*Rätsel*) for the unpretending admirer. (13:211–212)

Freud's modesty in this text is part of a strategy. The very structure of the beginning of "Moses" invites us to read it in the same way that a work of art should be read,[12] for every text is tissue that masks at the same time that it reveals. It invites us also to distinguish in it, as in a dream, a manifest and a latent content. As in a dream, it is the minute details that arouse suspicion and provoke interpretation. Here, the relevant details are the tone of the text, the irony directed at the "true" connoisseurs, and Freud's denial of his ability to appreciate a work of art as such—a denial that marks an instance of repression and invites us to assign it the opposite meaning of the one declared. What he does subsequently in interpreting the statue of Moses down to the smallest details—which the many "connoisseurs" to whom he refers have not succeeded in doing—totally cancels the opening statements and justifies our way of reading this text as a riddle to be solved, one that might not be seen as such if certain details are neglected.

The riddle of this text figures in miniature the riddle constituted by every work of art and is itself figured in miniature by the riddle that is openly presented here: who is speaking and from where is he speaking? Indeed, the text on Moses is anonymous; it is as though the author were playing a guessing game by creating a verbal portrait of himself in order to elicit his name ("I am no connoisseur of art, but simply a layman," etc.). Here Freud seems to be imitating Morelli, the Italian art lover who wrote under the Russian pseudonym Ivan Lermolieff; for Freud claims to have been "greatly interested" to learn that an Italian doctor was hiding behind the Russian pseudonym (13:222). Morelli set out to distinguish copies from originals—that is, to attribute to the work with absolute certainty the name of its father. To do this, he proceeded by pointing out what seemed to be the most insignificant details of the painting, such as the way the fingernails and ear lobes were drawn—in short, everything that was considered to be rubbish (*Refuse*). But Freud only plays at being

Morelli, the better to denounce the ideology in which the latter is trapped; for to consider it essential to find the name of the author is to conceive of him as the father of his works, as a creator. Yet it is precisely this theological conception of art that Freud sets out to unmask. To tell the name is not to understand the work. Michelangelo is known to all as the author of the statue of Moses, yet the "intentions" of the artist in sculpting it, and the reasons why it moves us, are yet to be understood. The "intentions" can be communicated only by the work in the writing that is specific to it,[13] its formal structure. What Michelangelo himself would have to say about them is of little importance, because true intentions are not conscious. If one can use the work to imagine the life of the author, as Freud does with Leonardo, one can conclude nothing about the work from the conscious life of the artist, of which the name is the symbol. Freud preserves the autonomy of the work as a text, but this is not incompatible with a method of generalized intertextuality. The text engenders its father, as Freud shows in more detail in his treatment of Jensen's *Gradiva*. The theological conception of art accepted the notion of an autonomous, conscious subject who was the father of his works, as God was of creation. By playing at being Morelli through his anonymity, Freud deconstructs the metaphysical conception of the subject: it is not he who is speaking, but the text (which does not mean that the text must be taken literally).

"The Moses of Michelangelo" as well therefore justifies the distinction we have introduced between what Freud openly says and what he in fact does. What he does is discernible through the structure of the text and the apparently trifling details. From this standpoint it is possible to do a better reading of the beginning of "Moses." The opposition between the connoisseurs of art and the mere laymen at first seems to function in favor of the former, since Freud humbly presents himself as a mere layman.[14] But at the end of the text, as in "The 'Uncanny,'" the "connoisseurs" are reduced to glib talkers caught up in subjective opinions, elevating their own fantasies about the works to the status of knowledge, yet unable to solve the riddle of the text in question. Freud's plea to them for lenient criticism should thus be interpreted ironically. What Freud means is that the art "connoisseur" criticizes without knowing what he is talking about, for he is talking about himself; only the psychoanalyst can disclose the "historical" truth, if not the "material" truth, of what the connoisseur says.[15]

A veritable reversal thus occurs between the beginning and the end of the text. Subsequently, Freud nonetheless seems to accord the connoisseur of art an expertise regarding the qualities of form and technique, to which Freud himself claims to be indifferent as he is interested principally in the "content." It would appear, then, that the art connoisseur grasps the specificity of works of art better than the psychoanalyst, because for the artist, the "value [of works of art] lies first and foremost in [their formal and technical qualities]." Likewise, "The 'Uncanny'" attributes to aestheticians the task of understanding how the artist obtains different effects from the same material by varying the means of expression: "[The poet] is able to guide the current of our emotions, to dam it up in one direction and make it flow in another, and he often obtains a great variety of effects from the same material. All this is nothing new, and has doubtless long since been fully taken into account by students of aesthetics. We have drifted into this field of research half involuntarily" (17:251). Yet these loquacious specialists fail where Freud, a mere amateur, succeeds: "The science of aesthetics investigates the conditions under which things are felt as beautiful, but it has been unable to give any explanation of the nature and origin of beauty, and, as usually happens, lack of success is concealed beneath a flood of resounding and empty words. Psychoanalysis, unfortunately, has scarcely anything to say about beauty either" (*Civilization and Its Discontents*, 21:82–83).

To what can this failure be attributed, then, if not to the fact that traditional aesthetics is trapped in the metaphysical distinction between "form" and "content," and trapped as well in the separation of the "faculties"—intelligence and sensibility—as if it were possible to understand the content without the form or the form without the content, even though the work of the artist is at the same time the "expression" of unconscious intentions; as if in order to enjoy art one absolutely must not understand it, even though intelligence itself is a form of enjoyment? In his analysis of the *Moses*, Freud brings together "form" and "content," affect and representation. Right after the introduction, he shows that the numerous interpretations of *Hamlet* failed because they did not account for the effect it produced. On the basis of a formal study that is attentive to the smallest details, he establishes the relations between the structure of the work—an expression of the unconscious ideas that he calls the "artist's intention"—and the effect it has on the spectator. Running counter to the ideology of traditional aesthetics, he establishes a concatenation between affect and representation, power and meaning, the economic and the symbolic.

"In my opinion, what grips us so powerfully can only be the artist's *intention*, in so far as he has succeeded in expressing it in his work and in getting us to understand it" ("The Moses of Michelangelo," 13:212). At the end of the text, Freud wonders whether Michelangelo succeeded at this perfect expression and writes that he was an "artist in whose works there is so much thought striving for expression" (13:236). He adds that Michelangelo went further than any other artist in this direction, to the utmost limits of what art can express. If Freud, as interpreter, has given a fallacious interpretation, the artist must share the responsibility for it. The problem here is to know the limits of expressiveness in a given artist's work and in art in general.

But in establishing a relation of expressiveness between "form" and "content," doesn't Freud himself remain imprisoned in the classical space of representation? Doesn't the concept of "expressiveness" belong to the sphere of metaphysics? Doesn't Freud denounce one aspect of it (the separation of form and content, signifier and signified) only to adopt its opposite (the union of the two), and therefore remain caught in the same closure? Or rather, even though retaining the language of representation, doesn't he cancel the two opposites in order to introduce a completely original conception of the status of form and content in the work of art? I shall examine this question later; here, my aim is simply to propose a reading of the beginning of "Moses," justifying my general method, a symptomal reading of Freud's discourse on art.

Freud says next that he cannot enjoy a work when he does not understand the effect it has on him. In his discourse, he accounts for this on the basis of his rationalistic or analytic disposition. And indeed, the very task of the analytic cure is to be able to link a meaning to an affect that has lost its meaning or never had any to begin with. But this necessity of linking affect to representation is not characteristic of every turn of mind; without this link, affect is transformed into anxiety. The status of representation and affect respectively cannot be understood independently of each other, though their fates may be different. Thus, one can read in this declaration the avowal of a conflictual relation between art and science. Is Freud a prisoner of the ideology that admits of a de jure opposition between art and science? Or is the opposition in question here merely one of two enemy brothers working toward the same goal but competing with each other? If this is the case, traditional ideology's substitution of a de jure opposition for a de facto conflict must itself be interrogated.

The Artist as Great Man and Hero, Substitute for, and Murderer of the Father

Indeed, Freud's oft-declared admiration for art and artists harbors a certain ambivalence and repeats the general public's admiration, all the better to denounce it. In many texts, he acknowledges artists' superiority in being able to "know" man, sparing themselves the detour through work taken by the man of science. In an 1884 letter, he writes, "I think that general hostility reigns between artists and researchers immersed in the details of a scientific investigation. As we know, art gives the former a key which allows them to enter easily into women's hearts, whereas we scientists remain baffled by that strange lock and must wrack our brains in order to find the key that fits."

Theodor Reik is surprised by Freud's harshness regarding Dostoevsky's morality and denounces it.[16] In his response to Reik, Freud acknowledges his ambivalent feelings toward Dostoevsky: "You are right in suspecting that, in spite of my admiration for Dostoevsky's intensity and preeminence, I do not really like him. That is because my patience with pathological natures is exhausted in analysis. In art and life I am intolerant of them" (21:196).

This ambivalence, which reflects people's general attitude toward artists, indicates a certain repression and a displacement of interest from art to artists. Freud's numerous declarations regarding the limits of the "application" of psychoanalysis to art—which, he insists, in no way diminishes the "grandeur," indeed the "saintliness," of the artist—have an essentially strategic significance. In his studies of Leonardo, Goethe, and Michelangelo, but also in that of Moses, he maintains that these great minds, because of their love of knowledge, would have been delighted with the psychoanalytic treatment to which he subjects them. In making this claim, he hopes to overcome the public's resistance, by inviting it to adopt the same attitude as that held by its own idols. Thus, the preface to the Hebrew translation of the *Introductory Lectures on Psycho-Analysis* written in 1930 (15:11) says that Moses and the prophets would surely have accepted his *Lectures* without resistance and warns the Hebrews of today against renewed idolatry of the Golden Calf, which would go hand in hand with a rejection of psychoanalysis. If Freud safeguards the ideological image of the artist in his declarations, he does so the better to denounce it. The same is true of his repeated references to the "fascinating" character of psychoanalytic studies of art,[17] and to the disturbing effect works of art have on whomever receives them. These repetitions are intended to reveal that the interest taken in art is not purely "disinterested" and that it implies a relation to the repressed that Freud proposes to bring to light.

On the one hand, the work of art is one of the offshoots of what is repressed in the artist, and as such is symbolic and symptomatic. It can be deciphered from traces, minute details that indicate that the repression is not entirely successful; this failure is the only thing that opens a space of legibility in the work.[18] One of these traces is the effect of the work on other people: what is repressed by the artist and can be read in his work produces a powerful and enigmatic affect. What is true of art is true also of religion and psychotic delusions, namely that the constraint imposed by the logical mode of thought is no longer in force. Only some element "which returns from oblivion asserts itself with peculiar force, exercises an incomparably powerful influence on people in the mass" (*Moses and Monotheism*, 23:85). What is expressed in art must have undergone repression "before it is able to display such powerful effects on its return" (23:101), which is to say that the work of art, like religion, implies the return of something universally repressed.[19]

On the other hand, the fact that the public's real interest in art lies not in art itself, but in the image it has of the artist as a "great man," is repressed. In light of this, it is easier to understand why the "application" of psychoanalysis to art meets with resistance. Thus, even Freud, who destroys the artist as idol in practice, if not in what he says, cannot completely stifle a feeling of guilt; for to a certain extent, to apply psychoanalysis to art is to commit a murder—that is, to do away with the artist as a genius or a great man. This murder comes in response to another one—the distortion of the repressed in its return, the traces of which are hard to cover up: "The distortion (*Entstellung*) of a text resembles a murder: the difficulty is not in perpetrating the deed, but in getting rid of its traces" (*Moses and Monotheism*, 23:43). During his first visits to San Pietro in Vincoli, where Freud went often to study the *Moses*,[20] he tried to avoid the gaze of the prophet as though he himself were guilty, and his "Moses" seemed to him to be the product of an illegitimate love engendered somewhat clandestinely: "My relationship to this work is something like that to a love child. Every day for three lonely weeks in September of 1913 I stood in the church in front of the statue, studying it, measuring and drawing it until there dawned on me that understanding which in the essay I only dared to express anonymously. Not until much later did I legitimize this nonanalytical child."[21]

Thus, Freud's anonymity in the "Moses" has an overdetermined meaning.[22] By remaining anonymous, Freud plays at being Morelli, inviting us to read his text as a riddle and demystifying the theological conception of the autonomous subject who is father of his works. But his anonymity is also that of the criminal who conceals his name for fear of punishment. In this sense, "The Moses of Michelangelo" foreshadows *Moses and Monotheism*. Just as the Jews killed Moses and repressed the murder, Freud, in his analysis of Michelangelo's statue, "kills" Michelangelo, thereby becoming, in a way, Moses himself, the destroyer of idols. Here, then, what Freud says about Moses in *Moses and Monotheism* could be said of Michelangelo and all other artists: "To deprive a people of the man whom they take pride in as the greatest of their sons is not a thing to be gladly or carelessly undertaken, least of all by someone who is himself one of them. But we cannot allow any such reflection to induce us to put the truth aside in favour of what are supposed to be national interests" (23:7).[23] But the murder of Moses, more than any other, is bound to arouse a strong feeling of guilt, for Moses is the very paradigm of the father. In the first place, he is father of the Jews: "We must not forget that Moses was not only the political leader of the Jews settled in Egypt, but was also their law-giver and educator and forced them into the service of a new religion, which to this very day is known after him as the Mosaic one. . . . I venture to say this: it was one man, the man Moses, who created the Jews" (23:18). But he is also the paradigm of the father in general. "Fate had brought the great deed and misdeed of primaeval days, the killing of the father, closer to the Jewish people by causing them to repeat it on the person of Moses, an outstanding father figure (*Vatergestalt*)" (23:88–89). As lawgiver, Moses is a father, but he is also the interpreter of God and thus a figure whose province is mediation. As such, he does not speak, but rather makes God's word intelligible by writing it down. Another trait attributed to Moses has a special claim to our interest. Moses is said to have been "slow of speech": "he must have suffered from an inhibition or disorder of speech" (23:33).

As an interpreter and destroyer of idols, Freud identifies with Moses. But he keeps at a distance from him as well, for he substitutes for the Mosaic law the law of ἀνάγκη, necessity. It is therefore understandable that the "murder" of Moses provokes in him an acute feeling of guilt. But this feeling must nonetheless persist as Freud "applies" psychoanalysis to art and artists, because each time he puts an end to the public's infatuation with an idol, he repeats the murder of the father. If Freud must proceed with great care when he speaks of art and the artist, it is because in their relationship to the artist, men repeat an infantile mode of behavior. In applying psychoanalysis to art, Freud advocates the murder of the father and his substitutes. Clearly, the public worships the artist and all other "great men." Yet in *Moses and Monotheism*, where Freud tries to define the nature of the great man, he shows that no thinker, artist, technical expert, or great chess player is worthy of the name (23:108). Success in a life of action is no more satisfactory as a criterion, as Freud shows by deliberately citing the examples of Goethe, Leonardo da Vinci, and Beethoven. The concept of the "great man" is vague and connotes nothing more than the presence of numerous human capabilities in the individual so designated. The interest this man arouses is due to the influence he has on other men, an influence that is made possible only by others' need to admire an authority, attracted as they are to all father substitutes.

The characteristics attributed to the "great man" are those of the father; thus, the concept of the "great man" is a pragmatic one whose coherence lies in the uniformity of infantile psychic reactions. But the psychic overvaluation of the actual father is limited to a short space of time. As a result of rivalry and disappointments, the child becomes detached from his parents and adopts a critical attitude toward the father. The child's "family romance," the source of all myth, divides the family in two, making one parent noble, the other humble—a development that marks a change in the child's affective relationship to his parents (23:12–13). And so the myth of the hero is born; the hero takes the father's place and always ends up killing him: "The hero . . . always rebels against his father and kills him in some shape or other" (23:87). People's attitude toward artists repeats this ambivalence. The cult of the artist is ambiguous in that it consists in the worship of father and hero alike; the cult of the hero is always a form of self-worship, since the hero is the first ego ideal. This attitude is religious but also narcissistic in character, and repeats that of the child toward the father and of the parents toward the child, to whom they attribute all the "gifts" and good fortune that they granted to themselves during the narcissistic period in infancy.

But if the artist is esteemed *like* a God, he is nevertheless not God himself, but a substitute. The religion of the father and the cult of art correspond to distinct moments in human evolution, which in turn correspond to different stages in the evolution of the libido. The artistic phase belongs to the animistic phase and corresponds to the narcissistic stage, whereas the religious phase is tied to the stage at which the libido is directed toward objects, the stage of fixation on the parents.[24] Epic poetry and tragedy take the place of the totemic meal and repeat it differently, opening a space that is specific to art. The fact that the deified hero may have preceded the deification of the father in no way weakens the argument, for the deification of the hero foretells the return of the primeval father transformed into a god. In "Group Psychology and the Analysis of the Ego," Freud suggests that the chronological succession would be as follows: mother goddess, deified hero, and god the father.[25]

The Biographical Illusion

This religious and narcissistic attitude toward artists can be observed at all levels of cultural production. It explains, for instance, people's interest in biographies—a fact that emerges clearly when biographies are lacking, as in the case of Shakespeare. Biographies never provide any insight into the hero, but rather reveal the infantile attitude that the biographer shares with the reader, one of admiration and narcissistic identification.

Biographers idealize the hero while trying at the same time to reduce the distance separating them from him. Yet it is essential that distance be preserved: the artist and his work must remain "taboo" in a sense,[26] in order to avoid murder and maintain the theological illusion of art.

> Biographers are fixated on their heroes in a quite special way. In many cases they have chosen their hero as the subject of their studies because—for reasons of their personal emotional life—they have felt a special affection for him from the very first. They then devote their energies to a task of idealization, aimed at enrolling the great man among the class of their infantile models—at reviving in him, perhaps, the child's idea of his father. To gratify this wish they obliterate the individual features of their subject's physiognomy; they smooth over the traces of his life's struggles with internal and external resistances, and they tolerate in him no vestige of human weakness or imperfection. They thus present us with what is in fact a cold, strange, ideal figure, instead of a human being to whom we might feel ourselves distantly related. That they should do this is regrettable, for they thereby sacrifice truth to an illusion, and for the sake of their infantile phantasies abandon the

opportunity of penetrating the most fascinating secrets of human nature. (*Leonardo*, 11:130)[27]

Freud lays equal emphasis, however, on biographers' desire to overcome distance:

> The biographer's justification also contains a confession. It is true that the biographer does not want to depose his hero, but he does want to bring him nearer to us. . . . And it is unavoidable that if we learn more about a great man's life we shall also hear of occasions on which he has in fact done no better than we, has in fact come near to us as a human being. ("Address Delivered in the Goethe House at Frankfurt," 21:211–12)

The double aim of biographers, to maintain and to overcome distance, is not a contradiction in Freud's discourse; it simply reflects the child's ambivalence toward his parents. The attitude of the biographer, like that of the art lover toward the artist, repeats the artist's attitude toward his father, which includes both admiration and the desire to kill. That is why, in the public eye, the artist is the image of father and hero alike. The ambiguous status Freud assigns him corresponds to the ambivalent attitudes of the artist and the public, who are both prisoners of their infantile prototype. In any event, to admire the hero is to continue to admire the father indirectly, for the hero acquires his status only through identification with the father and the desire to take his place. The "murder" of the father by the artist is achieved by means of regression to the narcissistic stage.

Freud's unmasking of this dynamic, however, consists in showing that the theological attitude of worship toward the artist is simply the other side of narcissistic identification. Both the religious and the animistic phase must be surpassed by the scientific phase—that of adulthood—characterized by renunciation of the pleasure principle and subordination of object choice to reality.[28] Freud substitutes the search for the laws governing not only the pathological and the normal, but also the "sublime," for biographers' idealization of artists. The continuity between the "great man" and the reader is established not by means of identification, but because the behavior of both can be explained by the same psychic mechanisms. The psychoanalyst acts as a mediator between the artist and the public, between the father and the son, because the son cannot bear to look his father in the face any more than he can confront his own unconscious, just as primitive peoples cannot safely look at their chieftain.[29]

The contribution of psychoanalysis to biography is to have shown that the artist is no more a great man or hero than we are. The "application" of psychoanalysis to art completely reverses the stance of traditional biographies. "Killing" the father means renouncing both the theological idealization and the narcissistic identification that prompts the subject's desire to be his own father. Yet it also means respecting the superego, which alone makes possible the renunciation of the pleasure principle.

A New Iconoclast

For Freud, then, the problem of art is linked to that of the father, that is, to the Oedipus complex. Art, like all cultural phenomena, is a reaction formation that stems from this complex (see note 9). The traditional ideology of art unmasked by Freud is both theological and narcissistic and is ultimately founded on the oedipal relation; it is the victim of infantilism and of an incompletely resolved Oedipus complex. Freud's attitude toward the artist repeats the attitude toward the father, admiring overvaluation, a reluctance to "kill" him, then the end of these illusions and also of childhood. The reign of pleasure and illusion gives way to that of necessity, and likewise, a period of admiration for the artist is followed by the analysis of his works: the "sublime" obeys the same laws as the normal and the pathological. Behind the great man one discovers the child, or even the neurotic. What is more, it is not only artistic "creation" that constitutes a reaction to the Oedipus complex. For Freud, the oedipal moment always forms the thematic core of works of art as well, whether it presents itself to the reader as a paradigmatic model, as in Sophocles' *Oedipus Rex*, or does so indirectly as a variation of, and difference from, a universal structure, as is the case with *Hamlet*, *The Brothers Karamazov*, *The Tales of Hoffman*, Jensen's *Gradiva*, and the works of Leonardo da Vinci.

In this light, it is clear why the "application" of psychoanalysis to art encountered such strong resistance despite Freud's cautious and modest declarations: art was the last bastion of narcissism. Psychoanalysis inflicted on man one of his three great narcissistic wounds by deconstructing the idea of the autonomous subject endowed with self-mastery and self-sufficiency, indeed a subject who is his own creator.[30] Narcissism, however, is essentially a death force, so to denounce it is to work in favor of Eros. We shall have to examine more closely the role played in art by Eros and the death impulses, respectively, as well as the situation of art in the economy of life.

If Freud's texts are read, then, by using the deciphering method he himself taught us, distinguishing what he says from what he actually does in his discourse,[31] one realizes that despite language that still belongs to the closure of metaphysics, Freud is not a prisoner of his ideology. He does not, however, demystify ideology as Marx does, because for Freud the epistemological rupture necessarily involves a psychic break: one can break with ideology only by renouncing the wish to be one's own father. Knowledge of ideology is futile if it is not accompanied by instinctual renunciation[32]—the latter is at least a necessary, if not a sufficient, condition of the former. Instinctual renunciation alone makes it possible to adopt a scientific attitude and accept necessity. In support of this claim, let me cite this fine passage from the *New Introductory Lectures*:

> The strength of Marxism clearly lies, not in its view of history or the prophecies of the future that are based on it, but in its sagacious indication of the decisive influence which the economic circumstances of men have upon their intellectual, ethical, and artistic attitudes. A number of connections and implications were thus uncovered (*auf-gedeckt*), which had previously been almost totally overlooked. But it cannot be assumed that economic motives are the only ones that determine the behaviour of human beings in society. . . . It is altogether incomprehensible how psychological factors can be overlooked where what is in question are the reactions of living human beings. . . . In an earlier enquiry I also pointed out the important claims made by the super-ego, which represents tradition and the ideals of the past and will for a time resist the incentives of a new economic situation. And finally we must not forget that the mass of human beings who are subjected to economic necessities also undergo the process of cultural development—of civilization as other people may say—which, though no doubt influenced by all the other factors, is certainly independent of them in its origin. (22:178–79)[33]

TRANSLATED BY WINIFRED WOODHULL

§ 2 The Impossible Profession

For Jean-François Lyotard

This Is Not a Profession

In "Analysis Terminable and Interminable" (1937), Freud pessimistically declares, on the basis of all his experience, that analysis, like the arts of educating and of governing men, is an impossible profession (*Beruf*).[1] It is a profession, in other words, in which one can be certain ahead of time of failing. Because a complete knowledge of the psychology of the unconscious and of the structure of the neuroses is a pure fantasy, the analyst cannot foresee the subsequent fate of a "successful" treatment. This distinguishes him from the obstetrician, who by examining the placenta can tell whether it has been completely expelled or whether noxious pieces are still inside. It is impossible to say whether the work of the analysis has been completed, or whether one should expect relapses or new attacks of the illness. There is apparently no way of resolving an instinctual conflict permanently and definitively, no way of inoculating the patient against any renewed possibility of analogous conflicts, no way of submitting a pathogenic conflict to preventive treatment so that it would never again betray itself by any indication. In addition, analytic experience itself reveals insurmountable resistances to curing the patient. Like a sculptor, the analyst works either on a stone that is too soft or on one that is too hard. Either he treats men who give the impression that instead of having worked with clay, he has written on water, so fragile are the results; or he treats patients who are unable to detach their libidinal cathexes from one object and transfer them onto another, and who remain forever fixated on the one object. Other, younger, patients display a certain amount of psychic inertia: all mental processes, all relations, all distributions of energy appear invariable and fixed. And finally, there are those patients who cling to their sickness and their sufferings, either through guilt and a masochistic need for self-punishment, or on account of a "negative therapeutic reaction" arising from the death instincts. Faced with the superiority of these forces that foil all his efforts, the analyst can only bow down and admit defeat. There is nothing to guarantee that the "end" [*fin*] of an analysis will coincide with its completion, nothing to guarantee that the analyst has at the end [*à la fin*] truly reached his goal.[2] In fact, the opposite is true. The profession of the analyst is impossible, and to practice it one has to be oneself a masochist.

But is psychoanalysis even a *profession*? The question also applies to Freud's two paradigms, the arts of educating and of governing men, which may not be only simple paradigms. Like these arts, psychoanalysis is an impossible profession that is impossible as a profession, if by this term we mean a *techne* having a particular aim that responds to a particular need, and having the appropriate means for achieving that aim. Failure is always of a technical nature, occurring at the level of means poorly adapted to the aim one has set for oneself. Now if it is true that Freud's texts by and large ascribe to analytic treatment a single purpose—curing the patient, a purpose that responds to the patient's demand and to his sufferings—the notion of "curing" itself remains vague and undergoes multiple variations from one text to another, sometimes even within one and the same text. "Analysis Terminable and Interminable" initially defines an ideal end for an analysis: "the patient shall no longer be suffering from his symptoms and shall have overcome his anxieties and his inhibitions; and . . . the analyst shall judge that so much repressed material has been made conscious, so much that was unintelligible has been explained, and so much internal resistance conquered, that there is no need to fear a repetition of the pathological processes concerned."[3]

Later in the same essay, Freud modifies those analytic ambitions he deems excessive: "Our aim will not be to rub off every peculiarity of human character for the sake of a schematic 'normality,' nor yet to demand that the person who has been 'thoroughly analysed' shall feel no passions and develop no internal conflicts. The business of the analysis is to secure the best possible psychological conditions for the functions of the ego; with that it has discharged its task" (23:250).

In earlier texts, Freud advised young analysts to be satisfied with having restored some of the patient's "capacity for work and enjoyment" ("Recommendations to Physicians Practising Psychoanalysis," 1912, 12:119), or simply with having restored the patient's "capacity for love."[4] All these formulations are quite vague and inexact.

On top of this, Freud's texts add an educational purpose to the therapeutic one, even as Freud advises physicians to give up all "educative ambition" ("Recommendations to Physicians," 12:119) and insists that they not aim for a sublimation of the instincts. The analyst's task is educational in that analysis is an apprenticeship in renouncing a certain primary, infantile type of defense against pain—namely, repression—for the sake of another, secondary, adult type of defense—namely, judgment.[5] Understood in this way, analysis would not be reserved exclusively for "sick" people. Freud goes to the point of saying that analysis works only with those who are normal, and that with them it should work every time. More than a treatment, then, analysis would be a school of judgment, albeit a school in which one would also witness the disappearance of certain pathological symptoms. In this educational mission, the analyst should not hesitate to offer himself as a model and guide. Whereas the medical profession does not require a physician to be in perfect physical shape (on condition that whatever illnesses from which he suffers do not prevent him from doing his job), analytic "practice," in order to be efficient and effective, cannot allow for "defective" practitioners. The model analyst should possess a certain superiority and, as proof of his ability, be endowed with "a considerable degree of mental normality and correctness" and a love for truth, qualities that cannot be acquired through an apprenticeship in a particular art (*bestimmte Kunst*) and its rules.[6]

This, then, is a funny occupation: where not only the analyst's attention but also the aim of his work is supposed to remain "aimless," where in order to succeed it is not enough to learn the rules of the "profession," where the practitioner is supposed to be a superior man at the same time that he is "allowed to be [a] human [being] like anyone else" ("Analysis Terminable," 23:247)—and where he is allowed to fail.

But it is also the very "aimlessness" of the aim of analysis that allows Freud to qualify his initial pessimism. The guarantee of failure—in this profession that is not one—applies only to the excessively ambitious analyst who seeks "extreme results." The wretched analyst, who has Freud's deepest sympathy, can escape the predicament of failure by modifying his aims and scaling down his ambitions. When he comes up against the biological bedrocks of female penis envy, on the one hand, and male castration anxiety, on the other, the analyst should above all else not try to overcome this factor, but be satisfied simply with "the certainty that we have given the person analysed every possible encouragement to re-examine and alter his attitude to it" ("Analysis Terminable," 23:253).

The plasticity of the analytic "profession's" aims make analysis less like a predetermined technique and more like a game, one with variable rules allowing for the peculiar temperament and inner preferences of each player. There is no discussion of the analytic method having a universal value or rules that one could simply, mechanically learn in order to become an analyst. To make reference to Freud, then, is not necessarily to appeal to an authority who has fixed once and for all the aims and rules of the "method." Freud, in any case, did not see himself in this way. He presented himself only as a model of an inventor of rules that were the most appropriate for his own idiosyncrasies, and he invited other analysts to imitate him, which is to say to invent other rules on their own, in an "inspired" and original way.

This is not to say that any practice whatsoever can arbitrarily be called an analytic game. In spite of the variability of the rules, there must be some fundamental, common principles that serve as the minimum requirement for the practice to count as analysis: these principles are free association for the analysand and aimless attention for the analyst.[7] Furthermore, the minimal condition for this practice to be a game is that not all moves [*coups*] are allowed and that any "blow" [*coup*] that mortally threatens the other is prohibited. Each player would have to invent—in an unregulated way—rules that prevent a harmful outcome. But how would such rules be decided a priori? Is not analysis a kind of game precisely because it implies a risky "blow-by-blow" progression?

> [T]he most successful cases are those in which one proceeds, as it were, without any purpose in view, allows oneself to be taken by surprise by any new turn in them, and always meets them with an open mind, free from any presuppositions. The correct behavior for an analyst lies in swinging over according to need from the one mental attitude to the other, in avoiding speculation or brooding over cases while they are in analysis, and in submitting the material obtained to a synthetic process of thought only after the analysis is concluded. ("Recommendations to Physicians," 12:114)

Is the progression of analysis not all the more risky in that the validity, the "truth," or rather the beauty, of each move is determined only after the fact [*après-coup*], insofar as there is no a priori criterion to follow, so that in order to make a move, one always has to place a bet, a wager without any guarantee? And on top of this, the analysand's speech cannot help to validate any one move, since his "yes" or "no" is only a symptom for the analyst and as such never ultimately decisive.

But is this risky method sufficient to turn analysis into a game, if its purpose remains otherwise serious, as analysis still aims at curing the patient, if in a limited way? Is play, which has been defined since Plato as a luxurious, superfluous, and frivolous activity, not opposed to the seriousness of a task punctuated by the demands and sufferings of the analysand? Unless, that is, the "cure" consists in ridding oneself of the seriousness of illness and in "playing"—in playing by oneself and with language.

When the patient addresses the analyst and eagerly awaits a response, there is nothing more shocking and painful than silence coming from the other side of the couch. However, the lack of response on the analyst's part is essential for the radical transformation of the patient's relation to language: for getting the patient to stop using language as an instrument of communication, of exchange and dialogue, and to start speaking "for the sake of speaking," without a purpose and without expecting a response. To recover, then, is to be capable of becoming indifferent to the speech of the other, to be capable of detaching oneself from it in order to play on one's own, while still in the other's presence. Winnicott, in a remarkable text, shows that "the capacity to be alone is a paradox; it is the experience of being alone while someone else is present," and that "the ability to be truly alone has as its basis the early experience of being alone in the presence of someone."[8] A child who cannot bear solitude is unable to play by himself in the corner even when his mother is present. He cannot stop bothering her, "clinging to her apron strings," and holding onto her. In his famous analysis of the *fort/da* game, Freud had already emphasized how the child playing with the bobbin has excellent relations with his parents and how, in spite of being very attached to his mother, he never cries when she is absent, even when she goes away for hours at a time. He can throw "the mother" away (*fort*), only because she is always there (*da*), even when she goes away. Because he has interiorized a good object—namely, the mother—he is capable of being alone—with or without her—of playing, and of playing with her, by sending her on a long walk.

If the aim of analysis is this ludic detachment that enables the patient to send the analyst out for a long walk, then the "seriousness" of recovery is no longer opposed to play, and play itself turns out to be a serious activity. In this way, Freud effaces the metaphysical opposition between play and seriousness.

The Sublation of Mysticism[9]

To tell the truth, none of Freud's texts explicitly ascribe this ludic purpose to analysis, any more than they explicitly compare analysis to a game. Nevertheless, the association is legible between the lines of a double gesture on Freud's part. On the one hand, for polemical and strategic reasons, and in response to the charge of mysticism, he insists on the scientific and technical nature of the methodological rules. On the other hand, and in the very same texts, he erases those claims by pointing to the radical difference between analysis and all other sciences and techniques. Analysis does not fit into any preexisting techne, even if most of the arts can serve as its metaphoric models. Freud compares the analyst in turn to a chemist, a gynecologist, a surgeon, a sculptor, a painter, an archaeologist, a musician, a chess player, and a player of solitaire. He also compares the analyst to a technical instrument, such as a mirror or a telephone. This permanent metaphorical sliding associates him with Plato's sophist (while "Constructions in Analysis" also turns him into a fisherman). That is, it associates him with an unclassifiable charlatan rather than with a professional man, with someone who works with magic and with play more than he does with science.

In his reconciliation of these two aspects of analysis, Freud lets go of neither. Analysis accomplishes the sublation [*relève*], the *Aufhebung*, of all the occult, mystical, and irrational powers that preceded it. Rejecting none of their "methods," it surpasses them in the act of preserving them. Depending on the given text, and on the requirements and specific moments of the given polemic, Freud puts the emphasis on either the surpassing or the preserving of these methods, on either the rationality or the irrationality—let us say the madness or delirium—of analysis. Correlatively, the figure of the analyst appears either as a superior being playing out his role on a stage entirely distinct from that of the analysand or as a human being like any other, as human, all too human, as someone capable of mistakes and aberrations, and as even more pitiable than his own patient, or, in any case, as someone working and playing side by side with the patient.

Is analysis, therefore, not, above all else, a modern form of mysticism? Is it not fundamentally unscientific? Is it not based on influence and suggestion, on uncontrollable psychic factors?

Freud responds to this accusation by saying that every treatment places the patient in a state of "expectant faith" and plays upon psychic functions that have a decisive role in the therapeutic process.[10] This uncontrollable psychic factor cannot, in any event, be eliminated, because "another person intimately concerned in the process of recovery—the patient—has no intention of discarding it" ("On Psychotherapy," 7:258), so psychoanalysis sets out to regulate and control it by responding with ever more rationality and efficacy. Instead of rejecting outright the old methods that are linked to suggestion and hypnosis, it transforms them in order to reach a better understanding of illnesses and how they work. Analysis, in this regard, is a technique for controlling the uncontrollable. Thanks to precise rules, the space of the cure is a laboratory, a space in which certain affects and infantile behaviors can be repeated under experimental conditions that have been determined and laid out beforehand. This kind of regulated and monitored repetition allows for the mastery, which is to say the termination, outside the space of the cure, of uncontrolled repetitions. It makes room for memory and the invention of new behaviors.

Transference is the best example of such an experimental repetition. This "invention," this major analytic technique, takes over from [*prend la relève de*] suggestion and influence, still making use of them, but in a way that is more regulated. Substituting for all the transferential relations of daily life (the spontaneous repetition, everywhere, of clichés and more or less stereotypical infantile prototypes), transference, the essential agent of analysis, is an "explosive material." As a new type of chemist, the analyst must know how to handle it aptly and according to precise rules, always at risk, in the worst-case scenario, of blowing everything up, of reinforcing the resistances instead of removing them, and of keeping the patient from ever renouncing the advantages of his illness. Transference requires that the analyst himself be analyzed, so that he will be able to control his own counter-transference and not fall into the trap of responding to the patient while forgetting that transference love, however "real," is the product of an artificial laboratory situation. Above all, the analyst should remember that the point of the treatment is to restore the patient with a capacity for love. To gratify transference love over the course of the therapy—in a manner that is entirely artificial, provisional, and defective—is to keep the patient from ever attaining real, lasting love. It contravenes conventional morality and ensures technical failure. Freud compares the analyst who does not know how to handle transference skillfully to the humorist [*farceur*] who throws a sausage into the middle of a greyhound race, distracting the dogs from the "garland of sausages" at the finish line, the reward for any analysis brought to term: "[The analyst] must not stage the scene of a dog-race in which the prize was to be a garland of sausages but which some humorist spoilt by throwing a single sausage on to the track. The result was, of course, that the dogs threw themselves upon it and forgot all about the race and about the garland that was luring them to victory in the far distance."[11]

The humorist is once more the analogue of the sophist in the *Phaedrus*, who over the course of the procession of souls toward the intelligible heaven of ideas forgets about the goal along the way, being seduced by the sensory and abandoning the pursuit of truth for the sake of the pleasure of argument and the struggle for power.

But who decides that a hypothetical garland of sausages, one reserved in any case for an uncertain future (because the end of analysis remains in principle unreachable), is worth more than a single sausage guaranteed *hic et nunc*? Is it simply the technical rules requiring that one place a risky bet on the future who decide? Even though Freud emphasizes technical constraints (e.g., the psychoanalyst should act like a surgeon who lets go of all emotional responses in order to pursue his one goal of completing the operation as skillfully as possible[12]), he recognizes that in analysis, moral obligations must augment [*doubler*] the technical necessities. Obedience to this double bind (in its nontechnical sense) is all that prevents analysis from becoming a grand farce in which the analysand turns out to be the turkey. If analysis plays with powers that have been known for a long time, if it plays with all the instinctual forces, it is only by rigorously controlling them that it can safely make use of them. The analyst who is unable to rise up to the task of sublating these forces can, instead of elevating and curing the patient, only cause him to regress and to flee.

Hence the need for strict rules, which are all that distinguish the psychoanalyst from the charlatan, the humorist, and the sophist. And yet these necessary rules are neither universal nor a priori. They are based on an empirical practice and are modified with the blow-by-blow experience of analysis. They cannot be learned from books and "cannot be discovered independently without great sacrifices of time, labour and success" (" 'Wild' Psychoanalysis," 1910, 11:226). Like every other medical technique, analytic "technique" is learned from those who are already proficient in it and who serve as models for others. The extreme diversity of psychic constellations, the plasticity of psychic processes, and the considerable number of determining factors all stand in opposition to any mechanization of psychoanalytic technique.[13] In its resistance to mechanization, the analytic game is like chess, that most noble of games. In chess, only the opening and closing moves can be described schematically and exhaustively; after the opening move, the game's immense complexity defies any further description. To become a chess player, one cannot restrict oneself to a knowledge of the game's mechanical rules. One has to study how the masters play.[14]

Paradoxically, proceeding "wildly" instead of following the rules can lead to positive results. In fact, "wild" analysis does much more harm to the reputation of analysis (which thereby loses all scientific authority) than to the patients themselves: "I have often found that a clumsy procedure like this, even if at first it produced an exacerbation of the patient's condition, led to a recovery in the end" (" 'Wild' Psychoanalysis," 11:227). And although a supposedly defective "method" can lead to the desired result, a procedure that usually works can sometimes prove ineffective (cf. "On Beginning the Treatment"). To follow the Freudian rules to the letter, then, is to risk failure, given that they were established only provisionally and according to Freud's own individual preferences and temperament: "I must . . . make it clear that what I am asserting is that this technique is the only one suited to my individuality; I do not venture to deny that a physician quite differently constituted might find himself driven to adopt a different attitude to his patients and to the task before him" ("Recommendations to Physicians," 12:111).

Like Descartes at the beginning of *Discourse on Method*, Freud simultaneously presents his method as a model for younger beginners, one that might spare them wasted efforts, and invites each one to follow his own path. Rather than offering rules, he gives advice based on his experience, experience that forced him to modify his own method over time. The invention of new rules potentially allows for the extension of the analytic field, as there is no absolute criterion for determining whether a given patient is in need of analysis: "I do not regard it as by any means impossible that by suitable changes in the method we may succeed in overcoming this contradiction" ("On Psychotherapy," 7:264). Neither an a priori judgment nor even a previously attempted treatment can determine whether a patient requires analysis. What ultimately decides, it seems, are the analyst's inherent preferences. If Freud refuses treatment to those "who do not possess a reasonable degree of education and a fairly reliable character" ("On Psychotherapy," 7:263), if the ideal, according to him, would ultimately be to accept only those people with a normal mental condition, indeed to accept the most highly developed personalities, is it not because he finds it preferable to welcome such an elite onto his couch? "It is gratifying that precisely the most valuable and most highly developed persons are best suited for [psychoanalytic] procedure" ("On Psychotherapy," 7:264).

This intellectual elite is also a social elite. Freud leaves to others the eventual possibility of offering analysis free of charge to those who do not belong to the privileged classes, having "no doubt that the validity of our psychological assumptions will make its impression on the uneducated too" ("Lines of Advance in Psychoanalytic Therapy," 17:167). But this would be possible only at the cost of adapting analytic technique to new conditions. Because the hard life awaiting the poor outside of analysis holds little attraction to them, and because illness gives them more claim to social support, they will be even less disposed than the rich to give up their neuroses. The application of analysis to their ranks will therefore require physicians to "alloy the pure gold of analysis freely with the copper of direct suggestion; and hypnotic influence, too, might find a place in [analytic technique] again" ("Lines of Advance," 17:168). Freud, for his part, keeps all to himself the "golden race"—those golden people who pay with gold to take advantage of "the pure gold of analysis," one that is "free of all bias." He exhibits a positively Platonic contempt for the "copper race" that makes the psychoanalytic task considerably more cumbersome and burdens it with the threats of lower fees and of introducing coarseness and vulgarity onto the couch. It is for others, then, to take up this threat, for anyone but the father of analysis, who was not always rolling in gold himself, and who, unlike Goethe, always had to pay his own way because no one would love him for his beautiful eyes alone.[15]

Analytic rules are a result of experience and thus have no general value. Their only purpose is potentially to supplement what Freud calls tact

(*Taktum*, a musical term denoting "musical touch"): "psychoanalysis provides these definite technical rules to replace the indefinable 'medical tact' which is looked upon as some special gift" (" 'Wild' Psychoanalysis," 11:226).[16] The analytic "method" is makeshift because nothing can truly supplement the tact that alone is ultimately decisive and that supplements the perpetually deficient rules more than they supplement it. There is, for example, no rule for deciding on the end of an analysis, for choosing the propitious moment at which to resort to the violent technical method of fixing a termination date and sticking to it, for employing that blackmailing device that is supposed to be effective only as long as "one hits the right time for it" ("Analysis Terminable," 23:218). Freud cites the case of the "Wolf-man," to whom he announced one day that the upcoming year of treatment would be their last: "the patient came to see that I was in earnest. Under the inexorable pressure of this fixed limit his resistance and his fixation to the illness gave way, and now in a disproportionately short time the analysis produced all the material which made it possible to clear up his inhibitions and remove his symptoms" ("From the History of an Infantile Neurosis," 17:11). This decision of putting an end to the analysis is always undertaken at risk, and miscalculations cannot be rectified. This is another verification of the adage that "a lion only springs once" ("Analysis Terminable," 23:219). But how to decide when the lion should spring? "The decision must be left to the analyst's tact [*Taktum*]" (23:219).[17]

What is ultimately decisive, then, is not a correct or mistaken, a more or less rational, "calculation." It is rather the "indefinable quality" of a special gift that is associated with intuition [*flair*], with an aesthetic touch.[18]

To base analytic judgments on an indefinable gift is to confer an uncanny aspect to the treatment, as nothing guarantees that a particular analyst in fact possesses this talent. It is to attribute the cure to some occult, unknown power granted by a good fairy or genie and to associate analysis less with science and technique and more with magic.

Freud himself says that psychoanalysis can be regarded as an *unheimlich* practice, not only because it revives in the patient mental processes deemed long overcome, but also because its "technique" brings seemingly archaic procedures back to life. It is neither science, nor medicine, nor religion, nor mysticism, nor magic, and yet is associated with all of these practices in its raising of [*relève de*] all the occult forces: it is an unusual, bizarre, atopical practice. "Indeed, I should not be surprised to hear that psychoanalysis, which is concerned with laying bare these hidden forces, has itself become uncanny to many people for that very reason. In one case, after I had succeeded—though none too rapidly—in effecting a cure in a girl who had been an invalid for many years, I myself heard this view expressed by the patient's mother long after her recovery" ("The 'Uncanny,'" 1919, 17:243–44).

Some of Freud's texts explicitly cast the analyst as a benevolent genie who can magically undo the curses cast by evil spirits. Illness is a spell that can be broken by calling things by their secret names, names that have been hidden behind the disguises that mask them:

> [The psychoneuroses'] capacity to exist depends on this distortion and lack of recognition. When the riddle they present is solved and the solution is accepted by the patients these diseases cease to be able to exist. There is hardly anything like this in medicine, though in fairy tales you hear of evil spirits whose power is broken as soon as you can tell them their name—the name which they have kept secret. ("The Future Prospects of Psychoanalytic Therapy," 1910, 11:148)

Like a magician, Freud enacts the most extraordinary reversals with just one wave of his wand, undoing the charms that have transformed realities and rendered them enigmatic and unrecognizable: "With a wave of the wand, as though we were in a fairy tale, we have stripped the astral garment from our theme; and now we see that the theme is a human one, *a man's choice between three women*" ("The Theme of the Three Caskets," 1913, 12:292).

Titles on Credit

Because it plays on secret forces and reveals "secret" names, psychoanalysis is a kind of initiatory and esoteric rite: people who see an analyst always expect some kind of revelation. Like Socrates' interlocutors, they assume the person behind the couch possesses a knowledge that will magically lead them out of their aporias, with a simple wave of his wand.

But what guarantees that the great magician is not a simple charlatan, that he is not more a sophist than a Socrates? This question was especially legitimate at the dawn of psychoanalysis, when it had no fame, no prestige, no title to show for itself; when it had not attained that powerful agency of scientific authority that single-handedly could guarantee its success; and when it appeared instead in the shabby figure of a poor Jew whom no one allows to borrow on credit.

> I can only say that when I assured my patients that I knew how to relieve them permanently of their sufferings they looked round my modest abode, reflected on my lack of fame and title, and regarded me like the possessor of an infallible system at a gambling-resort, of whom people say that if he could do what he professes he would look very different himself. ("Future Prospects," 11:146)

It is this lack of accreditation that makes analysis comparable to a game of chance in which one has to risk everything. Generally speaking, psychoanalysis is the last card on which one bets, when there is nothing left to lose. The analytic game is played only in desperation, after one has already resorted to practices that enjoy more authority and that are regarded as more infallible. Recourse to analysis is indeed an act of faith, a final bet. And yet in spite of his pathetic figure, the analyst, like the gambler, claims to have "an infallible system" for winning, as long as his patients agree to place a bet and to pay. His patients must consent not only to pay the price of the cure, but to pay with their entire person, to do the work themselves, to disclose their "secrets" (secrets they mistakenly believe the other already knows). They must deliver themselves, bound hand and foot, by making a show of their faith at every trial that arises, because the promised gains require prior losses in the form of aggravated symptoms and because the whole (magical) operation cannot be pulled off without some hemorrhaging.

As in any game, nothing ventured, nothing gained. If you go to a gynecologist and, like a Turkish woman, simply extend your arm through a hole in the wall to have your pulse taken, the success of the consultation will be proportional to the inaccessibility of the object. It is not surprising that in Turkey, gynecology enjoys no credit. Elsewhere, however, the gynecologist has become the helper and savior of women. And behind the pathetic figure of Freud the charlatanic gambler, there also hides (for those willing to look) a savior of women, a gynecologist of the psyche: in order to be saved, you simply have to bet on him and to lend him some credit. And this means offering him something other than a wrist through a hole in the wall, through the hole that leads to the dark room of consciousness. It means allowing your depths to be revealed directly and without distortion by the analyst's speculum trying to thread them like a camel through the eye of a needle.[19]

The lack of credit lent to analysis is due not to its actual lack of titles but to the disavowal of its importance and seriousness. Because women allow the analyst only to feel their pulse, psychoanalysis finds itself discredited and seems ineffective. The analyst appears as little more than a simple charlatan—someone who promises a cure in return for the patient's trust and confession, without actually possessing any technical knowledge. Such a charlatanic analyst can in fact only worsen the case of anyone who has "bet" on him, because analytic investigation is no simple affair. It implies at the very least that one puts oneself at risk for the sake of the cure. Just as one cannot examine a tumor without already having studied histology, one should not take on the analysis of a hysteria without having undergone an apprenticeship. The psyche is a musical instrument that is difficult to handle, and one should use caution in learning how to play it.

The difference between psychoanalysis and charlatanry was perceived long ago by Shakespeare, in his staging of a "neurotic" Hamlet who refuses to let himself be manipulated by incompetents.[20] The incompetent charlatans are the king's courtiers, Rosencrantz and Guildenstern, who have been assigned—for political reasons—the task of questioning Hamlet in order to extract the secret of his melancholy. The questioning is a true interrogation, a torture session carried out with the aim of extorting a secret from someone who has no intention whatsoever of giving it up, and who has not asked for anyone's help because his "madness" is a mask that it is in his best interest to keep on. The king's courtiers demonstrate their analytic incompetence by thinking that interrogating a "sick" person is sufficient for obtaining a response. They are unaware that in every hysteric there lies a criminal and that only the transferential machine could get him to open his mouth.[21] In trying to extort Hamlet's secret against his will, Freud says, the courtiers proceed as torturers do. Hamlet asks his torturers whether they would like to play the flute that has been brought on stage, telling them it is as easy a task as lying (an art in which they should be masters, like the charlatan who pretends to heal without having any technical knowledge). The courtiers refuse on grounds of musical incompetence, and Hamlet has thereby successfully pointed out their inconsistency: they claim to be able to play with his psyche, to play upon him, even though he is a much more complicated instrument than a simple flute.[22] In order to be a competent player of the psychic instrument instead of its torturer, in order to extract beautiful sounds from it, one has to know how to handle it, one has to be trained and to be willing to submit oneself to the rules of the analytic game.[23] One has to transform the "criminal" into a sick person, into a hysteric, by obtaining—through transference—his benevolent collaboration. One has to see to it that the patient manages to reveal his secrets on his own, so that the analyst feels like a savior, not a torturer. The beauty of the sound is in the freedom with which it is sung, a freedom that results entirely from work that is costly, regulated, and painful, and that necessarily takes place between two people. Without the analyst who knows the technical rules of the game, the psyche is an inert instrument that emits no sound. For his own part, however, the analyst must also know how to yield to his instrument, to its resistances and demands. As Aristotle said, one does not make the same statue out of gold that one makes out of plaster. One does not get the same sound out of every instrument, and must in each case submit to its specificity, introducing new variations into the technical rules.

It remains to be seen whether, as in the case of music, only he who has mastered the instrument can enjoy the beauty of its sound. It remains to be seen, that is, whether it is he alone who decides what is "beautiful," just as it is he who decides, thanks to his musical tact, where play begins and where it ends. This being the case, just who benefits from the analytic game? Does not the analyst conceal a will to mastery behind the guise of healing and educating the patient, behind the guise of simply allowing the patient to speak freely, of giving him the ability to "play" and to emit beautiful sounds? Is analysis not also a version of that famous game of heads or tails, a game in which the analyst wins every flip of the coin, never losing face regardless of whether it is the tail or the head that turns up?

"Constructions in Analysis," one of Freud's last essays, responds to this accusation. A veritable apology for the analytic "profession," it relegates the work of the analysand to the wings in order to place the spotlight on the astonishing performance of the analyst.

TRANSLATED BY PATIENCE MOLL

§ 3 Ça cloche[1]

Man: *anthropos* or *aner*?

It is well known that the title of this colloquium ["The Ends of Man"] is a citation of a title Derrida gave to a lecture he delivered in New York in October 1968, on the occasion of an international colloquium on the theme "Philosophy and Anthropology." Derrida straightaway emphasizes the political significance of any philosophical colloquium, a significance reinforced by the international nature of any such colloquium. Writing in April 1968, in a specific historico-political context—just before the events of May, at the moment when negotiations for peace in Vietnam were getting under way, at the moment of Martin Luther King's assassination—Derrida questions the political import of a colloquium that, by emphasizing the universality of the *anthropos* in its very title, aims at erasing singular ethnic differences in the name of a "humanism" that—whatever its form, atheist or not—is fundamentally metaphysical (as Derrida reminds us by citing Heidegger: "every humanism remains metaphysical,"[2] metaphysics being here another name for ontotheology).

To erase differences is to master them. The ultimate end behind organizing a colloquium on the universal *anthropos* may well be a need to master differences.

From New York in 1968 to Cerisy in 1980, the philosophical, historical, and political scene has changed somewhat. As the colloquium has retained a title so strongly marked by metaphysical humanism, one may suspect that a need to master differences has once again slipped in: a need to master all differences, but above all—because the scene has shifted in twelve years—to master sexual difference (even if this is obviously not the intention of the colloquium's organizers)? So how must the "Ends of Man" be thought today, if one is to avoid raising this suspicion? The suspicion that the colloquium has been designed to help, to assist, and (in every sense of the word) to raise up [*relever*] man—man now no longer understood as *anthropos*, as universal man, as sexually neuter, but as *aner* or *vir*?

It would seem that the subtitle of this colloquium, "Concerning the Work of Derrida," would straightaway dispel any such suspicion. Although it is true that the texts published in *Margins of Philosophy* do not emphasize the danger of mastering sexual differences, Derrida's other texts since *Of Grammatology* never stop denouncing metaphysics (and therefore humanism and any discourse on "the ends of man") as phallogocentric. *Glas* in particular, while also tolling, among other things, the death knell [*glas*] for phallogocentrism, tolls the death knell for any colloquium on the "ends of man" in which "man" would be understood as sexually neuter, universal *anthropos*. In this text, Derrida resoundingly claims that in the final analysis, the ends of man are always those of "masculine man." The benefits man derives from his speculations on the ends of man or on the "ends of nature" (another means of further concealing the true ends of such speculations) are always masculine benefits. From behind one of those judas holes through which he surveys the eagle and its sublime flights, in particular at the moment when he speculates about sexual difference, Derrida observes that such speculation sets out to base phallocratism and the most traditional of hierarchies—the opposition of passivity and activity, of matter and form—on what appears to be reason, by appealing to the epoch's scientific axioms, and especially to the notion of *Aufhebung*, a concept central to the relation between the sexes, and one that enables Hegel to articulate his entire discourse on ontotheoteleology. And Derrida then takes up [*relève*], as symptomatic of this aim of mastery, the equivalent of a "slip," the "we" (*wir*) Hegel uses at the moment when he explains what makes up the system of virility: "in the man on the contrary, we [*wir*] have there active sensibility, the overflowing swelling of the heart, etc."[3] Behind his judas hole, Derrida exclaims, "Who, we? Magisterial we, we of *Ça*, we men? And what if it were always the same? And who-we-assists-us here" (*Glas*, 113, text modified).

Similarly, Derrida reminds us about Kant that his anthropological discourse has not man in general but woman as its central object (*Glas*,

124–31) and that this anthropological and humanist discourse pursues phallogocentric ends that are disguised as natural purposes (even if the phallogocentric system is very complex and contains within itself that which undermines and neutralizes it, even if it is therefore, as always, also a feminism). The appeal to this hidden teleology is the means of justifying all the developmental inequalities, all the dissymmetries that Kant ascribes to sexual difference. It is the corollary of a denegation: what is characteristic of the female sex—namely, an inclination to appropriate the entire male sex—is said to be in no way indebted to the categories, aims, or forms of human consciousness and in no way guided by the principle of our ultimate purpose, by "what *we make* our end"[4] (another "we"). It is only said to be guided by that profound natural wisdom that always already prompts women to set up a kind of male reserve as compensation for their eventual widowhood, as man is by nature finite [*fini*]. This characteristic is said to be guided by nature's sole objective in the preservation of femininity: the conservation of the species and the refinement of society by femininity. It is said to be guided neither by a human purpose, nor, a fortiori, by some kind of male purpose—that of Immanuel Kant, for example, who in order to protect his sex from such female appropriation knew full well how to remain celibate, and who in *The Conflict of the Faculties* did not hesitate to recommend celibacy along with the fundamental dietetic principles to anyone wishing to be certain of a long and happy life, because

> It might be hard to prove that *married* people have a *better chance* of living to a very old age. . . . Again, it is not a bad political principle to promote marriage by commending married life as a long life, although experience provides relatively few examples of married couples who have lived to an exceptional old age together.[5]

The Ends of Freud[6]

I would like to demonstrate here that one finds the same operation at work in Freud's texts, at moments when Freud speculates about women: the pursuit of phallogocentric ends hidden behind a pseudo-scientific discourse that presents itself as exclusively based on observation and that disavows any "speculation." This discourse would be positivistic, if only so through an opposition between observation and a sterile, mad speculation (an opposition that in Freud's text is not a radical one except precisely at the moment when Freud "speculates" about women, whereas *Beyond the Pleasure Principle*, for example, recognizes without hesitation that the death drive is a purely and necessarily speculative hypothesis, one that forces Freud to take hobbling, limping [*clochante*] steps[7]. In this would-be positivistic discourse, several signs bring a phallogocentric purpose to light. Besides Freud's denial of any speculation, the clearest symptom is his appeal to this or that moment of "demonstration," to a natural teleology, to a benevolent Mother Nature who like a deus ex machina opportunely comes to the aid of man (*vir*), proving that he, and only he, is Nature's final end, that he is his mother's favorite, that he is the favorite of her who can be fully satisfied only by bringing a male child into the world—this is one of the results obtained by Freudian speculation. And if Nature is a grandiose sublimation of the mother, then appealing to nature is also a means of rendering the mother and women in general (even though they are so little favored by Nature, who provides them with only an incomplete sex and an incurable penis envy, from which all their misfortune is born) complicit in a discourse that turns them into Nature's refuse (this complicity is necessary to clear Freud of any suspicion of antifeminism). "Analysis Terminable and Interminable," Freud's last word about women, actually concludes with a rejection of femininity by both sexes, a rejection whose symptoms are, in the man's case, castration anxiety and, in the woman's case, penis envy, the bedrock against which every analysis strikes, an impassable biological fact. This would be the last word of every analysis, or Freud's last word, in any case, as "Analysis Terminable and Interminable" is one of his last texts. It is as though trying to have the last word (about women) inevitably led Freud to his last word (like Spinoza, whose death left his *Political Treatise* unfinished precisely at the moment when he was about to deprive women of all political rights). Besides, Freud had always dreaded this last word, seeing that a real fear of death accompanies his writings on female sexuality. It is not until 1921–23 that he writes specifically about women, and he then publishes in haste, out of a fear of dying, and, as he says, without waiting for his results to be invalidated or confirmed by experience. The same fear of death becomes manifest around the time of the publication of *The Interpretation of Dreams*, because it is in this text that he reveals for the first time the thing so horrifying to see, the thing that should not be looked at directly: the sex of the mother, horrifying because it is too desirable. For fear of having to gouge out his eyes, Freud is forced to cover this sex with a thick veil, forced, in other words, to speculate, to elaborate pseudo-solutions and fictions that screen what should not be seen and that transform woman into a permanently unsolvable enigma.

I will give several examples of this "ideological" recourse to nature or, alternately, to biological science, as a symptom of a speculation that is intended to justify an *"idée fixe"*—the woman's famous penis envy—and that is also intended to justify Freud's phallocentrism more generally.

It is only in 1923, in "The Infantile Genital Organization of the Libido," a text that affirms the primacy of the phallus, that Freud introduces the idea of a third stage, the phallic stage, a phase that allegedly recognizes only one kind of genital organ, namely, the male organ. In this phase, which already "deserves" to be called a genital phase, there is a sexual object as well as a certain convergence of sexual tendencies on that object. The introduction of this supplementary stage precisely at the moment when Freud discovers the radical difference of the little girl's pre-oedipal sexuality—the wholly other of Mycenaean civilization—can be read as an apotropaic defense intended to conceal the surprising and frightening nature of Freud's discovery. In fact, nothing in the text really justifies why Freud had to wait until 1923 to discover or invent the existence of such a third stage. Moreover, nothing explains the contradictions between the 1923 text and the 1905 text, the *Three Essays on the Theory of Sexuality*, contradictions that Freud acknowledges without hesitation in his later supplementary footnotes, in which he dedicates himself—from one edition to the next—to a fundamental revision of the theory of infantile sexuality. There is no explanation except for a vague affirmation of a "progression in knowledge" over the course of time, induced by an intentional difference in observation. No explanation, that is, except, as a final recourse, the appeal to a biological prototype (*Vorbild*), an appeal for which Freud moreover does not even take full responsibility himself: "According to Abraham, [the phallic stage] has a biological prototype in the embryo's undifferentiated genital disposition, which is the same for both sexes" (a footnote added in 1924).[8] This is in contrast to the "Femininity" lecture, in which Freud criticizes traditional psychology and its psychic determinations of masculine as active and feminine as passive; when these determinations are based on a biological model, he claims, they can only "lead to erroneously analogical reasoning." The appeal to Abraham and to his specific biological prototype is thus intended—in a manner that could not be any more speculative—to transform what is a simple theory of infantile sexuality (the belief in the nondifferentiation of the sexes, due to the child's inability to recognize the vagina's existence) into a fact of nature. It transforms a theory that is more or less fantasmatic, despite the kernel of truth it is always supposed to contain, into a fact of a benevolent nature that from the beginning, from the embryo on, would have shown its preference for the male sex.

Freud's appeal in the *Three Essays* to Abraham's embryonic prototype serves to ground the primacy of the phallus, while elsewhere his appeal to Ferenczi's paleobiology—which Freud himself also qualifies as fantastic and speculative—serves to ground penis envy (the corollary of the primal phallus) and to anchor it in an origin that could not be any more archaic—that is, in the epoch of sexual differentiation. Briefly put, Freud's appeal to paleobiology turns penis envy into an insurmountable primary phenomenon, an immovable rock. Freud offers this recourse to speculative paleobiology as a supplementary "proof," in addition to clinical proof (i.e., the dream of one of Freud's patients—or at least the interpretation of the dream, as Freud never gives us the dream's manifest content) and the proof offered by literature (i.e., Hebbel's *Judith and Holofernes* and Anzengruber's *Das Jungferngift* [*Virgin's Venom*], which once again confirms Freudian "theory" only insofar as it is always already being read in circular fashion, in light of analysis). In "The Taboo of Virginity," Freud writes:

> In a palaeo-biological speculation, Ferenczi has traced back this hostility of women—I do not know if he is the first to do so—to the period in time when the sexes became differentiated. At first, in his opinion, copulation took place between two similar individuals, one of which, however, developed into the stronger and forced the weaker one to submit to sexual union. The feelings of bitterness arising from this subjection still persist in the present-day disposition of women. I do not think there is any harm in employing such speculation, so long as one avoids setting too much value on them. (11:205–6)

This is true kettle logic of the kind customary with Freud since the dream about Irma: (1) I do not speculate but observe; it is Ferenczi who speculates; (2) in any event, there is no harm in speculating from time to time; (3) these speculations are valuable only to the extent that they support my own observations and corroborate my idée fixe. Ferenczi must not "set too much value" on them.

The idée fixe of penis envy, introduced as the deepest layer of the virginity taboo, is like a panicked reaction to this disturbing, strange, and fearsome woman, who is accused by Freud of castrating men at the very moment when he himself, and not nature, is in the process of castrating her by definitively endowing her with an incomplete sexuality and with simple penis envy. Freud retroactively [*après coup*] makes Mother Nature responsible for this castration, turning her once again into her son's accomplice. In "Femininity," penis envy is a primary phenomenon that is no longer derived from observation, but solely from Freud's inclination to decide in favor of its primacy (*Wir sind geneigt*—*Wir*, majestic we? *Wir*/*Vir*?). Freud recognizes that other psychoanalysts—in particular, female analysts—are inclined to make this envy a secondary phenomenon and that they have other inclinations (*Neigungen*), such as, for example, to diminish the importance of original, innate penis envy and to emphasize instead the patient's subsequent history. Who will choose from among these different inclinations, from among these opposed theses and opposed texts, each of which defends theses that are already anticipated by inclinations? Who will decide from among all these speculations? In the case of penis envy, it is simply Freud's male conviction, and nothing more, that tilts the balance in favor of its innateness. It tilts the balance in favor, once again, of a natural, biological foundation of a nature, a nature that itself [*elle*] tilts the balance in favor of man and that clearly indicates its preferences by bestowing an immediate, irresistible, and definitive penis envy on those said to be endowed with an incomplete sexuality.

I will offer one last example of this appeal to a natural teleology designed to camouflage a phallocratic purpose. It concerns the assimilation of activity to masculinity. The example is all the more interesting in that Freud's gesture at this point is very complex, is at least a double gesture. In opposition to an entire metaphysical tradition, he actually tries to distinguish active from masculine and passive from feminine by emphasizing, for example, that the pair active/passive precedes the pair masculine/feminine: the former pair appears in the sadistic–anal stage, whereas the latter appears only in the genital stage. By clearly distinguishing the biological and psychoanalytic meanings of the words *masculine* and *feminine*, Freud leaves open the possibility that a woman, in the biological sense of the word, could be masculine in the psychoanalytic sense, which is to say active, and vice versa. Active and passive are therefore not essential properties of either of the two sexes. The libidinal instincts of individuals of either sex are sometimes active, sometimes passive, over the course of their development, without this having to be attributed to their bisexuality. In the end, both sexes equally show a preference for activity. Briefly put, Freud emphasizes throughout that it is too easy to make activity correspond with masculinity, and passivity with femininity. And when he winds up doing so himself, he claims that he does so only in accordance with convention. This is the case, for example, when he qualifies the libido as masculine. Properly speaking (and no longer conventionally speaking), the libido does not belong to any sex (*Wir können ihr selbst kein Geschlecht geben*):

> There is only one libido, which serves both the masculine and the feminine sexual functions. To it itself we cannot assign any sex; if, following the conventional equation of activity and masculinity, we are inclined to describe it as masculine, we must not forget that it also covers trends with a passive aim. ("Femininity," 22:131)

And yet, on the other hand, a completely different gesture, sometimes in the very same (?) text, tends, as in all metaphysics, to assimilate masculinity to activity and femininity to passivity, and does so no longer by way of simple convention. The masculine is then said to encompass the subject, activity, and possession of the penis, whereas femininity is said to encompass the object and passivity; here the biological and the psychoanalytic meanings match up perfectly. Because the sadistic–anal opposition between active and passive fuses at the moment of puberty with the opposition between the sexes, it becomes possible to assert retrospectively [*après coup*] that there have been differences between the girl and the boy from the beginning, that the girl is always already the more passive one. If, for example, both sexes manifest a preference for the active role, they do not reverse roles with the same energy: the difference in their behavior in this regard allows one to draw conclusions as to the relative strength of the masculinity and the femininity they will manifest in their sexuality.

This is why the convention that qualifies the libido as masculine appears in the final analysis to be neither entirely conventional nor arbitrary. Freud rejects the idea that there could be a different convention that would authorize someone to qualify the libido as feminine; nothing, he says, can justify joining together the words *feminine* and *libido*. Ultimately, nature and its teleology provide the rationale for "convention":

> It is our impression that more constraint has been applied to the libido when it is pressed into the service of the feminine function, and that—to speak teleologically—Nature takes less careful account of [that function's] demands

than in the case of masculinity. And the reason for this may lie—thinking once again teleologically—in the fact that the accomplishment of the aim of biology has been entrusted to the aggressiveness of men and has been made to some extent independent of women's consent.

The sexual frigidity of women, the frequency of which appears to confirm this disregard, is a phenomenon that is still insufficiently understood. (22:131–32)

The weakness of women's sexual demands, it would seem, are desired by Nature itself [*elle-même*], so as to entitle man to sexual aggression, and thereby to the reproduction of the species, without the consent of women. The quasi-frigidity of women would therefore be, so to speak, constitutive of and essential to Nature's plan, a plan that could not be any less dissimulated. Under the guise of fulfilling the biological destiny of the human species—that is, reproduction—the ultimate ends of man are fulfilled: by subordinating woman's sexual desires to man's desire and by keeping women in a confined state of dependence. Under these conditions, when a woman has some sexual demands of her own, she is a true anomaly of nature and would not be able to fulfill the task for which she is biologically destined. In short, she is not really a woman. If she is not homosexual, such a "woman" has at least a considerable "masculinity complex" whose decisive factor is constitutional. Conflating this time the biological and the psychoanalytic meanings of "activity," Freud maintains that this type of woman possesses "a greater amount of activity," a characteristic ordinarily found in men: "The essence of this process is that at this point in development the wave of passivity is avoided which opens the way to the turn towards femininity" (22:130). If such a woman does not envy the man's penis, it is because she is by her own nature a man. Freud is unable to imagine any reason besides a natural one why a woman might not envy the penis, why she might not recognize the "fact of her own castration"—in short, why she might not subordinate her sexual desires to man's desires, as her natural or cultural purpose—to keep in place the traditional nature/culture opposition which Freud upholds—would have her do. In fact, "The Taboo of Virginity" allows one to conclude that the appeal to a natural teleology, to an injustice on the part of nature or on the part of the mother who, in one way or another, indicates her preference for man, is a way of making nature take the blame for the cultural injustice of men. For "The Taboo of Virginity" does concede that cultural rules are in fact designed to subjugate women sexually. In this essay, Freud shows that a certain degree of sexual subjugation is necessary to maintain the institution of civilized marriage and to contain the threat of polygamous tendencies. The necessity of subjugating the female sex rather than the male sex is not really explained; Freud simply notes it. The woman's subjection (which may go as far as her losing any independent will and tolerating the most severe sacrifice of her own interests) is more frequent and more intense than the man's, because the woman remains fixated on the first man who was able to appease her amorous desire and to overcome her resistances. Her first amorous experience would therefore guarantee her permanent and undisturbed possession. Beyond all of Freud's speculations that appeal to a natural teleology, these, then, would be the ends of man: to stabilize instability and feminine oscillation, to make the woman able to resist new impressions, and to incite her to sacrifice her sexual interests—all for man's benefit. The ruse of male culture would be the use of a psychic phenomenon, the repression of female sexuality, that is itself socially conditioned, to sacrifice the woman's interests, to submit her without her consent to the man's aggression, and to render her complicit in the man's desires, at the expense of her own desires. The frigidity of woman, which Freud in his "Femininity" lecture still considers an insufficiently understood phenomenon, could certainly be regarded not as the condition of possibility of this state of subjection, but as one of its consequences. Of course, Freud does not say this. "The Taboo of Virginity" explains frigidity as the reaction to a narcissistic wound that has its source in the organ's destruction during defloration, and, ultimately, by penis envy: "a woman's *immature sexuality* is discharged on to the man who first makes her acquainted with the sexual act" (11:206). The virginity taboo in primitive societies would be what saves man from such dangers as castration and female frigidity. At a higher stage of civilization, the recognition of these dangers yields to the promise of subjection.

> I think it must strike the observer in how uncommonly large a number of cases the woman remains frigid and feels unhappy in a first marriage, whereas after it has been dissolved she becomes a tender wife, able to make her second husband happy. The archaic reaction has, so to speak, exhausted itself on the first object. (11:206)

The ends of man would therefore be the subjection of women, the assurance of their permanent and undisturbed possession. This would be the only thing enabling him to overcome castration anxiety, the anxiety he experiences when confronted with women's bitter hostility, with their need to avenge themselves for having been so unjustly provided for, for having been so deprived by "nature"—in short, the anxiety he feels when confronted with their penis envy. What Freud does not say is that this famous penis envy, this idée fixe haunting the entirety of his text, is itself a way of putting women in a stable position, of ending their permanent oscillation between the masculine and the feminine position, the oscillation from which the whole enigma of their sexuality (as Freud defines it) originates. It is a way of mastering their bisexuality for the benefit of either their femininity or their masculinity, both of which come back to the same thing. It is a way of subjugating women by rendering them complicit with men's desires; this is because penis envy, even while it arouses men's castration anxiety, also reassures them by assuring them that they are the ones possessing the penis. The "theory" of penis envy is a speculation, a fiction, a reaction to the panic provoked by seeing the woman's sex, the mother's sex, a panic analogous to that incited by the collapse of throne and altar. In the face of castration anxiety, it is an apotropaic solution that allows for the circumvention of the homosexual solution; it alone allows for the combination of horror and pleasure and for the colossal erection of man. If the debasement of the sexual object—the love of the whore—is under civilized circumstances the necessary condition for man's sexual well-being, the condition for his sexual power in all of its components (including its perverse components), one can say that the fiction of "penis envy," despite Freud's denials, is what allows for the debasement of woman. It is what allows man to dispense with the whore, that woman so far debased that she no longer evokes the mother (even though the figure of the whore originates out of a splitting of the maternal figure), and to dispense with the costly solution of the brothel and with all the dangers it poses to man's health:

> The man almost always feels his respect for the woman acting as a restriction on his sexual activity, and only develops full potency when he is with a debased [*erniedrigtes*] sexual object; and this in its turn is partly caused by the entrance of perverse components into his sexual aims, which he does not venture to satisfy with a woman he respects. . . . Anyone who is to be really free and happy in love must have surmounted his respect for women and have come to terms with the idea of incest with his mother or sister. ("On the Universal Tendency to Debasement in the Sphere of Love," 11:185–86)

"My Excitement Is the Oscillation" for a Generalized Fetishism: Derrida

Freud's solution still makes it possible to dispense with fetishism. But fetishism, too, facilitates amorous relations. According to Freud, most of its devotees are very content with it. When they enter into analysis, it is not on account of their fetish, as in general they do not experience it as a painful symptom. This being the case, one may ask why Freud considers the fetishistic solution to be pathological (and why penis envy, which allows for heterosexual relations that are considered "normal," is a "better" solution). In short, why is it so bad to be a fetishist? It is because in fetishism, a certain oscillation, something "undecidable," remains, and "to speculate on the undecidable" is always to be the loser. Even if the fetishist is very content with his fetish on a conscious level, his analysis brings to light that the adopted solution is only a compromise and as such never perfectly satisfying. What resonates in Derrida's *Glas* is that the question of fetishism is linked to the question of an undecidable oscillation, and thus to a speculation in which one wins and loses at the same time. Beginning with a reading of Freud's text, *Glas* puts forth what may be called a generalization of fetishism, and therefore of undecidability and oscillation as well, as the first step[9] of a deconstruction of phallogocentrism: "My excitement is the oscillation" (*Glas*, 127).

After a reading of the Hegelian speculation on the fetish, from which he concludes that a certain undecidability of the fetish allows for an oscillation between a dialectic (of the undecidable and the dialectic) and an undecidability (between the dialectic and the undecidable), Derrida takes up a reading of Freud: "What is it to speculate concerning the fetish? For such a question, the headless heading [*le cap sans cap*] is undecidability" (*Glas*, 209, text modified). On the one hand, grafting the reading of Freud onto the reading of Hegel allows one to emphasize through this simple juxtaposition that the benefits Hegel derives from his speculation on the fetish are perhaps of the same order as the fetishist's. On the other hand, it allows one to reinscribe the Freudian notions of castration and fetishism in the circle of speculative dialectics, to place them in relation to the process of *Aufhebung* and to truth, and to show that Hegel puts forth a powerful systematic articulation of these concepts. In a more general way, it allows one to graft Freud's text onto the text of metaphysics, which has always attempted to master the undecidable and the intolerable, the oscillation, and for which being a fetishist is always a bad thing. Fetishism has always been unanimously opposed by the founders as well as the detractors of religions. To be against religion does nothing to upset the economy of metaphysics and of religion, as long as one continues to critique fetishism. Such a critique of fetishism by both the detractors and the founders of religions is a symptom of a common will: the will to unveil the column, to erect the thing itself, and to reject the substitute. This will is destined to fail because the undecidable can never be mastered. Fetishism, on the contrary, makes it possible to unsettle the metaphysical categories; it allows for an oscillating between a dialectic and an entirely other logic, that of the undecidable. It necessarily entails a speculation that oscillates between a gesture that tries to master the oscillation and a gesture that shakes up and attracts all oppositions, dragging along in its path the oppositions fetish / nonfetish, substitute / thing itself, and masculine / feminine, among others, to the benefit of a generalization of those terms that are most devalued by the metaphysical hierarchy: fetishism, the substitute, the *Ersatz*, supplementarity, and also the feminine (because the feminine is characterized by oscillation). It is this double gesture that Derrida deciphers particularly in Freud's text on fetishism, a text that is said to oscillate, to go awry [*clocherait*] in a very particular way, a text that is said to be particularly speculative in all senses of the term. Derrida goes as far as to say (this time going against what the text literally says) that when taking up the question of fetishism, Freud himself claims to be taking a speculative path, as when he attempts to weigh down his speculative hypothesis with some weighty arguments, among them the famous argument of the support belt. But contrary to that, Freud actually declares that he is leaving the speculative path at the moment when he takes up the description of fetishism, that he is leaving that risky path to which at another time he mistakenly committed himself, though in that instance apropos not of the fetishistic split, but of the distinction between neurosis and psychosis: "But soon after this I had reason to regret that I had ventured so far" (21:155). "Returning to my description of fetishism, I may say that there are many and weighty additional proofs of the divided attitude of fetishists to the question of the castration of women" (21:156). The fact that Freud, like the fetishist, does not openly declare his speculation does not mean he is not speculating. Even more than an avowal, a denegation is always symptomatic. Derrida, who apropos of Rousseau distinguishes between what a text *declares* openly and what it *does* in contraband, does not even need Freud's own avowals for his demonstration—on the contrary. So what is the purpose of this kind of a reading (as it cannot simply be a bad reading)? What strategy is Derrida pursuing here and to what ends? What is the benefit of this operation, and whom does it benefit?

The first thing is to show that Freud's text on fetishism is, like any text, heterogeneous. There are determined and decidable statements about the fetish as well as undecidable statements. The latter allow for the undoing of the system of oppositions on which the definition of the fetish as a substitute for the (mother's) penis is based, and for the reconstruction—on the basis of the fetish's generalization—of a "concept" of the fetish that would no longer be containable within any opposition. One such statement would be the argument of the support belt (as well as those arguments that are systematically linked to it), held up by Freud, despite its "subtlety," as a consequence of his definition of the fetish; this argument would in fact break with Freud's initial definition by virtue of the undecidability it introduces. The singularity and subtlety of the support belt would derive from the fetish's link to opposed tendencies, which would render it particularly resistant. Derrida concludes—which, according to him, Freud would not do—that the slightest consistency of the fetish already presupposes some link to opposed tendencies and that this link is also inscribed within a general economy of the undecidable. Briefly put, the fetish in general would consist by virtue of its undecidability in an excessiveness with regard to all oppositions, an excessiveness that would cause the opposition between *Ersatz* and *non-Ersatz* and between denial and affirmation to oscillate. This is what Freud could not acknowledge openly, because he had to maintain the definition of the fetish as a substitute for the penis, for the thing itself. Like the fetishist, then, Freud is said to oscillate between two positions, which in turn forces him to speculate.

> The fetish—in general—begins to exist only insofar as it begins to bind itself to contraries. So this double bond, this double ligament, defines its subtlest structure. All the consequences of this must be drawn. The economy of the fetish is more powerful than that of the truth—decidable—of the thing itself or than a deciding discourse of castration (*pro aut contra*). The fetish is not opposable. It oscillates like the clapper of a truth that rings awry [*clocher*] . . . in the gulf of a bell [*cloche*]. (*Glas*, 227)

It seems to me that Freud's text at this point perhaps does not ring awry [*cloche*] exactly as Derrida, who simultaneously grants Freud too much and too little, says it does. Derrida grants Freud too little when he assumes that Freud's definition of the fetish implies the (simple) distinction between the thing itself and its *Ersatz*, a distinction that is to the advantage of the thing itself, as throughout the entire metaphysical tradition. In fact, if at the end of his text Freud declares that the fetish's normal prototype is the man's penis, he says at the beginning of the text that his definition of the fetish as penis substitute would risk being a disappointment if one did not immediately add

> that it is not a substitute for any chance penis, but for a particular and quite special penis that had been extremely important in early childhood but had later been lost. That is to say, it should normally have been given up, but the fetish is precisely designed to preserve it from extinction. To put it more plainly: the fetish is a substitute for the woman's (the mother's) penis that the little boy once believed in and—for reasons familiar to us—does not want to give up. (21:152–53)

How is such a definition less disappointing than the preceding one (a question that Derrida, who attributes the disappointment to the second definition, does not take up), if not in that it breaks with metaphysics, with the idea of the penis as "thing itself," because the penis for which the fetish substitutes is a fantasmatic penis, one that was never perceived as such? The mother's penis, "the thing itself," is always already a fetish fictionalized [*fictionné*] by the child, a belief implying at once the disavowal and the affirmation of castration. There never was a "thing itself"; there was only an *Ersatz*, a postiche, a prosthesis, an original supplementarity, as the panicked response of infantile narcissism. Adult fetishism is a repetition of this spontaneous infantile fetishism, not the substitute for the "thing itself" or for truth. This is because as a substitute for the mother's fantasmatic penis, the fetish always already implicates the play of supplementary difference within the "thing itself."

If the *Ersatz* is originary, there can no longer be an opposition between *Ersatz* and *non-Ersatz*. The traditional logic of fetishism is thus undone by the new definition Freud proposes, a definition that is certainly less disappointing than the first because it alone authorizes the concept of a generalized fetishism. Understood in such a way, this definition no longer implies a real rupture with the argument of the support belt. Derrida is right to assert that "the slightest consistency of the fetish already supposes some link to opposed tendencies" (*Glas*, 211, text modified), but Freud does not say otherwise, as there can be no fetishism without compromise, without a compromise between the affirmation and the disavowal of castration. The split is the condition of possibility of maintaining two currents that, for any logic of consciousness, are mutually incompatible and contradictory. If there were a decision in favor of one of the two currents, there would be no need to construct a fetish. One would be faced with either psychosis—the complete disavowal of reality—or the recognition of what Freud calls the reality of castration. The argument of the support belt, as refined and subtle as it is, is thus nevertheless a consequence of Freud's definition of the fetish, for Freud declares right away that all cases of fetishism have the same general solution. It has only paradigmatic value, and the fetish in general is, for Freud too, clearly "undecidable" in its nature. Freud says that it has the quality of a compromise. To purely and simply assimilate the compromise to the undecidable is perhaps to grant Freud too much. In any case, the conduct of the fetishist, who both venerates and batters his fetish, shows that he is not for either of the two sides, that he is neither for nor against castration, or rather that he is for both at once, that he is "between" the two, that he oscillates between the two contradictory hypotheses without being able to decide between the two recognized functions of the fetish, no more than he could decide between the "thing itself" and its supplement, or between the two sexes. This oscillation could cease only if there were an absolute split between the two currents and if one of them were to disappear completely. But the advantage of the fetishistic operation consists precisely in playing on both sides at once, in speculating on the fetish's equivocality and ambivalence (its undecidability, in this sense), in accordance with the more or less complex needs of its economy. It consists in being more or less the loser in this game (because there always remains a doubt about the woman's castration or noncastration, and therefore about "his" own castration).

The strategy of Derrida's reading, which thus assimilates the compromise (possible only because of the split between the two currents) to the undecidable (which does not necessarily imply a logic of the unconscious), prompts him to emphasize this economic speculation on the undecidable and to underline that to speculate in this way is inevitably to lose. Keeping to Freud's literal text, one would have to say that like the fetishist, Freud is playing here on all sides: on that of decidability and that of undecidability. The heterogeneity of Freud's text can be brought to light only by a comprehensive strategy, by an operation of "subtle and refined" displacements.

It remains to be said that it is only through this strategy of reading that Derrida is able to introduce the concept of a generalized fetishism (of the *Ersatz*, the fake, the original prosthesis), which opens the space of play, of oscillation, and of undecidability, the space from which literature originates. In its very form, *Glas* is the mise-en-scène of this kind of fetishism, of this generalized undecidability that "overturns" phallogocentrism and all metaphysical oppositions. What does one win and what does one lose in this game? And who wins and who loses in this game, if that question still has any meaning? What end is Derrida pursuing? (Is "Derrida" really the "author" who signs *Glas* with this name? *Glas*, which tolls the death knell [*glas*] for the "author," for the "proper name," for the "signature"?)

The Double Band

First off, there is never a single end, but, as with the fetishist, always a playing on at least two sides at once: "Designs [*Desseins*] . . . are never reduced to one alone" (*Glas*, 257, text modified), for the happiness or unhappiness of the one who oscillates between the two, who situates himself in the "between." Hence the subdivision of *Glas*: its *colpos*, its double nipples, its two hills [*collines*], its double columns [*colonnes*], its double support belts, each of which is itself double (allowing for a potential double reading—struck with undecidability and "textualized"), divided, split by an antagonism, by a double bind. The support belt argument is erected into a general law, a law that Derrida elsewhere, apropos of Blanchot's *The Madness of the Day*[10] and *Death Sentence*,[11] calls the double invagination: it envelops everything that "like a glove or flower" (see Genet's *The Maids*) "turns in every sense and direction, over, inside out, upside down, without losing a certain form" (*Glas*, 229).

Double designs, a double posture or postulation, require a double discourse, a double writing, the writing of two texts at once, and a double gaze that is profound and stereoscopic: a cross-eyed reading, a squinting imposed on the reader, which, by dividing him, makes him nauseous, makes him spin and lose his head because he can no longer tell the discourse's head from its body. "When his head is here, he is to be reminded that the law of the text is in the other, and so on" (*Glas*, 64, text modified). By suppressing the margins and frames, by annulling and blurring the lines that would separate one text from another, one prevents all demarcation, division, domination, all hierarchy. "In writing two texts at once, what scene is being played here? Who plays it? Who desires what, or is afraid of what? Of whom?" (*Glas*, 64, text modified). These questions are inscribed in the columns of *Glas*. There is also a preliminary response that is refuted in advance: by writing two texts at once, by playing a double score (like the hysteric in crisis or the fetishist), by having a double erection [*bander double*[12]], one wants to make oneself impregnable, to make writing impregnable. This would be the height of mastery: to erect two columns, to claim to always uphold a double discourse, to have one eye crossing the other so as to let nothing escape—like the Stranger in the *Sophist*, who, in order to trap the animal he is pursuing, attempts to chase it with both hands at once, abandoning neither term of the dichotomy. On the one hand, it is true that writing two texts at once can be read as a powerful and paralyzing [*médusante*] apotropaic strategy, as the erection of a supplementary column that would protect against castration anxiety: "If I write two texts at once, you will not be able to castrate me. If I delinearize, I erect" (*Glas*, 65). But on the other hand, to write doubly is also and always at the same time to castrate oneself, to split oneself, to split one's desires by dividing them; it is to make oneself impregnable, undoubtedly, but always to lose in doing so. Wanting like the fetishist to play both sides, one loses on both sides. One never really comes [*jouit*], but only oscillates from one posture, one postulation, to the other; one only "play[s] at coming [*jouer à jouir*]" (*Glas*, 65); one writes.

> I divide my act and my desire. I—mark(s) the division, and always escaping you, I simulate unceasingly and take my pleasure [*jouir*] nowhere. I castrate myself—I remain(s) myself thus—and I "play at coming" [*je "joue à jouir"*].... For if my text is (was) ungraspable, it will (would) be neither grasped nor retained. Who, in this economy of the undecidable, would be punished? But if I linearize, if I line myself up and believe—silliness—that I write only one text at a time, that comes back to the same thing, and the cost of the margin must still be reckoned with. I win and lose, in every case, my prick... double posture. Double postulation. Contradiction in (it)self of two irreconcilable desires. Here I give it... the title DOUBLE BAND(S), putting it (them) into form and into play practically. A text laces [*sangle*] in two senses, in two directions. Twice girt. Band contra band. (*Glas*, 65–66)

In this strange and disturbing play, this *unheimlich* play,[13] this play of the double, one is always also the loser, because the duality of columns or embouchures necessitates passing from one signature to the other, from one breast [*sein(g)*] to the other. It implies the impossibility of getting one's hand or language on both at once, of mastering and manipulating all this as though it were a featherweight [*plume*]. For there is no death knell [*glas*] without the intervention of an entire machinery in which any absolute knowledge would itself be only one of the parts: "you count for nothing . . . at the very moment you think you are clutching/declutching, manipulating, orchestrating, making the liquid music rise or fall by playing the petals" (*Glas*, 223–24). And if you persist in wanting to manipulate, you run the risk of seeing—through the judas holes behind which you hide in order to spy on this primal scene—this double, these two columns, this entire disturbing machinery put in motion in order to crush you, to play with you, to threaten to collapse one column on top of the other, without leaving you any way out. This sight—seeing the columns of the synagogue collapse on you—is probably what you were already dreading when, as a Jewish child, you looked from afar, and probably from down low, on the stripped, unbound [*débandée*] Torah, its two legs/columns spread, held up, then rolled up again, and re-bound [*bandées*]. Before you yourself later lent a hand in the ceremony. A forbidden vision, a forbidden manipulation, one that you say made you dream and that ordered all the pieces of your life. Without a doubt, this is the origin of your generalized fetishism, your undecidable oscillation, your necessarily double liaisons. But who is "you"? Derrida? The one who signs *Glas* with this name? *Glas*, which puts into play the proper name, the signature as the mark of an identity, of a particular author? If the signature is "the network of (no) more than a name" (*Glas*, 170), then *Glas* tolls the death knell for autobiography, for a psychoanalysis of the author; it would not be possible to analyze the clapper of a bell [*cloche*].[14] Hence, "Derrida's" childhood memory is grafted onto the evocation of the Torah by the non-Jew Genet in *Our Lady of the Flowers*, a text that prescribes the form of *Glas*, much as the Torah does: "When the rabbi slowly unrolls the Torah, a mystery sends a shudder through the whole epidermis, as when one sees a colonist undressing" (*Glas*, 240). "Derrida's" childhood memory is not an explanatory principle of the writing of *Glas*, and the Torah is not a paradigmatic text. With *Glas*, there are no more paradigms, only series. The Torah is part of a series that includes *Our Lady of the Flowers* and *The Miracle of the Rose*, along with "What Remains of a Rembrandt" and Blanchot's *Death Sentence* [*L'Arrêt de mort*], a text with a fixed [*arrêté*] title that is suspended between two meanings, and which is itself part of a series that includes Kafka's "A Country Doctor," which in its turn is grafted onto *Madame Bovary*, and so forth. *Glas* is part of a series along with other texts that are signed "Derrida"—among them "The Double Session," *The Truth in Painting* and the question of the colossal double (of van Gogh's pair of shoes that is not truly a pair), "Living On" (about Blanchot's double narrative and the question of the double theory and the double triumph), and so forth. *Glas* is a pealing of bells [*cloches*] between texts, an oscillating pendulum that, in accordance with Blanchot's title, accompanies texts without accompanying them, that escorts them. "*Glas* is written neither from one side nor from the other. . . . [It] strikes between the two. The place the clapper will, necessarily, have taken up, let us name it *colpos*" (*Glas*, 71, text modified). "I write myself . . . on the top, between the two" (*Glas*, 229).

The relation between all these texts is not one of model and copy, but one of citation, plagiarism,[15] infatuation, translation, transference, re-edition, "apocalyptic superimposition," and "cryptic obsession" (all terms that can be found in "Living On"); it is a relation whose condition of possibility is the absence of a paradigmatic text, of an integral corpus, and of a fetish. Each text, according to *Glas*, is a machine with multiple reading heads for other texts that thus communicate with one another, keep surveillance on one another, and respond to one another: yoked, divided, and agglutinated at the same time, these texts become undecidable as to their code and their sex. They each speak in the language of the other without even knowing one another (like the two women in *Death Sentence*, according to the mad hypothesis of "Living On"): the procession of one text, one language, into another, the forceful crossing over by this procession to the banks of another language, into the language of the other, provokes a kind of overflow that afflicts all dividing boundaries. There is no more frame, no more border; there is no longer a sure boundary between a text and its outside, between the end and the beginning of a text, between the unity of a corpus, the title, the margins, and so forth. There is only a differential network, a tissue of traces that indefinitely refers to some other, that is referred to other differential traces. Every text that is transformed by another text, and a fortiori the text that is written between them, belongs to no form, no genre, no literary or philosophical mode. Toll the death knell for code and genre!

Everything that has been said of the text can be said of sex. In *Glas*, there is a sexualization of the text and a textualization of sex. The question of sexuality as undecidable oscillation repeats—is the same as—the question of the text, like the pealing of bells [*cloches*] between texts. The writing of the double column is the writing of a double, diabolical sex that in its duplicity breaks with all oppositions and all hierarchies. Like each text agglutinated to another text, each sex becomes undecidable, speaks the language, and in the language of the other, penetrates the other: neither feminine nor masculine, neither castrated nor noncastrated, not because it is bisexual, but because it strikes between the sexes, because it is always already a double sex, which doubly envelops and erects [*gaine et bande*] in keeping with a double bind. It is a sex with a double ligament, a double liaison, a double spur [*éperon*], a double style, a sex that becomes erect and smuggles [*bande et contrabande*], that becomes erect only in order to be erected [*qui ne bande qu'à être bandé*], that becomes all the more erect in that it is always already "castrated" (because even if castration never takes place, one still cannot say that there is no castration)—at all events, a sex that is sliced, incised, and slashed by the other, a sex that is all the more powerful in that it is divided and cut. Hence the oblique aspect of the erection, what Derrida calls the *antherection*, which accompanies any erection and makes it pour out, fall, and reverse itself.

The power of this erect [*bandé*] sex, which in seeking to become doubly erect [*à bander double*] can nevertheless only "play at coming," is like Tiresias, patron of actors, whose citation by Genet is cited in *Glas*: "because of his double nature . . . [f]or seven years a man's clothing, for seven years a woman's . . . his femininity followed in close pursuit of his virility, the one or the other being constantly asserted, with the result that he never had any rest, I mean any fixed point where he could rest" (*Glas*, 226–27). Tiresias–Dionysus: the power of *jouissance* and its play are not antinomies, and one can perhaps only "truly" come by playing at coming.

From "The Question of Style" to That of Stilitano or, *l'écriture du m'ec*

The power, the "potency," of *Glas* derives from its staging of the *double erection*, the *double band* [*la double bande*], the *double bind* that text and sex are. It results from the mise-en-scène of this generalized fetishism, from the writing that erases all oppositions (between the sexes and between castration and noncastration) in favor of affirmation, of double affirmation. Because it mixes up all sexes and genres, this writing implies a necessary lapse in taste. Let us replay, within the limitations of this lecture, the ritual ceremony of *Glas*—which is the opposite of a purification. It begins with the remainder [*le reste*], with the bit, the stump, with a citation that puts the remainder in play. It begins with two columns that are always already mutilated at the top and at the bottom and are slashed open at the sides: wounded columns, colossal columns that are double from the start. Stilitanesque columns (*Glas* can be perhaps be grafted directly onto "Nietzsche and the Question of Style," a lecture delivered here by Derrida in 1972), they stand straight up like the stems [*styles*] of a flower or like swathed heads that, after having been cut off, are sanctified and glorified by this decapitation, are raised up [*relevées*] by this very decapitation (like the heads of the decapitated, martyred saints in the Fra Angelico painting on display in the Louvre: bloody, glorious heads). They are the glorification of what expires, of what falls off like a turd.

> Our-Lady-of-the-Flowers opens up with the archive of all the heads that have just fallen, condemned to death.... But in letting itself fall, the head is already raised up again. It surges up, is erected precisely, decidedly in this case. To be decapitated is to appear—banded, erect [*bandé*]: like the "head swathed" ... like the phallus, the erectile stem—the style—of a flower. (*Glas*, 21)

The Stilitanesque columns are oblique columns, adhering to the logic of the antherection. After the cut, what remains becomes stronger.

> The more that (*ça*) remains, the better that (*ça*) bands erect [*bander*].... The logic of antherection must not be simplified. It (*Ça*) does not erect *against* or *in spite of* castration, *despite* the wound or the infirmity, by castrating castration. It (*Ça*) bands erect, castration. Infirmity itself bandages itself {*se panse*} by banding erect. Infirmity is what ... *produces* erection. (*Glas*, 138)

This is the entire history of the Jewish people from Abraham on, as Hegel–Derrida reads it. In the other column, it is the story of Stilitano, who derives his power, glory, and magnificence from his stump, from his mutilation, from his castration, one could say, if that "term" did not bring the text to a standstill. It is the story of Stilitano who goes erect and goes limp [*bande et débande*], who is more alive than dead because of his cuts.

A Stilitanesque column is not one erected retroactively [*après coup*] in order to veil a deficiency, a castration; it is a prosthesis that no castration event will have preceded. Nothing would remain standing without it. It erects [*bande*] all by itself. It is a machinery, a postiche and a pastiche, an ornament, a parade (an umbrella, a screen, a parachute, etc.), an original supplement. His sex undecidable, Stilitano asserts himself as much as a man as he does as a modest woman, or as a self-hating queer, or as a transvestite.

> The whole world bands erect and is incorporated in the transvestite, all kinds and genders of oppositions. . . . The incorporation of all sexes at once . . . assumes the cut and the supplement within the double band. But as soon as there are two bands because of the supplementary cut . . . it is a matter of a double, undecidable sex, which sheathes [*gainer*] father and mother all at once. (*Glas*, 246–48, text modified)

Stilitano's postiche bunch of grapes cannot be read as a fetish substituting for a penis (which he has, and a large and strong one at that), but only as a postiche wound. This feminine counterpart is the antherection. A Stilitanesque column is one that is also marked, covered with scars, inscriptions, and tattoos: "*Glas* is a ceremony that obeys, in its form, the 'Order of Tattoos' whose institution is recounted in the *Miracle of the Rose*" (*Glas*, 239, text modified). Each column is inlaid, marked with words and designs that mix the black of the ink and the red of the blood so as to transfer the contract into the skin and to process the text. And apropos of *Glas*, "in the stone of each column a variety of inlaid judas holes, crenels, Venetian shutters, loopholes, to see to it not to be imprisoned in the colossus, tattoos in the folded flesh of a . . . body" (*Glas*, 2–3).

> Tattooing—thousands and thousands of little jabs [*coups*] with a fine needle prick the skin and draw blood, and the most extravagant figures are flaunted in the most unexpected places. . . . The grimacing of all that blue on a white skin imparts an obscure but potent glamour to the child who is covered with it, like a neutral [*indifférente*] and pure column becoming sacred under the notches of the hieroglyphs, like a totem pole. (*Glas*, 240, text modified)

Columns slashed open at the side, cut into, tattooed, inlaid for supplementary strength, power, and jouissance—"feminine jouissance," one might say—if such a thing could still exist within this generalized fetishism that causes the opposition of feminine and masculine to oscillate—as "the tattoos also have the relief of brilliant and cutting precious stones, like those the Dayaks of Borneo used to insert . . . after an incision, into the surface of the penis, to increase . . . the woman's *jouissance*" (*Glas*, 239, text modified).

And if such a jouissance were the ultimate end of this entire machinery, of this ritual, it would be the very reversal of Freud's ends and of the ends of phallogocentrism, which are to subordinate the woman's sexual interests to man and his desires, as we have seen. These inlays in *Glas* are not ornaments added retroactively [*après coup*] to columns that were originally smooth and intact, as in the case of those phallic columns of India that open and close *Glas*'s Hegelian procession. Those columns were originally unbreached and seemingly unbreachable; they were columns whose grooves, cavities, openings, hollow spaces, holes, and deep, lateral marks were added retroactively [*après coup*]. *Glas* tolls, too, for the end of any boundary between a column and its ornaments, its *parerga*, its balconies, its flutes. Like the columns of the brothel in Genet's *The Balcony*, each column is false, always concealing judas holes, galleries, and balconies.

What relationship exists between these two columns, columns that may seem—and this is a metaphysical way of seeing—opposed, pitted one against the other and not communicating with one another, in the same antagonistic relationship that is said to exist between the feminine and the masculine and between literature and philosophy? The two columns are not opposed, but they are nevertheless heterogeneous. Generalized fetishism does not lead to a sexual or textual indifferentiation. One column does not speak the language of the other; it follows neither the same rhythm nor the same law. The two columns differ from one another like "the dialectic from the galactic": they are like two colossal towers erected in a double solitude, without any apparent relation. Not opposed but heterogeneous, they nevertheless communicate with one another. Because they are not unmarred, because they are double and oblique, and because there are judas holes and jalousies, a series of exchanges and of reciprocal winks is established between them; they attach to and detach from one another, a process by which each passes over into the other. They penetrate one another: every penetration suspends opposition (because it finds no truly opposable substance within it). Notably, the sexual opposition is compromised in this agglutination, this infatuation, this coupling of sexes, texts, and terms. "Each term divided in two agglutinates to the other term, couples in an unleashed manner, drunk like a bell-ringer hanging from his rope." This is the effect of the *Gl* (paste, glue, spit, sperm, chrism, ointment together make up the conglomeration-without-identity of this ritual), or put in still another way, this is *the law of the general equivalence of terms*, of opposites endlessly taking each other's place, where

> each sentence, each word, each stump of writing is related to each other, within each column and from one column to the other.... Each envelopes or sheathes [*gainer*], incalculably reverses, turns inside out, replaces, remarks, overlaps the other ... Infinite exchange between two columns that regard themselves in reverse.... It's always the flower and the gloves that lend their form to this general equivalence. (*Glas*, 1, 43, text modified)

> For alleged opposites to be equivalent to each other and reflect each other, the flower has to be turned inside out like a glove, and its style like a sheath {*gaine*}.... The gloves are not only artificial and reversible signifiers, they are almost fake gloves.... The maids, like the Jews in the other column, are at once castrated and castrating, spiders or umbrella case, full and void of the phallus of Madame that Madame does not have. (*Glas*, 47–48, text modified)

> The law of oscillation and indecision ... remarking the flower's incessantly instantaneous reversal: penis / vagina, castration / virginity, erection / relapse, natural organism / disarticulated artifact, total body proper / fetishized morsel, and so on.... There is no choice, no disjunction or accumulation here. My excitement is the oscillation. (*Glas*, 125–26, 128, apropos of *The Thief's Journal*)

Each column that seems to rise up to an impossible self-sufficiency—the belief in such a self-sufficiency is metaphysical ideology—is thus nevertheless interlaced, intertwined, and wrapped around the other like a vine; each flows into the body of the other. Precisely this is *écriture du m'ec*, the reverse of man's writing: the writing of the general equivalence of subjects and opposites, of the *mixing of genres*. Thanks to an entire machinery that is complex and depurifying, *écriture du m'ec* tolls the death knell for phallogocentrism. It tolls for the end of all oppositions, for the end of man as well as that of woman, in favor of a "feminine jouissance," if by "feminine" one means undecidable oscillation.

The generalization of fetishism reverses the hierarchy in favor of the most devalued term and allows for general equivalence, for the flowing of one term into the other, for the communication of what had seemed incommunicable. It is a "stage" that leads to affirmation (although affirmation is already there in the generalized fetishism that it alone makes possible) or rather to double affirmation, because affirmation is bound "to the one that engages in the language of the other."[16] It leads to a "Yes,

yes," to a "Come" that is said to the other. It is the sign of a hymen, of an alliance wherein one body flows into the body of another, transforming the one and the other, and leaving neither of these complementary, mutually "infatuated" poles intact. The "passage" from generalized fetishism to double affirmation is a step beyond [*un pas au-delà*], from Genet to Blanchot, from undecidable oscillation to the neuter that—even when it takes the form of the "neither . . . nor . . ."—is fundamentally affirmative. Perhaps it is in this step beyond that one can hear not only the death knell [*glas*] of phallogocentrism, but also new ends: no longer the ends of man nor those of woman, but those of an "I–we."

> What she is to me? The "we" that holds us together and in which we are neither one nor the other? . . . Perhaps he is only me, from the very beginning me without me, a relationship I don't want to embark upon, that I push away and that pushes me away.[17]

> I could distinguish myself from it, only hear it while hearing myself in it, this immense speech which always said "We." (Blanchot, *The Last Man*, 67)

> The happiness of saying yes, of endlessly affirming. (*The Last Man*, 4)

TRANSLATED BY THOMAS ALBRECHT

PART II

Nietzsche and the Scene of Philosophy

§ 4 The Evil Eye

What is tragic?—On repeated occasions I have laid my finger on Aristotle's great misunderstanding in believing the tragic affects to be two *depressive* affects, terror and pity. If he were right, tragedy would be an art dangerous to life: one would have to warn against it as notorious and a public danger. Art, in other cases the great stimulant of life, an intoxication with life, a will to life, would here, in the service of a declining movement and as it were the handmaid of pessimism, become *harmful to health* (—for that one is "purged" of these affects through their arousal, as Aristotle seems to believe, is simply not true). Something that habitually arouses terror or pity disorganizes, weakens, discourages—and supposing Schopenhauer were right that one should learn resignation from tragedy (i.e., a gentle renunciation of happiness, hope, will to life), then this would be an art in which art denies itself. Tragedy would then signify a process of disintegration: the instinct for life destroying itself through the instinct for art. Christianity, nihilism, tragic art, physiological decadence—these would go hand in hand, come into predominance at the same time, assist one another forward (*vorwärts*)—*downward* (*abwärts*)—Tragedy would be a symptom of decline.

One can refute this theory in the most cold-blooded way: namely, by measuring the effects of a tragic emotion with a dynamometer. And one would discover as a result what ultimately only the absolute mendaciousness of a systematizer could misunderstand—that tragedy is a *tonic*. If Schopenhauer did not *want* to grasp this, if he posited a general depression as the tragic condition, if he suggested to the Greeks (—who to his annoyance did not "resign themselves"—) that they had not attained the highest view of the world—that is *parti pris*, logic of a system, counterfeit of a systematizer: one of those dreadful counterfeits that ruined Schopenhauer's whole psychology, step by step (—arbitrarily and violently, he misunderstood genius, art itself, morality, pagan religion, beauty, knowledge, and more or less everything).[1]

Medical scene: What about the pharmaceutical value of tragedy? Is it, as Doctor Nietzsche maintains, a remedy favorable to life, a stimulant, a tonic? Or is it dangerous for the health, depressing, harmful to life, as would hope Doctor Schopenhauer, who, in a perverse manner, prescribes it as a tranquilizer?

Schopenhauer would be right if the goal of tragedy were to provoke terror and pity, as was imagined by that other doctor who was long the authority on the subject: Aristotle. To refute Doctor Schopenhauer implies therefore first of all to bring suit against that very bad doctor, Aristotle, who believed he was able to "purge" man, to relieve him of his depressing passions by prescribing a homeopathic remedy: the tragic spectacle.

Eye Against Eye

Aristotle, Schopenhauer, and Nietzsche together debate an aesthetic problem: *What is tragedy?* asks one of them, as a true philosopher. Is it really Nietzsche who asks such a question? Is it not more typical of Aristotle? If Nietzsche repeats it, is it not in order to displace it? And is it not to substitute for the question of essence the question of power: if you want to understand something about tragedy, stop trying to make it an aesthetic category with an immutable and universal essence? Tragedy is a vital phenomenon, a network of forces capable of producing predetermined effects on certain beings. The problem is not to know what tragedy is but what it can do, to evaluate whether its effects are beneficial or harmful to life, to health. It is more a question of medicine than of philosophy, because the meaning that you will give to tragedy, o philosophers, is itself an "effect" of the tragic effect, which is why there are as many interpretations of tragedy as there are types of forces among the spectators. Despite the differences between you, Schopenhauer and Aristotle, there is a common point to your readings of tragedy: they betray the fact that you both are quite poor spectators and that you both have bad vision, an evil eye that forces you to give a moral interpretation of tragedy, to make of tragedy the pagan, the ally of all the forces of decadence, of nihilism, of Christianity. Seen in this way, the force of tragedy is that of an illness, decadence, of which tragedy would be the symptom.

Most philosophers and aestheticians do take as a starting point for their research the effect of the spectacle on the spectator (this will also be the analytic approach that Freud follows): start from the effects to go back to the causes. However, to a certain extent, this starting point necessarily leads to a misunderstanding of the meaning of the art because it positions itself from the point of view of a third party considered passive, the spectator, instead of positioning itself from the point of view of the artist, the creator. And this poor start is even worse for the fact that it postulates in general the universality, as though by necessity, of "the effect" of emotion or of pleasure. You can, of course, start from the spectator, but on condition of seeing, on the one hand, that he, too, is active, and, on the other hand, that there is not one ideal spectator, but many [*des*] spectators who maintain a completely singular relation with the spectacle; that it is a question of substituting for universality a pluralism of effects, of introducing in aesthetics, like in ethics, a differential typology; and finally you must see that aesthetic pleasure is not "disinterested" and decipher it like a symptom of health or of illness.

Armed with this new art of interpretation, you must, o philosophers, transform yourselves into doctors.

And understand, then, that the readings of Aristotle and of Schopenhauer are symptoms of their evil eye that projects onto all things its baseness, its pettiness, its illness. To interpret tragedy otherwise is to possess another eye, a "true artist's eye," a Dionysian eye, capable of seeing in art and in tragedy a tonic, a great stimulus for life. This debate that pits me against Aristotle and Schopenhauer? It is a *story of the eye* [*histoire d'œil*].

One eye is certainly not more "true" than another, but it can be "worth" more than another and consequently can function as a standard of measurement to evaluate as bad or as "evil" the eye that proposes a moral reading of the tragic phenomenon: this is not to be taken for a refutation, because one cannot refute a point of view; one can only change the conditions of existence that made it necessary.

Can we henceforth really accuse Aristotle of having committed "a great mistake" and Schopenhauer of having "refused to understand" what tragedy really is, of having misunderstood and "systematically" falsified everything? Even more, can we declare that it is possible to refute in a scientific manner the "theory" (*diese Theorie*) of Schopenhauer with the aid, for example, of a dynamometer? Would that not be saying, in this case, that the perspective of the artist's eye is also the one that delivers the truth, the very essence of tragedy? That the very essence of art is to be affirmative and that to interpret art as a negation is a contradiction in terms?

How to reconcile the genealogical point of view with this will to refute a singular perspective in the name of an essence of art and of tragedy? And why this quite particular relentlessness against Schopenhauer? Is not this "criticism" even more violent by virtue of being a counterpoint to Nietzsche's prior attachment? Is the massive rejection of Schopenhauer not the rejection of the old Nietzsche by the new Nietzsche, the rejection of the "evil eye," of illness, of his illness? Is it not the rejection by Doctor Nietzsche of the sick Herr Nietzsche?

> But let us leave Herr Nietzsche: what is it to us that Herr Nietzsche has become well again? For a psychologist there are few questions that are as attractive as that concerning the relation of health and philosophy, and if he should himself become ill, he will bring all of his scientific curiosity into his illness. For assuming that one is a person, one necessarily also has the philosophy that belongs to that person. . . . [W]hen it is distress that philosophizes, as is the case with all sick thinkers—and perhaps sick thinkers are more numerous in the history of philosophy—what will become of the thought itself when it is subjected to the *pressure* of sickness? . . . I am still waiting for a philosophical *physician* in the exceptional sense of that word— one who has to pursue the problem of the total health of a people, time, race, or of humanity—to muster the courage to push my suspicion to its limits and to risk the proposition: what was at stake in all philosophizing hitherto was not at all "truth" but something else—let us say, health, future, growth, power, life.[2]

"Catharsis"

Doctor Nietzsche has a diagnostic reliability like no other, but no one is more deaf than the invalid who covers his ears so as not to hear the issuing of his death sentence. So the doctor is forced to repeat his condemnation over and over. Whoever has ears, listen! From *The Birth of Tragedy* to *Ecce Homo*, passing by *Twilight of the Idols*,[3] the sickly character of the Aristotelian interpretation of tragedy is denounced. Aside from the fact that it translates the profound continuity of an identical will, of an identical a priori (*The Birth of Tragedy* is already a first "transmutation of values," an affirmation of the eternal return of life), this repetition also expresses the perverse jubilation of the spoiled child of philosophy, the philosopher of *The Gay Science*, who takes pleasure in emphasizing the faux pas of the father of philosophy, in pointing out and ridiculing the one who, for a whole tradition, is the authority and passes for having had the last word on tragedy. It is an attentive and suspicious reading by the child who follows with his finger the text of his fathers in order to point out their mistakes, and who surveys the philosophical scene the same way one watches for the "primal scene."

Aristotle, venerated by all, the great Aristotle, committed a great misunderstanding (*Missverständnis*), a diagnostic error, by making terror and pity, depressing affects, the tragic affects par excellence. And yet he did perceive the necessity of judging tragedy from a medical point of view, because he identified the purpose of tragedy as purging the soul of pity and fear by arousing these emotions in small doses;[4] the purging, the tragic catharsis, should expel from the soul the terror and pity that weaken it, like a purge aids the body in discharging the excrements that burden it. Terror and pity are bad passions, caca of which the soul must be purged, all the more so because the soul desires to "keep" them and take pleasure in them, imagining that the "pity" that is aroused spontaneously and easily at the sight of the suffering of others is a virtue. The cathartic remedy would be homeopathic and prophylactic: by the representation, the "imitation" of objects intended to provoke horror and pity, tragedy would awake a pity and a fear unaccompanied by pain, which would vaccinate against a real pity and a real fear aroused by "real" objects, not by objects that are only "imitated." At a later point, Breuer and Freud will call the analytic method cathartic because it relieves the patient, through fantasy repetition in transference, of unbearably cumbersome unconscious memories. The goal of theatrical catharsis would be to avoid in some sense the "hysterization" of emotion that leads to a poisoning by auto-intoxication or by an accumulation without discharge. Purging the soul produces a lightening of a quantitative surplus of emotions, of an excess of tension that creates an imbalance and whose discharge procures pleasure.

Long before Freud, Aristotle envisions aesthetics from an economic and quantitative point of view: by catharsis, the soul must be relieved of an excess quantity of caca, of terror and pity. Both purgation and the purge and purging are remedies that must be used only by those who are too "burdened" [*chargés*] with respect to their soul or to their body. By feeling at the theater the same harmful emotions, but in a way that is intense and without pain, souls "find themselves once again back on their feet, recovered, as if they had taken a remedy and a purgative"; just in the same way as the soft sacred melodies, the enthusiasm provoked by ritual dances, purge and cure the soul fallen prey to Dionysian agitation, transported outside of itself under the effect of religious enthusiasm sent by the god: the soft melody and the enthusiasm "in little doses" settle the soul, permit it to experience an inoffensive joy and lighten its overflow of enthusiasm.

> For feelings such as pity and fear, or, again, enthusiasm, exist very strongly in some souls, and have more or less influence over all. Some persons fall into a religious frenzy, whom we see as a result of the sacred melodies—when they have used the melodies that excite the soul to mystic frenzy—restored as though they had found healing and purgation. Those who are influenced by pity and fear, and every emotional nature, must have a like experience, and others in so far as each is susceptible to such emotions, and all are in a manner purged and their souls lightened and delighted. The purgative melodies likewise give an innocent pleasure to mankind.[5]

Plato had earlier referred to the practice well known to mothers to calm their children, also used by healers to calm frenetic Corybants and to temper their violent, uncoordinated movements: they resort to a lullaby, accompanied by music and dancing.[6] And beyond Plato, Democritus had had the idea of homeopathic treatment, *omoion pros to omoion*.

If, in fact, theatrical catharsis affects everyone, the means used, the "purgatives," are themselves a function of the spectator class, because the class of free spectators and the class of "unrefined people" each takes pleasure in that which is appropriate to its nature.

If Aristotle had pushed the idea of a differential typology of spectators to its logical conclusion, he might perhaps have avoided this double medical "mistake": situating the motivating force of tragedy in two depressing affects and imagining, contrary to Plato, who in this case had much better vision, that tragedy could serve as a purgative.

Pity and terror, in fact, are depressing passions in the physiological sense of the word; they provoke a decline of tonus, as already seen by Spinoza, who, as a true ancestor of Nietzsche, classed these two affections among the sad passions, those that indicate the passage of the soul from a greater to a lesser perfection and signal the reduction of its power to act. Pity is sympathy for the weakness and the suffering of others; terror is the fear experienced before the horrors of existence: both postulate that man is too weak to be able to tolerate suffering and death and that life, because it implies one and the other, is not worth the trouble of being lived. The path to which these two affections lead, as symptoms of the degeneration of a sick will that turns against itself, is the path of nihilism. This was the path taken by Schopenhauer, that enemy of life, the very symbol of European

Buddhism. The morality of Schopenhauer, who makes pity the virtue par excellence, is in fact a vital danger for humanity because by following this morality one goes straight into the abyss: in divine rags, in a coat of sublime speech, Schopenhauer's morality expresses a fundamental inimity toward life; by way of love, gentleness, and benevolence toward humanity, it is the most certain path to nothingness, the only one capable of delivering us from suffering forever, of bringing peace, quiet, Nirvana. A morality of pity is a mortal illness for humanity: it marks the end of transcendence, and because it favors weakness, it favors that which is ready to disappear. Because it defends the disadvantaged and those who are condemned by life, it hinders the law of evolution, which is the law of selection. What is disturbing, and strange, is that a depressive illness like this one, which implies a veritable perversion of instincts because it takes the will to nothingness as a standard of living, has become a contagious illness that affects even the healthiest beings. Even philosophers who, despite their differences, have always until now united around their scorn for pity, their affirmation of the nonvalue of pity, from Plato to Kant, passing by Spinoza and La Rochefoucauld, all affirm that pity cannot be a virtue because, founded on a misunderstanding of the greatness of man, of man's capacity to tolerate pain, it debases humanity. Pity, for Plato, is worthy only of women; it is condemned because it develops the least noble part of the soul, the least virile part, the unreasonable part that reminds us of our unhappiness and makes us moan, the cowardly and indolent part. It is a "shameful feminization of sentiment," a Nietzschean phrase that could have been Plato's. Pity is not suited to strong souls, noble souls, well-made souls: La Rochefoucauld, for instance, reserves it for the miserable, common people incapable of submitting themselves to reason.[7]

To show pity for another is to despise him as a reasonable being; it is not to recognize, says Kant, the sublimity of human nature as reasonable beings—it is ultimately to lack respect for reason. Compassion is "an insulting kind of beneficence which expresses the kind of benevolence one has towards unworthy beings,"[8] beings who, because they act more according to sentiment than to reason, are more women than men, are miserable people deprived of all nobility. Scorn for pity, unanimous among philosophers, is also always scorn for woman and for the common people.

The strange overestimation of pity by modern culture is a disturbing phenomenon because it is a symptom of a transmutation of values in favor of weakness.[9] This new value accorded to pity renders suspect the value accorded to the morality that makes of pity "*the* virtue, the ground and origin of all *virtues*."[10] It compels a questioning of the value of value and dresses up "faith" as the value of morality. The conversion of philosophers to pity, this virtue of the weak, of the sick, of the decadent, of women, forces us to turn away from morality and in turn to carry out a transmutation of values; because pity acts in a depressing manner and is opposed to affections that raise the energy of the vital sense, the true love of men consists of bursting it like an abscess, of ridding ourselves of a virtue that acts more like a poison than a remedy, of uprooting pity from ourselves, implacably, surgically, and without pity. No pity for pity! "To be physician *here*, to be inexorable *here*, to wield the scalpel, this pertains to *us*, this is *our* way to love men, in this way *we* are philosophers, we the Hyperboreans!"[11]

Aristotle saw clearly that pity was a sickly, dangerous state and that it was good to attack it from time to time with a purgative; his error was to have believed that tragedy could be this purgative and could take the place of a scalpel, to have believed that pity and terror prescribed in small doses could protect against depression. In this he was less perspicacious than Plato, who understood that such a remedy was a poison: far from vaccinating against depression, it habituated the soul to acting detrimentally to the reasonable part. The noxious effect of tragedy is to place the *thumôs*, ambivalent by nature, next to the *epithumia*, to make it the ally of weakness: tragedy dis-courages [*dé-courage*], it disheartens the heart [*ôte tout cœur au cœur*], it disorganizes the soul by reversing the natural hierarchy among its different parts. Contrary to what should happen, the *thûmos*, this intermediary instance whose role is decisive (as the intermediary ego between the id and the superego would later be for Freud), finds itself, at the theater, seduced by weakness; by repeatedly identifying with the afflicted hero, it loses the good habit of valiantly tolerating suffering and death. Tragedy emasculates man, makes him act like a woman or a child. At the theater, man comports himself in opposition to what the law of reason commands: although we call unreasonable, cowardly, and indolent the part that reminds us of our unhappiness and makes us moan, this part is moved before a spectacle, and we sympathize with the hero in his affliction. "But when one of us suffers a private loss, you realize that the opposite happens. We pride ourselves if we are able to keep quiet and master our grief, for we think that this is the manly thing to do and that the behavior we praised before is womanish. . . . The pitying part, if it is nourished and strengthened on the sufferings of others, won't be easily held in check when we ourselves suffer."[12]

As a better physician of public health than Aristotle, Plato chases the tragic poets from his ideal city because they poison the entire body of the city by emasculating it. Later, Rousseau, repeating to a certain extent the Platonic gesture, declares theater harmful because it can only augment natural inclinations and give new energy to all the passions. And he rebels against the Aristotelian idea of catharsis that claims "to purge the passions in exciting them":

> Is it possible that in order to become temperate and prudent we must begin by being intemperate and mad? . . . Do the emotion, the disturbance, and the softening which are felt within oneself and which continue after the play give indication of an immediate disposition to master and regulate our passions? . . . The only instrument which serves to purge [our passions] is reason, and I have already said that reason has no effect in the theater. . . . Thus the Theater purges the passions that one does not have and foments those that one does. Is that a well-administered remedy?[13]

Even supposing that the theater were capable of awakening pity, it can be only a "fleeting and vain emotion which lasts no longer than the illusion which produced it; a vestige of natural sentiment soon stifled by the passions; a sterile pity which feeds on a few tears and which has never produced the slightest act of humanity."[14] For what distinguishes Rousseau from Plato and Aristotle is this overestimation of the pity that is symptomatic of modern decadence, of which he is a typical example. Far from reproaching the theater for being an inefficient remedy against pity, he considers it dangerous because by arousing a pure pity unadulterated by anxiety, it excuses man from having to feel actual pity and gives him the illusion of being virtuous at little cost:

> In giving our tears to these fictions, we have satisfied all the rights of humanity without having to give anything more of ourselves. . . . In the final accounting, when a man has gone to admire fine actions in stories and to cry for imaginary miseries, what more can be asked of him? Is he not satisfied with himself? Does he not applaud his fine soul? Has he not acquitted himself of all that he owes to virtue by the homage which he has just rendered it? What more could one want of him? That he practice it himself? He has no role to play; he is no Actor.[15]

Thus, the effect of the theater, according to Rousseau, is to give a new energy to all the passions, except pity, which on the contrary, thanks to the theater, could be done without: for this reason, it would be twice as dangerous.

In this sense, Rousseau might have understood better than Aristotle the "essence" of tragedy: if tragedy develops passions and is harmful to morality, it goes in the direction of an affirmation of life; it is a tonic, a stimulus to life. Moreover, pity and terror cannot, then, be tragic passions because if that were the case, tragedy would be the ally of moral and religious forces, of pessimism, of decadence. Taking the side of weakness against strength, it would lead straight into the abyss.

Although Aristotle did see that tragedy, like music, is not simply a pleasurable art but a type of medical art, he was nonetheless mistaken about the nature of the remedy: "*Not* so as to get rid of pity and terror, not so as to purify oneself of a dangerous emotion through its vehement discharge."[16] Aristotle's error is to have let himself be guided by a pathological and moral point of view instead of positioning himself from an aesthetic and Dionysian point of view: he expected of tragedy only a negative effect, relief, a lightening, a discharge, which shows that he did not know how to take pleasure in the spectacle in all its components. The effect of tragedy is positive, and tragedy plays the role of a tonic for the person who knows how to watch it with a true artist's eye. The Aristotelian conception of catharsis proves only that Aristotle lacked an aesthetic temperament, that he had quite an evil eye, not "one eye too many,"[17] but one eye too few. If he was able nonetheless to be a school unto himself for many centuries, if his point of view is also that of the majority, it is only because the aesthetic listener [*l'auditeur artiste*] had always disappeared in favor of the moral listener, of a sick listener. Starting with *The Birth of Tragedy*, Nietzsche carries out a genealogical reading of the tragic spectator.

> Of course, our aestheticians have nothing to say about this return to the primordial home, or the fraternal union of the two art-deities, nor of the excitement of the hearer which is Apollonian as well as Dionysian; but they never tire of characterizing the struggle of the hero with fate, the triumph of the moral world order, or the purgation of the emotions (*Entladung von Affekten*) through tragedy, as the essence of the tragic. And their indefatigability makes me think that perhaps they are not aesthetically sensitive at all, but react merely as moral beings when listening to a tragedy. Never since Aristotle has an explanation of the tragic effect been offered from which aesthetic states or

an aesthetic activity of the listener could be inferred. Now the serious events are supposed to prompt pity and fear to discharge themselves in a way that relieves us; now we are supposed to feel elevated and inspired by the triumph of good and noble principles, at the sacrifice of the hero in the interest of a moral vision of the universe. I am sure that for countless men precisely this, and only this, is the effect of tragedy, but it plainly follows that all these men, together with their interpreting aestheticians, have no experience of tragedy as a supreme *art*. The pathological discharge, the *catharsis* of Aristotle, of which philologists are not sure whether it should be included among medical or moral phenomena, recalls a remarkable notion of Goethe's. "Without a lively pathological interest," he says, "I, too, have never yet succeeded in elaborating a tragic situation of any kind. . . ." . . . Anyone who still persists in talking only of those vicarious effects proceeding from extra-aesthetic spheres, and who does not feel that he is above the pathological-moral process, should despair of his aesthetic nature. . . . Thus the aesthetic *listener* is also reborn with the rebirth of tragedy. In his place in the theater, a curious *quid pro quo* used to sit with half moral and half scholarly pretensions—the "critic."[18]

The point of view of Aristotle and of the greatest number of people, which as such is irrefutable, ends with a "mistake" [*méprise*] when it transforms its singular perspective, linked to a determined idiosyncrasy, into a truth that reveals the essence of tragedy at the very moment when it puts tragedy into the service of pessimism, when it ignores the fact that like all art, tragedy is "a great stimulus of life, a drunkenness of life, a will to live." If tragedy were in its essence harmful to life, it would be, as a form of art, in contradiction with what art is, at least usually (*sonst*).

Usually? Is not the usual effect of art, on the great majority of people, negative, purgative, or moral? If art is usually a great stimulus to life, it must be understood that its function as such is to be in the service of the affirmative forces of life, even if its effect on "degenerate" spectators is strictly negative. In order to know what art really is, one must interrogate a truly aesthetic spectator, the only one capable of not transforming an aesthetic phenomenon into a moral or religious one, of not perverting its most intimate nature. The point of view of the aesthetic spectator and the point of view of the truth naturally coincide, because art is at one with the affirmation of life; it is life itself representing its creative power, the eternity of its return beyond suffering and death. Rigorously speaking, an art that is harmful to life, that negates life, destroys itself as art and can only abusively be called "art." There is no art, strictly speaking, without intoxication, without an overflow of life that becomes creative by spilling its excess of life into the universe.

> For art to exist, for any sort of aesthetic activity or perception to exist, a certain physiological precondition is indispensable: intoxication. (*TI*, 71)
>
> In this condition one enriches everything out of one's own abundance: what one sees, what one desires, one sees swollen, pressing, strong, overladen with energy. The man in this condition transforms things until they mirror his power—until they are reflections of his perfection. . . . [I]n art, man takes delight in himself as perfection. (*TI*, 72)

The origin of art is the recognition of life by a strong life. Its function is to permit *l'amor fati*, the love of life as a changing, savage, ferocious, lying becoming; to learn to want the illusion as such, to divest oneself of the moral eye that condemns becoming, the multiple, appearance, in favor of another eye, a Hericlitean eye, capable of grasping life as a game of forces where constructions and deconstructions alternate in all innocence; to understand that the One and Being, far from being opposites, constitute the very law of evolution.

The tragic spectator guided by such a Dionysian, "truly aesthetic" eye is capable of enjoying a tragic pleasure that is neither a negative pleasure nor a pleasure of the negative.

If, observing from a genealogical point of view, Nietzsche distinguishes two types of art whose premises are physiological, one having as its origin an excess of suffering by an overabundance of life, the other by a deficiency, he nonetheless describes this last type of art as an anti-art because it creates not beauty but ugliness and because it can be appreciated only by a living being who is always already dead and whose depressive illness it reinforces.

> Every art, every philosophy, may be considered a remedy and aid in the service of either growing or declining life: it always presupposes suffering and sufferers. But there are two kinds of sufferers: first, those who suffer from the *overfullness* of life and want a Dionysian art as well as a tragic insight and outlook on life—and then those who suffer from the *impoverishment* of life and demand of art and philosophy, calm, stillness, smooth seas, or, on the other hand, frenzy, convulsion, and anesthesia. Revenge against life itself—the most voluptuous kind of frenzy for those so impoverished! Wagner responds to this dual need of the latter no less than Schopenhauer. . . . Regarding artists of all kinds, I now avail myself of this main distinction: is it the *hatred* against life or the *excess* of life which has here become creative?[19]

If tragedy were an art harmful to life, it would be a corrupt art: a radical perversion of art, symptomatic of a radical perversion of the vital instinct that turns against itself to the point of desiring death and of experiencing pleasure at the representation of that which is depressing, a negative pleasure of the negative, symptom of a will to nothingness.

The Eye of the World

However, for Schopenhauer, wanting death is a matter not of the perversion of art but of its very essence; every form of art is a means to renounce the will to live [*le vouloir-vivre*], and tragedy is perhaps the privileged example of this. This conception is the exact opposite of that of Nietzsche, for whom wanting death would be symptomatic of a corruption of art that would destroy itself by bringing about the triumph of values inimical to life. Allies of a Christian morality and the Christian religion, related to all reactive forces, art, and tragedy in particular, animated by a decadent will, would lead straight to the abyss. Joining hands as if in a macabre dance, these nihilist forces would triumph together—a derisory triumph, in that it would only in fact be the triumph of death.

For Schopenhauer, indeed, the goal of art, like that of morality (which extols pity as a fundamental virtue), is to teach resignation, to lead to the abdication of the will to live. Or rather, art, by its own proper path, the path of the beautiful or the sublime, serves the ends of morality by inviting us—at least temporarily—to renounce the will to live. By the beautiful, we are torn away from life, without resistance and without our knowledge: it is a gentle way of renouncing happiness, hope, the will to live; by the sublime, the tearing away happens violently, and we are fully conscious of it. By this double path, aesthetic contemplation succeeds in delivering us from servitude to the will, because it ravishes us, charms us, transports us into the state of pure knowledge, a state of bliss that makes us forget our individuality and the unhappiness attached to it. Aesthetic contemplation erases all subjective difference in favor of the knowledge of the object, of its essence or idea, which makes us understand the difference between will and wills [*la volonté et les volontés*], the profound unity of wills inciting a renunciation of the individual will to live. Transformed into a pure subject of knowing, into "the one eye in the world" [*l'œil unique du monde*], we enter another world where nothing appeals any longer to our will or disturbs us, a world analogous to the world of sleep and dreams:

> Whenever it presents itself to our gaze all at once, [beauty] almost always succeeds in snatching us, although only for a few moments, from subjectivity, from the thralldom of the will, and transferring us into the state of pure knowledge. This is why the man tormented by passions, want, or care, is so suddenly revived, cheered, and comforted by a single, free glance into nature. The storm of passions, the pressure of desire and fear, and all the miseries of willing are then at once calmed and appeased in a marvelous way. For at the moment when, torn from the will, we have given ourselves up to pure, will-less knowing, we have stepped into another world, so to speak, where everything that moves our will, and thus violently agitates us, no longer exists. This liberation of knowledge lifts us as wholly and completely above all this as do sleep and dreams. Happiness and unhappiness have vanished; we are no longer the individual; that is forgotten; we are only pure subject of knowledge. We are only that *one* eye of the world which looks out from all knowing creatures, but which in man alone can be wholly free from serving the will. In this way, all difference of individuality disappears so completely that it is all the same whether the perceiving eye belongs to a mighty monarch or to a stricken beggar. . . . There always lies so near to us a realm in which we have escaped entirely from all our affliction; but who has the strength to remain in it for long? As soon as any relation to our will, to our person, even of those objects of pure contemplation, again enters consciousness, the magic is at an end. We fall back into knowledge governed by the principle of sufficient reason; we now no longer know the Idea, but the individual thing, the link of a chain to which we also belong, and we are again abandoned to all our woe.[20]

> With the beautiful, pure knowledge has gained the upper hand without a struggle, since the beauty of the object, in other words that quality of it which facilitates knowledge of its Idea, has removed from consciousness, without resistance and hence imperceptibly, the will and knowledge of relations that slavishly serve this will. What is then left is pure subject of knowing, and not even a recollection of the will remains. On the other hand, with the sublime, that state of pure knowing is obtained first of all by a conscious and violent tearing away from the relations of the same object to the will which are recognized as unfavorable [to the will]. (*WW*, 1:202)

Tragedy is the highest degree of the sublime; the spectacle of the tragic catastrophe must ineluctably lead to our turning away from the will to live, by presenting us with the terrible side of existence, by putting before our eyes everything that clashes with our will. Especially by displaying the reign of chance, the fall of the just, the triumph of evil, "the irretrievable fall of the just and the innocent" (*WW*, 1:253), tragedy reveals the existence of a malevolent destiny that persecutes us and against which it is vain to want to struggle; it shows that the world and life are powerless to produce any true satisfaction and by that very fact are unworthy of our attachment. The tragic hero serves as an example: in tragedy, after long combats, after long suffering, the most noble natures renounce the goals pursued, sacrifice life's pleasures, or even existence itself, and all this thanks to the knowledge that, purified by suffering itself, finally arrives at the degree where Maya's veil can no longer abuse it, where it sees clearly through the phenomenal form or the principle of individuation; such a clear knowledge leads to a renunciation of egoism and to the abandoning of formerly powerful motives. The suitable lesson to draw from the tragic spectacle is not that the hero expiates some individual sin but indeed the original sin, that is to say "the guilt of existence itself" (*WW*, 1:254), and does so by the path of knowledge, which, substituting itself for all the prior motives of the will, acts like a sedative, brings resignation, the renunciation, and even the abdication of the will to live (not to be confused with a suicide by resentment toward a life that fails to procure the hoped-for pleasures, because that would be nothing more than a simple reversal of the will to live, whereas the tragic character dies purified by suffering and when all will to live is already dead in him).

So for Doctor Schopenhauer, tragedy does have a pharmaceutical function but neither the purgative one imagined by Doctor Aristotle nor the tonic one asserted by Doctor Nietzsche, but a calming, sedative one: tragedy, like sleep or dreams, must bring forth Nirvana. A new kind of dream, tragedy must awaken us from the "weighty nightmare of existence" by showing us that man's greatest crime is having been born and by inciting us to relieve ourselves joyfully of the great burden of existence.

The "sublimity" of tragedy is that it succeeds in transforming our spiritual disposition to the point of making us "take pleasure at the sight of that which is most repugnant to it." Like the dynamically sublime, it is capable of raising us beyond the will and its interests, thus revealing the "sublimity of our nature": "At this sight we feel ourselves urged to turn our will away from life, to give up willing and loving life. But precisely in this way we become aware that there is still left in us something different that we cannot possibly know positively, but only negatively, as that which does *not* will life" (*WW*, 2:433).

If Schopenhauer was right, if his "eye" that confused itself with "the one eye of the world" really did reveal to us the intimate essence of all things, tragedy would be then a symptom of decline, and only a decadent civilization could favor such an art, whose function would be to produce Nirvana, to provide a path that leads to resignation, to holiness, to religion, the will's only really "serious" sedative: it would be the only durable consolation, and one that is no longer ephemeral, because it definitively leads away from life, into the abyss.

> That pure, true, and profound knowledge of the inner nature of the world now becomes for [the artistic genius] an end in itself; at it he stops. Therefore it does not become for him a quieter of the will, as we shall see in the following book in the case of the saint who has attained resignation; it does not deliver him from life for ever, but only for a few moments. For him it is not the way out of life, but only an occasional consolation in it, until his power, enhanced by this contemplation, finally becomes tired of the spectacle, and seizes the serious side of things. (*WW*, 1:267)

But can Schopenhauer's eye be assimilated to the eye of the world? Can it reveal the essence of art and of tragedy to us in all objectivity? Is it separable, detachable from the individuality, from the idiosyncrasy of Mr. Arthur Schopenhauer? Is the fact that he could have related the tragic state to the depressive state, and art to pessimism, not a sign that Schopenhauer's eye is quite an evil eye that projects onto everything its own venom, its own ugliness? And is the affirmation of a universal suffering, a generalized and implacable persecution, not the projection of a sick man who, by his conception of a unique will, identifies the victim with the executioner?

Schopenhauer's vision of art and tragedy, far from being that of the only eye in the world, is the eye of the sick man who can outlive himself only by taking refuge in sleep, dreams, forgetting, and the extinction of the will to live: by wishing for the triumph within himself of this "sublime element," the desire for the negative that reveals itself only negatively, which Freud will later call, invoking Schopenhauer as one of his inspired predecessors, the "death drive."

The Eye of Science

From a genealogical point of view, we could stop there. But Nietzsche, miming the traditional philosophical point of view, claims that it is equally possible to refute Schopenhauer's theory by using technical means at science's disposal: in order to remove any passional character from the debate, the tragic effect could be measured by means of a dynamometer; it could thus be verified, irrefutably, that tragedy, far from being a sedative, plays the role of a tonic. Why this methodological rupture, and why the introduction, hardly customary in a debate between philosophers, of a measuring apparatus? It is, it seems, the last recourse, the only possible one, against the systematic prejudice of a philosopher whose "reason" is so perverted by the logic of his own system—that of his sick instincts—that the brutal and cold intervention of scientific measure is necessary to make him understand "reason."

To introduce the dynamometer is to replace "the eye of the world" with the only "objective," if not true, eye, the eye of science. The dynamometer is a supplemental eye, the eye of the referee who can separate the adversaries.

But is it possible to convince a sick person, to refute the prejudice of the illness on which the whole logic of the system rests? The system is both a symptom of the individual illness and an attempt to defend against this illness by generalizing it. The "system," in fact, allows Schopenhauer to do without paranoia because he substitutes for an "individual persecution" a general persecution that is perceived by the scrutinizing eye of the world; this persecution, because it is general, provokes not paranoia but depression, the desire to renounce the will to live: the system is an apotropaic machine that protects against paranoia by means of melancholy, by means of an evil eye cast on all things.

What is intolerable about Schopenhauer is the lack of loyalty characteristic of systematizers [*faiseurs de système*],[21] which means that for the needs of the system, that is to say of his illness, he got to the point of applying the premises of this illness to everything, little by little, and of corrupting his whole psychology by taking possession of all phenomena with the violence and arbitrariness of a prejudice, the prejudice of his sick instincts against life. Because a systematizer is necessarily a prisoner of his prejudice, of his violent and arbitrary evaluations, it is necessary to introduce into the debate the violence of a technical apparatus that has the effect of a cold shower, in order to put an end to a delirium whose gravity can be seen in the interpretation of the tragic state as a depressive state, in his radical incomprehension of the greatness of the Greeks, whom he accuses of not being sufficiently "resigned" [*résignés*], of not having known how to reach the heights of a *Weltanschauung*, and whom he accuses, ultimately, of not being sick.

The measure of tragic emotion by the dynamometer should, then, expose the false measures of a systematizer, his generalized counterfeiting.

But only on condition that the spectator who would submit to this experiment is the aesthetic listener discussed in the *Birth of Tragedy*, and not the most usual spectator, prisoner of a moral and pathological perspective. The dynamometer experiment would be really crucial if tragedy did provoke an augmentation of tonus in every spectator. But in that case, how could the readings of Aristotle and Schopenhauer have been possible; how could they have become schools unto themselves?

Suppose that the dynamometer experiment records a lowering of tonus in a given spectator: would this mean that Schopenhauer is right? No; it would mean only that we are dealing with a creature who is more dead than alive; and if, despite the depressing effect that the spectacle had on him, this spectator cried out, "It's so beautiful!," it would prove only that his judgment of taste, a conclusion whose premises are inscribed in his body, is completely perverted.

> The effect of the ugly can be measured with a dynamometer. Whenever man feels in any way depressed, he senses the proximity of something "ugly." His feeling of power, his will to power, his courage, his pride—they decline with the ugly, they increase with the beautiful. . . . In the one case as in the other *we draw a conclusion*: its premises have been accumulated in the instincts in tremendous abundance. (*TI*, 79)

One can conclude from the dynamometer experiment only that tragedy is a tonic for those who already have "tonus," or even that tragedy is a spectacle intended for the strong, made for the strong, a fundamentally Greek spectacle that only those Greeks prior to decadence could correctly enjoy. By displaying the sufferings and the death of the tragic hero, tragedy, understood correctly, does not invite, in an exemplary fashion, pessimism or an abdication of the will to live. Through the sacrifice of the most elevated types of life, tragedy teaches, on the contrary, the necessity of loving life enough to consent to such sacrifices as well as the necessity of wanting the eternal return of life despite suffering and death. Dionysus, the only true tragic hero, is lacerated, dismembered, but is eternally reborn. Tragic art is fundamentally affirmative: it leads neither to pessimism nor to optimism but to a "virile skepticism": it teaches us to love life the way one loves an unfaithful woman, whose beauty is still acknowledged despite her duplicity. The tragic hero leaves life not cursing it, but blessing it, the way

Ulysses leaves Nausicaa. The spectacle of horrifying things leads to pessimism only for the person who is not strong enough to want the eternal return of life. Tragedy is a tonic for those who are strong because they are powerful enough to affirm "the global economy of the universe, which justifies and then some the fearsome, bad, equivocal things."

> Art is essentially *affirmation, blessing, deification of existence*—What does a *pessimistic art* signify? Is it not a *contradictio?*— Yes.— Schopenhauer is *wrong* when he says that certain works of art serve pessimism. Tragedy does *not* teach "resignation"—To represent terrible and questionable things is in itself an instinct for power and magnificence in an artist: he does not fear them—There is no such thing as pessimistic art. (*WP*, 434–35)
>
> The *tragic* artist.—It is a question of *strength* (of an individual or of a people) *whether* and *where* the judgment "beautiful" is applied. The feeling of plenitude, of *dammed-up strength* (which permits one to meet with courage and good humor much that makes the weakling *shudder*)—the feeling of power applies the judgment "beautiful" even to things and conditions that the instinct of impotence could only find *hateful* and "ugly." The nose for what we could still barely deal with if it confronted us in the flesh, as a danger, problem, temptation—this determines even our aesthetic Yes. ("That is beautiful" is an *affirmation*.) From this it appears that, broadly speaking, a *preference for questionable and terrifying things* is a symptom of *strength*. . . . It is the *heroic* spirits who say Yes to themselves in tragic cruelty: they are hard enough to experience suffering as a *pleasure*. Supposing, on the other hand, that the weak desire to enjoy an art that is not meant for them; what would they do to make tragedy palatable to themselves? They would interpret *their own value feelings* into it; e.g., the "triumph of the moral world-order" or the doctrine of the "worthlessness of existence" or the invitation to "resignation" (—or half-medicinal, half-moral discharges of affects à la Aristotle). Finally: *the art of the terrifying*, in so far as it excites the nerves, can be esteemed by the weak and exhausted as a stimulus: that, for example, is the reason Wagnerian art is esteemed today. It is a sign of one's *feeling of power and well-being* how far one can acknowledge the terrifying and questionable character of things; and *whether* one needs some sort of "solution" at the end. (*WP*, 450)

Multiply Your Eyes

The judgments that we pass on tragedy, then, definitively judge us. They are symptomatic of our religion and our wisdom; our options concerning tragedy reveal our most general options concerning life, the meaning that we give to existence: a Greek, pagan, Dionysian meaning or a Christian meaning. In the former, life is religiously affirmed in its totality, with its contradictions and its doubts and without renouncing or eliminating anything. In this Dionysian ideal, it is life itself, its eternal fecundity, and its eternal return that are the causes of torment, destruction, and the will to nothingness. In the latter, the Christian ideal, the suffering and crucifixion of the innocent Christ bear witness against life and are sufficient to condemn it. Life is denied in favor of another world; it is a simple path that leads to holiness. From the Greek, pagan perspective, on the contrary, "being is counted as *holy enough* to justify even a monstrous amount of suffering" (*WP*, 543). Tragic man is strong enough to affirm the harshest suffering and to deify existence, whereas the Christian is incapable of affirming even the happiest lot on earth: "he suffers from life in whatever form he meets it" (*WP*, 543). This double evaluation of all things can also be found in the significance accorded to the torture of the two divinities: God on the cross signifies a curse on life, a signpost to seek redemption from life; Dionysus cut to pieces is, on the contrary, a promise of life: "[Dionysus] will be eternally reborn and return again from destruction" (*WP*, 543).

To choose Dionysus instead of the crucified one is to declare not that Schopenhauer is correct but that Nietzsche is, that Nietzsche is the first tragic philosopher, the antipode of the pessimist philosopher,[22] the opposite of Schopenhauer. Schopenhauer's work, "the greatest piece of psychological false-coinage in history" (*TI*, 80), is the sole heir to Christian interpretation, with the one difference that Schopenhauer approves what Christianity rejects, the great deeds of civilization, but still approves of them in a Christian—that is, in a nihilist—sense, because he conceives of them only as "roads to 'redemption,' as preliminary forms of 'redemption,' as stimulants of the thirst for 'redemption' " (*TI*, 80).

Armed with a Christian art of reading, Schopenhauer corrupted all of psychology, made a sort of upside-down genealogy of all phenomena by submitting them to his own arbitrary and violent system of evaluations. He gave a moral reading of morality, of knowledge, of art, of religion, that was the exact opposite of Nietzsche's. Fundamentally misunderstanding all things, he notably—and this is no accident—cast his evil eye on all that is Greek, including Greek religion, art, and tragedy; all that is pagan and Dionysian; and everything that is a form of recognition of life, that represents its vindication and its deification.

Because Schopenhauer's aim is ultimately to transform the individual subject into a pure subject of knowledge, stripped of will, pain, and time, his goal is to identify his evil eye with this eye of the world, which, insofar as it perceives the essence of phenomena, finds itself delivered from the burden of existence, all cultural phenomena acquiring for it meaning and value solely because, in the final analysis, they imply knowledge as their precondition and their goal.

For example, what is *genius*? Its sole origin is the knowledge of ideas, its sole goal the communication of these ideas; the essence of genius is an eminent aptitude for the contemplation of ideas that demands a complete forgetting of the personality and its relations. "For genius to appear in an individual, it is as if a measure of the power of knowledge must have fallen to his lot far exceeding that required for the service of an individual will" (*WW*, 1:186). "Whereas to the ordinary man his faculty of knowledge is a lamp that lights his path, to the man of genius it is the sun that reveals the world" (*WW*, 1:188). "The genius, with his unfettered intellect, could be compared to a living person playing among the large puppets of the famous Milan puppet-show. This person would be the only one among them who would perceive everything, and would therefore gladly quit the stage for a while in order to enjoy the play from the boxes" (*WW*, 2:386).

If it is the hypertrophy of imagination that gives genius access to knowledge, it is also the hypertrophy of knowledge that explains all the characteristics traditionally associated with genius: its awkwardness, its lack of practical sense, its power of concentration, its excessive sensitivity, its solitude, its untimeliness, and the relation it is alleged to have to madness or to childhood; all these characteristics are connected to an excessive and abnormal disproportion of the intellect with respect to the demands of a particular will. The childlike, simple, naive character of genius also finds its explicative principle in the predominance of the intellect, because Schopenhauer's systematic prejudice allows him to affirm that children are more disposed than adults to a theoretical occupation, that they have more intellect than will, penchant, desire, or passion, all of which makes childhood the kingdom of innocence and happiness: "The genius is such through that preponderance of the sensible system and of the activity of knowledge, natural to the age of childhood, maintaining itself in him in an abnormal manner throughout his whole life, and so becoming perennial" (*WW*, 2:395–96).

However, if Nietzsche's earliest texts,[23] which still rely on Schopenhauer, also emphasize naiveté, the simplicity of genius, its untimeliness, its power of imaginative intuition allowing it to anticipate science's laborious knowledge, later texts put the emphasis not on the privileged aptitude for knowledge that genius supposedly possesses, but on the intensity of its will to power. And Nietzsche then denounces the misunderstandings and misinterpretations committed by humanity toward its benefactors when it confuses the wasting of forces—by a person who is not afraid of putting aside his survival instinct—with sacrifice or with abnegation for the sake of an idea. The characteristics of the genius can be explained not in terms of the intensity of his knowledge but in terms of a spending without reserve, without precaution or prudence, of his forces. For a "moral" reading of genius, Nietzsche substitutes an economic point of view, the point of view of an economy that is no longer restrained but general.

> Great men, like great epochs, are explosive material in whom tremendous energy has been accumulated; their prerequisite has always been, historically and physiologically, that a protracted assembling, accumulating, economizing and preserving has preceded them—that there has been no explosion for a long time. If the tension in the mass has grown too great the merest accidental stimulus suffices to call the "genius," the "deed," the great destiny, into the world.... The *danger* which lies in great human beings and great epochs is extraordinary; sterility, exhaustion of every kind follow in their footsteps. The great human being is a terminus; the great epoch, the Renaissance for example, is a terminus. The genius—in his works, in his deeds—is necessarily a prodigal: his greatness lies in the fact that *he expends himself*.... The instinct of self-preservation is as it were suspended; the overwhelming pressure of the energies which emanate from him forbids him any such care and prudence. One calls this "sacrifice"; one praises his "heroism" therein, his indifference to his own interests, his devotion to an idea, a great cause, a fatherland: all misunderstandings.... He flows out, he overflows, he uses himself up, he does not spare himself—with inevitability, fatefully, involuntarily, as a river's bursting its banks is involuntary. But because one owes a great deal to such explosive beings one has bestowed a great deal upon them in return, for example a species of *higher morality*.... For that is the nature of human gratitude: it *misunderstands* its benefactors. (*TI*, 97–98)

Genius, but also art, beauty, religion, all of it, according to Schopenhauer, implies knowledge as the origin and the will to nothingness as goal. Therefore, to restore a healthy psychology, to give back to all these phenomena their right to existence, is to refute fundamentally the conception of knowledge proposed by Schopenhauer. Knowledge is not a pure and disinterested contemplation of essence by a pure knowing subject, freed of will, pain, and time. There can be no intuitive intelligence that would make us see things with an eye entirely different than our ordinary one, make us see things no longer according to their relations but "according to what they are in themselves and by themselves," make us perceive their absolute existence. Because we can never be entirely foreign to the contemplated scene, we can never remain completely "detached." The idea of a "pure" subject of knowledge is a pure illusion; the one eye of the world is a dangerous and absurd fiction, because how would such an eye be possible? To know is not to possess the one eye, without any particular point of view; it is to possess the greatest possible number of eyes, to multiply and diversify perspectives, to learn to see otherwise, to appreciate the pros and the cons, to change perspectives. Not only is the subject of knowledge [*le sujet de la connaissance*] incapable of not being implicated in the contemplated scene; not only is he not "pure"—he is moreover not *one*, but many. There is not one *single* [*unique*] eye, one Cyclopean eye, one single will; rather, there are multiple eyes, differentiated wills. To want to know with one single eye is to want to castrate knowledge.

> [T]o see *differently* in this way for once, *to want* to see differently, is no small discipline and preparation of the intellect for its future "objectivity"—the latter understood not as "contemplation without interest" (which is a nonsensical absurdity), but as the ability *to control* one's Pro and Con and to dispose of them, so that one knows how to employ a *variety* of perspectives and affective interpretations in the service of knowledge. Henceforth, my dear philosophers, let us be on guard against the dangerous old conceptual fiction that posited a "pure, will-less, painless, timeless knowing subject"; let us guard against the snares of such contradictory concepts as "pure reason," "absolute spirituality," "knowledge in itself": these always demand that we should think of an eye that is completely unthinkable, an eye turned in no particular direction, in which the active and interpreting forces, through which alone seeing becomes seeing *something*, are supposed to be lacking; these always demand of the eye an absurdity and a nonsense. There is *only* a perspective seeing, *only* a perspective "knowing"; and the *more* affects we allow to speak about one thing, the *more* eyes, different eyes, we can use to observe one thing, the more complete will our "concept" of this thing, our "objectivity" be. But to eliminate the will altogether, to suspend each and every affect, supposing we were capable of this—what would that mean but to *castrate* the intellect?[24]

"To refute" Schopenhauer's conception of knowledge implies that one has another perspective on everything; that one has learned to see otherwise, to abandon the evil eye in favor of multiple, differentiated eyes; that one is an adept of Dionysus and not of the Crucified One, which is to say that one is not always already castrated by the fear of not entering the Kingdom of God. Commenting on Mark 9:47–48—"And if thine eye offend thee, pluck it out; it is better for thee to enter into the kingdom of God with one eye, than having two eyes to be cast into hell fire: Where their worm dieth not, and the fire is not quenched"—Nietzsche writes, "It is not precisely the eye that is meant."[25] It is only through a change of gaze, of drives, and by multiplying perspectives, that one can cease to take hold of all things with the arbitrariness and the violence of a single point of view. The Dionysian eye is not better than the Christian eye just because it is more affirmative; because it is a "plural" eye, it is also more capable than the single, castrated eye of making itself of use to knowledge. Because it is more "subjective," it is more objective and consequently more apt to grasp, for example, the "essence" of the tragic.

TRANSLATED BY BEN ELWOOD

§ 5 Scorning Jews: Nietzsche, the Jews, Anti-Semitism

> A settlement (*Austrag*) of their [the Jews'] case (*Sache*) would still be premature!
>
> —*Daybreak* §205, "Of the People (*Volke*) of Israel"[1]

1. The Jewish Question and the Question of Nietzsche's Anti-Semitism

No! The Jewish question has not been disposed of! The age-old dispute between the Jewish people and other peoples is nowhere near a settlement. No one has mastered the Jews or their "case" yet; no one has solved the riddle of their strangeness. This affair, Nietzsche tells us, has by no means come to term; it is still too soon to put its perplexities behind us. One sign that the dilemma is still with us: from text to text Nietzsche seems to take wildly varying positions, just as he did in the case of Socrates,[2] and to deliver himself prematurely of more than just one "Jew."

To see this absence of a systematic and definitive exposition (which is in itself a perfectly valid observation about Nietzsche's handling of this question and of many others besides) as incoherence or contradiction is easy to do and has been done often, though clumsily. The current fashion is to lean toward a charge of anti-Semitism. The philosopher is accused in the most summary and crude manner (without any serious examination of the texts' diversity or complexity) of having been the spokesman, indeed the father, of Nazism, and of being responsible, among other things, for Auschwitz. No more, no less! This, too, looks like an effort to decide Nietzsche's case prematurely.

There is no doubt that certain texts, when taken out of context, isolated from the Nietzschean corpus as a whole, presented without any references, mounted on pins, and, what is more, purposely misrepresented, may lend themselves—may indeed have lent themselves—when deployed by a certain type of man (whose frog's-eye view of things rules out all possibility of seeing and hearing plainly), to a dangerous, scandalous misinterpretation and reappropriation.

Such is the fate of many books, as Nietzsche knew. In "Philosophy in the Tragic Age of the Greeks," speaking of the way the texts of the pre-Socratics were manhandled by subsequent philosophers, he emphasizes that the *fatum libellorum*[3] is in general quite a painful fate, for misfortune often lands books in inappropriate hands that take from them only what they can grasp—that is, only what they themselves have already put in.

Granted, all written works, as we have known ever since Plato's *Phaedrus* and his *Theaetetus*, are by definition subject to every kind of manipulation by everybody; even so, Nietzsche's writings have been particularly ill served. The falsifications carried out by his sister Elisabeth Förster, when she took charge of the Nietzsche archives in Weimar and assumed the role of authorized spokesperson and interpreter of his philosophy, are well known. Her anti-Semitism and that of her husband are famous; likewise her friendship with Hitler and Mussolini (the latter had read all of Nietzsche's books). A fervent partisan of Nazism, she welcomed Hitler at the entrance to the archives in Weimar on the occasion of her eighty-eighth birthday, a meeting immortalized by a historic photograph no less famous than that of Hitler posing in front of the bust of Nietzsche in 1934. At Elisabeth's funeral—which was practically a national ceremony—the Führer himself placed a laurel wreath on the coffin. Two years later, thanks to her cousin and collaborator at the archives, Commander Oehler, a monument to Nietzsche was dedicated in the presence of high Nazi officials (Mussolini offered a statue of Dionysus for the occasion). Hitler had proposed this monument as early as 1935. He wanted it to be equipped with an auditorium and a library and to provide a meeting place for German youth: young people would attend seminars there and receive, through lectures and study groups, the so-called Nietzschean doctrine of the superior "race." The archives had already become a propaganda center for Nazi ideology, and in a lecture held there, Alfred Rosenberg and Dr. Walter Frank had hailed Nietzsche as the father of National Socialism. Furthermore, *Zarathustra*, adopted by the Hitler Youth as their Bible, had been placed with great ceremony, along with *Mein Kampf* and Rosenberg's *The Myth of the Twentieth Century*, in the Tannenberg Monument (erected to commemorate Germany's victory over Russia in World War I).[4]

2. The Greatest Scorner of Germans

These "facts" are crushing. But for whom? Principally for those who lay claim to texts that are over their heads and who have used them in an "unsavory"[5] manner completely lacking in probity. The price of greatness—the "rancor" it provokes—is solitude and incomprehension. Nietzsche deplored being misunderstood by the Germans, in particular by the Germans of the *Reich*. He was proud, as he says in *Ecce Homo*, to surpass everyone else in his contempt for them. It was the Germans and not the Jews who were "impossible" as far as he was concerned: they are situated in his typology at the extreme opposite from himself; they are canaille, lacking all sense of nuance and discrimination.

> The Germans are impossible for me. Whenever I picture to myself a type of man that antagonizes all my instincts, it always turns into a German. The first point on which I "try the reins" is to see whether a man has a feeling for distance in his system, whether he sees rank, degree, order between man and man everywhere, whether he makes *distinctions*: with that one is a gentilhomme; otherwise one belongs hopelessly in the broad-minded—ah, so good-natured—concept of canaille. But the Germans are canaille. (*EH*, 323)[6]

Nietzsche never stopped vituperating against this stupid "race," which greeted him tactlessly and indelicately, which would not lend him so much as a single ear[7] (an ear truly attuned to his *Zarathustra*, which after ten years was still received with an absurd silence, ignored, and then misinterpreted). His scorn for the Germans of the *Reich* led him to deny his whole Germanic connection on his mother's side, as it might link him to that canaille and its base instincts. He invented instead an imaginary genealogy,[8] a "family romance," which conferred upon him far higher and nobler origins that were much more to his liking. He declared himself to have such a horror of his mother and sister, on the canaille side, that he would rather disown the deepest of his thoughts than contemplate the possibility of their eternal return. This declaration—formerly censored, no doubt by the above-mentioned Elisabeth—appears in section 3 of "Why I Am So Wise," which was first published in the Colli-Montinari edition of *Ecce Homo*.[9]

Just as he denied his mother and his Germanic roots, Nietzsche worked hard to reach non-German ears—ears not afflicted with "otitis and indeed meta-otitis"—and moreover to be read in a language other than his mother tongue. And although he may claim to be the greatest of German stylists, he also asserts the strongest affinity with the French language, even going so far, for example, as to declare that he would rather people read *The Case of Wagner* in French translation than in the original.[10]

His desire to be "reborn" French does not mean, however, that he would trade one nation for another. Nietzsche feels contempt for all brands of nationalism, without exception. Indeed, he never ceases denouncing what he calls the "national neurosis" afflicting all of Europe, and in particular the provincial politics of the Germans, their pan-Germanism, their overestimation of everything German, of everyone belonging to what they call the German "race," and all this at the expense of any broad cultural vision, any inclusive European politics:

> I feel the itch, I even consider it my duty, to tell the Germans for once how many things they have on their conscience by now. *All great crimes against culture for four centuries they have on their conscience.* . . . They have on their conscience all that followed, all that is with us today—this most anti-cultural sickness and unreason there is, nationalism, this *névrose nationale* with which Europe is sick, this perpetuation of European particularism, of *petty politics*. . . . I speak of their indecency *in historicis*. Not only have the German historians utterly lost the great *perspective* for the course and the values of culture . . . One must be "German" and have "race," then one can decide about all values and disvalues *in historicis*—one *determines* them. "German" has become an argument, *Deutschland, Deutschland über alles* a principle. (*EH*, 319–21)

Far from being the father of the "master race" ideology, Nietzsche never uses the term "race" in the text cited above except in quotes, the better to stress what in his view is the scandal of nationalism and of racism. In particular, he denounces his contemporaries' anti-Semitism, evidence of which he senses, for example, in the characteristically German way they have of writing history: "There is now a historiography that is *reichsdeutsch*; there is even, I fear, an anti-Semitic one" (*EH*, 319).

The German stomach, insensible to differences, undiscriminating—incapable of choosing between opposites but granting equal rights to all in the most plebeian fashion—effortlessly engorges, in fact relishes, contradictions that are utterly flagrant to anyone with the least flair for things of the mind: " 'Faith' as well as scientific manners, 'Christian love' as well as anti-Semitism, the will to power (to the *Reich*) as well as the *évangile des humbles*" (*EH*, 318).

The "neutrality" of the German stomach, its abnegation, its limp "impartiality," and its democratism are why it likes anti-Semitism—indeed, finds it just right. This keeps it from vomiting when it should, from throwing up the foods that make Nietzsche—the aristocrat, the nobleman with a keen sense of nuance—throw up. Nietzsche, whose stomach is subtle and delicate enough to distinguish, not between high and low "races," but between the more and less delicate types of ears and minds that get hold of his work,[11] does not ally himself with anti-Semitism. Far from it, he savors the knowledge that when no one else paid him any heed, his work and his name were defended by a Jew, a Jew all alone, the first of Nietzsche's readers to organize a seminar on his work, in Copenhagen. I allude to Dr. Georg Brandès, "a Dane, the wittiest of Danes, that is to say, a Jew." Only Brandès was able to bring Nietzsche's originality and his "aristocratic radicalism" to light: "That is well said, and well felt—Ah! those Jews" (Letter to Kösselitz of December 20, 1887).

3. Jews Against Germans

Nietzsche always contrasts the Jews to the Germans; he never stops pitting them against each other and comparing them, not as a superior race with an inferior one, but as two types separated by an abyss: the former imbued with an extreme moral subtlety, "sharpened by rabbinical intelligence" (witness their invention of a perfect God and their concept of sin); the latter, lazy, warlike, and rapacious. The differences between them are so great that Nietzsche wonders how the Germans, with the cold sensuality of beer drinkers and amateur hunters—unable, apparently, to rise above a religion barely suitable for savages and who, "a thousand years ago, had not yet lost the habit of cutting people's throats on sacrificial altars"—could, in some respects, have had an affinity with the Jews. This is because paradoxically, the invention of "two excellent Jews, Jesus and Saul, the two most Jewish Jews there ever were," awakened more familiar resonances among the Germans than among any other people: "Both [Germans and Jews] believed that the destiny of every man, in every era past and future, as well as the destiny of the Earth, the Sun, and the stars depended on a *Jewish event* (this belief is the Jewish *non plus ultra*)."[12] One of Nietzsche's answers to this paradox is this: if the Jewish element predominates among the Germans, who are proponents of the Protestant mentality more than of Catholicism's Roman element,[13] it is not because the Germans resemble the Jews; it is only because they are more distant from the Romans than is the Catholic population of southern Europe.[14] In this rivalry, Nietzsche never fails to take sides with Jewish subtlety and malice against bovine German heft, and he maintains this attitude in all cultural domains. Thus, in literature it is Heinrich Heine, with his divine malice, who represents perfection for Nietzsche and who provides him with the highest idea of what a lyric poet is. His music is the sweetest and the most passionate in the world; he and Nietzsche share the honor of being "the foremost artists of the German language—at an incalculable distance from everything mere Germans have done with it" (*EH*, 245). As for music, the Germans are simply incapable of recognizing it: "Those who are called German composers—the greatest above all—are *foreigners*: Slavs, Croats, Italians, Dutchmen—or Jews" (*EH*, 251). Nietzsche contrasts the pseudo-genius of Wagner, who became German, all too German, with the real musical genius of the Jew Offenbach, with whom he associates the aforementioned Jew Heinrich Heine:

> If by artistic "genius" one means the most extreme liberty exercised within the law, divine buoyancy, insouciance even in the worst difficulties, then Offenbach has more right than Wagner to be called a "genius." Wagner is heavy, weighty; nothing is more foreign to him than the instants of exuberant perfection that that joker Offenbach achieves five or six times in practically every one of his farces. (Posthumous Fragment, *KSA*, 13:497)
>
> The Jews have achieved artistic genius with Heine and with Offenbach, that witty, capricious satyr, who remains faithful to the great musical tradition and offers to whomever has anything like true ears a veritable deliverance, after far too many sentimental and, in short, *degenerate* musicians of the German Romantic variety. (Posthumous Fragment, *KSA*, 12:361)[15]

In a letter to Peter Gast of March 21, 1888, Nietzsche declares himself transported by *La Pericola*, *The Duchess of Gerolstein*, and *The Daughter of the Regiment*: "Four or five times in each of his works, he reaches a level of exuberant comedy, all the while staying well within the bounds of classical taste, yet managing at the same time to be marvelously Parisian." And perhaps because Mendelsohn was more Jewish than German, Nietzsche acknowledges, and this is altogether to his credit, that in Mendelsohn, and only in him, one finds something of that great German who, more than a German, was a European and a consummate human being—that is, Goethe.[16]

"The Jews against the Germans," one might say then, taking up the agonistic formula that concludes and sums up *Ecce Homo*, "Dionysus against the Crucified" (*EH*, 335, translation modified). And here again, *against* should be read in all the senses of the German word *gegen*: at once oppositional and comparative (each people measuring itself against and substituting itself for the other) and also as an expression of proximity—in, and in spite of, difference (right up against). In a posthumous fragment from *The Gay Science*,[17] Nietzsche notes that it is more an affinity than a dissimilarity with Jewishness that strikes him in haters of Jews such as Wagner, for example (who is not, as we will see, a simple example).[18] Anticipating Freud,[19] Nietzsche accounts thus for the Germans' anti-Semitism, which is evident in their excessively zealous wish to be "real Germans," always making a great point of the purity of their "race" for fear of being mixed up with Jews, to whom they actually feel very close (to the extent that only an insufficiently nuanced, oversimplifying judgment can split Germans into Jews and haters of Jews, as though it were a matter of a pure and simple opposition).[20] Indeed, Nietzsche explains this German anti-Semitism by what, in a posthumous fragment from *The Gay Science*, he calls "a huge jealousy" (*KSA*, 9:597).

4. The Jews, the Law

Later, in the "Second Essay" of *The Genealogy of Morals* (§11), Nietzsche—whose entire genius, as we know, lies in nostrils alert to the harmful, asphyxiating odors that are mixed in with divinely fragrant ideals—senses in anti-Semitism (which he locates on the same terrain as anarchism) the smell of a plant—resentment—which like the violet flowers in the shade but lacks the violet's delicate perfume.[21] In a text dedicated to unmasking Eugen Dühring's account of the genesis of justice (a perverse, reactionary, and servile genesis rooted in the feeling of vengefulness), Nietzsche—and this is no accident—shows that anti-Semitism and anarchism grow in the same soil, that their typological closeness is betrayed by a common reactionary prefix. Anti-Semitism opposes the Jew, while anarchism opposes the law ("neither God nor master"[22]); both underline *a contrario* in this way the affirmative and primary character of the "Jew" and the "law," which belong to the affirmative and aggressive forces of life.

Even more than the Greeks, the Jews cleave to life and are the least decadent of all peoples (we will return to this). By no means weakened by their unparalleled sufferings, they have found ways to be strengthened by that pain. Their vital instincts (*Trieb nach Leben*) are so strong that the threat of mortality as a punishment for sin—the ultimate threat of never returning to life (an image absent among the Greeks)—works fearfully on their imaginations, so much do they fear being separated from their bodies: "With their refined Egyptianism," they hope to preserve their bodies for all eternity ("A Jewish martyr... has no thought of renouncing possession of his torn-out intestines: he wants to *have* them at the resurrection—such is the Jewish way!" [*D* §72, 43]).[23]

The Law, for its part, is not a reactive, inhibiting force. Commanding authority (*archê*) is immanent to life which—lacking any hierarchical principle—would be immediately condemned to death. To sanctify vengeance under the grand name of justice, as Dühring did,[24] is to effect—by moralizing it—a real displacement of the meaning originally given to it by the strong and to cause that meaning to be "forgotten," to the benefit of the weak and their reactive sentiments. Juridical authority does not originate in a reactive need. On the contrary, it struggles against all forms of reaction; it is a means to dominate, to impede the overflow of reactive affects. It is an inhibitor not of desire as an affirmative force but of the forces of death and resentment. "Justice" is an attempt to establish a compromise with these forces in order to keep them at its mercy. It implies a relation of one strength to another, of the stronger to the weaker, which it tends to dominate. In order to curb the resentment of the weak, which it maintains under its authority, justice supplants the avenger, placing under its jurisdiction both the victim and the "guilty party." On the one hand, it appears to defend the weak by declaring war on the enemies of peace and order. But it also places itself on the side of the strong, by giving force of law to "prejudices." Resentment is no longer confronted by some "third party," against whom it could turn, but by the law, which is to say, the power of society itself. All crime is crime against the law, and it is only by reference to the law that there is any "crime." Order is the order of the law, which institutes the just and the prohibited in relation to, and in conformity with, its own degree of power. Legal principle is always positive but is not opposed for all of that to natural law (as Rousseau and Montesquieu, among others, think), since it is nothing but the erection as law of an aggressive, spontaneous will to power.

Nietzsche stresses that the consequences of "legality" are the reverse of those consequences sought by violence: attention is directed away from wrongs suffered and from the person who suffered them, toward the law and the positive obedience that is due to the law as the highest power, rather than to this or that aggrieved individual. Legal principle detours away from the immediate, demanding impersonal appreciation. It trains us in "objectivity"—a clear gaze that does not pre-judge. It requires not the suppression of all particular points of view—which is just optical nonsense—but rather a changing vantage point. It does not cut off the individual from his or her desires, but habituates him or her to new priorities perceived from a new perspective, subordinating the perspective of the weak to that of the strong. It is only from the viewpoint of an individual who is at odds, rather than integrated, with the global power that legal procedures can be considered restrictive and inhibiting. In fact, they are aggressive and affirmative curbs that enable a superior power to dominate weaker powers. Juridical authority and the law are not opposed to life, they are life's very definition: partial restrictions on the will to power in the service of a greater will to power.

If I emphasize the common belonging of both Jews and the law to the affirmative and aggressive forces of life, it is not just because this aspect of Nietzschean thought has been insufficiently stressed. First and foremost, it is because Nietzsche sees the Jewish people as both the most affirmative of all people and the very people of the law. (That is why anti-Semitism and anarchism are not just born on the same terrain—that of resentment. Each is necessarily implied by the other.)

Jewish Law is not social law: it is ordained by God, the supreme power who, by singling out, by choosing the Jewish people among all peoples to be the people of his Law, confers on the Jews a propensity to the sublime (*Neigung zum Erhaben*) that no other people possess.[25] They are the chosen people, supremely distinguished by God; that, at least, is what the Jews were capable of imagining—"this people which had taken the fantasy of moral sublimity (*sittlichen Erhabenheit*) higher than any other people and which alone achieved the creation of a holy God, together with the idea of sin as an offence against this holiness" (*D* §68, 40). The essential, in fact, is this ingenious correlation between a God to whom all humanity's power is transferred and "sin," conceived not as a harm done to humanity bereft of all its power but as a wrong done to God alone, the most high and the all powerful (as we have just seen, "crime" and "injustice" understood correctly [in a Jewish way?] are not crime or injustice against some aggrieved individual, but against "deified" society and its law).

5. Saint Paul, or Hatred of the Law

The figure of Saint Paul, that "Jewish Pascal," drawn splendidly by Nietzsche in *Daybreak*,[26] can serve as a counterexample, furnishing by way of contrast an illustration of the Jews' "sublime" representation of their Law, while at the same time it lays bare the origins of Christianity.

What is the Law of the Jews all about? For Nietzsche, that was the question permanently lodged in the mind of Saint Paul, who was a sorry figure of a man: tormented, as unpleasant to others as to himself, ambitious, superstitious, and sly. At first, he, too, would have liked to serve the Law. Saint Paul was, in Nietzsche's description, "the fanatical defender" of the Jewish God and of his Law—"constantly combating and on the watch for transgressors and doubters."[27] But here is the rub: consumed by the basest passions, he found himself unable to serve the Law. Worse, his unbridled will for domination perpetually tempted him to transgress (*übertreten*) it. His suspicion (which was also an easy way to deflect his well-deserved self-reproach) was this: it was not so much "carnal urges" that spurred him with an irresistible charm to transgress, but, behind those urges, the Law itself, which "*had* (*muss*) ceaselessly to prove its unrealizability." At the same time that he threw himself into the veneration and defense of the Law with the utmost fanaticism, he said to himself: "It is all in vain! The torture of the unfulfilled law cannot be overcome." He began to hate that revered Law, which never stopped tormenting him: it was "the cross to which he felt himself nailed," and he "sought about for a means of *destroying it* (*es zu vernichten*)." It was Jesus and his cross—Jesus the destroyer of the Law (*der Vernichter des Gesetzes*) and also its fulfillment (*vernichtet nämlich erfüllt*)—who saved Paul from that cross and brought him out of the aporia (*Ausweg*). Jesus's crucifixion, his ignominious death, had to occur, Saint Paul suspected, in order to abolish (*abzutun*) the Law, to annihilate it, to evaporate it by spiritualizing it, thereby making Saint Paul the happiest of men. That is how he became the "doctor" of the Law's destruction (*der Lehrer der Vernichtung des Gesetzes*):

> To die to evil—that means also to die to the law; to exist in the flesh—that means also to exist in the law! To become one with Christ—that means also to become with him the destroyer of the law; to have died with him—that means also to have died to the law! . . . The Law existed so that sins might be committed, it continually brought sin forth. . . . [With the] death of Christ, . . . guilt as such has been destroyed; now the law is dead, now the

carnality in which it dwelt is dead—or at least dying constantly away, as though decaying. (*D* §68, 41)

What did Saint Paul want, then, when he invented Christianity with all the force of his hatred (which was just the reverse side of his veneration) for Jewish Law? Becoming the first Christian not only put an end to his torments, but also excused the exercise of his implacable will to dominate. The benefit for him was that he could imagine—in a manner unthinkable for a Jew and strung out by an insatiable sensual intoxication—that he was one with Christ, able to return to life with him, to participate in his divine glory and become, like him, the "son of God." Fundamentally, what Saint Paul could not stand was the idea of divine transcendence and the uncrossable gulf[28] it implies between the divine and the human. This gulf rules out the very thought of any communion whatsoever with God. For union with the Father would be a shameless, lewd abolition of all barriers (an incestuous union with the father?) and of all rank. Nietzsche stresses the mad sensuality[29] in Saint Paul (the revealing obverse side of which is the need to disseverate oneself[30] from the flesh and to annihilate it), which predictably will bring him to an "orgy" of divine splendors. In the final analysis, Nietzsche discerns in the invention of Christianity by this man whom he calls an "epileptic"—a man so tormented by the flesh that he wanted to end his tortures by annihilating it—nothing but the mask of an unprecedented will to power. (For Nietzsche, the dream of erotic promiscuity between man and God is really the dream of abolishing all subordination to the divine.)

Thus, at the origin of Christianity, one finds Saint Paul's "personal history": his tendency to separate himself from the Jews and from Jewish Christians—to separate himself, that is, from the flesh and from the Law, the perpetual thorn in his flesh ("The Law makes *hamartia*, the *sarx*, present to man at full force and thus makes it unbearable to man. 'To live in the flesh,' means also to live in the Law. To die to evil, is also to die to the Law" [*KSA*, 9:155]). Christianity is founded on Saint Paul's own story, then, Nietzsche says—or rather, only this story can explain how Christianity can have located itself beyond Judaism, bypassing the concept of a "finally realized Judaism" or of a "special branch of Judaism," while the Jews themselves refused to believe that their ideal had been fulfilled: "That it was possible to become Christian without becoming Jewish first—*that* was *his* invention" (*KSA*, 9:163–64). The madness of Saint

Paul—the "error" of his "invention," since Christians did, after all, become Jews[31]—is to have supposed that it was possible to dispense with Judaism, to become outlaws without passing through the Law. What he wanted was to escape the Law, which was structurally the spur to transgression and sin. To annihilate the Law meant wanting to abolish the natural necessity of sin[32] (considered sometimes as a weakness and imperfection by comparison to a perfect God, and sometimes as an absolute autonomous principle). By becoming "Christian," Saint Paul wanted to quit measuring himself against the Law and feeling himself a "sinner" no matter what he did. He wanted the death of the Law, of the flesh, and of insurmountable sin. Granted, these "murders" do not eliminate hamartia, sin; still, the presence of Christ in Christians, their union with him—this, at least, is their belief—makes sin no longer "necessary," no longer insurmountable.

The hatred of the Judaic tradition, which Nietzsche paradigmatically describes in the first Christian, Saint Paul, is inseparable from a hatred of the "flesh," of the Law, of the Law's omnipotence and of its sublimity, which keeps man forever a sinner. One might add, invoking a term that Nietzsche uses only with reference to Saint Paul, that it is no accident if the profound aversion to the "Jew" can be read in the horror linked to circumcision. For this custom symbolizes the alliance of the Jewish people with a God whose absolute transcendence entails man's radical inability to fulfill "his" Law and the necessity that he always be "cut off" from God and subordinated to him. Without hope of reconciliation, union, or communion. No matter what he does.

6. An "Oriental," Jewish Specialty

The "sublime"[33] conception of the Law is what "sets apart" the Jewish people from all others. Their "specialization in morality," which is the "Jewish specialty" par excellence, places them higher than any other people. Indeed, in their eyes, it is the sign of their election. Their invincible belief that they were chosen by God[34] enabled them to endure all the sufferings that the contempt of other peoples had visited upon them, and to triumph over that contempt by finding ways to profit from it, increasing their strength and fortitude.

For that, anti-Semitism would never forgive them. Anti-Semites have always wanted to get hold of that coveted divine "election" for themselves, forfeiting only "circumcision," which they regarded with horror and disgust,[35] to the Jews and "forgetting" that it is the mark of a covenant with God and not of infamy. Anti-Semitism's "error" is to introduce a split between election and the Law whose corollary is circumcision,[36] and to believe that it is possible to be the father's "favorite" while dispensing with submission to a Law that cannot be circumvented, that always puts you in the wrong. The "error" consists of believing, as Saint Paul did, that it is possible to dispense with the "Judaic" and to crush it.

What Nietzsche, for his part, understood very well was this: only the fiction of a sublime Law such as the Jews were able to imagine could have served them as the "guarantee" that they had never been abandoned by their God, but had remained his favorites and his chosen, despite material vicissitudes and the setbacks of history. Only this fiction could have safeguarded what the Jewish people and all other peoples who envied them cherish most—that is, the belief that they are the elect. The "fiction" of a sublime, divine Law, incommensurable with all other laws, a law that by definition no man could "fulfill," in effect enabled the Jews, when misfortune struck or in times of military defeat, to invent the correlative fiction of sin and to transform themselves into a people of infinitely guilty sinners, rather than acknowledge the possibility that God had abandoned them or that their supreme distinction had expired. The "misfortunes" that befell them at particular moments of their history were read by them not as symptoms of a divine "withdrawal," but as signs of their guilt toward God and toward him only—a God whom they pictured as hungry for honors, as "oriental," as one who "could not care less" about all the harm sin caused men: "sin is an offense against him, not against humanity."[37] A powerful God, so powerful that no injury except that which touches his honor can affect him, yet who paradoxically would take pleasure in vengeance:

> Too oriental.—What? A god who loves men, provided only that they believe in him, and who casts an evil eye and threats upon anyone who does not believe in this love? What? A love encapsuled in if-clauses attributed to an almighty god? A love that has not even mastered the feelings of honor and vindictiveness? How Oriental this is! "If I love you is that any of your concern?"[38] That in itself is a formula sufficient to criticize Christianity in its entirety. (*GS* §141, 190, translation modified)

From this perspective, all sin is a crime of divine *lèse-majesté*, an injury done to a sovereign who will never forgive except at the price of humiliating penitence. Enthroned at the summit of heaven, separated from humanity by an abyss, the divine king cannot be bothered about the natural consequences of sin. Given the Jewish fiction of a divine sovereign whose splendor, authority, and omnipotence are without equal and without compare, actions can be weighed from the viewpoint only of supernatural consequences, because all that is natural has become in itself unworthy (this is what makes Jews strangers to art, Nietzsche notes, and to the pleasures of tragedy, whereas the Greeks, thanks to the invention of tragedy, were able to lend dignity even to acts of sacrilege: for example, Prometheus's theft of fire and the massacre of the herds by Ajax[39]).

7. "Spernere se sperni"

The Jewish "specialty"—invincible belief in their divine election—and the Jewish concept of an "oriental" God, of a sublime Law, and the corollary of that concept, the idea of insurmountable sin inherent in humanity, are inventions that add up to a system. They make the "Jew" a strange, ambivalent, paradoxical figure. On the one hand, he maintains a very lofty image of himself, which enables him to greet scorn with scorn; on the other hand, he scorns himself and hates himself more than any other people has ever done, and he extends this hate and this scorn to all humanity. This "good" and this "bad" self-image give him a double countenance, like Janus.

In fact, the Jewish people feel superior to all others and have quite a high opinion of themselves. They do not consider this opinion the least bit arbitrary, for they have been able to fashion a superhuman ideal, by which they possess supreme power, distribute rewards and punishments, and prefer themselves to all other peoples.[40] This "good" image of themselves, this positive face, protects them against the contempt other peoples have shown them throughout history and enables them to scorn others' scorn and to overcome all the frightful, impossible obstacles that have confronted them (without resorting to drink or suicide, as so many other peoples have done, notes Nietzsche in *Daybreak* [§207]). Nietzsche cites as an example sordid occupations such as usury[41] to which Jews have been assigned on the grounds of their well-known "uncleanness"[42] (an assignment that, whatever else might be said of it, was not likely to make the Jew clean, any more than punishment could ever improve the criminal[43]). Far from rendering the Jew despicable, as his tormentors hoped it would, usury on the contrary strengthened his feeling of power and thus his self-esteem. Usury, in effect, gave him the power of revenge. In the fundamental text of *Daybreak* (§205), entitled "Of the People of Israel," Nietzsche writes:

> For two millennia an attempt was made to render them contemptible by treating them with contempt, and by barring them from all honours and all that was honourable, and in exchange thrusting them all the deeper into dirtier trades—and it is true that they did not grow cleaner in the process. But contemptible? They themselves never ceased to believe themselves called to the highest things, and the virtues which pertain to all who suffer have likewise never ceased to adorn them.... They have known how to create for themselves a feeling of power and of eternal revenge out of the very occupations left to them (or to which they were left); one has to say in extenuation even of their usury that without this occasional pleasant and useful torturing of those who despised them it would have been difficult for them to have preserved their own self-respect for so long. For our respect for ourselves is tied to our being able to practise requital, in good things and bad. (*D* §205, 124)

And in a posthumous fragment of the same year, he writes: "Man can bear the most dreadful scorn (as the Jews have), provided that from some angle or other he feels powerful (for the Jews it was from a money angle)" (*KSA*, 9:185).

In the same passage from *Daybreak*, Nietzsche shows that, fortified by a thousand-year ordeal of uninterrupted persecution, the Jews managed to acquire an unshakable sangfroid and tenacity. So cleverly did they contrive to turn their misfortunes to good effect that, under cover of a pathetic servility, their courage and "their heroism in the practice of '*spernere se sperni*'[44] outshines the virtues of all the saints" (§205, 124, translation modified).

That is how the Jews conspired to avenge themselves for the sordid occupations that were thrown to them and to outsmart fate. But that, after all, would only have been the usual expedient of the weak—a symptom of impotence more than of power—if their originality had not proved itself in their refusal to let themselves get drawn too far down the road of resentment, the road taken by the weak. Their vast experience in human relations, and their practice in flexibility and guile, so useful in such relations, taught them to exercise prudence even in their passions. They came to possess extraordinary resources, admirable qualities of mind and heart that equipped them to do great things. Nietzsche predicted that their destiny was either to be Europe's undoing as once they had been Egypt's or to become Europe's masters and guides.

8. The Becoming "Führer" of the Jew

In §205 of *Daybreak*, the passage we are now in the process of reading, Nietzsche is delighted to analyze, with extreme precision, the quasi-Hegelian reversal of servitude into mastery: the Jew's becoming master, that is, and becoming noble and fine, starting from, and thanks to, his initial and ancestral state of servitude. Nietzsche stresses throughout that it is still too soon, still premature, to settle the "case" of the Jews in Europe. They have not yet said their last word; they have not finished "becoming" what they are. The future that Nietzsche predicts for the world's most reviled people is that they will turn into the most noble, the most distinguished. Starting out as the shame (*Scham*) of Europe, they will cease being "dirty Jews," a "circumcised" people, and will instead be called the inventors (*Erfinder*) and the guides (*Wegzeiger*) among Europeans, no longer offensive to the Europeans' sense of propriety.

This metamorphosis of the Jew will not be achieved by means of violence or wars of conquest: the Jew has never earned his bread by physical force nor has he ever taken up arms in the grips of chivalrous and aristocratic sentiments (he seems, rather, up till now, says Nietzsche, to have been notable only for effusive, embarrassing obsequiousness).

The intellectual suppleness of the Jew, his highly evolved adaptability arising from his homelessness and his awful trials, has nurtured his gift for acting out mimetically (hysterically) any and all roles and has made him the typical comedian (the theatrical instinct in him has crowded out all others). He has become not only the artist and clown par excellence (cf. *The Gay Science* §361) but, more than anything else, a man able to take any position at all: for example, to act like an aristocrat by imitating the intellectual and physical manners of the best European nobility, the class with which he has gradually allied himself and whose heir he has become. Nietzsche predicts that in a hundred years the Jew will have absorbed enough aristocratic tone to be no embarrassment whatsoever to his subjects when he becomes master and lord of Europe. And that is what matters. It is by practicing the art of the blacksmith that one becomes a blacksmith; it is by practicing virtue that one becomes virtuous, Aristotle said.⁴⁵ By acting the part of distinguished men, and then—once their customs and manners have acquired a distinction of their own (which they swiftly do: "the way they honor their parents and their children, the reasonable character of their marriage practices and matrimonial traditions stand out among all Europeans" [*D* §205, 124, translation modified])—by excelling in everything that does credit to Europeans, by ranking everywhere among the best, the Jews will succeed in earning real distinction (*Auszeichnung*) for themselves. They will enunciate their own values and impose them on others (and it is in precisely this way that they will become decadent artists, in the sense that Nietzsche applies that term to Wagner⁴⁶: a decadent artist, he says, identifies with his fictional character and disowns appearance, hoping to become a real person). The Jews will not simply hold up a mask of distinction; they will become distinguished, discriminating men: nobles and masters, guides and inventors. And this will be achieved without a hint of violence: they will have only to cup their hands for Europe to drop in automatically, "like a well ripened fruit." The Jews will have crossed their Rubicon.

Not only will their empirical situation have been transformed; they themselves will have changed. They will have created themselves anew and thereby will have turned their eternal vengeance into an eternal blessing for Europe. Only then, concludes Nietzsche, will the God of the Jews really be able to rest, to rejoice in himself, in his creation, and in his chosen people. "And all of us want to rejoice with him!" he adds, saying "amen," as it were, to that day whose coming he had prophesied—the day the Jew becomes noble, a master and a great man.

9. Origins of the Jewish God

Why does it please Nietzsche so much to picture this emergence? Because the true Sabbath day will celebrate not the birth of a new Adam, but rather a reappearance by the Jew of the great biblical era, the Jew at the height of his powers, capable of forging in his own image, in the image of his prophets and of Moses,⁴⁷ a majestic, all-powerful, angry, and jealous God. Does Nietzsche in *Daybreak* not interpret the Jew's transfiguration through the course of his history as a recuperation of past greatness? This, in any case, is my hypothesis. Nietzsche sees it as an "oblique," not "outright," way of taking back from God what had initially been assigned to him. Would it not involve reappropriating the "good image" of himself that the Jew had lost, and lost only at the time of historic defeats? At that time, hard-pressed by events and wanting to preserve at all costs the invincible faith in his election, he transformed his image of God, made God "moral" and good. Through the same process, he came to see himself as an abject and contemptible sinner, consumed by hatred for himself (reduced thus to his "negative image," to being less than nothing) and for humanity. Did he not degrade himself even further by transferring all his own greatness, all his "superhumanness," onto the divinity, exhausting, as it were, his narcissistic libido for God's sake? The Jew's ascent to greatness, as Nietzsche imagines it in *Daybreak*, should therefore be accompanied by a revival of man's superhuman dimension and by the "death of God" as Jews and Christians imagine him (the Christians having done no more than push Jewish instincts to their limit, where they recoiled against themselves, thereby producing, with the aid of a systematic falsification of Jewish history, the illusion of a new and original perspective).[48]

This Jew, having become a great man, would serve as an even better model for the "superman" than would the Renaissance man and would bode well for the coming of that figure, so far strictly "ideal" and fictive, represented solely by Zarathustra. Nietzsche does not say it outright, but perhaps this explains his joy and his exultation at the prospect of the Jews' arrival or return to greatness, as guides and masters of Europe. If Nietzsche does not simply assimilate the Jewish "great man" to the superman, maybe it is because on the true Sabbath, when after many disasters the Jews regain their past glory and their powers, they will not realize that they are reclaiming for themselves a greatness they had transferred to God, for they have never really "known" that they created their God in their own image; they could only just barely feel that they were God's creators, Nietzsche says in a posthumous fragment from *Daybreak* (*KSA*, 9:330). In order to believe themselves "chosen" by God—in order to preserve that indispensable feeling of election—they had to fall back on mystification and self-deception (one even suspects that having become a great man and master of Europe, the Jew will not turn to atheism but will perforce continue to attribute his success to "election" by God). But beware of oversimplification: Nietzsche also shows that throughout their history, despite their abject submission to God, the Jews have always had a penchant for independence.[49] They have endured abjection only because they knew very well "somewhere," without really knowing it, that they themselves were behind the ever-growing power of their God, and that in return they had "elected" themselves. They knew (without really knowing it) that they had given themselves the fine privilege of exclusive access to this sublime majesty whom they themselves had raised up and whom their own blood had raised up ever higher, while, on an opposite course, they had lowered themselves, scorning and hating[50] man more deeply than any other people ever had.

In a comparison emphasizing the typological "nobility" of the Jews, Nietzsche likens their submission to a God whose power they themselves built up through transference and projection to the submissiveness of the French nobility under Louis XIV: the noblemen of France had surrendered their rights to a king whose power they had themselves created, but they were the only ones allowed into his presence. This "trade-off" gave them license to denigrate every other right or privilege and helped them endure the contempt they felt for themselves.

> The Jews' enjoyment of their divine monarch and saint is similar to that which the French nobility derived from Louis XIV. This nobility had surrendered all of its power and sovereignty and had become contemptible. In order not to feel this, in order to be able to forget this, one required royal splendor, royal authority and plenitude of power without equal to which only the nobility had access. By virtue of this privilege, one rose to the height of the court, and from that vantage point one saw everything beneath oneself and found it contemptible—and thus one got over an irritable conscience. Thus the tower of the royal power was built ever higher into the clouds, and one did not hold back even the last remaining stones of one's own power. (*GS* §136, 188)

Only "nobles"—with the pathos of apartness that characterizes them—could create, by transferring and projecting power, an abyss between "God" and man (and between man and man) that generates holy terror. They alone could have imagined this pure, distant, inaccessible figure—in short, the "Most High." And only "Jews," inversely, could have imagined a being who would jump into that abyss as mediator and bridge between God and man; only "Jews" could see that such a being must also be God, and not just a hero, for the Jews could envisage nothing truly elevated that did not come from God. "That very man who felt himself to be the mediator, had first to consider himself God in order to impose upon himself this mediating task" (*KSA*, 9:657). As a corollary, only the

Jews could have invented two "worlds," radically separated, heaven and earth, one placed absolutely high, the other absolutely low; they alone could have turned values upside down, given nature a moral interpretation, and awarded to everything that goes against nature and against life the highest esteem.

10. The Mask of Decadence

And yet this overturning operation did not transform the Jews into a race of decadent people. Quite the opposite, according to Nietzsche. They gave a decadent appearance, because they are such good actors. They knew how to play the part without actually being decadent, and they did so to safeguard the idea of their election and their strength. Faced with a new historical situation that threatened them with their own disappearance as a people and the loss of their autonomy, they preferred to survive, even at the cost of turning their moral values upside down. Their intelligence, sharpened by these perilous predicaments, saw a way of putting the decadents to good use. Above all, the priestly caste—the strongest faction among them—borrowed the evaluations of the weak for its own purposes, systematized these evaluations, and transferred divine authority to them in order to turn them into an implement of power. In order to stay alive, the Jews employed this priestly ruse, donning the mask of decadence: The Jews are nothing like any kind of decadent; they have so successfully imitated decadents, however, that they've fooled everyone and have been able to place themselves at the head of all the decadence movements in order to make these into something stronger than any affirmation of life (*The Anti-Christ* §24).[51] And this mystifying falsehood, initiated by the priests, was refined to perfection by Saint Paul's properly Jewish flair for the stage. He was driven by unbridled "ambition": "His need was to be powerful; with Saint Paul once again the priest wanted power."[52]

If, then, one can perceive the complexity of the Nietzschean argument—at the same time "historical," "typological," and "psychological"—and the transformations that this reading works on the figure of the Jew and, as a corollary, his God, mapping his response over the course of time according to changes in his empirical circumstances, then one can no longer charge Nietzsche with incoherence or contradiction. On the contrary, one can only admire the consistency of this entire construction whose different, apparently contradictory elements in fact reflect the Jew's own ambivalence—his Janus face. These elements interlock to form a system. It is simply that depending on the particular text and the circumstances, Nietzsche emphasizes either the positive or the negative face of the figure he has fashioned.

11. Jews versus Greeks

Thus, when he undertakes a differential typology, juxtaposing one people to another, or one religion to another, in critical comparison, Nietzsche ranks the Jews among the least decadent, the most affirmative of all peoples, even next to the Greeks. The Jews are more attached to the body and to life than are the Greeks; they simply cannot imagine—and they are unlike the Christians in this regard—a resurrection that would not revive flesh and organs. Thus, in many texts, the Jews are typologically compared with the classical Greeks and contrasted with the Christians, the first of whom, Saint Paul, had dogmatized an "error" of his master, Christ. This "error" was to have mistakenly believed (feeling himself to be without sin and lacking experience in this matter) that nothing made men suffer more than their sins. "It is thus that his soul filled with that wondrous and magical pity for a pain which his people, who had invented sin, rarely suffered very deeply from at all."[53] On the other hand, the majority of Nietzsche's texts have a different emphasis. They show Jews behind the triumph of the ascetic ideal and the corresponding figure of man as "sublime runt," responsible for overturning values and splitting the world in two—"terrestrial" and "celestial." In this version, the typological and agonistic confrontation clearly opposes "Jew" and "Greek." *A contrario*, the decadent Greeks—for example, Socrates—are pronounced "more Jewish than Greek."[54] This time, then, the Jew is paired with the Christian, who becomes a mere successor of the Jew, born on the same terrain.[55] When this is the leading comparison, Nietzsche uses the origin of the idea of God as his typological dividing line. The Jewish God, not Plato, is the basis for all metaphysical oppositions[56]; he is described as an "oriental" despot, exacting submission from his enslaved people. They become contemptible in their own eyes because they transferred their strength and their grandeur to an ideal placed so high that an abyss separates them from it. The Jewish God is thus opposed to the Greek gods, who were created as a projection of the Greeks' own strength, out of gratitude for life, to magnify their own affirmation of life. This projection of their strength did not drain their "narcissistic libido" to feed their divinities, for they did not feel diminished or humiliated. They felt, on the contrary, closely related to these gods whom they had endowed with the same passions they themselves felt, and who were not separated from men to some incommensurable extent. They made their gods simple delegates of the most refined human types:

> The Greeks did not see the Homeric gods above them as masters and themselves below them as servants, as did the Jews. They saw, as it were, only the reflection of the most successful specimens of their own caste, that is, an ideal, not a contrast to their own nature. They felt related to them, there was a reciprocal interest, a kind of symmachia. Man thinks of himself as a noble when he gives himself such gods.[57]
>
> *Jewish*, a religion of dread, of contempt and, occasionally, of Grace (for example, the ancient patriarchs). *Greek*, a religion of joy felt in might and in personal perfection, occasionally a religion of envy towards those who want to rise too high (Agamemnon, Achilles).[58]

From this perspective, Greeks and Jews (and Christians *as Jews*) are opposed to each other on every point, notably in their attitude toward the passions: deified by the former, brutally rejected by the latter.

> Color of the passions: "evil eye" for the passions in Paul and among the Jews: they see in passions only their own unclean side, which disfigures and breaks the heart;[59] their idealistic tendency aims at the annihilation of the passions, and they find perfect purity in the divine. Very differently from St. Paul and the Jews, the Greeks directed their idealistic tendency precisely toward the passions and loved, elevated, gilded, and deified them.... And the Christians? Did they want to become Jews in this respect? Did they perhaps succeed? (*GS* §139, 189–90, translation modified)

As we have seen, this "evil eye" for the passions makes the Jews utter strangers to tragedy, which the Greeks, with their "good eye" for the passions, invented.[60] The "aesthetic" category proper to the Jews is not the tragic but the sublime (in the Kantian sense). And this "propensity for the sublime" makes them the only possible inventors of a morality that was totally foreign to the Greeks: "oriental," says Nietzsche, because they moved morality into a divine world inaccessible to men and treated this deified moral element just as Asian peoples did their princes, groveling with devotion, anguish-ridden, full of adversarial contempt and dissatisfaction with themselves.

Meanwhile, these "typically" Jewish characteristics have been reappropriated by Christianity and passed on to Europeans, who ended up thinking of inner torment as the definition of humanness:[61] "Everyone thinks that the moral sentiments of today are moral sentiments par excellence—universal—but they are Jewish sentiments" (*KSA*, 9:385). "Morality (Judeo-Christian morality) is now the morality of civilization itself" (*KSA*, 9:393).[62] By civilization, Nietzsche means here the civilization of the weak, the "cowardly," the lazy, the outcasts—those whose "goal" is equality and whose state is built on "sand."

"Granted," to be at ease in such a moral element, "it does not do to be the happiest or sanest of peoples," says Nietzsche in one posthumous fragment from *Daybreak* (*KSA*, 9:89), in which he seems not yet to suspect, as he will later in the *Antichrist*, that the Jewish people wore the mask of decadence only to serve their own ends. And yet, even in the texts of this period, he does not boil down the "genealogy" of Jewish morality to a matter of its inventors' typological weakness. This morality is far too elevated, too sublime to have so base an origin. Nietzsche admits to confusion on this subject: "I cannot explain why among all the nations it is the Jews who have lifted moral grandeur to the highest level in theory as well as in practice. They alone have produced a Jesus of Nazareth, a holy God, and the notion of sin against that God. Moreover, the prophet, the savior—these are their inventions" (*KSA*, 9:75). This is a hopeless contradiction, as Jewish morality, having, via Christianity, become the morality par excellence, apparently favors universal equality and yet declares loudly that it is the highest morality, hierarchically superior to all others. Wanting to set up a hierarchy among moralities, believing it is even possible to find the necessary criteria, is a vain pretension, a sign not of weakness but of an unbounded will to power:

> What is the character of this morality? . . . And what is the hierarchical criterion of different moralities? . . . Perhaps it is part of the essence of the Jewish morality to consider itself the first and the highest. Perhaps this is a pretentious illusion: does a hierarchy of moralities even exist? Is there any such thing as a canon that determines everything and defines what is moral without consideration of the people in question, of the times, of the circumstances, of the level of cultivation? (*KSA*, 9:23)

12. The Strangeness, the Familiarity of the Jewish People

The superiority of Jewish moral philosophy is an illusion, of course, yet it has prevailed among practically all peoples. It was adopted in Europe and—everyone having forgotten its Jewish origins, its foreign, "oriental" character—it has become the moral system par excellence. Whereas Europe feels that Greek civilization is as distant and foreign (*fremd*) as can be, Jewish morality feels close to home.

Christianity's tour de force was to appropriate the inventions of a "very particular and peculiar Asiatic race, to place its literature, its Psalms, the sacred book of a Semitic people into the hands of an 'Indo-European race'" (*KSA*, 9:22), to have allowed the assimilation of so small and strange a universe, to have caused it to be cherished and sanctified (presenting its literature as superior because more "moral," a better fit with the currently accepted ethical system, better adapted to refined mores). This move was so successful that non-Semitic Europe no longer finds anything surprising in that "small, foreign universe" and has no sense of estrangement from it at all. The tour de force was the drastic reorientation of Europe's sense of foreignness, to Greece's detriment. The figure of Abraham acquired more importance for Europeans than that of anyone in Greek or German history, and the Psalms of David are more "familiar," more *heimlich*, than Pindar or Petrarch.

The foreignness, the singularity of the Jewish people, which is now "covered over," would not have been lost on the Greeks, a people who were exempt from the feeling of sin: they would have been bemused or irked, as if by a slave's idea, at the thought of a God who forgives provided only that one repent.[63] The Romans, in due course, felt this "singularity" very strongly. We know of their suspicion of and distaste for "outlandish" Jewish rituals (and those of the Christians, who were lumped in with the Jews). They charged the Jews with believing in absurdities and practicing secret cannibalism.[64] Nietzsche (who emphasizes that anyone embarking on an impartial study of Jewish history will have a hard time pulling back from too long and too great a familiarity with the Jewish world in order to perceive its strangeness, given that Europe, on top of its reappropriation of Judaism via Christianity, has projected a good deal of itself into the Bible [*KSA*, 9:21–23]) does all he can to make this foreignness plain while at the same time attempting a "return" to Greece, now a foreign country for

Europe. "In general, European morality is Jewish, and a deep foreignness separates us from the Greeks" (*KSA*, 9:656).

> Sin, as it is now experienced wherever Christianity holds sway or has held sway, has a Jewish origin. It is a Jewish feeling and a Jewish *invention*. Regarding this background of all Christian morality, Christianity did aim to "Judaize" the world. How far it has succeeded in Europe is brought out by the fact that Greek antiquity—a world without feelings of sin—still seems so very strange (*fremd*) to our sensibility, although whole generations as well as many excellent individuals have expended so much good will on attempts to approach and incorporate this world. (*GS* §135, 187, translation modified)

Nietzsche's suspicion is that the "generalization" of Judaism by Christianity, the effort to "make the whole world Jewish," was neither altogether "disinterested" nor altogether favorable to the Jews. For not only did Christianity thus efface the singularity of the Jews: the effort also amounted to nothing other than a raid by the Christians on the Jews. It was a way to subdue an opponent: Christians absconded with the sacred book of the Jews by claiming that it contained only Christian tenets, that it only foretold Christianity, in short that it belonged to the Christians, the only real people of Israel, and that the Jews were keeping it under false pretenses. In this "assimilation" of Judaism by Christianity, Nietzsche sees a typical example of a dishonest, burlesque philology, giving in with a clear conscience to self-serving interpretive and interpolative madness.[65] The success of this interpretive violence brought another benefit, however: Europe thereby overcame itself, winning a great victory over the "racial limitation and complacency according to which only what one's own father and grandfather have said and done is of any real value for anyone" (*KSA*, 9:22).

13. The Race Question

Although Nietzsche repeatedly uses the term "race" (e.g., Semitic race, Indo-European race, "racial" limitation), it is not in a "racist" sense, to mark the superiority of one "race" over another. If "race" had a biological meaning, the overcoming of racial limits that Nietzsche stresses, the assimilation of one "race" by another, the subsequent loss of that race's singularity—its originality, its historical and typological specificity, its "specialness"—would all be impossible. It would be impossible to associate Christians and decadent Greeks with "Jews." Nietzsche's concern is not the "innate" superiority or superior "blood" of any race or people; his concern is the struggle for power, the submerged play of wills in a fight to survive or predominate, and the see-saw shifts of power in the course of history, since one group's domination over another is never definitively won or assured. Over and above all "racial limitations," Nietzsche postulates a universal principle of intelligibility—the will to power—which explains, regardless of the differences, the will to be a "chosen people," to be first in everything everywhere, to be a "superior race" living in other peoples' countries. According to Nietzsche, this "universal" leads not to a generalized leveling and erasure of differences, but to the untenability of a canon that would decide the hierarchical superiority of anything—any morality, any race, any type—"without taking into consideration the particular people, the times, the circumstances, the level of cultivation."

That is why Nietzsche uses the term "race" in a critique of racism and of anti-Semitism in particular: to displace the meaning of the word. He signals this by putting the word in quotation marks.

Thus, in *Ecce Homo*, "Why I Am So Wise" (§3), announcing that he is going to treat the question of race, he stresses that he has not a single drop of German blood (*Blut*). And *Blut* is repeated three times. But he slips from this apparently biological point of view to a typological one by linking "bad blood" to bad, loutish instincts (the canaille), and "good blood" to aristocratic instincts. Then, substituting an economic reading of kinship for a physiological one[66]—a reading of inheritance where the line is not transmitted through blood but rather through instinctive drives, forces cultivated for centuries by the preeminent, finally exploding in the genius—Nietzsche creates a fantastic genealogy for himself, going back to the very highest and most ancient: all the way to Dionysus.

The "divine" Nietzsche, a man without a country, feels nothing but contempt and horror for all notions of "race" and "nation" (as well as "class").[67] If the beginning of "Why I Am a Destiny" apocalyptically foretells "wars such as there never were before," these wars, like Saint Paul's (which Nietzsche parodies), are "wars between minds,"[68] and that is what politics ought henceforth to be. Such politics will no longer put existing forms of power into play. Those forms are all based on deception, for "real" wars with their martial posturing are still just "idealism." In their stead will come a "great politics" demanding great efforts of societies, great overturnings, real revolutions of a kind undreamed of by practitioners of present-day, petty politics. Revolutions will not originate in war between nations, or between classes, or between races. Nietzsche predicts that all these notions will fly apart. The only war conceivable will hierarchically oppose one type of man to another, in a sort of merciless duel to the death:

> I come bringing war. Not between nations; I have no words to express the scorn I feel for the abominable politics of European dynastic interests which make a principle and practically a duty out of the overwrought egoism and antagonistic vanity of nations. And *not* between classes: for we have no superior classes and consequently no inferior classes; those who are on top today are physiologically doomed.... I come bringing war, a war that will cut straight down the middle of these random absurdities called nation, class, race, profession, education, culture. (*KSA*, 13:637)[69]

> We have just entered upon a great politics, and even the greatest politics ... Everything that today is most exalted, "the Triple alliance," "the social question," will disappear in favor of an *individual oppositional position*: we will have wars such as were never seen before, but not between nations or between classes; all these distinctions will come to pieces.... We will have overcome the absurd frontiers between races, nations, and classes: there will be no more hierarchy except between man and man.[70]

The "great politics" that is supposed to eliminate all narrow-minded nationalisms, whose sole inventor Nietzsche declares himself to be—after acknowledging Napoleon's paternity—will entail a radical reconsideration of the very ideas of civilization and humanity as they have so far been conceived. Only the ecumenical task which Nietzsche assigns to himself will be grand enough to succeed ultimately in linking all the peoples of the world together.

Still, it cannot be denied that the texts of "Why I Am a Destiny," along with the others I have cited in corroboration, promising spiritual wars instead of the martial or military ones Nietzsche despised, do resonate in a particularly strange and disquieting manner for those of us who have experienced nationalist and racist wars attributable to men who appealed, wrongly, to Nietzsche in order to legitimate an ideology that he found horrifying. They misused his texts: for example, in spite of the author's numerous warnings,[71] they misinterpreted his notion of the "superman," changing him into a new "lord of the earth." The "great politics"—and Nietzsche had made this perfectly unmistakable—was not meant to imply political domination by any one nation or race, or by any man over another. Nietzsche is, of course, no humanist, and he makes no bones about it. But the "hierarchical relation between man and man"—the only hierarchy he contemplates after the elimination of the absurd frontiers dividing races, nations, and classes—is not a political hierarchy. It involves two types of humans: one forged by the ascetic ideal, which up to that point had been so successful, it seemed to have fixed once and for all the features and characteristics of humankind; the other the superman, whom Nietzsche had fashioned in the figure of his son Zarathustra and who was to serve as a model of a new type of man yet to come. This new type would put an end to the dangerous supremacy of a single, unrivaled type[72] that led to leveling and decadence. Granted, Nietzsche does not hesitate to establish a real "apartheid"[73] between these two "human" types ranged competitively against each other. But this segregation is not "racial," nor does it have as its goal the domination of the strong over the weak. On the contrary, it is a question of trying to protect the strong against the weak (and life from the decadence that threatens it), against the risk of overwhelming disgust that could infect the strong with nihilism, against the risk (greater than the risk of syphilis[74]) of contamination and corruption, a risk the strong run when they let themselves be seduced by the ascetic ideal and its morality. That ideal is a dangerous Circe who hides her vampirism beneath a goddess's finery. To be protected from the poison of a guilty conscience and from any hint of pity, the superman must be isolated, consigned to the icy, pure heights, kept at a distance, there where only his peers can join him.

Assuming he has any. Nietzsche knows very well that Zarathustra, his son, is a fictive character and that only fiction can forge a type of man strong enough, beautiful enough, "wicked" enough, immunized enough against disgust and pity by his great pity for faraway mankind, to succeed in a transvaluation of values. As for "Nietzsche," at the end of the "Second Essay" he explicitly distinguishes himself from his character. He will publish only a single chapter, under the title *The Anti-Christ*, from the work that was to mark the beginning of a new era, *The Transvaluation of Values*. In 1888, the most fecund year of all,[75] he collapsed into "madness," which is another name, according to Foucault, for the absence of work.

If Nietzsche cites cleanliness and purity as his own most characteristic instincts, and water as his element, he goes on to reevaluate these notions. In any case, it requires a violent interpretive stretch to see him as the father of National Socialism and its racism. A text from *Daybreak* (§272), "The Purification of the Race," has an important bearing on this point. Nietzsche (who is not to be confused with Gobineau, even if he did read the latter's *Essai sur l'inégalité des races humaines*) writes there as plain as day that there are no pure races—that a better hypothesis would be that of races *become pure*. What one encounters most often are mixed races that form mixed cultures, which are generally more wicked, more cruel, more unstable, and more diabolical (the devil, he says ironically, created people of mixed blood, while God created whites and blacks). "Purity" is not original but is rather the final result of innumerable adaptations, absorptions, and eliminations (*Auspassungen, Einsaugungen*, and *Ausscheidungen*). Progress toward purity consists of selecting certain functions from an excess of often contradictory ones, for this contradictory plurality tends to dilute the strength present in a "race." And, Nietzsche writes, although the process of elimination presents the appearance of an impoverishment, when it is complete, all the strength that before was dissipated in the conflict among discordant qualities becomes available to the entire organism. That is why when they become purer, races have also become stronger and more beautiful. Need I mention that for Nietzsche it is by no means the Germans who exemplify a race and civilization that have become pure? On the contrary, he always emphasizes their "many-colored" instincts and "soul." His example is the Greeks; they are a model and a hope for the constitution of a "pure" European race and culture.

In a text from *Human, All Too Human* (§224), "Ennoblement Through Degeneration," Nietzsche writes that the growth of an individual or a race has two components: on the one hand, an increase in basic, innate strength, thanks to bonds linking minds together in a community of beliefs and feelings; on the other hand, the possibility of attaining lofty goals, promised by the appearance of degenerating natures and, consequently, the weakening and partial erosion of the innate strength. And he recalls—which, for me, has the highest importance—that it is precisely the weaker nature that makes progress of any kind possible because the weaker nature is subtler and more free: "A people that begins to rot and weaken in one area but remains strong and healthy on the whole, is capable of sustaining the 'infection' of newness and can turn this newness to its advantage by absorbing it."[76]

If one believes this text, one sees that far from heading in the direction of Nazism and its belief in the purity and superiority of the German race,

Nietzsche discovered Germany's "weakness" in advance, for the German culture could not absorb or assimilate newness; it could only eliminate it, could only exterminate it as refuse, nothing but refuse.

In general, if one reads Nietzsche's texts as I have tried to do, in their multiplicity and their complexity, it is impossible—barring bad faith and a willful disregard of their strictly literal sense—to decide in favor of a Nietzschean anti-Semitism.

14. A Youthful "Error"

There is one more thing: the man who signs his texts with the single name "Nietzsche" did not arrive at his "purity" and his "unity" until he had completed a long process of selection and catharsis. He had to win a struggle of emancipation from, and disavowal of, his identificatory models and to break his symbiotic relation with them. As we see in my reading of *Ecce Homo*,[77] the process by which Nietzsche became "Nietzsche," the fulfillment of the "promise" that he had made to himself to win his own terrain and his secret garden and to bring about his own (re)birth, implies the cutting of the umbilical cord joining him to the Germany of the Reich, to his mother and sister, and to his parent substitutes—Wagner and Schopenhauer, among others—and thus to their mad anti-Semitism. To have it out with "anti-Semitism" was for Nietzsche part of the same "vital" undertaking as settling accounts with Wagner, among others. It demanded a systematic opposition to Wagner's negative judgments of Jews, notably of Jewish musicians in his famous text "Judaism in Music." (Thus, in *Ecce Homo*, in "Why I Am So Clever" [§7], *klug* (clever) is precisely, like *weise* (wise), one of the traits popularly attributed to Jews in Lessing's *Nathan the Wise*, and these are traits that Nietzsche appropriates to define who he is.) This move is all the more necessary because Nietzsche continues to love and revere Wagner.[78] He manages when Wagner dies to split his image in two: a "bad" Wagner and a "good" Wagner reincarnated in *Zarathustra*. And he even goes so far as to save him in the last analysis from his anti-Semitism by transferring full responsibility to Schopenhauer alone, on the pretext that an artist is always a philosophy's mere valet:[79]

> Wagner is Schopenhauerian in his hatred of the Jews to whom he is not able to do justice even when it comes to their greatest deed; after all, the Jews are the inventors of Christianity. . . . Of course, the philosophy of an artist does

not matter much if it is merely an afterthought and does not harm his art. . . . Let us remain faithful to Wagner in what is *true* and authentic in him—and especially in this, that we, as his disciples, remain faithful to ourselves in what is true and authentic in us. (*GS* §99, 154–55)

To break with anti-Semitism is "vital" for Nietzsche because all his "role models" set out to permeate him with it, him and all those Germans of the Reich who were fascinated by Wagner and Schopenhauer and who saw them as models for a revival of German culture (for example, Nietzsche's friend Gersdorff, who wrote him in a letter of March 11, 1870, that Wagner's "Judaism in Music," written in 1850 and published in 1869, had opened his eyes).

The traces of anti-Semitism in the "young" Nietzsche are easy to spot in his correspondence between 1866 and 1872 (the year when the *Birth of Tragedy* was born and also when "Nietzsche" himself was born—that is, when he rejected Wagner and Schopenhauer, even though, as he says in *Ecce Homo*, he still had to accentuate the novelty of his own voice by borrowing the voice of those two masters, using them as straw men and metaphors[80]).

Let me present here a few pieces of incriminating evidence:

- Letter from Leipzig, April 22, 1866, to his mother and sister, the first letter he sends from his new lodgings: "Gersdorff and I finally found an inn where neither melted butter nor Jewish faces were offered for our delectation."[81]
- Letter from Leipzig, April 27, 1866, to Hermann Mushacke: "No matter where you look, it's Jews and Company."
- Letter from Naumburg, April 4, 1867, to Paul Deussen: "There aren't any more of those Hebrew clouds between us that used to keep us from advancing together at the same pace, our thoughts in perfect agreement."
- Letter from Leipzig, October 18, 1868, to his mother and sister: "Today the Fair is over, and we're glad to be rid of the smell of burnt fat and the crowds of Jews."
- Letter from Leipzig, December 9, 1868, to Erwin Rohde: "I am powerfully attracted to the figure of Democritus; granted, I reconstructed him for myself from the ground up, since the historians of philosophy have been unable to do justice either to

him or to Epicurus, bigots that they are, and righteous Jews before the Lord, but Schleiermacher the least able of all, that false and obscure, tricky little woman."

It is interesting to note that in *Ecce Homo*, Nietzsche, having by now come into his own, repeats these charges against historians of German philosophy, whom he always treats as tricksters, and continues to take Schleiermacher (whose eloquent name means "veil maker") as the prime example. But the allusion to Schleiermacher's Jewishness and to his femininity (two traits that anti-Semitism and a whole philosophical tradition commonly conjoin) is now suppressed. Schleiermacher ceases, as it were, to be a "proper" name (and "proper" to an effeminate Jew), the better to become, thanks to a famous play on words, the general name for all philosophers, including the most anti-Semitic among them. "The Germans are inscribed with nothing but ambiguous names; they have always brought forth only 'unconscious' counterfeiters (Fichte, Schelling, Schopenhauer, Hegel, and *Schleiermacher* deserve this epithet as well as Kant and Leibniz: they are all mere veil makers)" (*EH*, 321).

In a letter to Wagner from Basel, dated May 22, 1869, Nietzsche stresses what a lucky German he is to have met the composer who has given him a more soulful and more serious vision of the world—and that he is pleased in large part given the "Jewish invasion." Thanks to Wagner and to Schopenhauer, he is hewing faithfully to the serious Germanic approach to life.

In a letter to Gersdorff on March 11, 1870 (in which Nietzsche once again associates everything best and most beautiful in existence with two names, Schopenhauer's and Wagner's), he draws a line between Wagner's ardent, chivalric combat and the Jews who detest his idealism, stressing above all Wagner's kinship with Schiller (later, in *The Twilight of the Idols*, Schiller will be classed with the "impossibles"). It should be noted that in this letter, the word "Jew" is put in quotation marks. In Nietzsche's view (if not in that of his correspondent, who, responding to Nietzsche's letter of December 23, 1872, from Naumburg, alludes to an icy Berlin as the "capital of the new Jewish empire"), the word "Jew" is losing its purely empirical meaning and acquiring a broader application ("For our 'Jews'—and you know how embracing that concept is..."[82]). In this broadening of the term, one anticipates what Nietzsche will later call a typological meaning: it associates the Jew with the plebeian and the everyday commotion of plebeian German politics, the complete opposite of Wagner's chivalric, idealist, and Schillerian circle of combat.

It is nonetheless true that the letters Nietzsche writes after the one announcing an "extension of the concept" are studded with comments that arise from the most vulgar kind of anti-Semitism (always supposing there could ever be some other "more refined" anti-Semitism that would be more acceptable) and are aimed at perfectly real Jews.

Thus, in a letter to Oskar Oehler on February 13, 1870, he asks for news of a Doctor Volkman, whom he says he met once without speaking to him, for "his clothes were in such fantastically bad taste and he resembled a type-cast Jew."

In a letter to his mother and his sister on December 23, 1871, apropos of a Christmas present to his sister, an art history book by Wilhelm Lübke, he writes without hesitation: "How can you expect me to order a book *from a scandalous Jewish antiquarian bookseller!*" (my emphasis).

In a letter to his mother from Splügen (a vacation spot) on October 1, 1872, he writes: "I dine at my hotel where I already find a few companions for the Splügen trip the next day: *they include, unfortunately, a Jew*" (my emphasis).

And finally, in a letter to Gersdorff, written on February 4, 1872, we make the stupefying discovery that Nietzsche has refused to go on a scholar's trip to Crete with Karl Mendelsohn because he is the son of Felix Mendelsohn-Bartoldi. Although Nietzsche blames the excessive amount of work he has to do, the son of the composer of Jewish origin (whom Nietzsche will later rehabilitate, again taking a position exactly opposed to Wagner's) has no illusions and does not overlook the more personal sources of Nietzsche's refusal, in particular his policy on Wagner and Wagner's music. Karl, it is true, judges that music "the greatest thing this century has produced," but he reacts with studied reticence to Wagner's negative judgment of the musical influence of Jews. "That in his writings he condemns the influence of Jews on the modern development of music, and that he considers my father a Jew, is a point we could discuss. I believe we could examine the pros and the cons of it while sailing across the blue waves of the Ionian sea," he writes to Nietzsche.

The turning point for Nietzsche with respect to the Jews seems to date from *The Birth of Tragedy*, that is, from the time he distances himself from Wagner and from the Germans, whom he henceforth calls "Teutons" or "horned beasts," and whom he thereby contrasts with the cultivated and intelligent Jews, who were the first to have grasped the originality of *The Birth*—even if, as Nietzsche remarks with some ambivalence, one of them wanted to take credit for the novel ideas that come to light in it. In a letter to Erwin Rohde from Basel on December 7, 1872, Nietzsche writes, in fact, apropos of his first book: "Jacob Bernays has declared that they are *his own* ideas but highly exaggerated. I find that damned insolent, coming from this cultivated and intelligent Jew, but also a very agreeable sign of what the 'country foxes' are already sniffing in the wind. Here as everywhere, the Jews are first in line while the good Teuton . . . , with his good horns, lags behind in the fog."

What are all these citations supposed to prove?

I have not provided them in order to denounce Nietzsche's "youthful errors" before what tribunal I could not say, but to stress that one cannot divorce Nietzsche's relation to the Jews and to anti-Semitism either from the history of Germany or from his own history, the history of becoming "Nietzsche," which urgently required him to break with his milieu and his prejudices, to divorce himself from Wagner and Wagner's violent condemnations of Jews and Judaism (so violent that Nietzsche half suspects such tyrannical hatred of being the symptom in Wagner of an unrecognized "Semitism").

Perhaps, indeed, Nietzsche's numerous texts on the Jews and their religion are the work of a "genealogical" historian, trying to be "impartial," and able, with his great flair, to detect what is or is not a Jewish "specialty." Nevertheless—and could he deny it?—these texts are inseparable from the personal question that he had to settle, if not with the Law and the torments of the flesh, at least with Wagner, his esteemed master.

That is why the alleged anti-Semitism of "Nietzsche" refers us back to that of the composer, and from there—if one wants to give Nietzsche a chance to "save" someone he never stopped loving—to that of Schopenhauer.

But that would probably be a whole new story.

TRANSLATED BY ANN SMOCK

PART III

With Respect to Woman

§ 6 From *The Enigma of Woman: Woman in Freud's Writings*

1. The Battle of the Sexes

Didn't Freud himself predict it? Feminists would take to the warpath against his texts, which, on the subject of women, would be seen as rife with masculine prejudice. The woman question has indeed provoked opposition not only from without but from within the very heart of psychoanalysis, has unleashed a veritable internecine war: women analysts are turning psychoanalysis against its founder, accusing him of taking sides, of siding with his sex, because of his sex. In brief, they say, on the question of woman, a man, even a Freud, cannot produce objective, neutral, scientific discourse: he can only *speculate*, that is, philosophize, construct a system destined to justify an idée fixe, a tendentious view based not on observation but on self-perception. So he cannot help verging on madness, paranoia.

In his lecture "Femininity" ("Die Weiblichkeit"),[1] a text recently denigrated—to put it mildly—by a woman psychoanalyst,[2] speaking to men and women ("Ladies and Gentlemen," he says at the beginning of his talk, repeating an apparently banal formula in order to bring out all its enigmatic strangeness later on), Freud emphasizes—not without irony— that every time any point is made against women, female psychoanalysts suspect men of deeply rooted masculine prejudices that prevent them from being impartial.

Freud avails himself of various arguments in an effort to dispel such suspicions. He maintains that the use of psychoanalysis as a weapon in the controversy is not enough to decide the issue, does not make it possible to choose between himself and the women analysts. Psychoanalysis is a two-edged sword that may well be used against women's discourse, he argues, for it allows us to understand that the female sex cannot accept, or wish to accept, anything that runs counter to its strongest desires, anything that contradicts, for example, the equality with men that women so ardently seek. Psychoanalysis thus allows us to understand why "feminists" adamantly reject the Freudian concept of the feminine superego, for according to them this concept originates merely in man's "masculinity complex" and serves as a theoretical justification for men's innate tendency to belittle and repress women.[3]

Almost always, in fact, it is the concept of the *feminine superego* and its corollary, women's intellectual and cultural inferiority, that give rise to controversy. It takes real heroism for Freud to make his explosive conclusions public:

> I cannot evade the notion (though I hesitate to give it expression) that for women the level of what is ethically normal is different from what it is in men. Their super-ego is never so inexorable, so impersonal, so independent of its emotional origins as we require it to be in men. Character-traits which critics of every epoch have brought up against women . . . would [all] be amply accounted for by the modification in the formation of their super-ego. . . . We must not allow ourselves to be deflected from such conclusions by the denials of the feminists, who are anxious to force us to regard the two sexes as completely equal in position and worth.[4]

And with regard to the different outcomes of the Oedipus complex in girls and boys, outcomes responsible for the differences in their respective superegos, "here the feminist demand for equal rights for the sexes does not take us far."[5]

I, Freud, Truth, I speak, and Truth will soon be able to resist all pressures, all more or less hysterical "feminist" demands; for, O women, if you seek to use psychoanalysis against me, I shall be much better prepared to turn it back against you, even while I pretend to be granting you some concessions, agreeing to some compromises in order to put an end to the battle of the sexes between us and to reestablish among male and female psychoanalysts a "polite agreement": in my lordly fashion, I freely grant you that "pure femininity" and "pure masculinity" are purely theoretical constructions and that the content of such speculative constructions remains quite uncertain. I am prepared to grant, too, that most men fall far short of the masculine ideal, for "all human individuals, as a result of their bisexual disposition and of cross-inheritance, combine in themselves both masculine and feminine characteristics" ("Consequences," 258).

In this internecine war, the thesis of bisexuality is a weapon that is supposed to put an end to the accusations made by women psychoanalysts: Freud's injurious discourse on women no longer concerns them, for they are exceptions to the rule, more masculine than feminine.

> The discussion of [femininity] has gained special attractiveness from the distinction between the sexes. For the ladies, whenever some comparison seemed to turn out unfavourable to their sex, were able to utter a suspicion that we, the male analysts, had been unable to overcome certain deeply-rooted prejudices against what was feminine, and that this was being paid for in the partiality of our researches. We, on the other hand, standing on the ground of bisexuality, had no difficulty in avoiding impoliteness. We had only to say: "This doesn't apply to *you*. You're the exception; on this point you're more masculine than feminine." ("Femininity," 116–17)[6]

More masculine than feminine, if not homosexual. "The Psychogenesis of a Case of Homosexuality in a Woman" emphasizes that the patient "was in fact a feminist; she felt it to be unjust that girls should not enjoy the same freedom as boys, and rebelled against the lot of women in general."[7]

The thesis of bisexuality not only is the thesis that Freud is defending; it also serves as his defense against accusations of anti-feminism; and it, too, is double-edged. It allows Freud to repeat the most tenacious, the most traditional, the most metaphysical phallocratic discourse: if you women are as intelligent as men, it is because you are really more masculine than feminine. Thus, it allows him to shut women up, to put an end to their demands and accusations. But this thesis also makes it possible to displace the metaphysical categories that it renders problematic, since it proclaims the purely speculative character of the masculine/feminine opposition. The thesis of bisexuality thus implies that Sigmund Freud himself could not have been purely and simply a man (*vir*), that he could not have had (purely) masculine prejudices. That charge only reveals the metaphysical prejudices of those who press it.

Freud never appeals to this argument in his own defense, however, never exhibits his femininity as he indulges in exposing the masculinity of his female colleagues. The thesis of bisexuality, declared valid in principle for all humans, is in the last analysis used only as a strategic weapon in connection with women; we shall have the opportunity to verify this. And it is as though Freud were loudly proclaiming the universality of bisexuality in order better to disguise his silent disavowal of his own femininity, his paranoia.

2. Speculation, Observation

It is indeed against the potential suspicion of paranoia that Freud seeks in particular to defend himself whenever he distinguishes, like a typical positivist, between (philosophical) speculation and (scientific) observation, or whenever he denies having any sort of gift for philosophy. It is always his opponents—Jung, for example—who are speculative. Thus, what is fundamentally at stake in "On Narcissism: An Introduction"[8] is the demonstration that narcissism, particularly with regard to paranoia, lends itself to sterile and insane speculations. This text is a polemical denunciation of Jung's philosophical monism[9]—Jung, who thinks he can dispense with the libido's sexual specificity, with the distinction between the energy of the ego's drives and its libido, between the ego's libido and that of the object, between sexual libido and nonsexual energy. This speculative economizing can be achieved only at the expense of observation and to the benefit of "barren theoretical controversy" ("On Narcissism," 77). By way of contrast, Freud's distinctions, his persistent dualism,[10] result from his elaborations based on close observation of neurotic and psychotic processes and from his pursuit of a hypothesis "to its logical conclusion, until it either breaks down or is confirmed" (Ibid., 78). To barren speculation, Freud opposes the productive model of physics:

> That is just the difference between a speculative theory and a science erected on empirical interpretation. The latter will not envy speculation its privilege of having a smooth, logically unassailable foundation, but will gladly content itself with nebulous, scarcely imaginable basic concepts, which it hopes to apprehend more clearly in the course of its development, or which it is even prepared to replace by others. For these ideas are not the foundation of science upon which everything rests: that foundation is the observation alone. They are not the bottom but the top of the whole structure, and they can be replaced and discarded without damaging it. The same thing is happening in our day in the science of physics, the basic notions of which as regards matter,

centres of force, attraction, etc., are scarcely less debatable than the corresponding ideas in psycho-analysis. ("On Narcissism," 77)

"I am not Jung, I am not paranoid," Freud reiterates endlessly.

What Freud seems to need to prove in the "Femininity" lecture is that he, Freud—he insists on this at the end of his talk (a classic denegation!)—is not the victim of an idée fixe,[11] even though he never ceases to stress the importance of the role the lack of a penis plays in the formation of femininity. It is no accident that the lecture begins, here again, by contrasting observation with speculation: you cannot evaluate the sexual position of my discourse, for it is not the pathological subject Sigmund Freud that is speaking or speculating; it is the transcendental subject of science, whose affirmations are based entirely on observed facts: "To-day's lecture . . . brings forward nothing but observed facts, almost without any speculative additions" ("Femininity," 113). With respect to those facts, "I" play no role, do not take sides.

If we recall that in *Beyond the Pleasure Principle*[12] Freud does not hesitate to present the hypothesis of the death wish as purely speculative, as possibly having only mythic roots,[13] the strenuous hostility to speculation he displays here may seem suspect: the whole campaign he is waging against the speculative no doubt in some way works to his advantage; perhaps it is to enhance one's own stature that one claims not to be playing a role or taking sides. In any event, the appeal to observation has the immediate object of cleansing Freud of any taint of partiality by making women psychoanalysts his accomplices. He repeats this endlessly: the observations of these "excellent female colleagues" furnished his most important material, first enlightened him on female sexuality. He has only added some clarifications, has better isolated certain points that they have already brought to light. His work is only one contribution among others, and he has limited himself to bringing out the most important points of agreement or disagreement.[14] Whereas elsewhere Freud insists on the priority of his own discoveries even while recognizing that they have often been foreshadowed by some brilliant poets,[15] here for strategic reasons he has to deny the paternity of his ideas and openly to display his debt to the female analysts.

> Since [my] subject is woman, I will venture on this occasion to mention by name a few of the women who have made valuable contributions to this investigation. Dr. Ruth Mack Brunswick [1928] was the first to describe a case

of neurosis which went back to a fixation in the pre-Oedipus stage and had never reached the Oedipus situation at all.... Dr. Jeanne Lampl-de Groot [1927] has established the incredible phallic activity of girls toward their mother by some *assured observations*, and Dr. Helene Deutsch [1932] has shown that the erotic actions of homosexual women reproduce the relations between mother and baby. ("Femininity," 130–31, emphasis added)

The appeal to observation has a fundamental strategic value here, and Freud does not seem to consider that it may be incompatible with the haste he is demonstrating elsewhere by publishing, against all scientific caution, results that by his own admission have not been completely verified, on the grounds that little time remains to him, though earlier he managed to hold back the Dora case for four or five years before divulging the secret of his patient out of pure duty to science;[16] on the grounds, too, that the women psychoanalysts will in any case be able to exploit and complete his work: "I feel justified in publishing something which stands in urgent need of confirmation before its value or lack of value can be decided," he writes at the beginning of "Some Psychical Consequences of the Anatomical Distinction Between the Sexes" (249).

3. Freud's Delays

In haste to write about women in order to outdistance women once again, in haste to write for fear that death may outdistance him: it is as though up to the very last moment Freud had been shrinking from the impossible task of writing about women; the texts on female sexuality, stressing the new importance of the preoedipal relation of daughter to mother and casting doubt on the status of the Oedipus complex as the core of neuroses, are all late texts, "a product of the very last few years" ("Femininity," 130). A retreat in the face of the task at hand, which is perhaps a retreat in the face of female sexuality itself, because of the horror/pleasure it provokes, because of the death threat that it is thought to bear. For neither death nor woman's sex can be faced directly. To write about female sexuality is to disclose a dangerous secret, is in one way or another to display openly, to dis-cover, woman's fearsome sex. A sex that is all the more fearsome and threatening for man in that he feels vulnerable—and guilty.[17]

Here we cannot help thinking of Spinoza, whose death left his *Tractatus Theologico-Politicus* unfinished just as he was about to confront the question of women in the political sphere and just when he had deprived women, along with servants, of all political rights, even under the ideal democratic regime.

Wanting to have the last word on women—doesn't that always mean running the risk that goes with last words? Doesn't the desire to get to the heart of the matter, to bring the riddle to an end, entail the risk of reaching the end? This accounts for Freud's extreme restraint on the subject of women over a long period of time, the period during which he set up a simple parallelism and a simple symmetry, for example, between the girl's Oedipus complex and the boy's; only later, with the preoedipal phase, came the discovery of the woman as totally other, and then there was the ultimate haste to publish, the anxiety in the face of death.

It was not the first time in Freud's career that anxiety over death underlay his decision to publish a text that he had held back a long time (five years). He had done the same thing with *The Interpretation of Dreams*,[18] at a time when his age alone could not justify an objective fear of death.

This becomes clear in the famous dream in which Brücke proposes that Freud dissect his own pelvis (*Dreams*, 452–55 and 477–78). The crucial feature of this dream—showing that, its manifest content notwithstanding, it is indeed a dream of wish fulfillment—is that the dreamer does not experience the *feeling of horror* (*Grauen*) that ought objectively to be connected with the dissection, with such a "strange task." Freud interprets the dream as follows:

> The dissection meant the self-analysis which I was carrying out, as it were, in the publication of this present book about dreams—a process which had been so distressing to me in reality that I had postponed the printing of the finished manuscript for more than a year. A wish then arose that I might get over this feeling of distaste; hence it was that I had no gruesome feeling ["*Grauen*"] in the dream. But I should also have been very glad to miss growing grey—"*Grauen*" in the other sense of the word. I was already growing quite grey, and the grey of my hair was another reminder that I must not delay any longer. (477–78)

This fragment of interpretation with the crucial wordplay on *Grauen* is not part of the central analysis of the dream, but is tacked on through association of ideas to the analysis of the dream of the journeyman tailor who became a famous poet (*Dreams*, 473–75). This latter dream seems to contradict the general law of dreams as wish fulfillment: it appears, indeed, to be a dream of punishment, but analysis reveals that the unconscious desire underlying the dream is the desire to remain young—a painful desire in the aging man, and one that is never appeased.[19] With the dream of the journeyman tailor Freud associates, in addition to the Brücke dream, another of his own in which he finds himself back in the "gloomiest and most unsuccessful year" of his medical career, when he did not yet have a job and did not know how he would manage to earn his living. Even so, this return to an unhappy time of life is indeed wish fulfillment, since it is a return to the period of his youth: "I was once more young, and, more than everything, *she* was once more young—the woman who had shared all these difficult years with me. . . . I had a choice open to me between several women whom I might marry!" (476). Nostalgia for youth, as this last association proves, is always nostalgia for sexual potency, just as ideas of death and old age are always connected with the idea of impotence: this is confirmed by the interpretation of the dream of "an elderly gentleman [who] was awakened one night by his wife, who had become alarmed because he was laughing so loudly and unrestrainedly in his sleep. . . . The dream-work succeeded in transforming the gloomy idea of impotence and death into a comic scene, and his sobs into laughter" (*Dreams*, 472–73).

In other words, the death anxiety that assails Freud and leads him to publish *The Interpretation of Dreams* is not "pure" death anxiety; it is inseparable from anxiety related to the limitation of sexual potency. And to publish *The Interpretation of Dreams* is not only to outdistance the death that is to come; it is in every sense to recapture youth, potency, even omnipotence: this publication, in fact, should confer immortality on its author, the immortality of the heroes and great men who could set out for an "unknown land which scarce an alien foot has pressed"[20] from time immemorial, could reveal "strange things," defy all taboos, including that of incest. By its unheard-of revelations, the publication of *The Interpretation of Dreams* is to transform Freud into a superman, make him a rival of that Oedipus who "resolved the dark enigma, noblest champion and most wise."[21] A superman, indeed a demigod: the dream in which Freud identifies with Hercules cleaning out the Augean stables (with a "long stream of urine" he would cleanse the science of neuroses of all its errors and prejudices) ends with the megalomanic affirmation: "in short . . . I was a very great man" (470).

Through the publication of this work, Freud was to achieve not only his infantile desire of immortality but also what his father, the Jew Jakob, had been unable to accomplish, so that his son had to accomplish it in his stead. To the son's great disappointment, Freud's father—as we know from the famous anecdote of the cap knocked to the ground by a Christian—was not a hero, although later, in his dreams, the son gives shape to his nostalgia for a heroic father modeled on Hannibal's: " 'To stand before one's children's eyes, after one's death, great and unsullied'— who would not desire this?" (*Dreams*, 249). After telling the story of the cap, Freud writes:

> This struck me as *unheroic* conduct on the part of the big, strong man who was holding the little boy by the hand. I contrasted this situation with another which fitted my feelings better: the scene in which Hannibal's father, Hamilcar Barca, made his boy swear before the household altar to take vengeance on the Romans. Ever since that time, Hannibal had had a place in my phantasies. . . . To my youthful mind Hannibal and Rome symbolized the conflict between the tenacity of Jewry and the organization of the Catholic church. (*Dreams*, 197, 196, emphasis added)

Against this background we can understand the complex factors that may have led Freud to put off publishing *The Interpretation of Dreams*, even though the work was destined to confer immortality on its author (in one passage, Freud alludes to a request made by Louise N. the previous evening to borrow one of his books, whereupon he proposed instead a book by Rider Haggard, for his "own immortal works" had not yet been written) and even though another dream confirms his desire to be done with *The Interpretation of Dreams* in order to become independent at last and to fulfill all his desires. (This is the botanical dream in which the initial situation is the same as in the Brücke dream: in the one case, Freud sees before him his own pelvis; in the other case, he sees before him the monograph he has written on the genus *Cyclamen*: "I saw the monograph which I had written *lying before me.* . . . I had had a letter from my friend [Fliess] in Berlin the day before in which he had shown his power of visualization: 'I am very much occupied with your dream-book. *I see it lying finished before me and I see myself turning over its pages.*' How much I envied him his gift as a seer! If only *I* could have seen it lying finished before me!" [172]. "The dream . . . [was] a passionately agitated plea on behalf of my liberty to act as I chose to act and to govern my life as seemed right to me and me alone" [467].) We can now understand why Freud, despite his strong desire for publication, nevertheless postponed it, why the idea of publication was so painful to him, stirred up in him a feeling of horror (*Grauen*), gave him gray hair (*grauen*); we can understand why the dream about Brücke, in which he seems finally to satisfy his desire, is at the same time a dream of anguish in which, far from attaining the immortality he desires, he sees himself in a wooden house identified by association with a grave (although the grave is Etruscan, this being a dream ruse to make him accept the unacceptable, to transform "the gloomiest of expectations into one that was highly desirable" [*Dreams*, 455], just as the heroine, the woman guide, of *She*, the book lent the evening before to Louise N., instead of retrieving immortality for herself and others, meets death in a mysterious subterranean fire). The only consolation the dream affords is that perhaps the children will obtain what was denied the father, those children who are their parents' sole access to immortality, those children who are one with their parents, in a way, as that "strange book" also indicates, that novel in which a character's identity is maintained through successive generations over a period of two thousand years.

By conferring immortality on myself through publication, I make a gift of it also to my father, with whom I identify, as my own children will one day confer it on me by living after me: such may be the meaning of this dream. But it may also be interpreted differently: I deny myself immortality and bequeath it only to my children out of guilt toward my father, who was unable to attain it himself for lack of heroism.

Guilt at having succeeded where the father failed thus explains Freud's delay in publishing (he waited five years)[22]—as Hannibal delayed before entering Rome, as Moses waited to enter the Promised Land. Generally speaking, guilt explains why Freud always postponed fulfillment of his desires or his ambitions, why he put off his marriage for five years, why he waited five years to take his medical examinations. The delays can thus be attributed to inhibition, but also to the fact that Freud always had the strength to postpone the immediate satisfaction of his desires in order to satisfy them more fully later on. As if five years of life did not count for him, as if he had all the time in the world ahead of him, as if he knew that in spite of his delays he would nevertheless achieve his aims. Symptomatically, he sets five years as the length of treatment of the patients to whom he is closest: what are five years of life in comparison with all the benefits that analysis offers? Freud knows that in spite of having a poor Jew for a father (whom he replaces in the dream by the professor Meynert, thanks to whom Freud, had he been the professor's son, would have advanced more rapidly), indeed thanks to his own—Jewish—tenacity, he will succeed in the end. "And just as I succeeded in the end in *that*, though you would not believe it, so I shall achieve *this*, too" (*Dreams*, 438), he notes in interpreting the "absurd" dream in which his father declares he was married in *1851* after getting drunk and being locked up. This marriage resulted in the immediate birth of his son Sigmund—in *1856*.

This dream proves that father Jakob did not have the strength to postpone the satisfaction of his own desires, that he was unable to accomplish the psychic exploit that matters most to a man, that of rising above his own nature (cf. the conclusion of "The Moses of Michelangelo").[23] He got drunk (which in the symbolic language of dreams means that he made love), got his future wife pregnant, had to get married in a hurry, and had to falsify his son's birth date by two months in order to conceal his guilt (two months transformed in Freud's dream into five years, the better to cleanse the father's stain),[24] as Freud declares that the paternal figure in this dream, an exception to the rule, plays the role of straw man, that this figure merely represents Professor Meynert, who had said of himself: "You know, I was always one of the clearest cases of male hysteria" (*Dreams*, 438). Thus, Freud conceals the paternal hysteria and takes it upon himself to accomplish the feat that his father was unable to perform: the "heroic" postponement of the satisfaction of his desires, giving the lie to the proverb "like father, like son," while contriving to do just the opposite in his dreams so as to create a father in his own image.

So Freud always postpones the satisfaction of his desires, killing two birds with one stone: he shows his superiority to his father, and he punishes himself for succeeding where his father failed.

That is why, in the Brücke dream, in order to publish his book, to make himself independent and immortal, he needs paternal authorization, even an order emanating from that substitute father, old Brücke. For why did he choose old Brücke if not because "even in the first years of my scientific work it happened that I allowed a discovery of mine to lie fallow until an energetic remonstrance on his part drove me into publishing it" (*Dreams*, 454), and because the evening before, when he went to see Louise N., he felt that she was pressing him to publish, transmitting someone else's orders: " 'Well, when are we to expect these so-called ultimate explanations of yours which you've promised even *we* shall find readable?' she asked, with a touch of sarcasm. At that point I saw that someone else was admonishing me through her mouth" (453).

All this, however, cannot in itself explain the delay in publishing *The Interpretation of Dreams*, the shame that Freud says he felt in making public a work that would betray such a large part of his most private character:

> Das Beste was du wissen kannst,
> Darfst du den Buben doch nicht sagen.[25]

A work that would reveal "such strange things," things that horrify him and that threaten to horrify others: how is it that taking the father's place "heroically" could be so shameful and terrible? Unless this "heroism," like that of Oedipus, consists not only of "killing" the father (Oedipus's father, according to Plato, also begat his son while he was drunk) but also of sleeping with the mother. Unless the son's heroism can be achieved only by virtue of the mother's complicity and preferential love.

In the Brücke dream, it is a maternal figure, Louise N., who presses him to publish, to become a hero (even though the interpretation casts her in the role of simple intermediary). Similarly, the dream of the three Fates casts the mother in the role of an educator who teaches her son to defer his desires by making him wait before appeasing his hunger: it is she who teaches him "heroism." In a note to *The Interpretation of Dreams* concerning the oedipal dreams of some classical heroes (Julius Caesar's dream of relations with his mother, Herodotus's dream of Hippias), dreams already interpreted in the classical period as favorable signs, signs of possession of (Mother) Earth, or of a reconquest of lost authority (like the Tarquinian oracle affirming that the first man to kiss his mother would be master of Rome), Freud remarks that "people who know that they are preferred or favoured by their mother give evidence in their lives of a peculiar self-reliance and an unshakeable optimism which often seem like heroic attributes and bring actual success to their possessors" (*Dreams*, 398, n. 1). Finally, in Supplement B of "Group Psychology and the Analysis of the Ego,"[26] at the point where Freud is showing how the first epic poet invented the myth of the hero—"A hero was a man who by himself had slain the father"—he adds: "The transition to the hero was probably afforded by the youngest son, the *mother's favourite*, whom she had protected from paternal jealousy, and who, in the era of the primal horde, had been the father's successor" (136, emphasis added).[27]

Now Freud, although the eldest son, indeed thought he was his mother's favorite. With respect to the dream in which he aspires to the title of *professor extraordinarius*, he wonders:

> What, then, could have been the origin of the ambitiousness which produced the dream in me? At that point I recalled an anecdote I had often heard repeated in my childhood. At the time of my birth an old peasant-woman had prophesied to my proud mother that with her first-born child she had brought a great man into the world. Prophecies of this kind must be very common: there are so many mothers filled with happy expectations and so many old peasant-women and others of the kind who make up for the loss of their power to control things in the present world by concentrating it on the future. (*Dreams*, 192)

If Freud hesitates to publish *The Interpretation of Dreams* and experiences death anxiety on his own account and his mother's, it is because this publication entails the formidable risk of exposing to everyone his double crime and revealing his mother's complicity. The dream of the dead mother that Freud had when he was seven or eight years old (the age at which the incident between his father and the Christian over the cap is supposed to have occurred) confirms that the death anxiety on his mother's behalf refers to the son's incestuous desires: in this dream he sees his

> *beloved mother, with a peculiarly peaceful, sleeping expression on her features, being carried into the room by two (or three) people with birds' beaks and laid upon the bed.* . . . I was not anxious because I had dreamt that my mother was dying; but I interpreted the dream in that sense in my preconscious revision of it because I was already under the influence of the anxiety. The anxiety can be traced back, when repression is taken into account, to an obscure and evidently sexual craving that had found appropriate expression in the visual content of the dream. (*Dreams*, 583, 584)

To publish one's dreams is to make known to everyone one's own (phantasmatic) incestuous relations. Freud is himself another Oedipus, not only because he, too, has been able to solve famous riddles, to head for unknown regions where no one has ever before set foot, but also—for the one is always a corollary of the other—because he has (although only in dreams, and that is what distinguishes him from Oedipus) "killed" his father and slept with his mother. He who seeks to know the deep mysteries of nature must not be afraid to violate natural laws, to appear to everyone as a monster, *horribile visu*: such is the lesson of the Oedipus myth, as Nietzsche had already exposed it in *The Birth of Tragedy*. Supreme wisdom requires supreme monstrosity. To be a hero is always also to be a monster who runs the risk of arousing a feeling of horror (*Grauen*) and of being cast out of society like a *pharmacos* instead of acquiring the immortality one has been seeking.

Moreover, if we recall that Freud uses the same term, *Grauen*, to designate the feeling experienced by most men when confronted by a woman's (the Mother's) genitals (represented symbolically by the Medusa's head)[28]—a feeling of horror that may well make one's hair turn gray (*grauen*) overnight—we may wonder whether "these strange, unknown things" that Freud reveals in *The Interpretation of Dreams* are not more specifically concerned with woman's sex, the Mother's, upon which the dreamer has dared to cast his glance, at the risk of being blinded, of being castrated, and of seeing his mother, like Jocasta, hang herself.

Throughout his work, Freud notes the horror and terror that women's genitals inspire and the disastrous influence that woman is thought to have on man. By virtue of her sex, woman cannot fail to bring about man's ruin. The *Autodidasker* dream offers a simple alternative: woman brings to man either organic ailments (syphilis, general paralysis) or functional difficulties (neuroses). Freud seems to have settled on the second choice, and like another Hercules he devotes his life to attempting to rid humanity of its "waste products"—that is, the neuroses, for which woman is considered primarily responsible. That these strange things revealed by Freud in *The Interpretation of Dreams* indeed concern woman's (the mother's?) sex is indicated by several features of the Brücke dream: the parallel established with the dream of the botanical monograph concerning the "genus *Cyclamen*," his wife's favorite flower, and the occasion that dictated the dream's formation: the book lent the previous evening to Louise N. was titled *She*. Freud calls it " 'a *strange* book, but full of hidden meaning . . . the eternal feminine' " (*Dreams*, 453); moreover, in this novel, a woman plays a major role. To publish *The Interpretation of Dreams* is to expose—along with his own criminal incestuous relations—woman's sex, the mother's sex; for such a book not to arouse horror, the reader would have to be familiar with the representation of incest and to have overcome castration anxiety. Freud's willingness to publish this book implies that he himself has overcome such anxiety and by the same token is no longer afraid to expose his own femininity as well, that most secret part of his most private being. The Brücke dream identifies Freud with the heroine of *She*, that woman guide who heads toward the unknown with the intention of winning immortality and who meets death in a subterranean fire. Another detail of the dream flaunts castration even while resisting it: Freud sees part of his own body (his pelvis) before him (detached from him, as it were), but at the same time he does not have the sensation that that part is missing from his body. To expose a "supplementary" pelvis is tantamount to a duplication of the genital organs; it has apotropaic value. Publishing *The Interpretation of Dreams* is a way for Freud simultaneously to display his castration and to defend himself against it. *The Interpretation of Dreams* is an apotropaic defense that is to protect Freud against castration and death, against his detractors, against anti-Semitism. We know, indeed, that circumcision for Freud is equivalent to castration and that he attributes the same unconscious origin to misogyny and anti-Semitism: the horror provoked by female genital organs, the fear of castration.[29] And we may perhaps relate the *Grauen* of the Brücke dream to the *Grauen* that we find in the famous dream about Uncle Josef (who bears the name of that biblical figure with whom Freud often identifies). Uncle Josef, that "simpleton," as Freud's father Jakob used to call him, that criminal, that Jew who had made Freud's father's hair turn gray (*grauen*) in just a few days because of grief over his criminal conduct (*Dreams*, 138). The Uncle Josef for whom Freud, at the level of dreams, feels a great affection, revealing in fact a deep hatred, a strange repulsion—in another dream Freud identifies that same Uncle Josef with colleagues who have been denied the post of professor by the ministry, yet he does not hesitate to identify himself with the minister and thus to mistreat those learned and eminent colleagues simply because they are Jews. His Uncle Josef's greatest crime, in the last analysis, was the fact that he was Jewish. This, even more than his misdeeds, is what made him an object of horror and revulsion to his own society—just like women, and for the same reasons.

By playing in his dream the role of persecutor, the role of the minister, Freud shows that he will not submit to the fate of his uncle or his Jewish colleagues, that he will become a professor precisely because of his "Jewish tenacity" and the love of his Jewish mother.

> In mishandling my two learned and eminent colleagues because they were Jews, and in treating the one as a simpleton and the other as a criminal, I was

behaving as though I were the Minister, I had put myself in the Minister's place. Turning the tables on his Excellency with a vengeance! He had refused to appoint me *professor extraordinarius* and I had retaliated in the dream by stepping into his shoes. (*Dreams*, 193)

The intimate, shameful secrets that Freud fears to expose to the public, because of the horror they are very likely to arouse, are thus inseparably linked with his Jewishness and with femininity, with castration anxiety. In this sense, *The Interpretation of Dreams* is another Medusa's head.

This long detour by way of Freud's dreams will prove not to have been useless, for these dreams are the royal road that may lead us to a better understanding of the status of female sexuality in Freud's theoretical texts. The detour has in any case allowed us to explain both Freud's delay in publishing on the subject of female sexuality and his ultimate haste, for fear of being overtaken by death.

4. The Other

To the fear of death is added a supplementary anxiety: the discovery of the radical otherness of woman, which threatens to bring about a thoroughgoing upheaval in psychoanalysis. Freud compares this revolutionary discovery of the *entirely other* to finding the Mycenaean civilization behind that of the Greeks: "Our insight into this early, pre-Oedipus, phase in girls comes to us as a surprise, like the discovery, in another field, of the Minoan–Mycenaean civilization behind the civilization of Greece" ("Female Sexuality," 226).

This comparison with the history of civilizations is designed to stress the fact that a great gap separates the two phases of the little girl's libidinal development, since the historians of Freud's day posited a radical break between the fourteenth to twelfth centuries B.C., when Mycenaean culture, so close to the Minoan, was flourishing, and the beginnings of archaic Greek culture in the eighth century B.C. Between the two there was thought to have been a dark age, the Hellenic Middle Ages, in which little-known upheavals separated the pre-Hellenic world from the Greek world proper. The Mycenaeans were thus seen as pre-Hellenes, just as the earliest period of the girl's development was seen as preoedipal; and just as the two peoples, pre-Hellenes and Hellenes, had nothing in common, so a real gulf separates the preoedipal and oedipal periods and thus the sexual development of little girls and little boys. "We have, after all, long given up any expectation of a neat parallelism between male and female sexual development" (Ibid.). Mycenean civilization was considered to be a simple preface, external to Greek history; in the same way, the preoedipal period was seen as merely a preamble to the Oedipus complex.

To be sure, this comparison would not hold up today, since the discovery of the Linear B script has shown that the Mycenaeans were Greeks, or at least spoke Greek, that the Mycenaean civilization is part of Hellenism, that it is the first chapter of its history and no longer a simple preface: ancient Greece is no longer looked upon as a beginning but as an extension, or a Renaissance. In short, today's historians stress the continuity between the two periods rather than the break.

Between the old interpretation and the new, we can see the same difference as that between Freud's reading and Melanie Klein's. While Freud thinks he is stressing the break between the two periods, by calling the first one preoedipal he is still taking the Oedipus complex as the telos of all development. It continues to dominate the preoedipal period: the Oedipus complex remains the final referent, just as the preface to a book is a preamble to that book and cannot be totally external to it. The Oedipus complex, like the book, remains the standard for what is declared to be without a common standard. Melanie Klein subordinates the Oedipus complex to preoedipal development, which, strictly speaking, should no longer bear that name since in this case the Oedipus complex is no longer the referent, the principle by which all development is understood (and this is as true of girls as it is of boys): Melanie Klein reverses direction in favor of the preoedipal period. But whether one takes the preoedipal period to be a preface to the Oedipus stage or as the first chapter of its history, whether one stresses discontinuity or continuity, the gesture of dominance remains the same: in both cases, one loses the specificity, the radical strangeness of the totally other; one overcomes the astonishing "surprise" that the discovery of feminine sexuality elicited if one reinstates it within the process of a history that must lead to the Oedipus complex in every case. If he has indeed discovered Mycenaean civilization, Freud refuses to be Theseus, refuses to plunge into the labyrinth, into the palace, with a "double-bladed axe," to rescue Ariadne, the fiancée. Freud's heroic model continues to be Oedipus, and for him woman is never the fiancée but still and always the mother.[30]

At the level of the text, the insistence on the surprise caused by the discovery of the preoedipal period corroborates the positivist character of Freud's undertaking, proving once again that it is not a matter of speculation: when observation requires it, Freud is capable of giving up earlier hypotheses, abandoning the strict parallelism between boys and girls. At several points in the lecture "Femininity," he insists that his observations, confirmed by those of women psychoanalysts, have run counter to all expectations (and thus to every prejudice) in forcing him to admit, for example, that the little girl has no reason to envy the boy as far as his activeness or aggressiveness is concerned; or, another surprise, that the girl may wish to have her mother's child, or even to get her mother pregnant. Indeed, don't the entire charm and attraction (*Reiz*) of analysis arise precisely from the surprises it produces with respect to the most widely held opinions and prejudices?

5. An Exciting Enigma

These popular opinions are the ones Freud claims to be denouncing in the lecture "Femininity" as he follows a procedure closely analogous to the one Descartes used to attack habitual prejudices. In this way, he hopes to arouse a new interest in woman, to surprise, charm, and excite (*Reiz*) his audience. From the very beginning, as if to apologize for taking up such a hackneyed topic, he stresses that the subject of woman has always been interesting to men (*Menschen*), more likely to rouse their interest than any other. Men and women alike find it exciting, especially when a debate is in progress between them, between male and female psychoanalysts! The question of woman cannot help arousing debate; perhaps men need this conflict about sex, this incessant war between the sexes, to continue to be "excited." For if "throughout history people have knocked their heads against the riddle of the nature of femininity" ("Femininity," 113), this enigma is quite a singular one (even though it is the prototype of every riddle): indeed, finding a solution seems impossible and even inappropriate—and not just for methodological or theoretical reasons. It is by virtue of her sexuality that woman is enigmatic, for sexuality is what constitutes that "great riddle" of life[31] that accounts for the entire difference between men and women. This does not mean that Freud reduces woman to her sexuality: at the end of the "Femininity" lecture, he reminds his listeners that women as individuals (if not as a species!) may equally well be considered human beings ("Die einzelne Frau auch sonst ein menschliches Wesen sein mag").[32] Woman as "female sexuality" is a purely theoretical construct, a mere object of study: "Do not forget that I have only been describing women in so far as their nature is determined by their sexual function" ("Femininity," 135). Even though he considers that function quite important, Freud nevertheless believes that what he has said on the subject of femininity is "incomplete and fragmentary," and he recommends other sources for further information: personal experience, poetry, biological science. To be sure, as we shall see, this modest declaration may be interpreted as a strategy, and perhaps Freud is once again doing something quite different from what he is saying.[33] Even so, it is still the case that what interests him in woman is what constitutes her difference, and that this difference lies in her sexuality—which thus acquires a privileged status as the object of study.

MAN'S PRIVILEGE

This object is particularly obscure and enigmatic, first of all because it has been little studied previously, for purely methodological reasons, or so it seems. The positivist rule requires one to start with what is most immediately accessible to knowledge. Because it is man (*vir*) who engages in scientific investigations, it is natural for him to start with himself. Freud is no exception: man has served as his point of departure and model. That is why at first he viewed woman only as symmetrical to man—why, for example, he established a strict parallelism between the boy's Oedipus complex and the girl's.[34] This "positivist" starting point, as always, led him to construct as telos and *arché* what was a simple epistemological beginning; it led him, following the example of Aristotle and Comte, to subordinate woman to man hierarchically, to think of woman, as far as her sex is concerned, as a lesser man. That is why it is not until his very late writings that he acknowledges in woman a difference exclusive of any parallelism or symmetry, and confronts the "Minoan–Mycenaean" riddle for its own sake. This does not, however, prevent him from continuing, even then, to invoke the masculine model. Thus, we find that immediately after comparing the surprising discovery of the girl's preoedipal period to the discovery of the Minoan–Mycenaean civilization, at the very point where a methodological revolution might be expected, Freud declares that in the study of female sexual development he is about to undertake, "it will help our exposition if, as we go along, we compare the state of things in women with that in men" ("Female Sexuality," 227). Even more paradoxically, in

"The Economic Problem of Masochism," after stating that feminine masochism is more accessible to observation and less enigmatic than the masculine variety, that it can be grasped in all its aspects, and that it is therefore going to be the point of departure for this discussion, he takes man as the unique example of the masochism he has called *feminine*: "We have sufficient acquaintance with this kind of masochism in men (to whom, owing to the material at my command, I shall restrict my remarks)."[35]

Man enjoys a privileged status, then;[36] he is taken as model or as point of comparison even when the irreducible specificity of female sexuality is acknowledged. For the latter does not in any event cease to be obscure, strange, incomprehensible, less completely known, more difficult to penetrate than the man's, which is much more "logical," easier to interpret.[37] In short, female sexuality is still covered by "a thick veil." Thus, with regard to the dissolution of the Oedipus complex: "How does the corresponding development take place in little girls? At this point our material—for some incomprehensible reason—becomes far more obscure and full of gaps" ("Dissolution," 177).

Similarly, when he makes a general law of the primacy of the phallus (the fact that in the infantile genital organization of both sexes only one genital organ—the male organ—is involved), Freud regrets that he can describe this state of affairs only in the male child: "Unfortunately . . . the corresponding processes in the little girl are not known to us."[38]

In short, "it must be admitted . . . that in general our insight into these developmental processes in girls is unsatisfactory, incomplete, and vague" ("Dissolution," 179).

WOMAN'S INACCESSIBILITY

Freud gives several disparate reasons for the fact that psychoanalysis has been slow to penetrate women. Not only is female sexuality more complex than that of the male (it has to solve two supplementary problems, changing both the woman's erogenous zone and her object cathexis), it also offers greater "resistance" to violation by science. It is less accessible to research, for several reasons: woman has a lesser sexual life; she is in an atrophied condition, as it were, owing to "civilization." Because of her education and cultural repression, woman speaks less freely about her sexuality than man does. Society makes modesty or "shame" woman's fundamental virtue, requires her to adopt a "reserved" way of speaking that is detrimental to science. Freud's whole effort consists precisely, through analysis, in attempting to pull women out of their reserve by giving them the right, even the obligation, to speak: about everything that comes into their heads, including what has always, from earliest childhood, been a forbidden topic. Girls' sexual curiosity, indeed, has always been subject to more repression than boys',[39] and such repression is the source of their intellectual inhibition, of their supposedly inborn and indelible intellectual inferiority.

Because woman has been reduced to silence, because her sexuality has necessarily been less "glaring" than man's, she has been "neglected" by research, or else misinterpreted. Freud says so over and over:

> The significance of the factor of sexual overvaluation can be best studied in men, for their erotic life alone has become accessible to research. That of women—partly owing to the stunting effect of civilized conditions and partly owing to their conventional secretiveness and insecurity—is still veiled in an impenetrable obscurity. ("Three Essays," 151)
>
> Homosexuality in women, which is certainly not less common than in men, although much less glaring, has not only been ignored by the law, but has also been neglected by psycho-analytic research. ("Psychogenesis," 147)
>
> [Women's] upbringing forbids their concerning themselves intellectually with sexual problems though they nevertheless feel extremely curious about them, and frightens them by condemning such curiosity as unwomanly and a sign of a sinful disposition. In this way they are scared away from *any* form of thinking, and knowledge loses its value for them. The prohibition of thought extends beyond the sexual field, partly through unavoidable association, partly automatically, like the prohibition of thought about religion among men, or the prohibition of thought about loyalty among faithful subjects. . . . I think that the undoubted intellectual inferiority of so many women can rather be traced back to the inhibition of thought necessitated by sexual suppression.[40]

As for this repressive education of women and its disastrous consequences, one wonders whether Freud knew Nietzsche's wonderful text "On Feminine Chastity"—a text considered misogynistic by some people,[41] just as Freud is considered "phallocratic"; in each case, things are perhaps not quite that simple.

> There is something quite astonishing and extraordinary in the education of women of the higher class; indeed, there is perhaps nothing more paradoxical. All the world is agreed to educate them with as much ignorance as possible *in erotics*, and to inspire their soul with a profound shame of such things,

and the extremest impatience and horror at the suggestion of them. It is really here only that all the "honour" of woman is at stake; what would one not forgive them in other respects! But here they are intended to remain ignorant to the very backbone:—they are intended to have neither eyes, ears, words, nor thoughts for this, their "wickedness"; indeed knowledge here is already evil. And then! To be hurled as with an awful thunderbolt into reality and knowledge with marriage . . . : to have to encounter love and shame in contradiction, yea, to have to feel rapture, abandonment, duty, sympathy, and fright at the unexpected proximity of God and animal, and whatever else besides! all at once!—There, in fact a psychic entanglement has been effected which is quite unequalled! . . . Afterwards the same profound silence as before: and often even a silence to herself, a shutting of her eyes to herself. . . . In short, one cannot be gentle enough towards women![42]

THE SUSPENDED TONGUE

Confronting this "profound silence" of women, which he compares to "a locked door" or "a wall which shuts out every prospect,"[43] Freud tries to bring it to an end, if not through "gentleness" toward women, at least by means of a treatment that cannot proceed without a simulacrum of gentleness, in transference, "the strongest lever" (*Studies*, 282) for lifting the bolt, knocking down the wall, stifling resistance, bringing into the open the secret that is buried in the depths.

Because woman, in fact, lacks the right to speak, she may merely have "secrets," "love secrets," which make her ill: hysteria is nothing else. "From the beginning it seemed to me probable that Fräulein Elisabeth was conscious of the basis of her illness, that what she had in her consciousness was only a secret and not a foreign body. Looking at her, one could not help thinking of the poet's words: 'Das Mäskchen da weissagt verborgnen Sinn' "[44] (*Studies*, 138–39). "The principal point is that I should guess the secret and tell it to the patient straight out" (Ibid., 281). Dora is ill because she loves a man "secretly," because she reveals her "secrets" only to her cousin and to Frau K., confides only in a doctor—the one person who will not be able to "guess her secret"—as she finds herself anxious in front of anyone else for fear that he may "guess," "tear" from her the shameful secret, the cause of her illness: masturbation.

Because woman does not have the right to speak, she stops being capable or desirous of speaking; she "keeps" everything to herself and creates an excess of mystery and obscurity as though to avenge herself, as though striving for mastery. Woman lacks sincerity:[45] she dissimulates, transforms each word into an enigma, an indecipherable riddle. That is why the "patient's" narrative is always full of gaps, foreshortened, defective, disconnected, incomplete, lacking in "links"; it is disordered, comparable "to an unnavigable river whose stream is at one moment choked by masses of rock and at another divided and lost among shallows and sandbanks" ("Fragment," 16). It is as though the pathogenic materials formed a spatially extended mass that had to cross a narrow cleft, like a camel passing through the eye of a needle, so that it arrived fragmented and stretched, as it were, in consciousness (cf. *Studies*, 291).

> The patients' inability to give an ordered history of their life in so far as it coincides with the history of their illness . . . has the following grounds. In the first place, patients consciously and intentionally keep back part of what they ought to tell—things that are perfectly well known to them—because they have not got over their feelings of timidity and shame . . . ; this is the share taken by *conscious* disingenuousness. In the second place, part of the anamnestic knowledge . . . disappears while they are actually telling their story, but without their making any deliberate reservations: the share taken by *unconscious* disingenuousness. In the third place, there are invariably true amnesias—gaps in the memory into which not only old recollections but even quite recent ones have fallen—and paramnesias, formed secondarily so as to fill in those gaps. . . . That this state of affair should exist in regard to the memories relating to the history of the illness is *a necessary correlate of the symptoms*. . . . In the further course of the treatment the patient supplies the facts which, though he had known them all along, had been kept back by him or had not occurred to his mind. ("Fragment," 16–18)

The psychotherapist has only to play a waiting game in order to try to decipher a riddle that might well appear insoluble if, despite her silence, the patient did not finally betray her own secret:

> When I set myself the task of bringing to light what human beings keep hidden within them, not by the compelling power of hypnosis, but by observing what they say and what they show, I thought the task was a harder one than it really is. He that has eyes to see and ears to hear may convince himself that no mortal can keep a secret. If his lips are silent, he chatters with his finger-tips; betrayal oozes out of him at every pore. And thus the task of making conscious the most hidden recesses of the mind is one which it is quite possible to accomplish. (Ibid., 77–78)

Because the patient's "insincerity" not only is unconscious but also involves willfully holding back things she is perfectly well aware of, the analytic treatment cannot be seen as a simple restitution of women's right to speech; it is also an attempt to "tear" from them their secret, to make them "admit" or "confess"—in short, an attempt not to give them speech but to extort speech from them. Woman is not only a patient, a hysteric; because she dissimulates, she is always also a criminal, and the psychoanalyst is a policeman on the alert for the slightest clues that may betray her, or at best he is a father confessor "who gives absolution, as it were, by a continuance of his sympathy and respect after the confession has been made" (*Studies*, 282). And if he no longer uses the constraint of hypnosis, then it is by means of another constraint, an affective one this time (that of transference), that he can manage to extort admissions, stifle resistances, replace defensive motives with other more powerful ones, and, as the situation warrants, play the role of instructor in cases where ignorance has led to fear, play the role of professor, "the representative of a freer or superior view of the world" (Ibid.). He can instruct the patient by substituting frankness for her "insincerity," by calling things by their names— "J'appelle un chat un chat"[46]—though he pays the price of looking like a criminal himself to his colleagues, looking like a lubricious pervert for daring to engage in such conversation with young girls. But then, "pour faire une omelette il faut casser des oeufs."[47]

On the other hand, he guarantees the patient that he will keep the secret extorted strictly to himself, and that if for the benefit of science he should be led to publish her case, he will change her name, so as to avoid putting any lay reader on the scent; he will not turn her over to the police, nor will he expose her to the unhealthy curiosity of those doctors who read his presentations like romans à clef, even if it is true that his case histories "read like short stories and . . . lack the serious stamp of science" (*Studies*, 160).

Thus, Freud makes himself an accomplice of the hysteric, the criminal, by dissimulating in his turn, by keeping the (professional) secret, but on condition that the woman first agree to be his accomplice. When she consents to reveal her secret, to "abandon [her] rejection" (*Studies*, 281), it is the same as consenting to collaborate with the doctor and recognize his word as the voice of truth:

> She suddenly confessed of her own accord that she had not told the truth: what had occurred to her had not been "*colour*" but "*incarnation*"—THE WORD I

HAD EXPECTED.... This lack of straightforwardness showed that it was at this point that resistance was greatest. (*Dreams*, 375, emphasis added)

> A psychical resistance, especially one that has been in force for a long time, can only be resolved slowly and by degrees, and we must wait patiently.... We may reckon on the intellectual interest which the patient begins to feel after working for a short time. By explaining things to him, by giving him information about the marvellous world of psychical processes ... we make him himself into a collaborator. (*Studies*, 282)

> After we have worked in this way for some time, the patient begins as a rule to co-operate with us. A great number of reminiscences now occur to him, without our having to question him or set him tasks. (Ibid., 292)

Consenting to collaborate with the doctor is finally what distinguishes the hysteric from a true criminal.[48] So beware of the patient, the woman, who refuses to collaborate, refuses to let "truth" be imposed! Beware of the woman who, through her "suspension" of speech, spoils the psychotherapist's policeman-like pleasure, analogous to that of a reader of a serialized novel who is exasperated when "immediately after the heroine's decisive speech or after the shot has rung out, he comes upon the words: 'To be continued' " (*Studies*, 297).

The indomitable women who refuse to open their mouths, those "[cavities] filled with pus,"[49] because they do not accept the pernicious "solution" of their psychoanalyst, if they are not turned over to the police like criminals, are at least to be abandoned, quickly replaced by the analyst, who bestows his gentleness only on "nice" women, on those who do know how to open their mouths, those he finds "wiser" because they are better prepared to follow his advice, to accept his solutions. In the famous Irma dream, Freud substitutes "her friend" for Irma: "For Irma seemed to me foolish because she had not accepted my solution. Her friend would have been wiser, that is to say she would have yielded sooner. She would then have *opened her mouth properly*, and have told me more than Irma" (*Dreams*, 111).

> I at once took her on one side, as though ... to reproach her for not having accepted my "solution" yet. I said to her: "If you still get pains, it's really only your fault." ... It was my view at that time (though I have since recognized it as a wrong one) that my task was fulfilled when I had informed a patient of the hidden meaning of his symptoms: I considered that I was not responsible for whether he accepted the solution or not—though this was what success depended upon. (Ibid., 107–8)

It is always the ladies' fault. I, Freud, am irreproachable. The dream is a thoroughgoing plea in favor of Freud's innocence: it piles up reasons for excusing him, in a way reminiscent of the defense of the man accused by his neighbor of returning a borrowed kettle in a damaged condition (*Dreams*, 119–20).

> "I am not responsible [according to the dream's latent thoughts] for the persistence of Irma's pains; the responsibility lies *either* in her recalcitrance to accepting my solution, *or* in the unfavourable sexual conditions under which she lives and which I cannot alter, *or* in the fact that her pains are not hysterical at all but of an organic nature." The dream, on the other hand, fulfilled *all* of these possibilities (which were almost mutually exclusive), and did not hesitate to add a fourth solution, based on the dream-wish. (Ibid., 316–17)

If Freud has such an urgent need to excuse himself, it is because he knows perfectly well that he himself is the criminal—not only because he has not yet cured Irma, but, as another part of the dream indicates, because he himself (a transgression attributed in both the dream and the interpretation to his friend Otto) has infected her with his symbolic-spermatic "solution"—trimethylamin—injected with a dirty syringe. The term *trimethylamin* brings to mind the learned solutions he has thrown in his patients' faces: if Irma and all indomitable women refuse to open their mouths and their genitals, it is because Freud has already transformed each of these organs into a "cavity filled with pus,"[50] has closed the women's mouths himself, has made them frigid, by injecting them with a learned, malignant, male solution. What could they have left to say, to disclose, except that they have been infected by the person who is claiming that they are ill, that they have been contaminated by the person who, under the pretext of curing them, is compelling them to collaborate, because he needs their complicity in order to believe in the value of his "solution" himself, because he knows perfectly well that they are the only ones who know their own secret and that a solution injected from the outside could only be inappropriate, "unclean,"[51] pernicious?

Thus, although psychoanalysis may inveigh against the sexual repression to which women are subject, although it may invite them to shed their inhibitions and restore their right to speech, the remedy it offers is at the same time a poison, because it can cure women only by contaminating them, by forcing them to "collaborate," to espouse the viewpoint of the other, of men, who are supposed to possess truth. The psychoanalytic solution restores speech to woman only the better to rob her of it, the better to subordinate it to that of the master.

That is why there is no crime worse than silence, for it covers women's sex with its "thick veil," renders it inaccessible, indomitable, implacable: terrifying [*ef-frayante*], in Blanchot's sense.[52] The enigmatic woman neither speaks nor "betrays herself" through any of her pores. It matters little to her if psychoanalysis withholds its gentleness. She has no need of it; she is sufficient unto herself.

SHAME

And it is this self-sufficiency that is unbearable: because he "envies" her unassailable libidinal position, man projects his own insufficiency, his own "envy," onto woman. If woman is silent, if she keeps a "thick veil" drawn over herself and her sex, she must have her reasons, and good reasons, for wishing to remain enigmatic: she has to hide that "cavity filled with pus," she has to hide the fact that she has "nothing" to hide. By seeking to make herself enigmatic, woman is only continuing the work begun by nature, which covered over her sex with pubic hair. Woman, in inventing weaving, was only "imitating" nature. Thus, near the end of his lecture on femininity, Freud does not hesitate to attribute the invention of weaving to penis envy (at the risk of being taken for a madman obsessed by an idée fixe):

> Shame [*Scham*], which is considered to be a feminine characteristic *par excellence* but is far more a matter of convention than might be supposed, has as its purpose, we believe, concealment of genital deficiency. We are not forgetting that at a later time shame takes on other functions. It seems that women have made few contributions to the discoveries and inventions in the history of civilization; there is, however, one technique which they may have invented—that of plaiting and weaving. If that is so, we should be tempted to guess the unconscious motive for the achievement. Nature herself would seem to have given the model which this achievement imitates by causing the growth at maturity of the pubic hair that conceals the genitals. The step that remained to be taken lay in making the threads adhere to one another, while on the body they stick into the skin and are only matted together. ("Femininity," 132)

In a gesture that is at the very least ambiguous, Freud asserts that modesty, or "shame," is both a conventional virtue (more or less linked to cultural repression) and a natural one, since, in her invention of weaving, woman was only "imitating" nature: shame is seen as the natural/conventional artifice used by women to mask the natural—too natural—defectiveness of their genital organs. By this artifice they can excite and charm men, who would otherwise recoil in horror before that gaping wound that threatens to contaminate them, and who would then be condemned to homosexuality. Feminine modesty is thus a trick of nature that allows the human species to perpetuate itself;[53] it is the corollary of fetishism in men, that spontaneous fetishism on the part of the little boy, prompted by castration anxiety, who at the first sight of the little girl's genitals throws a veil over the lack of a penis by saying, "She has one, but it's small; they've cut it off, but it will grow back."

Woman's physical vanity also has its source, then, in penis envy: when nature is good enough to endow woman with an extra portion of beauty in addition to pubic hair, then she has every chance of seducing men; for this boon of pleasure, of seduction, that beauty offers deflects attention from the horror inspired by the genital organs (whose ugliness is indisputable) and makes ultimate pleasure possible. Beauty alone reconciles horror and pleasure. Women, too, get a boon: "they are bound to value their charms [*ihre Reize*] more highly as a late compensation for their original [*ursprüngliche*] sexual inferiority [*Minderwertigkeit*]" ("Femininity," 132).

The good reasons women have for "veiling" themselves thus all correspond with men's need for a certain fetishism. If woman makes herself man's accomplice, it is because it is in her own interest as well as his to do so: men and women alike benefit from the fact that the feminine "riddle" is not solved. Woman's "ulterior motive" remains penis envy, castration, fetishism. Such, at least, is what the bulk of Freud's discourse tells us.

TRANSLATED BY CATHERINE PORTER

§ 7 The Economy of Respect: Kant and Respect for Women

> *Nec femina, amissa pudicitia, alia abnuerit.* (When a woman has lost her modesty, she will have nothing more to refuse.)
>
> Tacitus, *Annals* IV, 3 (quoted by Rousseau in *Émile* with the following commentary: "Did ever an author better understand the human heart in the two sexes than the one who said that?")

To respect women, is this simply to obey the categorical imperative that requires respect with regard to the other as moral personage? Are women solely and simply special cases, models, or examples of the moral law, which they present and make visible, acquiring by that same law, as all moral persons do, an unalienable dignity that puts them above all price? It is, in effect, as moral personage that man (in general) possesses dignity, that is to say an interior and absolute value that forces man to respect (moral) man in his own person and in that of others, beyond all considerations of social rank, age, or sex, and permits him to contend with all other rational creatures in terms of an original equality. Kant moreover distinguishes respect as a *comparative sentiment* and respect as a *moral sentiment*.[1] The first arises when we compare our personal value with that of another, as, he tells us, in the sentiment "which a child, by simple habit, bears toward his parents, a pupil with respect to his master, or an inferior in general toward a superior." The second implies the restriction of the esteem that we bear for ourselves by the taking into consideration of the human dignity of another person. As a moral sentiment, respect is the effect of a maxim by which each is obliged to remain within limits—in his place—so as not to deprive the other of any value to which his humanity gives him the right. While as a comparative sentiment respect implies a measurable and appreciable distance between men, which can go as far as an estimation that one man is susceptible of being a means for the other who is judged superior, and of being treated as somehow a simple commodity having a certain price, as a moral sentiment respect implies not so much the absence of distance as an incommensurable distance, requiring that no man be reduced to playing the role of simple means for the ends of another, nor a fortiori be constrained into so abnegating himself as to become a slave to the ends of another.

This is why, after having distinguished these two kinds of respect, Kant, so to speak, lets drop comparative respect: it cannot and should not be classed among the first metaphysical principles of the doctrine of virtue, "which consider only the pure principle of reason," while "the different forms of respect which should be observed with respect to the other according to the difference in qualities or contingent relations among men, that is to say age, sex, birth, strength or weakness, even social position and nobility, are grounded in part on arbitrary institutions."[2] These different contingent forms of respect should not therefore be the object of a detailed account in the *Doctrine of Virtue*. All the same, Kant does return to them in the paragraph that follows in order, paradoxically, to erase in some way the distinction introduced between the comparative and the moral sentiment of respect, for this time both kinds are described as simple applications of the principle of virtue to particular cases of experience, implying particular rules "modified according to the difference between subjects."[3] They would be only "a schematism for setting forth pure principles of duty." These special cases—which seem to restore respect as comparative sentiment—"would not represent new kinds of ethical obligation (for there is only one, that of virtue in general) but only forms of application, consequently they should not be developed as sections of the Ethics and members of the division of a system (which must follow *a priori* from a concept of reason) but merely added on to it." It is only in the complete exposition of the system that these "special cases" should be examined in more detail.

Are these special cases of experience really a "schematization of the pure principle of duty"? Can they, as such, all be put on the same level? Is not the respect of one sex for the other, in particular that of men for women, a more special case, supposing it to be a simple "case of application," which must, on this basis, be relegated to some addendum or appendix and, in the name of moral rigorism or critical rigor, be reserved for the exposition of the complete system? What if this "special case" were not an example among others, but a model, a very prefiguration of moral respect? Would it not then come to stain by its empirical impurity the purity, if not of the principle, then at least of the motivation of the moral, the purity, that is, of respect for the moral law? And if, in the name of the law that commands respect—for example, that of one sex for the other—it were a question of something quite other than a moral relation of one man (in general) to another man (in general), if the question were, in the name of respect, that of holding women in respect—at a certain respectful distance—would morality not serve as a cover for an operation of a completely different order, an operation of mastery?

Apotrope, umbrella, would respect not always permit the realization of a certain economy, the gaining of respite (one knows that *respect* and *respite* are both derived from *respicere*)?

The Preliminary Respect or the Premium of Nonseduction

If one refers to the *Anthropology*—addendum or appendix to the *Doctrine of Virtue?*—the description that Kant therein gives of the relation between the sexes is not one of moral relations wherein each respects the other as representative of the sublimity of the moral law; it is rather one of warlike relations in which each struggles for domination, this last being defined as the using of another for a private end, the motivation of which is the fear of being dominated.[4] In this war, it is the so-called weaker sex that has the upper hand—just because of its weakness; men are thereby disarmed, constrained to respect as well as to a whole series of compensations: the right of women to respect seems from the beginning to be a right acquired by their weakness, a measure of protection granted to the weak by the strong.

As always, there arises a downright reversal: the weakness of women and all the traits that characterize them[5] are so many levers for controlling men and using them at their will. If women cannot dominate by force, they dominate by indirect means, by the obliqueness of ruse, the art women have to use men for their own ends. Thanks to their charms, to the love they inspire, women enchain their victims and master them through their particular abilities. Two traits, says Kant, quoting Pope (but he could as well have quoted Rousseau, and perhaps he quoted the one to hide what he owed to the other, to the author of *Émile*, which he knew well), characterize the feminine sex: the tendency to dominate and the tendency to please, mainly in public (these are such that the second trait can be assimilated to the first: in trying to please, a woman wishes always to get the upper hand over an eventual rival). The tendency of women is to dominate, but at the same time that of men is to be dominated. This double tendency explains in the last analysis the particular nature of the respect the masculine sex has for the feminine: it cannot be simply reduced to a right accorded to the weak by the strong; it is the will to dominate that drives the arrogance of women, the desire to avert all importunity on the part of man; women require, in the very name of their sex, consideration, even if they do not deserve it—that is what respect is. To the woman, this permits the eventual economy of virtue; and to the two sexes, a sexual economy, a certain respite: the woman refuses, the man demands. When woman concedes, it is a favor, and if an inversion were to occur, that would degrade, even in masculine eyes, the value of her sex. The woman must appear cold, not respond too easily to the demand, under pain of her own dishonor. In brief, that which goes to make up the value of her sex and renders woman as such respectable is, as for an entire tradition, her reserve, her modesty: "woman must be sought after, so it is required by the attitude of reserve necessary to her sex." Because of her modesty, woman protects herself and protects man; she avoids being demeaned, being for the other sex solely a means of satisfaction. At the same time that she satisfies her will to dominate in educating man to chastity, she educates him to morality; by preventing him from giving himself up to sensuality, "this vice which results from the love of the flesh,"[6] by saving him from the risk of shamelessness, that repugnant vice whereby man makes "use of his person in such a way as to demean himself below the level of the beasts," for he thus gives way entirely to animal inclination, reduces himself to a simple orgiastic object [*objet de jouissance*], woman prevents man from becoming an object of disgust to himself: from changing himself into a thing against nature, no longer deserving of respect; in brief, from defiling himself and, in his own person, from defiling the whole of humanity.

This transgression of morality, which violates duty to oneself at the highest level, brings forth such repugnance, says Kant, that it is even held as immoral to call such a vice by its name, as though to name it were to expose it to every eye in all its horror, as though it were openly to display the union of the sexes or, at least, the sex of the woman, laid bare, without discretion, of all disguise: that which can never be looked upon as such without provoking disgust; that which cannot therefore be named without disguise, clearly, without risk of defilement.

> Everything happens as if in a general way man feels the shame of being capable of making use of his person in such a way as to demean himself below the

level of the beasts, to such an extent that the carnal union of the two sexes in marriage, which is permitted (it is in itself obviously purely animal), demands and requires great care in order to disguise it whenever it must be discussed in civilized society.[7]

Defilement, disgust: a simple transgression of the duties of man to himself, if it does justify a moral condemnation, does not justify such violence in the terms in which it is made. Kant himself remarks that no other transgression of duty to oneself, suicide for example, provokes the same repugnance. Is this not to acknowledge that this vice that is born of the union between the sexes, sensuality or shamelessness, gives rise not only to disgust and moral defilement? If feminine modesty renders woman respectable, prevents man from becoming disgusted with himself, and permits him to remain a moral person, it also prevents man from having a completely different disgust: disgust for the sex of woman, to which the full and entire satisfaction of man's inclinations inevitably leads him: feminine modesty permits man to remain man, to remain virile, without succumbing to instability.[8]

The ardor that the sexual drive arouses must therefore be inhibited, curbed by the restrictive conditions that are imposed by both practical reason (the respect for oneself and others as moral persons) and pragmatic reason (calculation of interest within the sexual economy, which modesty imposes, the respect of women: let man hold them in respect, at a distance; let woman hold her sex in safekeeping from the importunities of man and dominate him thereby).[9]

These restrictive conditions are found best realized in marriage, toward which one should not be skeptical, says Kant, because it is through marriage that "woman becomes free" although also "man loses his liberty therein."[10] This is perhaps why in *The Conflict of Faculties* celibacy figures among the fundamental principles of dietetics for whoever desires to assure himself of a long and happy life, as "it would be difficult to prove that those who have reached a great age have been married for most of the time."

In this economy of respect, there are therefore no benefits without loss, and these are not of the same nature for the two sexes.

On the one hand, thanks to respect, in spite of her weakness, woman dominates, like a queen. But at the same time, she, who represents feeling, does not govern. It is man, the minister, who governs through his understanding:

The behavior of the husband must show that the well-being of his wife is closest to his heart. But he shall be like a minister to a king who, mindful of his pleasure, organizes a fête. He begins by explaining to him all the deference he owes him, but that, for example, there is no money in the coffers, in such a fashion that this all-powerful master does what he wants on condition that his minister suggests his will.[11]

On the other hand, all that characterizes the feminine sex, its weakness as well as its mastery—more or less illusory—are, for Kant, to be situated in a more general economy of nature and to be thought in terms of its design: through the device of the war between the sexes for domination, and hence through the device of what Kant calls human folly, nature directs the education of man toward morality. Such is the final goal. From this point of view, respect for women would be, in a way, a preliminary respect, a premium on nonseduction being required to lead to the final respect, moral respect, which it prefigures and recommends. Respect for women, in this sense, would be the law of laws, a law sacred among all, the condition sine qua non of the existence of the moral law, or at least of apprenticeship for submission to it. If woman ought not to provoke disgust, it is because she "constitutes herself as an object of taste for everyone," because she educates in terms of taste, decorum, fine language, and disguise—of sex and of language; moral apprenticeship passes through that of decency, of which the corollary is the passage from vulgar parlance to the delicacy of expression that throws a veil over everything "repugnant," the object of disgust and defilement. Woman's veil—the prohibition of her sex—leads, one could say, to the veil or mask of words, to substitution in language, to the opening of the infinite chain of supplements, to a supplementarity erasing all "correct" meaning—that is, improper, always already defiled.

In the *Conjectures on the Origins of Human History*, Kant insists on the importance of decency (of which the fig leaf in the Bible is a symbol) as fundamental to the formation of man as a moral creature, decisive in giving a new orientation to the form of thought, more important "than the whole interminable series of subsequent cultural developments." Decency, defined as the "propensity to provoke in another consideration toward ourselves by means of our good manners" (masking what could incite contempt), the real foundation of all true sociability, is also the first *sign* of the morality of man, of his capacity to respect the other: if "preliminary" respect is a "humble beginning," it nevertheless marks a new era because it prefigures moral respect; it is the index not of arbitrary conventions but of the rational nature of man, just as the refusal of woman, which screens the sexual object from the senses, is a "cunning artifice" educating man to reason and at the same time showing it: "the fact of rendering a feeling stronger and more lasting by withdrawing its object from the senses denotes already a certain conscious supremacy of reason over feeling." By refusal, modesty, and decency, man is led from purely animal excitations toward ideal excitations, and little by little from animal desire to love and morality. The progress of civilization is, as always, described as a passage from the senses to reason, from sensuality to morality. And this passage, just as later in Bachofen and Freud, is also described as separation from the mother, from the maternal breast of nature, which man, through his imagination, represents to himself by hindsight as paradise.[12]

Man's education toward reason and morality leads, therefore, to an emancipation with respect to Mother Nature, to women, and to feelings, and yet all education necessarily passes through them. Man cannot do without such a passage. Nature's ruse is to use women and their characteristics to arrive at an end to their reign in favor of that of man, all while leaving them the illusion of continuing to rule.[13]

It is, in effect, nature that, fearing for the survival of the species, is supposed to have implanted in woman's nature fear for bodily harm and timidity before physical dangers, weakness that authorizes her to ask men for protection. Moreover, wishing to inspire in men the refined sentiments that bring about culture, those of sociability and decorum, nature would have given the feminine sex ease of speech and expression, the claim to receive from men a welcome of gentleness and politeness, thus according her mastery over men for moral ends. Men would find themselves "through their own generosity enchained without being aware of it by a child and led in this way, if not to morality, at least to that which clothes it, to that decorum of manners which serves it as a preliminary and an introduction."[14] The order of nature, by the tendency of human folly—by the tendency of women—prefigures in this way the moral order; respect for women announces and prepares for respect for man.

If the final goal of nature is moral, if her concern is the safekeeping of humanity, if in this respect she seems not to privilege either of the two sexes, it remains nonetheless that in this general economy woman seems certainly the loser, because she does not hide, in the last analysis, her wish to be a man (to be able to give more room and more freedom to the play of her feelings), while in return no man wishes to be a woman.[15] This rejection of femininity by both sexes leaves room for the suspicion that the benefits of this whole "natural" enterprise, this economy of respect, are essentially masculine, that behind the goals of nature lie concealed the goals of man (*vir*). Behind the proclaimed respect for women, it is indeed very much a question of holding women in awe, and this because they represent a double risk: (1) that of letting oneself fall into sensuality, that is to say the abuse of the sexual faculty, and therefore an excessive spending that could lead to death—whence celibacy as the fundamental dietetic rule; (2) that of allowing the triumph of feeling over reason in oneself, the triumph of the "feminine" over the "masculine": risk of emasculation through loss of reason; risk of forgetting the sublimity of human nature and of being reduced to a natural object, to animal nature, and becoming an object of horror and disgust (*horribile visu*).

The risk of femininity is thus, on the one hand, the risk of death and, on the other hand, the risk, which respect protects one against, of no longer remaining within human limits, of losing dignity as man, of losing virility, by returning in a regressive way to the breast of Mother Nature.

The Double Fascination

And yet this return to the maternal breast is nostalgically called return to paradise by man.[16] That is to say, the violent terms that Kant makes use of, those of defilement, repugnance, horror, and disgust, serve perhaps as a countercathexis to a violent desire to return to the maternal breast. These terms, in their violence, would serve to camouflage this desire just as they would be its sign. Repugnance and horror would be the simple reverse of an unconscious fascination for women (for the mother), which in Kantian language, refined and civilized, expresses itself in the most modest expressions of an inclination for feeling, for self-love, and of an inclination for evil. This last, inherent in a finite and fallen creature, is defined by the spontaneous preference for feeling at the expense of the law, by the impossibility of having a holy will. Respect as moral sentiment is the other side of our unworthiness, which we disregard as such, fascinated as we are by our feelings. Thus, respect is a negative sentiment. In opposition to love, which attracts, it implies a repulsion, the distancing of that which fascinates; or better it implies quasi-simultaneous attraction and repulsion: that the object that fascinates and seduces is found concealed and at the same time discovered. The *Critique of Judgment*, in bringing up the sentiment of the sublime, which always implies respect, describes it as an emotion comparable to a shock in which repulsion and attraction rapidly alternate, both having as origin the same object.[17] Respect—*respectus*—is a new way of looking, looking behind. It follows the fascinated look, equivalent to contact at a distance, bound to an impossibility of not seeing, to an immediate proximity, which, as Blanchot says,[18] "absorbs you in an immobile movement and a depth without profundity," and leaves you disarmed, losing mind or senses as well as the possibility of making sense, which would put you in jeopardy of being crushed, confounded if you did not oppose this look precisely with that other look, respect. The latter gives you respite, permits you to hold yourself apart, keep your distance, to introduce a decision that separates in order to avoid contact and confusion, returns to you your mobility—this is respect also as motivation (*mobile*). Respect distances the horror that is provoked by that depth without profundity; it stops the petrifying and immobilizing movement: it has an apotropaic function.

Respect for the moral law still has traces of the original fascination. It is described as frightening,[19] and the moral law itself seems to be another "object of fascination" that is substituted for the fascination exercised by feeling—by the maternal breast?—by that which in Kant always returns to the "feminine," to a feminine face, even if this is precisely not a face, but rather a faceless depth, without a gaze, perhaps only a voice. The moral law, by its power and majesty, at first disregarded because of the original fascination, because of the "inclination for evil," counterbalances the power and majesty of that feminine "face." This also, in its sublimity and transcendence, is for the imagination "like an abyss in which it dreads its own loss."[20] In the *Critique of Practical Reason*, Kant describes the law as a holy and "solemn majesty" before which men recoil in their unworthiness. They do everything to get rid of this "frightening respect." They try to hold in respect the respect that so severely shows them their own unworthiness, from fear of feeling themselves disarmed, confounded, crushed, humiliated. Such is their presumption. But because they have only an inclination for evil, a fragile will that is neither perverse nor diabolical, respect can become a practical sentiment, the moral law a motivation, to mobilize and no longer immobilize them. In this case, a veritable conversion is brought about: men can no longer be satiated in the contemplation of the majesty of the law, which crushes them only inasmuch as they are presumptuous but which raises them all the more as they recognize its holiness and sublimity and, correlatively, the fragility of their own nature but also their own sublimity as rational beings.

Everything takes place, then, as though the respect for women, preliminary to moral respect and the inhibitory rules that it introduces in order to curb and defer desires, has as corollary a cleavage of the original fascinating figure whence results a double image: that of sensuality, charged with all evil, a repugnant and disgusting image; that of the holy law, sublime, inheritor of the power and majesty of the original fascinating figure.

Sublime and Sublimation

Should one, and could one, say, taking it from there, that the figure of the law and of its sublimity is a "grandiose sublimation" of the figure of the mother? Freud could no doubt effect such a reading, genetic or genealogical, of the moral law, or rather of its figuration, for he has shown how the respect for the mother that is ordained by the prohibition of incest is at the origin of the cleavage of the maternal figure into a double figure: that of the prostitute, demeaned sexual object with which man can satisfy his sensuality, the perverse constituents of sexuality—to yield oneself to sensual pleasure and to defile oneself; and that of the sublime and eminently respectable figure, raised on a pedestal of holiness, the immaculate and untouchable Virgin.[21]

Such a question seems legitimate to the extent to which the moral law implies a preliminary apprenticeship, passing through respect for women; and if we admit that the first woman all men should respect is "the mother," if the condition of the possibility of moral respect is the prohibition of incest, one may ask oneself whether respect does not still keep something of its empirical origin even if, sentiment a priori, it could not, for Kant, be so derived.

Kant himself insists on the fact that the word *respect* (*Achtung*) given to the specific sentiment that determines the a priori relation of man to the moral law envisaged as motivator is certainly the word that fits, that it corresponds to the common experience of respect and the usage of language that is criticized by Schopenhauer, according to whom the Kantian conception of respect essentially depends on a "Judaic" relation of submission to the law. The word *respect* would have as its object the dissimulation of the theological origin of Kantian morality and the "Jewish stench" that issues from it.²² The common experience of respect, of which the representation of the law as the figure of a "solemn majesty," fascinating and frightening, is the witness. More generally, the personification of the law, or even its aestheticization, sends one back, incontestably, to the common experience of respect, and notably to "preliminary" respect for women, for the mother.

Now Kant considers that aestheticization, if it is an aesthetic artifice (*Maschinerie*), could still have a moral sense, and that the aesthetics of morals, without being part of the metaphysics of morals, is a subjective representation of it.²³ But again it must be understood just what he means by the aestheticization of the law; it is not to be confounded with a delimitation and a precise determination that would serve as a measure; the law, because it is sublime, is without common measure, "absolutely great under all relations," beyond all comparison, and it could not have an appropriate measure outside of itself because by comparison with it everything else is small.²⁴ The personification of the law in a figure must precisely figure its incommensurability, its unfigurability, in the sense in which no determinate figure could be adequate to it; that is to say that the figure of the law could not be reduced to the figure of the mother, unless this itself were to figure unfigurability, that is to say, sublimity. There is nothing to figure "aesthetically" but the sublime or the unfigurable. In the *Critique of Judgment* (§49), Kant defines the aesthetic idea as a "representation of the imagination which gives much to be thought, without, however, any determinate thought, that is to say any concept being adequate to it; no language could completely express it nor render it intelligible." The aesthetic idea suggests with respect to a concept many inexpressible things of which the sentiment animates the faculties of knowledge, inspiring a soul to the letter of language. This is why the passage from the book of Jewish Law²⁵ that forbids the representation of God would be the most sublime of all, because it forbids the representation of the infinite divinity in any sensible or finite form, which could come to limit and delimit it, and leaves room for the infinite movement of the imagination, indeed to enthusiasm, dangerous only when it is abused. The same applies to the representation of the moral law. It must be forbidden. To believe that, deprived of all that recommends it to the senses, it would find nothing more than a cold, lifeless approbation, as though by itself it was incapable of impulsive force or emotion, is to be needlessly concerned. On the contrary, when the senses no longer see anything before them and when only the idea of morality remains, it would rather be "necessary to moderate the transports of an imagination without limits in order not to let it swell into enthusiasm than to call in the help . . . of images or some puerile appearance," which would come to arbitrarily impose limits on the power of extension of the faculties of the soul. Kant says as much in "On a Recently Assumed Aristocratic Tone in Philosophy"; it is the empirical representation of the law that castrates and paralyzes reason, emasculates it by taking away its (virile) power of impulsive force. This from the subjective point of view is called respect. Respect prevents the emasculation of reason by setting in motion the transcendental imagination. As motive force, it is the equivalent of a schema, because it permits the passage from simple knowledge of the law to its effectuation, the making of the law in general into a singular maxim—in short, that one should be truly mobilized by the law thanks to the setting in motion of the transcendental imagination. More than an a priori sentiment, respect, in this sense, would be an aesthetic idea.

In a footnote to paragraph 49 of the *Critique of Judgment*, Kant writes, "Perhaps no one has ever said anything more sublime or expressed a thought in a more sublime manner than in that inscription on the temple of Isis (mother nature): I am all that which is, has been and will be, and no mortal has ever lifted my veil."

This inscription, reproduced in a vignette of Segner, was destined, says Kant, to fill with sacred trembling and solemn trepidation he who would begin the study of physics, that is, who would introduce himself into the temple of Mother Nature. Rather than the content, it is the form of the expression that is sublime, because it sets the imagination in motion infinitely, promises the discovery of infinite mysteries without revealing any, presents the study of physics as an infinite task, interminable because always already prohibited. It is impossible to completely dis-cover Mother Nature; she is inexhaustible, impenetrable. Behind one veil, there will always be another veil.

Kant therefore forbids the (empirical) representation but not the aestheticization of the moral law, which, by the infinite movement of the imagination that it provokes, is adequate to the sublimity of the law.

All the same, "On a Recently Assumed Aristocratic Tone in Philosophy"[26] seems to contradict these analyses from the *Critique of Judgment*: there Kant sets himself against the aestheticization of the moral law, against, to be precise, its personification in the form of the veiled goddess

Isis. Here he puts the accent on the risks and abuses of such an aestheticization. He demands, as he takes on those he calls mystagogues, that the law not be personified as a beautiful and sensible form, so as to prevent men from being seduced by it, seduced by its voice as though by the pathological voice of a siren, on pain of becoming deaf to the voice of the law of reason. One must avoid the fascination of a sensible and finite voice in order to hear what must be substituted for it: "a ringing voice" that demands resistance to passion, to feeling; a sublime voice that promises nothing in return. But to speak of the voice of the law is to continue to personify it, appealing to a sensible metaphor at the very moment when what is demanded is a turning away from fascination exercised by the senses and the exclusion of all empirical representation as unacceptable and pathological. There would be, therefore, a good and a bad personification: one that arrests and paralyzes, another that mobilizes. The inscription on the temple of Isis, by the infinite character of what it evokes, by its grandeur, "I am all that which is, has been and will be," makes Isis herself pronounce the prohibition of her finite representation; it is sublime because it prevents anyone from lifting the veil of Isis, that is to say from giving her an exact and determinate figure. If one fully understands the inscription, it becomes permissible to personify the moral law in the figure of Isis because it would be that of the unfigurable. If in "On a Recently Assumed Aristocratic Tone" Kant nevertheless refuses such a personification, it is because a veiled Isis might give mortals a desire to raise this veil and to master what is not to be mastered, "like those mighty men who claim to have seized this goddess by the train of her veils and thereby made themselves masters." In other words, such a figuration may always run the risk of *fixing* the figure of Isis, of reducing her, for example, to the goddess who murdered Osiris, who recovered every morsel of him except the penis; of reducing her to a phallic castrating mother by taking an analogy for reality, by confounding a sensible representation that gives life to an idea with that same idea—and thus losing oneself "in an exalted and mystic vision" in straying from the bounds of the principles of pure reason.

In order to avoid these risks of mastery, Kant requires—and this is the minimal condition of a good personification—that an aestheticization be moral and not pathological, in other words that the personification should come after the idea of the moral law and not before it: "The aesthetic state (affection of internal sense) is either a pathological sentiment or a moral sentiment. The first is the sentiment which precedes the representation of the law; the second can only be its consequence."[27]

> The veiled goddess before whom one way or another we kneel, that is the moral law in us in its invulnerable majesty. Certainly we perceive its voice and even understand very well its commandments, but in listening we doubt whether it comes from man and if it originates in the all-powerfulness of his own reason or if it emanates from some other being whose nature is unknown to him and which speaks to him through his own reason. In the end we would do better perhaps to dispense entirely with this inquiry, since it is simply speculative, and what it is incumbent upon us to do remains the same, whether one founds it on the one or the other principle. The only difference is that the didactic method of bringing the moral law in us under distinct concepts according to a logical method, is alone *properly philosophical*, while the method which consists in personifying that law and making of the reason which commands morally a veiled Isis (as long as we do not attribute to it other properties than those which the first method discovers) is an *aesthetic* manner of representing [*Vorstellungsart*] exactly the same object, a manner in which it is certainly permitted to trust provided one has already started by reducing the principles to their pure state, to give life to this idea by means of a sensible representation [*Darstellung*], although this is only by analogy, not however without always running some risk of giving in an exalted vision that which is the death of all philosophy.[28]

Kant would not thus admit the moral law to be a grandiose sublimation of the figure of the mother. To believe this is to confound that which comes after with that which comes before: personification and a priori moral principles.

All the same, if the moral law is not derived from experience, does not find its principles there, apprenticeship to morality and respect certainly begin there. Because there is a childhood of the individual and a childhood of peoples, moral respect certainly "begins" with respect for women, for mothers, a necessary "preliminary" for reaching "terminal" moral respect, and education to morality grows from that of religious myths, that is to say from the personification of the moral law. Chronologically, the "personification" always comes first, before the knowledge of a priori moral principles, and thus indeed risks the contamination of all subsequent "representation" of the moral law. This contamination is present in Kant's own work, in spite of the rigor of the critical enterprise whose goal is precisely to purify the law of all empirical and pathological contamination, and this in order to avoid the paralysis and castration of reason, its emasculation: the metaphors are well and truly Kant's own. The word for "respect," if it is truly the one that fits this double sentiment that humiliates me at the same time that it elevates me, is like a "trace" of that first relation between an infant and that solemn and frightening majesty his mother is to him, the phallic mother figured by Isis, personification of the law.

That the figure of Isis should have been chosen as an analogical representation of the law permits inversely a better comprehension of what it is to respect women: to respect them is to hold them in awe at a distance, in order not to be tempted to lift their veil or master them, an act culpable because of the prohibition of incest, but above all dangerous and doubly dangerous. The lifting of the veil would risk confounding man, crushing him, paralyzing him, and depriving woman, the mother, of all her phallic dignity, emasculating her. To put women/mothers on high, to respect them, is to avoid seeing that they have no penis, "that they have nothing to hide."[29] The economy realized by respect is that of the agony of castration, communicated with a gesture of fetishism.

Likewise, to unmask the law would perhaps be to become aware that its authority does not emanate purely and simply from its a priori character; that the a priori is always already contaminated by the a posteriori, the masculine by the feminine; that there is no moral purity any more than there is a phallic stage—a stage that would be only masculine and not yet feminine—phantasm of all children, dream of all philosophy.

Respect—for women as for the moral law—is therefore to be seen in connection with that panic reaction of which Freud speaks in "Fetishism," analogous to that which takes hold when throne and altar are in danger. Respect is the economy of this panic; bound to the anguish of castration, it avoids the death of the human species—and that of philosophy, which has always identified the logos with the phallus.

This economy of death requires, therefore, the rejection in oneself and beyond oneself of femininity, from fear of being in one way or another contaminated by it and perishing from it. Respect for women is always the glorious, moral obverse of the "misogyny" of men.

But this distancing of women does not happen without loss: that of sensual pleasure; and with it, that which Freud calls the necessary unhappiness of the sexual life of man, who, not familiarized with the representation of incest with the mother or the sister, cannot fully satisfy his sexual desires, notably in their perverse constituents, except by going to find "the" whore, the sexual object demeaned enough not to evoke the mother: the whore who would not be a moral person worthy of respect, above all value and price, but who belongs in the mercantile circuit of exchange, is not to be respected but appraised; in brief, she is a simple means for the ends of man. In this case, the respect men have for their wives in marriage, if it is a necessary preliminary to their morality, is also that of their immorality toward other women not worthy of the name of mankind.

Yet the Kantian morality denies sensual pleasure as well, be this at the price of neurosis[30] and misery, except perhaps for those capable of procuring themselves substitute satisfactions by the route of sublimation. This was no doubt the case with Kant, who, in spite of the theoretical importance accorded to marriage, managed to remain celibate. And died at a great age.[31]

TRANSLATED BY NICOLA FISHER

PART IV

The Truth in Painting

§ 8 The Melancholy of Art

To write about art—is this not an impossible task? What is art in general? Can one even address what is called "representational" art and "modern" art in the same breath? And is each of these domains truly a homogeneous whole? Is it possible, moreover, to talk about music, architecture, sculpture, painting, poetry, film, photography, and such in a way that would be univocal? Is there one kind of art that could be privileged and that could serve as model, as paradigm?

All of these questions rest on a primary assumption: that there are works of art and a hierarchical classification of the arts. This assumption in turn presupposes that the initial ontological question has been resolved: what is art? The question itself is replete with metaphysical presuppositions.

I would like simply to show that "the question of art" may be what forces us to shift this type of inquiry, to dismantle the notions of model and of paradigm, and that this question may be what compels us, more generally, to appeal to [*solliciter*] the entire system of metaphysical oppositions on which philosophical discourse on art classically depends: the opposition between art and nature, sensible and intelligible, form and content, surface and depth, appearance and reality, signifier and signified, and so forth.

To make art a philosophical question, to hold a discourse on art that conforms to this system of oppositions—is this not to repeat the gesture of mastery by which philosophy has always sought to subordinate art to the logos and to truth? And which has, revealingly, always placed poetry and the arts of language at the top of the hierarchy?

The Sublation of Art

Hegel, for example (if Hegel is really just an example here), makes art a moment of the development of Spirit that finds its fulfillment and its sublation [*relève*[1]] in religion. Art is defined as the sensible expression of spirit, and expressivity (whose condition of possibility is the opposition of form—sensible material—and content—meaning, the Idea, Spirit) is the criterion that justifies a hierarchical classification of the arts from the least to the most spiritual. At the lowest level is architecture, whose form—raw material, heavy, mechanical mass—has with its content—Spirit, God—only a relation of pure exteriority and is thus incapable of making this content appear, incapable of representing it or making it manifest. Architecture is a symbolic art that is satisfied with a mere allusion to Spirit, as it prepares the way for an adequate expression of Spirit in the elaboration of external materials. At the top of the hierarchy is poetry, the most spiritual art: in poetry, the sensible material, articulated sound, is no longer a symbol; rather it has become only a sign of content, of representation, of spiritual interiority. It is in itself devoid of any intrinsic value: but just as poetry is the ideal of art or its fulfillment, so is it at the same time its end. When form as matter is completely erased in favor of its value as spiritual expressivity, then art—which must present objective content, Spirit, in sensible form—disappears as such, and poetry finds its fulfillment and its sublation in prose.

This is why the intermediate arts—sculpture, painting, and music, arts in which form remains sensible—although hierarchically inferior to poetry, best correspond to the exigencies of the specific "moment" of art, which is to be the mediator that enables the revelation of spirituality at the very heart of naturalness.

> The sensible must indeed be present in the work of art but should appear only as the surface and as a pure appearance of the sensible.... What Spirit wants is sensible presence which indeed should remain sensible, but liberated from the scaffolding of its pure materiality. Thereby the sensible aspect of a work of art, in comparison with the immediate existence of things in nature, is elevated to a pure appearance, in opposition to the immediate reality of natural objects. It is *not yet* pure thought, but, despite its sensible character, it is *no longer* a purely material existent either.[2]

In sculpture, form and content exist in perfect adequation. Corporeal form no longer expresses anything in itself; it reflects only an inward depth because sculpture cannot represent a spiritual content without giving it a sensible form that would be available to intuition. In painting, art is freed from the material element, and content meets with a high degree of particularity: its domain is that of the life of the soul, of all that agitates it, all that seeks to externalize itself in action. Music expresses the abstract and spiritual interiority of feeling, and its material is still less "material" than that of painting: the sound that makes feeling resound is a quasi-spiritual element; it is the very ideality of the material that finds its fulfillment in "articulated sound," the raw material of poetry.

All art, therefore, whatever its place in the hierarchy, expresses Spirit more or less adequately, more or less spiritually. Art is always a language that—though mute—speaks to Spirit; and its purpose, from which it derives its dignity and its nobility, is to address itself to spirits, to speak to them, to awaken in us an echo of Spirit since art is Spirit's mirror, its double or ghost: "The sensible concrete thing in which an essentially spiritual content is expressed speaks also to the soul, and the external form by which that content becomes accessible to our intuition and to representation aims only to awaken an echo in our soul and in our spirit."

In this perspective, the culmination of art is to make itself forgotten as art so that Spirit can appear alienated in nature, and we can remember ourselves as spirits, beyond our alienation in the immediacy of desire.

A Story of Ghosts and Corpses

Indeed, it seems that the philosophical discourse on art also aims to make us forget art, to occult it, to ensure its controlled sublation in the interest of reason and truth. And why such an occultation, if not because art strangely disquiets [*inquiète étrangement*] "Spirit," disturbs it, like a ghost, an *unheimlich*[3] phantom that will not let itself be bound to Spirit's familial (*heimlich*), all too familiar, home? Why this occultation, if not because there is in art a nonsublatable "remainder"?

There are remainders, ghosts, and phantoms wandering in limbo, things neither living nor dead, neither sensible nor intelligible, neither present nor absent, but rather present in such a way that presence gives the misleading impression of absence, absent in such a way that an oppressive plenitude emanates from absence, a plenitude that occupies and entirely takes over the spectator's gaze. With art, it is a matter not of the simple abolition of the real (which could still be mastered), but of its sacrifice, in the sense in which Bataille says that sacrifice alters and destroys the victim, kills but does not neglect it.[4] It is about shifting the real, about the real being suspended in such a way that it loses all immediate meaning: the real is there without being there; it is derealized, rendered indifferent, empty of meaning, which is why art abolishes all conventional or expected feeling in the spectator. For example, when the spectacle of death is presented as its double in painting, it becomes bearable or insignificant. There is an *a/pathy* on the part of the spectator—or, at the very least, a transformation of affect with cathartic value—that corresponds to the absence of meaning and the silence of the painted object: the spectator takes pleasure in what in ordinary life would provoke horror and terror, tolerates the intolerable, or remains indifferent to what should provoke enjoyment. The spectator takes no interest in the existence of the painted object, which, detached in splendid isolation, ends up—whatever its subject matter—transformed by the magic of art into a still life. This is what, in his own way, Kant is suggesting when he claims that the beautiful is the object of a *"disinterested" pleasure* or that it is a *purposiveness "without purpose."* The *paradoxical pathos* elicited by "art" is the flip side of its paradoxical essence, the essence of the double, of the colossus that substitutes for the absent corpse, the "unwonted and ambiguous presence which is also the sign of an absence" and which plays on both sides at once.[5] The moment the colossus becomes present, it reveals itself as something not of this world, as belonging to an inaccessible elsewhere. It is thus ungraspable and devilishly deceptive. Like every double: "In the double of the beloved woman, beneath the seductive mask of Aphrodite, the elusive Persephone shows through."[6] In "The Sandman," the student Nathaniel discovers that behind the perfection of his fiancée Olympia is a mere automaton with fixed, dead eyes, with no life but the life he is willing to impart to it,[7] and which, like every double, has devoured the life of its "model," sucked its blood down to the last drop. In Hoffman's *Kater Murr*, the painter Ettlinger compares himself to a vulture: "I am the red vulture and I can paint when I have eaten rays of color. Yes, I can paint when I have the hot blood of the heart for paint."[8]

There is no double without devouring, without *cutting into* [*entame*] what, without it, might have passed for a full, self-sufficient presence. The double makes the original differ from itself; it dis-figures the original, calls up and disturbs what, without it, might simply be identified, named, classed in this or that determinate category. Art is not a matter of some "shadow world" that could be opposed, in any simple sense, to the real world of the living. Art upsets the opposition between these two worlds, causes each to slip into the other. A shadow henceforth haunts the living form "itself" (if the latter could still be identified as such). The petrifying foundering of all oppositional categories and of any decidable meaning—this is what fascinates and frightens, like the head of the Gorgon. Vernant reminds us that Persephone sent this head to greet those who, while still living, sought to enter the realm of the dead.

With art, there is always fascination: "The one who is fascinated perceives no real object, no real figure, because what he sees does not belong to the world of reality but to the indeterminate realm of fascination."[9]

This fascination produced by the uncanniness of art is the same fascination that is provoked by the corpse, the double of the living who perfectly resembles the living being, to the point of being confused with it, without, however, being the same: more imposing, more colossal than the other, the corpse is the victor in this combat with the enemy brother, who takes the place of the devoured one and becomes the greater for it. Let us read this fascinating text by Blanchot:

> The image does not, at first glance, resemble the corpse, but it may be that the corpse's strangeness is also that of the image. What we call mortal remains escape ordinary categories: something is there in front of us that is not the living person, nor is it anything real—it is not the same as he who was alive, nor another, nor something else. . . . It is striking that, at the moment when we are confronted, in the presence of the corpse, with the presence of the unknown, the mourned deceased begins to resemble himself. . . . Yes, it is really he, the cherished living person, but all the same it is more than he: he is more beautiful, more imposing, already monumental and so absolutely himself that he seems to be *doubled* by himself, united, by resemblance and by the image, to the solemn impersonality of the self. The corpse is the reflection coming to master the life it reflects, absorbing it, identifying with it in its substance by taking it beyond its use value and its truth value to something incredible—unusual and neutral. And if the corpse is such a good resemblance [*si ressemblant*], it is because it is, at a certain point, resemblance par excellence, resemblance itself, and also nothing more. It is likeness [*le semblable*] to an absolute degree, distressing and marvelous. But what is it like [*à quoi ressemble-t-il*]? Nothing.[10]

It is in order to escape this frightful fascination—a fascination elicited by a shift in the real and in all the categories by which identity is distorted (in the *Sophist*, Plato demonstrates how the concept [*genre*] of the Other can cut into [*entamer*] the self-identity of the Idea simply by asking questions about simulacrum, resemblance, that particularly slippery concept [*genre*])—and to escape this panic that there is philosophical speculation, infinite specularization, with a view to final mastery.[11] Perseus can only triumph over Medusa by making her contemplate her own fascinating image in a mirror. Philosophical speculation is such a mirror, an inveigler of images that are too overwhelming, too intolerable. Without this speculation, philosopher and philosophy both would risk death or madness.[12]

The Shattered Mirror

This is why beauty is never free from melancholy: it seems to be in mourning for philosophy. With art, it is not about the simple work of the negative, but about a work of mourning unsublatable by any master dialectic.

Let me insert here, in emblematic fashion, that painting by Greuze depicting a crying girl, entitled *The Broken Mirror*.[13] In his *Salons*, Diderot compares this painting with another painting by Greuze, *Young Girl Crying over Her Dead Bird*, in order to counter a naive reading, one based on the immediately obvious: a girl is crying over the loss of her dead bird. Diderot writes:

> Greuze painted the same subject once before: in front of a cracked mirror, he placed a tall girl dressed in white satin and overcome by a profound melancholy. Do you not think that it would be as ridiculous to attribute the tears of the girl in this salon to the loss of a bird as it would be to attribute the melancholy of the girl in the preceding Salon to her broken mirror? I tell you, this child is crying over something else. ("Salon of 1765")[14]

Were you to ask what this "something else" was, you would be as naive as those who hold to the bird or the broken mirror, to whatever seems to be "truly" rendered, restored in painting. As for Diderot, he does not reply and will, ironically, denounce this "projective" reading: the girl is crying over the loss of her bird "or of anything you like." At a deeper level, in comparing the two paintings, he is suggesting that there is no need to reply, no need to talk about it, that the painting is not a mirror that could reflect an immediate or hidden meaning, Spirit or nature, some natural or cultural object, a bird or a mirror. The bird is always already flown, the mirror broken, cracked, and it is this shattering of meaning that the girl is crying over—the loss, along with the mirror and the bird, of all reference and thus of all discourse. She is crying over the "sacrifice" of the subject or the loss of the object, of that which indeed, according to Freud, produces melancholia until the work of mourning is done.[15]

"But is this not to give yet another meaning to the painting?" *The Broken Mirror* would be thus an allegory of painting. And so yet another discourse, even if it is one that condemns all discourse.

Figurative Order and Discursive Order

And so it is not the painting that "speaks." A painting does not mean (to say) anything. Were speaking in fact its aim, it would certainly be inferior to speech and would need to be "sublated" by language to receive meaning, and a clearly communicable meaning at that. Between the figurative order of the painting and the discursive order of language there exists a gap that nothing can bridge. Painters used to mark this structural impossibility of expressing meaning in painting by giving their figures streamers with rolled-up ends bearing captions: what are called *phylacteries*. It is no accident, moreover, that Freud takes painting as his paradigm to show that dreams are a kind of figurative writing with laws and untranslatable codes of their own:

> [D]reams have no means at their disposal for representing these logical relations between the dream-thoughts. . . . The incapacity of dreams to express these things must lie in the nature of the psychical material out of which dreams are made. The plastic arts of painting and sculpture labour, indeed, under a similar limitation as compared with poetry, which can make use of speech; and here once again the reason for their incapacity lies in the nature of the material which these two forms of art manipulate in their effort to express something. Before painting became acquainted with the laws of expression by which it is governed, it made attempts to get over this handicap. In ancient paintings small labels were hung from the mouths of the persons represented, containing in written characters the speeches which the artists despaired of representing pictorially.[16]

(This does not prevent Freud from repeating elsewhere philosophy's reappropriating gesture by giving in to an interpretation that turns the figurative writing of dreams and art into a discourse. Nonetheless—because he knows the gap between the figurative and the discursive can never be filled—he conducts an "interminable" analysis that presents itself as a fictional or hypothetical construction, or even as an analytic novel, an expression he uses in his work on Leonardo da Vinci.) What Freud grasped at least was that to the extent that there can be discourse on art or on dreams, it will never be univocal and conclusive. If one wants to recount one's dreams and interpret them, if one wants to make a painting or a statue speak in order to extort its pseudo-secret, one must consent to a certain wavering, to the fact that one's language will always slip from one meaning to another in an endless movement of supplementation. The resistance of the figurative to being spoken binds one at the very least to a polysemic and interminable language, which has a greater affinity with poetry or fiction than with the univocal language of science or philosophy. The gap between the figurative and the discursive prevents one from stopping at any single, determinate meaning, as one might at an answer or last word to a riddle.

The addition of a title to the outside of the painting, usually on the frame, is like a supplementary "caption" intended to force the painting to speak—a painting that, in and of itself, for structural reasons, can never be eloquent or escape its own muteness.

This gap between the figurative and the discursive order opens a double possibility of reading: the most common, which is also the most "philosophical" and the most psychoanalytic, consists of trying to fill the gap with a proliferating discourse that subjects the painting "to questioning," as if violently to wrest from it a secret that it kept silently and discreetly in reserve. A long-winded discourse that dissembles the painting more than it reveals the key to the riddle, and that seems rather driven by the anxiety to which these uncanny "voices of silence" give rise (in exactly the same way that the psychoanalyst's silence forces the "patient" to speak).

A resounding discourse of this kind, which in its clamor covers over the muteness of the work of art, is what most guides inflict on museum visitors, who are content to cast a vague glance, when they can, at the title and painting before moving on to the next. The same cover-up operation is performed by the catalogs in which the spectator takes refuge to read a description that is ostensibly objective and nonetheless laced with value judgments and projective interpretations that cut into [*entament*] the supposed purity of the "description." The implicit postulate of such descriptions is that of the perfect homogeneity between the figurative and the discursive order, a homogeneity that would make it possible to move from one to the other, from one sign system to another, while at the same time preserving an identical content, without remainder. Ultimately, it should be possible to reconstitute, even to generate, the painting on the basis of these discourses.

This first type of long-winded reading seems called for by the painting itself when it "represents," when it seems to refer to a model outside of itself that it "imitates." When it is *mimetic*, painting seems eloquent and to call for eloquence. Resemblance elicits a judgment of identification and predication that is based on the purely obvious—this is that, this is a bird, a girl, et cetera—and this affirmation continues in an enumerative description that is meant to exhaust the painting's "content." The birds that peck at Zeuxis's painted grapes, or Büttner's ape who devours a precious natural history collection because it is illustrated with maybugs (examples cited by Hegel when he critiques the idea that art is an imitation of nature), produce in their own way this kind of identification by demonstrating "the excellence of a reproduction," one that would be truer than nature. Man, on the other hand, according to Hegel, leaves the object its independence when he contemplates a work of art; he maintains a respectful distance from it and does not devour it. The beautiful object is not the desired object, subject to gluttonous consumption. Of course, to hold a discourse on painting is still, in another way, to devour it, to consume and destroy it [*de le consommer et consumer*] without leaving a trace. But Hegel does not say this, and he is content—as is an entire philosophical tradition—to critique the imitation of nature, this futile and superfluous, frivolous task, worthy of an animal but not of a Spirit. A matter of cunning more than of creation, imitation neglects the true content of art, objective beauty, and benefits only the vanity and narcissism of the psychological subject. Imitation is a presumptuous and diabolical game and one that is necessarily doomed to failure because, limited in its means of expression, it produces only partial illusions that deceive only one of the senses. In the place of the real and the living, it presents only a caricature of life:

> The Turks, as Muslims, do not, as is well known, tolerate any pictures or copies of men, etc. James Bruce in his journey to Abyssinia showed paintings of a fish to a Turk; at first the Turk was astonished, but quickly enough he found an answer: "If this fish shall rise up against you on the last day and say: 'You have indeed given me a body but no living soul,' how will you then justify yourself against this accusation?"[17]

In the *Republic*, Plato had already condemned art as simulacrum, this supreme danger, this poison that, because it confuses all genres, causes those who do not at least possess the antidote of reason and knowledge to mistake the philosopher for the sophist, and illusion for truth: animals, children, and the ignorant, all those who look on from "afar."[18] Philosophy has always condemned without appeal the diabolical production of the simulacrum that gives rise to *apate*, deception, and the judgment of illusory identification that exposes one to the risk of seeing the grounds [*l'assurance*] of all identity founder: the risk of madness itself.

It is against this risk that Plato protects himself by distinguishing, within this troubling genre of the mimetic, between a bad mimesis, which delights in illusion as such, and a good mimesis, which subordinates illusion to truth and to the philosophical logos.

This philosophical condemnation of the simulacrum is, to a certain extent, lifted by Diderot, who congratulates the magician Chardin for reproducing the truth in his painting so eloquently that he deceives not only animals and children but also the philosopher himself:

> In the Salon are several small paintings by Chardin: almost all of them depict fruit along with the accoutrements of the table. It is nature itself. The objects come out of the canvas and are so true to life that they deceive the eye. . . . Oh, Chardin! It is not white, red, and black that you crush on your palette: it is the very substance of objects, it is air and light that you apply to the canvas with the tip of your brush. . . . Ah, my friend, you can spit on Apelle's curtain and Zeuxis's grapes! Ardent artists are easily fooled, and animals are bad judges of painting. Haven't we seen the birds in the King's garden go and break their necks against the worst painted perspectives? But Chardin can deceive both you and me whenever he chooses. ("Salon of 1763")[19]

Diderot seems to have let himself be deceived by the magic of Greuze's art in *Young Girl Crying Over Her Dead Bird*, a painting that appears so "true" to him that he wants to go up to it and kiss the girl's hand. And if he refrains from doing so, it is not because it would be an absurd thing to do but because he "respects the child and her sorrow." So he keeps his distance, does not devour her with his kisses but engages her in a real dialogue, asks her about the meaning of her tears, proffers a series of hypotheses that he rejects successively because the girl seems to shut him up each time, as if objecting to his answers. Diderot appears increasingly to forget that he is dealing with a young girl in a painting. As if suffering from hallucinations, he replaces the scenography with a real script, a bourgeois family drama, in which fiancé, father, and mother are all summoned in turn. And as in every good bourgeois drama, there is a moral lesson: the bird was forgotten and died because the girl forgot herself. The painting's figurative economy carries with it a delirious discourse that proliferates endlessly: the painting is the pretext for speech, the outline of a poem, of an elegy, or of a drama, the canvas of an entirely different text. Since the young girl can only remain quiet when pressed with questions, the discourse of the philosopher would in principle be interminable—were it not that, by some fiction, it finally forced her to respond: "Speak—I shall never be able to fathom you."

Diderot is not really fooled. A burst of laughter here, perhaps from some Thracian servant,[20] recalls the philosopher, the madman, from heaven down to earth and puts an end to his raving and his distraction: laughter at the seriousness of the philosopher who is not afraid to amuse himself by consoling a painted child for the loss of her painted bird. This laughter shatters all earlier readings; it makes a mockery of all interpretative hypotheses and opens onto an entirely different space, a space of indeterminacy and play. Not only does this laughter replace a naive reading with an interpretive, polysemic one, like the one Freud offers us—a reading that still comes under the same logic of the sign and mimesis—but it breaks with the very space of meaning, however plural; it breaks with all eloquence: it "wrings its neck."

Strangled Eloquence

This space is the very one that modern art meant to introduce when it decided not to "express," not to "represent," not to "imitate" anything anymore—anything that might lend itself to a spontaneous identification and to an alleged discursive equivalent, anything that would let painting to *be made to* or even *to be allowed to* speak.

In this regard, a whole set of sacrificial operations characteristic of the style of each "artist" tried to reduce the work of art to a pure play of forms, to a series of differential traces. There are the symptomatic modifications of titles such that titles no longer designate this object or that one but rather pure music, simple rhythmic games of force: *Composition I, II, III* (Kandinsky's, for example). Or else there is a displacement of the title that is inscribed in the painting and loses its overhanging, referential position;

the title becomes a figurative element like any other, in exactly the same way that, in dreams, speech is not a privileged element and is more important [*joue plus*] for its figurative than for its significative value. This inscription of the title contests the apparently unequivocal identity of a figure: a "shoe" in Magritte tips over into strangeness, is rendered unspeakable or nameless [*innommable*] by the inscription "moon," an inscription that prevents any foot from slipping into it, unless one's head is in the clouds. Or, again, a "pipe" in Magritte is no longer really a pipe: the caption "This is not a pipe" is inscribed in the painting beneath a "pipe" that is painted on a canvas and propped on an easel, in the painting within the painting above which there is another "pipe," analogous but more imposing, the "model," which loses its paradigmatic and referential function when reintroduced in the painting. In a painting where there are two "pipes," inscription replaces the resemblance between copy and model with a relation of similarity, a relation no longer of signifier to signified but of signifier to signifier, and it opens up a chain of substitution that is without end and without originary signified, in a movement of infinite referral from one signifier to the other.

> In the same painting, two images bound thus laterally by a relation of similarity are enough for exterior reference to a model—through resemblance—to be disturbed, rendered floating and uncertain. What "represents" what? Even as the exactness of the image functioned as a finger pointing to a model, to a sovereign, unique, and exterior "pattern," the series of similarities (and two are enough to establish a series) abolishes this simultaneously real and ideal monarchy. Henceforth the simulacrum runs across the surface, in a direction that will always be reversible.[21]

Generally speaking, *series* deal a fatal blow to the paradigm, which finds itself reinscribed in a serial chain in which each object in the series is both self-sufficient and at the same time in a relation of infinite, reciprocal supplementarity with others: there is no reason for the series to stop.[22] A painting in a series will never be, any more than it is the reproduction of a model, the "reflection" of the artist. The artist can no longer be considered the "father" of his work, the heroic rival of God or of the father, as he is in a theological and narcissistic conception of art. In *Totem and Taboo*, Freud shows how the traditional space of art takes the place of religion and repeats, in a differential fashion, the totemic feast, that is to say, the ritual murder of the father and his deification. The first epic poet was the man who broke away from the crowd and assumed the burden of the collective murder of the father. He is the first hero. One component of aesthetic pleasure is to be found in the spectator's identification with this hero, because we have all committed this murder, unconsciously, in our dreams. Pleasure is possible only because there is, thanks to the magic of art, both recognition and misrecognition of this crime, and the assumption of collective guilt by the lone artist. In this perspective, the work of art is like a gift to the mother who is always, out of love, an accomplice to the murder of the father: this gift is the "child" the son gives his mother.[23]

Serial painting puts an end to this oedipal scene: each object in the series is desacralized, reduced to mere play, the analogue not of divine creation but of one of nature's countless "attempts" that heeds not purposiveness but only chance and necessity. The child, if there is one, is always already aborted and disfigured: see, for example, Bacon's serial portraits, in which the face is distorted and mutilated by an aggressive layer of paint.

These operations of modern art enable us to "read" what we call "representational" art completely differently: modern art "belatedly" ushers the painting of the past, too, into permanent silence and leaves room only for a boundless play of possible forms. What we call representational art can no longer be thought of as the mere repetition of a preexisting model but only as an originary double that causes all of our assumptions to waver—our assumptions about the identity of the "object" as well as that of the subject—by doubling every "real" thing with its unwonted and fascinating "presence."

TRANSLATED BY JENNIFER BAJOREK

§ 9 The Resemblance of Portraits: Imitation According to Diderot

To Keep the Eyes That Nature Gave Us, or to Make Oneself New Eyes?[1]

Can we draw from his many texts on art an aesthetics of Diderot? And were we to formulate its basic rule, would this rule be a classical one, of the rigorous imitation of nature? Does Diderot not actually praise those painters who, like Chardin, present nature more than they represent it, and who paint objects, so to speak, outside the canvas and so true as to deceive our eyes? To deceive not the eyes of birds (as did Apelle's curtain and Zeuxis's grapes), birds who are, in any case, "bad judges of painting." For "have we not seen the birds in the King's garden go and break their necks against the worst of painted perspectives?" And not the eyes of children and the ignorant, like the mimetician in Plato's *Republic*, who deludes only those who "look from afar," that is to say, those who are removed from truth by at least three if not in fact by an infinite number of degrees.[2] No, "it is you, it is I," it is the philosopher himself, whose knowledge is no longer an antidote, whom "Chardin will deceive whenever he likes" (*OE*, 485). This great magician, this charlatan, this deceiver, this cunning maker of simulacra—we should not chase him from the city in the name of truth; we should urge aspiring painters to follow his example and to take his painting as a model, for it is the strict equivalent of nature (*OE*, 483). Any composition that so conforms to nature in its every detail that the spectator might exclaim, "I have never seen this phenomenon, but it exists" (*OE*, 773), deserves the greatest praise. The rule of the imitation of nature is imperative, and it can never be too rigorously obeyed.

One could cite multiple texts in which Diderot uses the word *rigorously* to emphasize the imperative nature of this rule, whose corollary indeed seems to be, on the one hand, the refusal of any "poetic" embellishment, of any alteration, and, on the other, the critique of academic painting. In looking at Chardin's paintings, it is enough to keep the eyes that nature gave us and to use them well; academic painting, in contrast, actually forces the spectator to "make himself new eyes" in that it interposes, between the eye and nature, a set of conventions and rules that alter the natural model, deform and impoverish it under the pretext of embellishing it. All those rules that scholarly painting follows are merely the symptom of our laziness, our inexperience, our ignorance, and our bad eyes. "If we really knew how things fit together in nature, what would become of all those symmetrical conventions?" (*OE*, 734). And yet no man—not even Chardin—will ever have perfect eyes, that is to say, divine ones, and the artist's studio will never be the equivalent of nature. To want to imitate nature too rigorously is to be doomed, necessarily, to failure. The rule of imitation must therefore not be understood naively, as it is by the ignorant dauber on the Pont Notre-Dame, who aims only to "make it resemble" utterly rigorously. Because man is man—neither God nor Nature—because his eye is always ever so slightly off [*mauvais*], imitation in painting will never be utterly rigorously reproductive; and painting would not be an art if it were not, ever so slightly, productive.

And so the rule of rigorous imitation is not the only and not the last word on Diderot's aesthetics. In the first place, this is because, generally speaking, Diderot, a philosopher who is as variegated as life itself, is far removed from any dogmatism; he knows that in one moment he is never the same as what he was in another; he knows that he never agrees with "himself," never has the same taste or the same judgments about the true, the good, and the beautiful,[3] and so never decides categorically, never pronounces the last word but says only: "Such are my thoughts for the moment, at the risk of having to go back on my error, if it is one" (*OE*, 506). Because generally speaking Diderot does not see things as definitively right or wrong and is always capable of reversing, paradoxically, the views that he seems finally to espouse, the rule of rigorous imitation that is massively affirmed in most of his texts is just as suspect in other texts that offer a completely different conception of mimesis. "In art as in nature, there are no sudden leaps: *nihil per saltum*; and this to avoid making shadow holes or circles of light, and of being cut up [*découpé*]. 'Aren't these shadow holes and circles of light to be found in nature?' 'Yes, I think they are. But who ordered you to be the rigorous imitator of nature?'" (*OE*, 805). But it is mostly for specific reasons stemming from the very structure of art that Diderot, even if he never completely erases the importance of the rule of imitation, is ultimately compelled to attenuate its "rigor" in favor of a mimesis that is not reproductive but creative.

Good and Bad Portraitists
La Tour: Is He Good or Is He Evil?

The passage devoted to La Tour in the "Salon of 1767" is, it seems to me, particularly emblematic of this double conception of mimesis.

When it comes to the portrait, the rule of rigorous imitation seems at first to be absolutely essential: the portraitist must make the portrait resemble and in this way arouse general admiration (that of both the wise and the ignorant), without his even needing to know the model. The rigor of the rule makes the portrait a particularly difficult genre, which the portraitist— if we are to believe Pigalle (*OE*, 839)—is so often tempted to renounce. Thus, it is not surprising if there are so few good portraits in this "Salon." Among these are certainly La Tour's portraits, whose great merit—even if it is neither their only nor their principal merit—is to "resemble."

From the start, then, Diderot introduces a distinction between a bad mimesis and a good mimesis, the latter of which alone is capable and worthy of arousing admiration. But why "admire" resemblance? Is it because, as Aristotle thought, man takes pleasure in resemblance, just as he takes pleasure in learning? Is it not, on the contrary, because resemblance—when it is rigorous—produces a feeling of anxiety, which it is necessary to camouflage with admiration, admiration then serving as a force of counterinvestment? Resemblance is indeed, as Plato says in the *Sophist*, a particularly slippery, atopical genre, for it can be situated neither in the place of being nor in the place of nonbeing. The good portrait possesses all the strange, uncanny, *unheimlich* characteristics of the double: a phantom wandering in limbo, it is neither living nor dead, neither present nor absent; present in such a way that its presence gives the misleading impression of absence, absent in such a way that there emanates from its absence an oppressive plenitude that occupies and takes over entirely the gaze of the beholder. An unwonted and ambiguous presence, which is also the sign of an absence and belongs to an inaccessible elsewhere—hence ungraspable and diabolically deceptive. Resemblance upsets all the categories that clearly distinguish between model and copy, life and death; it causes all oppositional categories and decidable meaning to founder.[4] And it is this shift in the real, and in all the categories whose identity has been undermined, which fascinates and disquiets. To admire that life, flesh itself, should be so well rendered is to conceal from oneself the fact that there is no life, no flesh, that is not always already touched [*entamées*] by death. Diderot does not underscore this pharmaceutical function of admiration, but the term returns insistently in the text, as if art's ultimate objective were precisely to arouse this admiration, even going so far as to suggest a resemblance where there is none. "One sees the model where, strictly speaking [*à la rigueur*], it is not, and one cries out in admiration" (*OE*, 507–8).

Indeed, if this is the function of art, would it not be essentially pharmaceutical for Diderot? Would its aim not be to camouflage everything that produces anxiety and that disquiets? We shall see this confirmed in what follows. Even if Diderot does not speak of anxiety directly in the face of the work of art, one might say that this anxiety reveals itself in a way that is displaced, through a series of theoretical questions: How does one distinguish between a good and a bad mimesis? Between a portrait and a work of imagination? What makes us think that these are in fact portraits, and without being mistaken? What is the difference between a fantastical head [*une tête de fantaisie*] and a real one? In the case of La Tour, it can be decided without hesitation: we are definitely dealing with portraits, and with good ones, although "all the conventional rules of drawing are broken: in the posture, the dimensions, the form, and the proportion of the parts" (*OE*, 505). For in La Tour's works, as in Chardin's, "it is nature itself; it is the system of nature's imperfections such as we see them every day" (Ibid.).

La Tour is a good portraitist because he is a *true* painter (one who paints truly), because he is a painter and nothing else. He rigorously reproduces nature without embellishing it, without transforming it through the rules of art. What he does "is not poetry; it is nothing but painting" (Ibid.). The bad portrait confuses genres, painting and poetry. The term *poetry* must be taken in its etymological sense here: to be a poet is to *produce* with complete freedom, without slavishly submitting to a model in order to *reproduce* it as rigorously as possible. The opposition between painting and poetry is the traditional opposition that comes to us from Aristotle,[5] between a mimesis that reproduces nature, a given model, and a productive mimesis, which supplements some deficiency in nature—nature's inability to do everything, to organize everything, to produce everything—and that perfects nature by ennobling it [*en l'agrandissant*], by embellishing it. The poet does not imitate "natured nature" but "naturing nature," nature as a productive, creative force. And this requires something more than talent: genius, a creative or divine gift, the gift made by nature itself of its own power to create.

What this means is that a good portraitist should in no way alter, change, correct, or remedy natural imperfections or embellish the model. If he "produces" instead of reproducing, he executes not a portrait but a caricature, even if it is a "flattering caricature [*caricature en beau*]." This means that the last thing he should be is ingenious, or rather that his only genius should be technical. Thus, La Tour is a "marvelous" technician [*machiniste*] in the theatrical sense of the term—but only in the sense in which Vaucansson, and not Rubens, is one. Known precisely for his technical genius, as the inventor of numerous machines and, in particular, of strange and disquieting automatons, Vaucansson had constructed, among other things, a mechanical scorpion for Marmontel's *Cleopatra*.[6] The portrait that Diderot sketches of La Tour is the symmetrical and inverted counterpart to his portrait of the artist as a genius. La Tour "has never produced anything spirited [*de verve*]"; his productions are only a result of "long and dogged study" (Ibid.). His coldness, his calm, his lack of enthusiasm are contrasted with the genius's lack of sangfroid, which has its source in an extreme sensitivity and falls prey to enthusiasm. La Tour does not paint under the effect of delirium; he is not inspired; he "does not imitate the furious gestures of the madman, he is not ecstatic, he is not indifferent to the rest of the world." The genius, distracted by a thousand objects, never gets an idea that does not awaken a feeling; he does not limit himself to looking; he is moved. He does not seek to reproduce nature; he wants only to give body to the phantoms that are his work: "In the heat of enthusiasm, he has at his disposal neither nature nor a consistency of thought; he is transported into the situation of the characters he creates; he has taken on their traits."[7] La Tour lacks this force of enthusiasm that would allow him to identify with his subjects: "He performs none of those contortions that are made by the enthusiastic modeler, in whose face one can see the succession of all the works he is preparing to render—works that seem to pass from his soul to his face and from his face to his clay or his canvas" (Ibid.). And yet, despite his coldness, La Tour's imitations are "warm." There is "flesh and life" in his painting, and he knows how to "animate dead things," a quality he shares with few: "For those who know how to preserve the life of those things to which it has been granted can be easily counted" (*OE*, 727).[8]

La Tour is the analogue of the great actor, who, far from being possessed by momentary inspiration, from falling prey to a passive mimesis (as does the hysterical woman), only plays at mimesis, which is, for him, the product of study, technique, and knowledge. The absence of any real identification (what, in the *Paradox of Acting*, Diderot calls his lack of feeling [*sensibilité*]) allows La Tour to imitate everything, to be outside of himself without being mad—allows him, on the contrary, to maintain a perfect mastery over himself. The painter "who never produces anything spirited [*de verve*]" actively imitates a model that is not in him but outside him. This is why he alone can paint portraits that are lifelike—that are the image of their models and not his own. He alone can reproduce nature in its diversity instead of dragging around everywhere "the same little corner of canvas," which betrays only a sterile and narcissistic self-repetition, a practice that had already been denounced by Leonardo da Vinci, for whom "the greatest failing of the painter is to repeat in a composition the same movements, the same faces and drapery, and to make nearly all faces resemble their author's."[9] The man of feeling will never be "a sublime imitator of nature, unless he can forget and be distracted from himself." The good portraitist, like the good actor, is therefore the least feeling of creatures. He must be nothing in order to imitate everything in a way that is lifelike. He must be unfeeling, cold, so that his imitation will be warm. Where the "Conversations on 'The Natural Son' " describe the mimetic tribe as an "enthusiastic and passionate bunch that feels keenly and reflects little," the *Paradox* suggests a parallel between the great actor and all great imitators of nature in general: "Great poets, great actors, and perhaps all the great imitators of nature in general, whatever their art—those gifted with a good imagination, superior judgment, exquisite tact, and infallible taste—are the least feeling of creatures."

In the *Paradox*, the great actor is described in almost the same terms as La Tour in the "Salon of 1767": "This man must be a cold, calm spectator. Consequently, I expect him to have great penetration and no feeling: the art of imitating everything or, what amounts to the same thing, an aptitude for playing all kinds of characters and roles." "They (actors) are equally capable of too many things; they are too busy looking and imitating to be keenly affected within themselves." The actor's performance, like La Tour's, is the result not of some gift of genius but of long study and assiduous work. The good portraitist and the great actor must therefore lose themselves to be as close as possible to nature in its diversity. They must not have their own tone; they should be nothing more than excellent instruments, "marvelous" technicians, if not, in fact, like the automatons invented by Vaucansson, marvelous and fantastic machines themselves. The actor, says the *Paradox*, "shuts himself up in a big wicker mannequin, whose soul he is, and he moves this mannequin in a most frightening way." For only a machine can be truly devoid of all feeling, only a machine can be perfect, and therefore only a machine can rigorously imitate nature and be a perfect portraitist. A machine or God. As prodigious and marvelous as any painter's technique may be, be he La Tour, Vernet, or Chardin, this technique will necessarily be "particular [*propre*] and limited"—even if the painter is not slave to a facile and narrow technique, even if he has nothing to do with some "adherent to protocol," that humble servant to the rainbow, even if he does not spend his life moving the same little corner of canvas around everywhere (like a great lord who has but one outfit and keeps his valets in the same livery). No matter how intrepid their brush, "which delights in mixing together all of nature's colors, in all of their hues, with the greatest boldness, the greatest variety and the most sustained harmony," the greatest and most rigorous imitators of nature will never be perfect: "because man is not God, and because the artist's studio is not nature" (*OE*, 679). God's true rival is thus not the painter who devotes himself to a poetic, creative mimesis, who seeks, in a more or less ingenious fashion, to perfect and embellish the divine or natural creation (the bad portraitist), but the painter who devotes himself to a reproductive mimesis: the true rival is the good portraitist. If Leonardo da Vinci thought he had found an antidote to the desire to rival God in the rule of the imitation of nature, Diderot, for his part, anticipates Hegel, who will condemn the strict imitation of nature as presumptuous, sacrilegious, demonic, and unworthy of spirit because it is the work of pure, technical skill rather than of a truly creative power. Far from eliciting admiration, a perfectly executed imitation ought to produce only boredom, displeasure, and nausea.[10] And yet both those who are wise and those who are ignorant admire portraits that are lifelike, an admiration that can therefore be explained only by the need to camouflage the uncanniness [*l'inquiétante étrangeté*] that a strict resemblance awakens.

La Tour, that marvelous technician [*machiniste*], does seem at any rate to be a disquieting, diabolical character, a wily creature with more than one *trick* [*tour*] up his sleeve; he is a veritable "traitor," "who respects none of his fellow painters enough to tell him the truth," who holds himself above all others because he is the only one, besides Chardin, to make "flesh"—magically, diabolically—"whenever he pleases" (*OE* 679–80).

Diderot, in the style of Vasari, relates one of the tricks that this diabolical character plays on his fellow painters. This trick is symptomatic of his vanity, of his desire not only to be the best—the rival of God—but to be recognized as such by all, and it precisely betrays his weakness. The painter's mimetic rivalry, his extreme jealousy, his desire to appropriate first place for himself, everywhere, always, and immediately, without waiting for posterity, the only true judge, to confer it upon him (for he seems to deserve it), betrays his extraordinary fragility. It betrays, on the part of this admirable technician [*machiniste*], the absence of a stable and secure identity (which is, on the other hand, the condition of his ability to imitate nature rigorously, as it is necessary to be nothing in order to be able to imitate everything). Diderot suggests that the ultimate aim of this "technical genius" is to transform himself into a stiff automaton, into a perfect machine (an impregnable *tower* [*tour*]!), so as to intimidate the audacity of his assailants, his rivals, and his fellow painters. Making use of the genealogical method, as Nietzsche would do later,[11] Diderot, in fact, deciphers, behind La Tour's coldness and calm, the jealous uneasiness the sick man feels when faced with a potential rival, even when this rival is modest enough to admit his inferiority. This uneasiness drives him to devise a test of public recognition, so that he may see his own superiority ratified by all and publicly demonstrate the great distance that separates him from his rival—as if he were afraid of being confused with him, with his double, and of perishing as a result.

Hence the trick he plays on his innocent fellow painter by forcing him to become his unwilling rival, that is to say, by forcing him to paint his portrait at the same time that he paints it himself—without saying anything. Exhibited in the same Salon, the two portraits of La Tour expose, for all the world to see, "the difference between master and pupil," and this clever—or dirty—trick [*tour*] of La Tour's publicly establishes, yet again, his mastery. Diderot, who paints the scene in moralizing tones, admits the trick's subtlety but does not appreciate it: "The trick is subtle and displeases me." And yet he shows himself to be indulgent with respect to the prank of this vain artist, "vexed at seeing himself brought down to the level of a man who did not come up to his ankles," and cannot help lecturing him:

> Oh, La Tour, was it not enough that Perronneau told you, "You are the best"? You could not be happy without the public saying so, too? Well, if you had only waited a bit, your vanity would have been satisfied, and you would not have humiliated your colleague. In the long run, everyone gets what he deserves. Society is just like Bertin's house: a fool is seated at the head of the table the first time he shows up, but, little by little, he is displaced by the new arrivals; he makes the full tour of the table and ends up in the least desirable place, to one side or the other of the Abbé de la Porte. (*OE* 506–07)[12]

This lesson does not encourage La Tour to renounce his mimetic rivalry but only to have patience and to spare his rival humiliation. La Tour's fragility probably prevented him from hearing this lesson because it prevented him from "waiting even for a moment"; his fragility prevented him from waiting his turn [*tour*], from deferring even for a bit the satisfaction of his vanity, that is to say, the public proclamation of his omnipotence necessary to reassure him, to guarantee him first place. La Tour—and this was his weakness—could not submit to the tribunal of history, could not wait for the last judgment, where "in the long run, everyone gets what he deserves." He needed to be recognized immediately and to sit at the head of Bertin's table.

Double Mimesis

Had he been able to leave it to the judgment of history, to the judgment of posterity, would posterity indeed have guaranteed him first place? Was La Tour's haste to be recognized not justified? Did he not know, deep down, that posterity would prefer his rivals—his true rivals, not the imaginary rivals he had invented for himself and over whom he was sure to triumph? That is, not the Perronneaus, but the painters who, far from simply yielding to the imitation of nature, exaggerate, alter, and correct its forms—in a word, the painters who are veritable creators. For the man of taste actually prefers what Diderot calls a "flattering caricature [*caricature en beau*]" to a painting that is only a painting, a painting that "so resembles it is nauseating [*ressemblante jusqu'à la nausée*]." And posterity confirms this choice: it actually prefers the bad portraitist to the good, the one who, like a history painter, poetizes, embellishes, ennobles [*agrandit*] nature, supplements its deficiencies—who devotes himself to a creative mimesis, painting portraits in the same way that "the great ancient sculptors made busts," in the same way that Voltaire writes history: a monumental history that portrays men not as they are but as they should be,[13] that is to say, as they are worthy of remaining in human memory.

In his "Essays on Painting," Diderot distinguishes the history painter from the genre painter as two hierarchically opposed types. Only the history painter deserves first place: first, because his task is much more difficult: "The genre painter has his scene continually before his eyes; the history painter has never seen or has only seen his for an instant." What is more, and most important, the genre painter is reduced to a servile condition,[14] whereas the history painter is a free man, a veritable creator: "The one is an imitator pure and simple, the copyist of ordinary nature; the other is the creator, so to speak, of a nature that is ideal and poetic. He walks a line that is difficult to maintain. On the one hand, he risks falling into something trite; on the other, into something overdone." Once again, like Nietzsche, Diderot performs a true genealogical reading of these two types of painting, of these two radically opposed types of mimesis. Genre painting, slave painting, which is purely technical, like La Tour's, is also painting for old men—for men too old to express life, too old to repeat it, not through a slavish mimicry, but in its ingenious power of invention: "This painting that is called genre painting should be for old men, or for those who were born old. It requires nothing but study and patience. No verve, little genius, hardly any poetry, lots of technique and truth, and that is all. . . . Because one begins to look for truth, for philosophy, at that age when one's temples turn grey" (*OE*, 486). It is between these two types of painting, which share nothing but their name, that the mimetic rivalry gets played out—as between two enemy brothers, two doubles who bear one another a reciprocal and more or less avowed fatal grudge. The creative painter looks down on the pure mimetician as a "pitiful copyist" "without genius," a lowly artisan, a "nothing." The pure mimetician, for his part, denigrates the creator in the name of a desire for truth at any price: the creative painter is, in his eyes, a romantic, a dreamer, a madman. Lacking genius, the mimetician covers over his creative weakness with the moral imperative of truth, which governs so-called "realist" painting:

> Genre painters and history painters never openly avow the contempt they feel for one another, but it can be detected. The latter see the former as

narrow-minded men without ideas, poetry, grandeur, elevation, genius, who go slavishly trailing after nature, not daring to let it out of their sight for a moment. They see them as pitiful copyists, whom they readily compare to the Gobelins artisan who picks out strands of yarn, one at a time, in order to reproduce the exact shade of the painting by the sublime man that hangs behind him. To hear history painters talk, one would think that genre painters were people concerned with trite, little subjects, with little domestic scenes taken from the street corner, who can be credited with nothing beyond the mechanics of the trade, and who are themselves nothing unless they have taken this one merit to the extreme. The genre painter, for his part, sees history painting as a romantic genre, in which there is neither resemblance nor truth, in which everything is overdone, which has nothing in common with nature, and in which falsehood can be discerned in its exaggerated figures that never existed anywhere; in the incidents, all of which are imaginary; in the entire subject matter that the artist has never seen outside his empty head; in the details that he has taken from who knows where; in this so-called great and sublime style that has no model in nature; and in the actions and movements of its figures, which are so far from any real actions or movements. You will certainly understand, my friend, that this is the quarrel of prose and poetry, history and epic poetry, heroic tragedy and bourgeois tragedy, bourgeois tragedy and gay comedy. (*OE*, 724–25)[15]

Each double proclaims its own superiority. As for Diderot, he does not exactly adopt either of these two points of view, whose radical opposition is the product of polemic and rivalry alone. For here again, like Nietzsche, Diderot shows that there can never be "realistic" or naturalistic art in the strict sense of the word. For even the pure imitator, if he is truly an artist, is always a bit of a poet, always puts on a bit of a show. The opposition between the two rival genres is, in the final analysis, only that between two literary genres, one slavish, the other noble: the opposition between prose and poetry, history and epic poetry, heroic tragedy and bourgeois tragedy, bourgeois tragedy and gay comedy. Even if he does not admit it, a good portraitist like La Tour, the pure technician—because he is not truly a machine—is also an inventor, an artist, even if only a minor one, a mere actor rehearsing the roles handed out by that great director, Nature or God.

The pictorial stage, no more than the theatrical one, is not the world stage. It always represents something other than what is given; it obeys a set of conventions or principles, an entire protocol—"a three-thousand-year-old protocol," says the *Paradox*. "Nothing takes place on the stage the way it does in nature," and the portrait that is the most lifelike always implies a necessary supplementarity. It is no accident that among the literary genres he cites to designate the necessary supplementarity of painting, Diderot privileges the theatrical model, the model of tragedy or comedy: it is because, since Plato, theatrical mime and its supplementing function has always exemplified mimesis.[16] There can be no theater without a set of conventions, a set of rules that govern good taste and exclude everything that might offend or nauseate the public. To want to transport the world stage onto the theatrical stage is to believe, mistakenly, that a gathering in the street constitutes, in and of itself, a marvelous and harmonious spectacle: it is to believe, mistakenly, that the "magic" of art is useless, even corrupting, and to think that brute nature and a chance arrangement are in themselves enough. It is to forget, precisely, that art is needed to embellish nature, that a woman is only beautiful because she resembles a virgin by Raphael, and that without art's artifices and conventions, all one would get is a "strange cacophony." It is to forget that there is a specificity to art, that it has its own time and its own duration. ("You speak to me about a real thing and I am speaking to you about an imitation. You speak to me about a fleeting moment of nature, and I am speaking to you about a projected, sustained work of art that has its own progress and duration.") In short, it is to confuse a horde of savages with an assembly of civilized men. Thus, in the theater, truth never consists of imitating things as they are in nature, for that would be like modeling public taste on vulgar—that is to say, bad—taste, rather than bending it to an ideal model invented by the great artist, who does not slavishly copy nature precisely because nature is always overdone, ugly, discordant, and twisted. The spectator with delicate taste rejects these natural, much too natural flaws, the truth laid bare, the plot unadorned:

> We want man, in the most extreme of moments, to retain his human character, the dignity of his species. . . . We want this woman to lose her virtue with decency, gently, and this hero to die like an ancient gladiator . . . with grace, with nobility, in an elegant and picturesque pose. . . . The ancient gladiator, like the great actor—the great actor, like the ancient gladiator—does not die in bed, as we do, but is obliged to act out another death for our pleasure. (*OE*, 317–18)

In painting, there can never be, any more than there can be in the theater, an absence of conventions, rules, poetry. It is in the name of the very nature of art as such—of the necessary magic of all art—that Diderot reconciles, as it were, the two rival genres and puts an end to the polemic:

> I believe that genre painting faces all the same difficulties as history painting, that it calls for just as much spirit, imagination, even poetry; that it calls for an equal knowledge of drawing, perspective, color, shadows, light, characters, passions, expressions, drapery, composition; that it calls for a stricter imitation of nature, and more meticulous details; and that, by showing us better known and more familiar things, it has more and better judges.... What does this mean, if not that history painting calls for greater elevation, for perhaps more imagination, for another, stranger poetry? That genre painting calls for more truth? And that the latter, even when limited to a vase and a basket of flowers, would not be practiced without all of the resources of art and some spark of genius, if those whose apartments it decorated had as much taste as they do money? (*OE*, 726–27)

Between the two types of painting there would therefore be a difference not in kind but of degree. In every case, it would simply be a matter of a little more or a little less poetry, even if this poetry was stranger, more fantastic in one case and concealed behind a more prosaic appearance in the other.

The radical opposition between the two genres of art, their division into two groups that are antithetical in nature, as genealogically distinct as the noble and the slavish, as a creative and a reproductive mimesis, comes, on the one hand, from the rivalry that exists between the two types of painter and, on the other, from the buyers' bad taste, from bourgeois, vulgar taste, which insists on truth at any price and is ready to pay any price provided that the art be lifelike, and which wants, like birds and apes, to consume still lifes. The opposition comes from the buyers' desire to impose their eyes, their bad eyes, their indecent frog perspective that flattens everything out—in a word, their antiartistic perspective—on the artists themselves.

There will never be lasting art—and, by definition, there can be no art without this duration that is its own time, as opposed to the fleeting instant of life—without a minimal distance between the imitation and the imitated. The "poetic" minimum of all art stems precisely from the fact that art introduces duration and fixity where there is nothing but a fleeting and evanescent life—to the great despair of the good portraitist. What finally drives the rigorous imitator of nature mad is that he is unable to render the vicissitude of flesh, the ephemeral and fleeting character of all things, the absence of identity of the model that continually changes before his eyes and tortures him:

> What ends up driving the great colorist mad is the vicissitude of this flesh; that it comes to life and fades from one instant to the next; that, while the artist's eye is on the canvas, his brush engaged in rendering me, I disappear; and that when he turns to look at me again, he can no longer find me. The Abbé Le Blanc comes to mind, and I yawn with boredom. The Abbé Trublet appears, and I take on an ironic expression. My friend Grimm or Sophie appear to me, and my heart skips a beat; a tenderness and serenity spread across my face; the pores of my skin begin to exude happiness, my heart rejoices, my little reservoirs of blood tremble, and the imperceptible tint of the fluid that escapes them spills rosiness and life from all sides. Fruits and flowers change under La Tour's or Bachelier's attentive gaze. What torture a man's face must be for them, that restless canvas that moves, stretches, slackens, blushes, dulls according to the multitudinous alternations of the light and invisible breath we call the soul. (*OE*, 680)

If the painter does not want to go mad, he must take only "enduring beauties" as models; that is, he must invent an ideal, conventional model of beauty, whose essential merit is precisely permanence, for "if one depicted beings in their rapid vicissitude, every painting would represent only a fleeting instant, and every imitation would be superfluous" (*OE*, 160).

The Tribunal of History

This is why a portrait that "truly" resembles will never last. The portrait done by the dauber on the bridge of Notre-Dame, who makes a better likeness than an academician, "dies with the person; the portrait by the man of skill lasts forever" (*OE*, 507). Without knowing the technical rules, without introducing a minimum of distance or convention between imitator and imitated, a minimum of poetry, the dauber strictly obeys the rule of imitation, painting only an "unflattering caricature [*caricature en laid*]" (Ibid.), the analogue of the cacophony produced by the simple transposition of a street scene onto the stage. Unflattering caricature and cacophony both err on the side of "wildness," through their lack of unity, their failure to subordinate the detail to the whole, to the perspective of the whole,[17] through their "naiveté."[18] The uncultivated dauber is the savage of painting. He makes "wild paintings" in the sense in which one speaks of a "wild" analysis. He disregards all technical rules—he is subject only to the rule of rigorous imitation. The dauber is nonetheless not a good portraitist, for the absence of any poetry does not amount to truth, nor to beauty, but to an unflattering caricature. To him Diderot opposes, as his symmetrical, inverted counterpart, not the good portraitist (La Tour, for example), but another type of bad portraitist, who errs through excess not of fidelity but of infidelity: the academician, who is closer to the history painter than he is to the good, learned, skilled portraitist. Free from the subjection to nature that characterizes the ignorant dauber, he is, however, not as free as one might think, for a set of conventional rules guide his brush and chain his eye to his art. His work results from a mixture of what he has learned at the École, what he has seen and admired, and what he presently sees with an eye that has always already lost its innocence and virginity, that is always already chained, seeing only through a strange camera obscura. All this cultural knowledge constitutes the painter's particular "manner," to which is added his particular technique—what Diderot calls "his way [*son faire*], his tic" (Ibid.)—and also his color, which is strictly dependent on his idiosyncrasy, his temperament, and the master he has imitated.[19] Manner, way, tic, color[20]—so many distinct elements separate the painter from nature and make it such that a portrait painted by an academician will never be a good portrait but merely a caricature, a flattering caricature that errs through excess of poetry, whereas the dauber's portrait, an unflattering caricature, errs through its lack of poetry. In contrast, however, to the ignorant man's work, the skillful man's work lasts forever. "It is according to the latter that our descendants will form their images of the great men who came before them." For the aim of art, as always for Diderot, is to transmit to posterity only what deserves to be transmitted. In his article "Encyclopedia," he says that it is the better part of ourselves that is snatched away from death, and that only those moments of our existence of which we are truly proud are rescued from the abyss: "Man shows himself to his contemporaries and sees himself as he is, a bizarre composite of sublime qualities and shameful weaknesses. But the weaknesses follow his mortal remains into the grave and disappear along with them; the same earth covers them. Nothing remains but the qualities immortalized in the monuments that he erects to himself or that he owes to public veneration and recognition."[21]

The tribunal of history chooses the "flattering caricature" done by the skillful man as an ideal of beauty that covers up and buries the shameful or disgusting deficiencies of nature. The criterion on which the judgment of the tribunal is based is not the truth of the work of art but its pharmaceutical power. Aesthetic pleasure is not a response to a rigorous equivalence between imitator and imitated; rather, it corresponds to the "anticipated jouissance" of man before the consciousness of his own worth, which is mentioned in the *Encyclopedia*—a "jouissance as pure, as strong, as real as any other jouissance."

The rules of taste to which the Académie painters are subject exist to prevent the disgust that certain natural objects might provoke from coming to interfere with this jouissance. Chardin's *Gutted Skate*—also gutted, it would seem, of all artifice, for "it is the fish's very flesh, its skin, its blood"—affects one as would "the very aspect of the thing," and "the object is disgusting." And yet it takes nothing less than all the magic of art to make it so that this "skate," gutted as it may be, produces not nausea but a true aesthetic pleasure—the specific pathos whose paradoxical character is emphasized by Aristotle (even if his solution to the paradox is not the same as Diderot's, given that he reduces this pleasure to the pleasure of cognition, and ultimately asserts the superiority of natural beauty over that of art).[22]

The Académie should therefore teach painters—if it can—what Chardin's genius and technique achieve magically: "the secret of redeeming, through talent, the disgusting qualities of certain natural objects" (*OE*, 484).[23] It is for this same reason that the Académie should ban the profound study of anatomy and of *écorchés*, which has, despite its benefits, "spoiled more artists than it has perfected" (*OE*, 815). "In painting, as in morals, it is dangerous to see beneath the skin" (*OE*, 815). Like Nietzsche once again, Diderot invites the artist to remain on the surface of things, on the outside, and denounces interior observation as indecent, perfidious, and perverse:

> Should we not be afraid that this *écorché* will remain perpetually in the imagination, and that the artist will persist in his vanity in wanting to show off his knowledge; that his corrupted eye will no longer be able to stop at the surface, that despite the skin and the fat, it will always be making out the muscle, its beginning, connection, and insertion; that it will make everything much too pronounced; that it will become hardened and cold; and that I will start to discover this wretched *écorché* even in the figures of women? Since it is only the outside that I have to show, I would much prefer to be taught to see it well, and to be spared a perfidious knowledge that I would have to forget. (*OE*, 668–69)[24]

It is true that this passage on the *écorché* occurs in the context of a critique of the Académie in the name of rigorous imitation: far from teaching the artist to look at nature, this kind of study teaches him to see it other than it is by putting between the artist's eye and his brush a series of "gloomy ghosts" that he rarely succeeds in exorcising. In this text, good taste consists, rather, of trying to get rid of academic models that make one forget the truth of nature and replace it with postures and figures that are posed, stiff, and ridiculous. "My God, save me from these models," cries "a young man with taste, before putting so much as a stroke on his canvas." But in this general critique, the argument against the study of *écorchés* has a very different significance. Diderot reproaches the study of *écorchés* not only for corrupting the eye by making it hallucinate ghosts but also for perverting it by making it look into the depth of things in an indecent, disgusting way. In this, the Académie transgresses its own rules about taste, which ought to encourage the artist to stay on "the surface" in order not so see "what is aesthetically offensive inside the man without skin."

Good taste therefore demands that we not try to see "everything," and the good eye is the aesthetic eye that knows how to keep to the surface. Good taste ultimately decides against the rule of the rigorous imitation of nature—even if this rule is recommended by the school and its pedants—in favor of a creative mimesis that poetizes, exaggerates, aggrandizes, and corrects and embellishes its forms. The pharmaceutical function of art justifies the man of taste against the pedant, for nothing can remain in men's memories but what is destined to last—that is, beauty.

In a very beautiful text,[25] Freud emphasizes the distress produced by the following thought: beauty—which is meant to camouflage the evanescent nature of all things—is itself ephemeral. What is at issue in this distress is a foretaste of the mourning that would be occasioned by the decline or loss of beauty:

> It is impossible that all this loveliness of Nature and Art, of the world of our sensations and of the world outside, will really fade away into nothing.... Somehow or other this loveliness must be able to persist and to escape all the powers of destruction. But this demand for immortality is a product of our wishes too unmistakable to lay claim to reality: what is painful may none the less be true.[26]

This refusal to mourn beauty, which reveals the intolerable nature of all ephemeral things, explains the sentence pronounced by the tribunal of history that rejects the portrait by the dauber and preserves the one by the man of skill.

"We have art so as not to die of truth." There is no art without poetry. And if certain natural forms must be more "poetized" than others—for example, this exceedingly disgusting skate—is this not because, in its very obscenity, the skate's flesh figures in an emblematic way the evanescence and the contingency of life? So much so as to be nauseating. Only the magic of Chardin's art makes the intolerable tolerable, transforms the skate into the *Gutted Skate*, a masterpiece that deserves to last for all eternity because it precisely camouflages the ephemeral and evanescent quality of all flesh by staging the obscene [*en mettant en scène l'obscène*].

And yet the tribunal does not openly declare that it was really a pharmaceutical criterion that determined its judgment, for posterity claims truly to know the great men of the past. It is in the name of truth and of resemblance that posterity admires historic portraits: it sees resemblance where there is none, where there is exaggeration, alteration, embellishment—a delusion made possible by the generalization of good taste that has transformed the eye of an entire people: "The eye of the people conforms to the eye of the great artist, and for it exaggeration leaves resemblance intact." "It sees the model where, strictly speaking, it is not, and it cries out in admiration." The people think they have found the resemblance they are looking for, not because art has in fact imitated nature rigorously but because art has succeeded in changing its own essence [*sa propre nature*]. The eye of the people is not the wild and naive eye of the dauber. It is falsely naive, unwittingly cultured, and does not see all these things that knowledge has introduced into the painting. The skilled academician succeeds in imposing his perspective on an entire nation because this perspective is complicit with the ideology of an entire society that wants to impose a certain image of its great men, a pretty picture that immortalizes them and that could serve as the model—the ego ideal?—for future generations. That is why Diderot rejects "immoral subjects," even if he knows that "the man who suppresses a dirty book or destroys a voluptuous statue is like the fool who is scared to go in the river for fear that a man may drown there." An immoral painting is necessarily destined to disappear, for one can be sure that there will always be some father who will want to remove such a painting from his daughter's sight. It does not deserve to last, to be taken as a model.

> Artists, if you are eager to see your works endure, I advise you to stick to honest subjects. Everything that preaches depravity to men is fit to be destroyed, and all the more surely to be destroyed the more perfect the work. . . . Who among us would dare to blame the honest and barbaric hand that will have committed this kind of sacrilege? Not I, who am nonetheless not unaware of the objection that can be made to it: namely, how small is the influence that the productions of fine art have on public morals. (*OE*, 471–72)

If the true criterion of posterity's judgment is not therefore resemblance or truth but its dissimulation, what sentence will the tribunal pass in the end on La Tour, on one who is neither the dauber eliminated by history nor the academician whose longevity is assured? What place will this diabolical technician [*machiniste*] occupy at Bertin's table if it is true that, in the final analysis, posterity prefers a creative, "poetizing" mimesis to a reproductive one? If it prefers God to the devil, lies to truth? Diderot does not decide, but the whole of the "Salon of 1767" implies it: he will never be in first any more than in last place, given that the rigorous opposition between the two types of mimesis is purely fictitious.

TRANSLATED BY JENNIFER BAJOREK

§ 10 Conjuring Death: Remarks on *The Anatomy Lesson of Doctor Nicolas Tulp* (1632)

It is a lesson.

A professor—recognizable right away, as he is the only one wearing a hat (this is Doctor Nicolas Tulp, Amsterdam's top surgeon, a world-renowned man of learning who presides each year over the ceremony of a public lesson before his confreres)—is situated at the far right of a group of seven doctors, his audience, arranged in a pyramid. At the base of the pyramid, and in contrast with this group, there is stretched out horizontally a cadaver. Standing just behind it, the professor (though his mouth is closed, as indicated by the gesture of his left hand) is about to describe and explain what had until then eluded their gazes but is now beginning to be made visible by the dissection he is performing on one of the hands and forearms: by the opening he is making—for that is what the word *anatomy* means[1]—in the body, thereby bringing into the open what the skin had covered and concealed, and what would have best been not seen, so that its discovery seems to be the betrayal of a frightening secret.[2]

The gazes of the seven doctors, each depicted with his own unique personality by Rembrandt—who, in accordance with their request and an entire tradition,[3] has painted a veritable portrait of each—diverge: they are not all looking in the same direction, though they are all inhabited by a common inner concentration, a particular quality of attention, which is tense less out of fright than out of an intense curiosity animated by the singular desire to learn and to know. It is through this common "scientific" gaze that these men belonging to the same corporation or practicing body *form one body* [*font corps*]: they are held together there, standing, staring down into some inaccessible depth, "holding eyes" in the way that others hold hands in a circle. Theirs are luminous eyes, turned toward the light of truth.

Except for the hands of the professor and those of the person who seems to be taking notes (along with those of the individual situated near the top, the most distracted of them all, who lets one of his hands show outside his cloak), just about all that is visible of these persons' bodies is the head. Encircled by a white ruff,[4] put into relief by it, the head stands out, detached, and rises above the rest of the body, which is covered up by dark clothing.

And with this dissimulation of the body, its fragility, its mortality, comes to be forgotten, even though it is exhibited in full light by the pale cadaver that is right there, purely and simply lying there, naked (only the sex is modestly veiled), in the most absolute anonymity. Those around him seem to be unmoved by any feelings for him, for someone who, just a short time ago, was still full of life, had a name,[5] was a man just like them. Their gazes display neither pity, nor terror, nor fright. They do not seem to identify with the cadaver stretched out there. They do not see in it the image of what they themselves will one day be, of what, unbeknownst to themselves, they are in the process of becoming. They are not fascinated by the cadaver, which they do not seem to see as such, and their solemnity is not the sort that can be awakened by the mystery of death.

They have before them not a subject but an object, a purely technical instrument that one of them manipulates in order to get a hold on the truth of life. The dead man and the opening of his body are seen only insofar as they provide an opening onto life, whose secret they would hold. The fascination is displaced, and with this displacement, the anxiety is repressed, the intolerable made tolerable, from the sight of the cadaver to that of the book wide open at the foot of the deceased, who might now serve as a lectern.

This opening of the book in all its light points back to the opening of the body. For the book alone allows the body to be deciphered and invites the passage from the exterior to the interior. It is this book (and the opening it provides onto the science of life and its mastery) that attracts the gazes, much more even than does the point of the scissors that has begun to peel away the skin from the body stretched out there.

The book of this *Lesson*, which, on its own, balances out the rest of the painting, communicates with the many other books found in Rembrandt's paintings: for example, with that held open by Jan Six (in *Jan Six Standing at the Window* [1647]), who is depicted leaning against the opening of a window, his back turned to it, thereby suggesting that only the book provides a true opening onto the world and access to knowledge. It can also be compared with the one found in the *Minerva* at the Hague Museum; there, too, the book is open and luminous, supported by a closed book (the equivalent of the feet of the cadaver), while a draping droops downward, symbolizing the dispelling of darkness through knowledge.

The doctors of *The Anatomy Lesson* are gazing down at the book of science with the same attentive fervor as that found in other paintings in which the evangelists are poring over the sacred books from which they draw the confirmation of their message (see, for example, Jordaens's *The Four Evangelists*, mentioned by Claudel[6]).

In *The Anatomy Lesson*, the book of science takes the place of the Bible; for one truth, another has been substituted,[7] a truth that is no longer simply confined to books, since it finds its experimental confirmation in the opening of a cadaver. The cadaver of Christ (for example, the one by Mantegna in the Brera Art Gallery in Milan, alluded to by the second *Anatomy Lesson*, that of Amsterdam) has been replaced by that of a man recently hanged, a purely passive object, manipulated, displaying no emotion, signaling no Resurrection, Redemption, or nobility. The cut into the flayed body thus also cuts into the religious illusion of a glorious body.

The lesson of this *Anatomy Lesson* is thus not that of a *memento mori*; it is not that of a triumph of death but of a triumph over death; and this is due not to the life of an illusion, but to that of the speculative, whose function, too, is one of occultation.

What is most astonishing about this *Lesson* is that with the help of a cadaver that is fully exposed but that no gaze sees as such, the cadaveresque that each living being, already from the origin, carries within itself comes to be hidden. If the spectator of *The Anatomy Lesson* does not shudder in anxiety at the sight of this painting and can even admire it in complete serenity, it is because he is dealing with an image, a representation with a pharmaceutical function. At the very moment when an opening toward the inside and the depths of the invisible is offered to the gaze, the painting as such remains sheer exteriority, a visible, colored, and luminous surface: Apollonian.

Just as Raphael's painting of Saint Cecilia breaking human musical instruments, spurning them for the sake of celestial music, does not allow the spectator of the painting to hear the divine music, so Rembrandt does not show everything. He is attempting to show what painting has always wished to mask and to reveal what must not be shown according to the laws of an aesthetics of good taste, Diderot being here a prime example. (Diderot recommends that the Académie teach painters "the secret of using their talent to redeem the distastefulness present in certain natural objects,"[8] and he asks it to ban the in-depth study of anatomy and flayed figures,[9] and to remain on the surface of things, on the outside, denouncing any views of the inside of the body as indecent, perverse, and treacherous.[10]) But Rembrandt does not, in truth, exhibit the entrails.

The same is true of the second *Lesson*, in which the cadaver nevertheless occupies a central place and is shown eviscerated, the operating physician having detached with a cut of the scissors the dome of the scalp in order to observe the cortical convolutions of a brain soaked in blood (something that is more difficult to bear with a neutral scientific gaze). The seduction offered by the colored envelope of the painting makes tolerable the sight of the flesh. Rembrandt's painting does not reveal the secrets of the living any more than those of its own creation. It does not admit that it, too, has entrails.[11]

I would thus oppose to this first *Anatomy Lesson* by Rembrandt not, as is normally done, the second one, but rather a painting by Goya, either the *Witches' Sabbath* or the *Pilgrimage of Saint Isidore*. In those disquieting gatherings, everyone forms a single body through a certain quality of their gazes, oriented this time, however, not by an extreme interest in science but by a common horror and terror. Their eyes are turned not toward some present object, like the cadaver in Rembrandt's painting, but toward something absent, threatening, and unnameable.

The luminosity of Rembrandt's gazes, which express the luminosity of intelligence and science, has given way to the obscurity of the night and the expression of anxiety. The fascination of the gazes points this time to something absent that imposes itself and can be related to fascination as it is defined by Blanchot in *The Space of Literature*:

> What happens when what you see, although at a distance, seems to touch you with a gripping contact . . . when seeing is *contact* at a distance? What happens when what is seen imposes itself upon the gaze, as if the gaze were seized,

put in touch with the appearance? . . . What is given us by this contact at a distance is the image, and fascination is passion for the image. . . . Fascination is solitude's gaze. It is the gaze of the incessant and interminable. In it blindness is vision still, vision which is no longer the possibility of seeing, but the impossibility of not seeing, the impossibility which becomes visible and perseveres—always and always—in a vision that never comes to an end. . . . Whoever is fascinated . . . doesn't perceive any real object, any real figure, for what he sees does not belong to the world of reality, but to the indeterminate milieu of fascination. . . . This milieu of fascination, where what one sees seizes sight and renders it interminable, where the gaze coagulates into light . . . light which is also the abyss, a light one sinks into, both terrifying and tantalizing. . . .

Whoever is fascinated doesn't see, properly speaking, what he sees. Rather, it touches him in an immediate proximity; it seizes and ceaselessly draws him close, even though it leaves him absolutely at a distance. Fascination is fundamentally linked to . . . the immense, faceless Someone. Fascination is the relation the gaze entertains—a relation which is itself neutral and impersonal—with sightless, shapeless depth, the absence one sees because it is blinding.[12]

TRANSLATED BY PASCALE-ANNE BRAULT

PART V

Judaism and Anti-Semitism / Autobiography

§ 11 *Shoah* (or Dis-grace)

> From the sovereignty of the monarch derives the right to pardon criminals; for it alone can realize this power of the spirit that makes what has happened un-happened (*das Geschehene ungeschehen zu machen*) and nullifies the crime by forgiving and forgetting it (*und im Vergeben und Vergessen das Verbrechen zu vernichten*).
>
> —Hegel, *Principles of the Philosophy of Right* §282[1]

    Shoah! this word full of tenderness,
        Now terrible,
        Compels us to silence:
Scha, still,
        one says in Yiddish,
Shh! shh! one says in French.
Shoah makes all voices stop speaking.
Open mouth screaming in anguish,
Shoah, brief as lightning,
Is this mute cry that no word
Could soothe,
that bears witness, while suffocating,
To the unnamable, to the ignoble immensity
Of this event without precedent, Auschwitz.
      This happened: *ist geschehen.*
      It *must* be said.
Because the "final solution," the *Vernichtung,*
is the diabolical will
Wanting what happened not to have happened
Das Geschehene ungeschehen zu machen
It is wanting to turn the Jewish people to nothing.
Without preserving anything. Without remainder. Without *Aufhebung.*
It is wanting to make the Jews' existence null, to make them
      un-happened,
To gather up the Jews, one by one, to nullify them
      Up to the last one.
It is wanting to erase, as fast

>   As a gas jet
> As though by magic (the very height of technology)
> This stain, the dirty Jew, this nothing.
> As fast as a "*Fiat Lux!*"
> Inverted in a sinister way.
> Dis-grace that the Nazis
> Believing themselves gods
> In their insane will to power
> Thought they had the power to grant:
> Extermination of the Jews, elimination without trace
> Of these dregs, these lice
> An end preceded (for reasons of efficaciousness and to avoid any panic)
> By a scandalous deceit, by a vile masquerade.
> We will not pardon [*faire grace*] the Nazis for this crime,
>   Render it null, make it un-happened,
>   Nullify it in forgiveness and forgetting.
> We will not listen to Faurisson:[2]
> He does not *deny* the existence of the gas chambers—
> He repeats, accomplishes the Nazi deed.
> He negates the event, turns it into nothing,
> Nullifies the crime, pardons [*grâcie*] Hitler:
> *Das Geschehene ungeschehen ist!*
> So that those who died at Auschwitz
>   May not be the last of the Jews
>   that their memory may not be murdered
>   Let us not forget this Event!

Translated by Georgia Albert

§ 12   Autobiographical Writings

Damned Food

Damned food! And twice damned.

"You must eat," said my mother. And she stuffed and stuffed and stuffed us. Not a chance of being deprived of dessert with her.

"You must not eat everything," said my father. Not mix milk and meat; not eat just any meat; not eat off just any dish; not mix plates and silverware, *milchig* and *fleischig*; purify them once a year at Passover, in case of a mistake made misguidedly.

My mother, the high priestess, officiated in the kitchen, where it was not uncommon to see a cut of salted beef dripping blood for hours or a carp wriggling in a deep pan while my father, a ritual slaughterer, killed chickens in the toilet according to the law.

Was it fear of transgressing some taboo, or the consequence of being stuffed, the fact that I had hardly any appetite and resisted with all my might the maternal categorical imperative? To accomplish her ends, my mother would follow me to school with her bowl of *café au lait*, taking the teacher as witness of my crime: "She didn't eat this morning!!!"

During the war, things became complicated. How to find anything to eat? How to continue eating kosher?

During the exodus, in the train that took us to Brittany, the Red Cross distributed cocoa and ham and butter sandwiches. "Don't eat that," said my mother. "Let the children eat," my father intervened, "it's wartime." The ham and butter, once decreed impure, I found delicious, now purified by circumstances and parental authority.

247

A few years later my father was deported.

We could no longer find anything to eat.

Being hidden, we didn't even have food ration cards or the means to get a few grams of the bran-filled bread that could trigger an attack of scabies, or any ersatz chocolate, sugar, or coffee. For fear that I might be "picked up," I no longer went to school and didn't even have the right to those curd cakes, or those pink vitamin candies, or the skimmed milk given out by the teachers.

After countless turns of fortune, I was "saved" just in time by a woman who kept me in her home in the middle of Paris until the end of the war.

At the same time that she taught me what it was "to have a Jewish nose," she put me on a totally different diet: the food of my childhood was decreed bad for my health, held responsible for my "lymphatic state." Very rare red meat (raw horsemeat in bouillon) was supposed to "restore my health." From then on, it was my daily ration (until the day when we really no longer had anything to eat and had to go begging at the soup kitchen for a mess tin of macaroni or beans).

Put in a real double bind, I could no longer swallow anything and vomited after each meal.

TRANSLATED BY FRANCES BARTKOWSKI

Tomb for a Proper Name

Dream: on the cover of a book, "I" read:
KAFKA
translated by
Sar . . . Ko(a)f . . .

Why had "I" become translator of Kafka? Why had "I" thus changed my names? Coupling the letter *a* with the letter *o*, "I" was suggesting an affinity between my name and Kafka's: what secret kinship could unite me with him whose name I quickly associated with *The Trial*, with guilt, and . . . with caca? The dream inserted an *a* in parentheses: wasn't that in order to disclose a guilt-inducing tie between my name and anality, dissimulated by its usual spelling? Didn't the dream, far from producing a whimsical translation, reestablish what is held to be the correct way of writing my *proper* name?

(The error of a city hall employee, which always delighted me, had distinguished *Kofman* from *Kaufman*, more common; and from *Kaufmann*, which can't help but suggest commerce, money, shit [caca], the Jew.)

Kof makes me think of *Ko(p)f*, the head: the "incorrect" spelling dissimulates what is low and dirty; it allows me to bear a quite proper name, my head held high. But why were the last syllables cut off?

- *ah*, in Hebrew, designates the feminine.
- *Man*, *Mann* designates the masculine.

Isn't the cutting "elision" the equivalent of a double castration, punishment for the one who meant to deny her blood, to erase her lowly origins, to hold her head high?

Sar . . . Kof . . . Sarkof?

Both sexes wounded, cat-rat [*chat-rat*],[1] I devour my own flesh: sarcophagus.

Sar . . . Ko(a)f . . .

TRANSLATED BY FRANCES BARTKOWSKI

Post-scriptum—1992 [to "Tomb for a Proper Name"]

A short time after I wrote this text ["Tomb for a Proper Name"], a friend informed me that he had consulted the computer in the Museum of the Jewish Diaspora in Jerusalem about the meaning of my last name. To my great surprise and satisfaction, here is the computer's response: if your name is spelled KAUFMANN and you are not Jewish, your name means merchant. If you are Jewish, KAUFMANN is a name that was borrowed to hide your Jewish origins because of the persecutions. The correct spelling is KOFMAN, which derives from the biblical name YACKOV (Jacob). Originally, the name was YAKOVMAN, but over the course of time, through usage and wear, it turned into KOFMAN.

If one believes the computer in Jerusalem, then, the mistake made by the city hall clerk had in fact reestablished the real origin of my name: an origin that, by making me the descendant of the patriarch Jacob, finally gave me the right to walk with my head held high.

TRANSLATED BY GEORGIA ALBERT

"My Life" and Psychoanalysis

To Jean-Luc

I always wanted to tell the story of my life. The entire beginning of my analysis was me telling a story. A linear, continuous story. I never lost the thread; I "strung things together," always knowing ahead of time what I was going to say: never the slightest break, the slightest gap, never the slightest flaw where a slip of the tongue might have a chance to sneak in, where something might happen. And thus nothing happened. From the other side of the couch, nothing. "My life" was met with indifference.

Everything "started" when I had nothing more to say, when I no longer knew where to start or how to end. At that moment, what I had recounted before came back, but in a way that was entirely other, in a discontinuous way, in different forms (memories, dreams, slips, repetitions), or it never came back. I understood that I had tried, by telling the story of "my life," not to recount it—it is too much for words—but to master it. I had been at once foolish and unfaithful.

My mouth then stopped being the place from which flowed a reassuring discourse—*bocca della verità*—and became a cave from which more or less articulate and intelligible words burst forth, cries whose extremely variable tone (booming, evanescent, barely audible, halting, melodious, etc.) surprised even me. I had never heard myself speak like this, and "I" did not recognize "myself." Generous mouth, spilling its offerings of semen. Closed mouth, mouth sewed shut, pursed, sealed. Constipated. What my discourse had undoubtedly also wanted to dissimulate is that the mouth, at different moments of the analysis, can mimic the other erogenous zones of the body: that it can consecutively or simultaneously be mouth, sexual organ, anus. And not simply in an analogical manner: I knew that if, for instance, on a given day I was constipated, I would not be able to "talk" on the couch either, that "it" would not produce anything, that nothing would pass.

What passes through my mouth in analysis, then, has nothing to do with truth or meaning. It comes up from my guts to be offered like a gift: it is up to the other to appreciate it. Thus, the analyst's silence is intolerable. It is the sign not of an indifference to the events of my life, but of a depreciation of my most intimate possession. A blunt refusal of my gifts, of what comes out of my stomach, of what I produce: my merchandise, then, is shit! So it is just as well not to give anything, not to say anything; silence, at least, is golden. But this silence, too, is intolerable to me. Hence the imperious need to hear my words taken up and *taken*. Not in order that they be given meaning, interpreted. But to establish an exchange that might transform "caca" into gold. That might allow me to get up, to remain standing, and to leave. (January 1976. Fragment of analysis)

TRANSLATED BY GEORGIA ALBERT

Nightmare: At the Margins of Medieval Studies

For Bernard

"By their frequency and by their character of emotional sign, a number of incantatory expressions are arrayed in the modern reader's memory, engraving this strange adverb from another age. The 'tant *mar*, i fustes ber' ['unlucky Lord, indeed'] before the battered hero, the '*mar* fui née' ['woe is me'] of the heroine in tears; that is about all that is left of Old French after it has been forgotten."[2]

I will be speaking here of this strange, *unheimlich* remnant of another age: *mar*. A relic neglected by traditional medieval studies, *mar*ginalized, considered unclassifiable, intractable. At best, with a reductive gesture common to grammatical description, it is placed in a well-known genre, that of negation, among the negative maledictions, imprecations, and interjections of all sorts available to Old French. It is placed in an unfixed class, constructed through proximity, a class that is marginal with respect to grammar, and this only after etymological research.

The work of Bernard Cerquiglini is meant to show that the "unmanageable" can be managed, the "unclassifiable" can be classified, all the while retaining its irreducible specificity. He points out the tie between the adverb *mar* and discourse, regulated discourse at that—a connection that had not been made previously. Abandoning the notion of etymological explanation (according to traditional philological practice, a branch of genealogical and patriarchal thought), which at its origin had turned away from syntax and substituted a systematic and structural philology, B. Cerquiglini demonstrates that the lexeme *mar*, that "segment of a vanished language," is a constitutive element of medieval discourse, that it plays a role from which we can construe some of the major precepts, and that it heeds a number of strict and complex constraints. In short, "syntax is where we least expected it." The adverb *mar* reveals itself as an extremely coded sign of a discourse, an exemplar of the multiplicity of codes that govern, in a sometimes contradictory fashion, medieval language. Indeed, the analysis of the "*mar* phenomenon" serves as a paradigm to demonstrate, more generally, the constrained mechanism of early thirteenth-century prose, the rigor of the prose form.

Where B. Cerquiglini takes the greatest pleasure, and what motivates his entire procedure, is the exposition of the mechanics of a lost language which he brings to life before our eyes—a language dead and voiceless only for those who do not know how to take it literally. "A syntax thought to be inert, rises up alive, from the heart of alterity, not animated by our feelings but by the respect, and by the meticulous examination of that which founds its difference. The rare pleasure of discovering an old forgotten tool box, filled with words, and seeing how happily it all works" (*La parole médiévale*, 249).

A fantastic pleasure, a diabolical pleasure of bringing to life what is dead? What if this whole syntactic attempt at scientific classification and rigorous filing had as its aim the triumph over death? The mastery of death and all that might evoke its specter?

A worrisome and strange specter of death that may be one with the struggle that haunts B. Cerquiglini: the specter of marginality.

The good fortune of the living to triumph over misfortune (*la mala hora*).

For it is no accident that the adverb *mar* is the case developed and analyzed. And not only because it is paradigmatic. In it there is a formula that figures the *medieval uttering of misfortune*. Whence "the terrible force of this adverb,"[3] which must be strangled, made manageable and bearable by reducing it to a part of a mechanical toy that is pleasurable to manipulate, that makes us study the variety of its possible and impossible positions, the necessary distribution inside the rule-bound and codified game that constitutes medieval discourse (a game whose structures we lovingly strain to discover, to expose its moving parts).

Medieval uttering of misfortune, familiar element of the literary language of the Middle Ages, *mar* "evokes the misfortune of an essentially dramatic fate; a word of hatred or anguish spoken quasi-ritually in certain texts."

In the epic text, it designates the intensity or excess of the scene. It is a sign of the epic code, "a sort of minimal signifying unity which can allude to the epic register in the midst of another literary code." In noncourtly lyric poetry, *mar* is the sign of anguish and weakness, of impossible or unrequited love. A masculine formula for love rejected, it is an especially important figure of the feminine lament.

"Woe is me" is a painful utterance that, at the heart of the literary code, becomes the word of the "woman" whose distress it translates.

Essentially, the speaker signifies with this medieval formula that a designated individual (placed in the position of subject) is in a "distressed situation." *Mar fui* is the regulated formulation of the expression of misfortune and one tied to a present situation.

Neither a linguist nor a medievalist, I would like just to underline the "profound" interest that "I" took in reading this book (which at first I read rather superficially) by reporting a dream here—an epic dream?—a dreadful night-*mare*.

The particle *mar*, that segment of a vanished language, induced the return of an entire buried past, belonging to an entirely other age, to my dark ages; it reappeared in a text ruled by a singular code, an entirely personal syntax and grammar.

> *I am in a room from my childhood, with my mother, my brothers and sisters, at night. A bird enters, a kind of bat with a human head, pronouncing in a loud voice: "Woe unto you! Woe unto you!"*
>
> *My mother and I, terrorized, run away. We are in tears in the Rue Marcadet; we know we are in great danger and fear death.*
>
> *I awaken very anxious.*

CONTEXT

I must take a plane on Tuesday [*mar*di]. An airplane strike forces me to delay my departure, to reserve a seat on a night flight. I am worried.

Night flight—night bird—bird of misfortune . . .

I associate this with a sinister event from my childhood. In February 1943—almost forty years ago—a Tuesday [*mar*di] perhaps, at 8 o'clock in the evening (the evil hour, *la mala hora*), a man from the *Kommandantur*—the bird of misfortune—comes to warn us, me and my mother (we are eating a vegetable soup in the kitchen), "to go hide as quickly as possible because we were on the list for that night": my mother and her six children (my father having already been "picked up" the 16th of July 1942). My mother and I fled in all haste (my brothers and sisters were hidden in the country). We lived in the Rue Ordener, and in order to get to the Rue Labat, where there was a woman who generously took us in on the nights of roundups, we took the long Rue Marcadet. During this forced nocturnal walk, clenched in anxiety, I vomited my dinner onto the Rue Marcadet.

For the rest of the war, we lived hidden in the Rue Labat, marginally. "Woe is me!" [*Com mar fui!*]

This hideous nightmare, I later understood, had as its purpose to reassure me in the face of the present anxiety: "You won't die this time any more than the last when you feared the worst." Only the spectacle of an old anxiety—despite the enormous affect of anxiety that accompanied it—could allow me to overcome the current anxiety. Only the union of two anxieties—in a unique category—allowed me to deal with the unmanageable.

As we always dream for the one to whom we want to tell the dream, Bernard, I dedicate this nightmare to you.

POST-SCRIPTUM

Three months after having this nightmare, I discover in reading *Lilith or The Dark Mother*[4] that one of the privileged representations, in Jewish folklore in particular, of Lilith, the first seductive and devouring Eve, is the bat. One of the avatars of Lilith is *Marewip*. *Mare*, found in night-*mare*, designates a nocturnal spirit. The Indo-European root of *mare* is *mer*, from which all sorts of words evocative of death derive, and, more precisely, of slow death by eating or suffocation—for example, undoubtedly the word *Maredewitch*.

The spirit of *Maredewitch*—that other avatar of Lilith—haunted my entire childhood. When I was bad, my mother locked me in a dark closet where "Maredewitchale" was supposed to come, if not to eat me, at least to take me far away from home: that was the threat. I imagined her to myself, not as a bat, but as a very old woman. My unconscious possessed an "unofficial knowledge" that knew much more than the "official knowledge."[5] The dream-work was able to condense in one image the two terrifying figures of my childhood: the man from the *Kommandantur*, the bird of misfortune; and the old sorceress *Maredewitch*.

TRANSLATED BY FRANCES BARTKOWSKI

Notes

Editor's Preface

1. Full bibliographical references to Kofman's original texts and, where applicable, their English translations are given in the actual chapters.
2. Besides *The Childhood of Art*, two of Kofman's books on Freud have been translated into English: *The Enigma of Woman: Woman in Freud's Writings*, trans. Catherine Porter (Ithaca: Cornell University Press, 1985) and *Freud and Fiction*, trans. Sarah Wykes (Boston: Northeastern University Press, 1991). For another text on Freud that has been translated, see " 'It's Only the First Step That Costs,' " trans. Wykes, in *Speculations After Freud: Psychoanalysis, Philosophy and Culture*, eds. Sonu Shamdasani and Michael Münchow (New York: Routledge, 1994), 97–131.
3. Only one of Kofman's books on Nietzsche has thus far been translated in its entirety into English: *Nietzsche and Metaphor*, trans. Duncan Large (Stanford: Stanford University Press, 1993). However, a considerable amount of the work on Nietzsche has been translated in the form of journal articles and book chapters. See "Nietzsche: The Painter's Chamber," in Kofman, *Camera Obscura: Of Ideology*, trans. Will Straw (Ithaca: Cornell University Press, 1998), 29–48; "Descartes Entrapped," trans. Kathryn Aschheim, in *Who Comes After the Subject?*, eds. Eduardo Cadava, Peter Connor, and Jean-Luc Nancy (New York: Routledge, 1991), 178–97; "Nietzsche and the Obscurity of Heraclitus," trans. Françoise Lionnet-McCumber, *Diacritics* 17 (1987): 39–55; "Nietzsche's Socrates: 'Who' Is Socrates?," trans. Madeleine Dobie, *Graduate Faculty Philosophy Journal* 15 (1991): 7–29; "Explosion I: Of Nietzsche's *Ecce Homo*," trans. Large, *Diacritics* 24 (1994): 51–70; "A Fantastical Genealogy: Nietzsche's Family Romance," trans. Deborah Jenson, in *Nietzsche and the Feminine*, ed. Peter J. Burgard (Charlottesville: University of Virginia Press, 1994), 35–52; "Wagner's Ascetic

Ideal According to Nietzsche," trans. David Blacker and Jessica George, rev. Alban Urbanas, Richard Schacht, and Judith Rowan, in *Nietzsche, Genealogy, Morality: Essays on Nietzsche's* Genealogy of Morals, ed. Schacht (Berkeley: University of California Press, 1994), 193–213; "The Psychologist of the Eternal Feminine (Why I Write Such Good Books, 5)," trans. Dobie, *Yale French Studies* 87 (1995): 173–89; and "Accessories" (*Ecce Homo*, 'Why I Write Such Good Books,' 'The Untimelies,' 3), trans. Large, in *Nietzsche: A Critical Reader*, ed. Peter R. Sedgwick (Oxford: Blackwell, 1995), 144–57.

4. For English translations of Kofman's writings on the figure of woman in psychoanalysis and philosophy, see also "The Narcissistic Woman: Freud and Girard," trans. Porter, in *Diacritics* 10 (1980): 36–45; "Baubô: Theological Perversion and Fetishism," trans. Tracy B. Strong, in *Nietzsche's New Seas: Explorations in Philosophy, Aesthetics, and Politics*, eds. Michael Allen Gillespie and Strong (Chicago: University of Chicago Press, 1988), 175–202; and "Rousseau's Phallocratic Ends," trans. Mara Dukats, in *Hypatia* 3 (1989): 123–36. The latter essay, like "The Economy of Respect," has been frequently anthologized.

5. Kofman's writings on visual art have thus far remained untranslated into English. On the topic of the portrait, see "The Imposture of Beauty: The Uncanniness of Oscar Wilde's *Picture of Dorian Gray*," trans. Large, in *Enigmas: Essays on Sarah Kofman*, eds. Penelope Deutscher and Kelly Oliver (Ithaca: Cornell University Press, 1999), 25–48.

6. On Judaism and the Holocaust, see Kofman's autobiographical text *Rue Ordener, Rue Labat*, trans. Ann Smock (Lincoln: University of Nebraska Press, 1996) and the autobiographically inflected *Smothered Words*, trans. Dobie (Chicago: Northwestern University Press, 1998). Readers interested in surveying the wide extent of Kofman's original-language publications and in locating existing English translations should consult "Sarah Kofman: A Complete Bibliography, 1963–1993," comp. Large (with the assistance of Sarah Kofman and Alexandre Kyritsos), in *Nietzsche and Metaphor*, 91–207. See also an updated version, "Sarah Kofman: Bibliography, 1963–1998," in *Enigmas*, 264–75.

Introduction

The French version of this text was published in *Les cahiers du Grif* 3 (1997): 131–65, in an issue devoted to Sarah Kofman. The translators wish to thank the members of a 1999 French reading group at DePaul University for their many judicious suggestions on an early draft: Christopher Boland, Benjamin Borgmeyer, Pleshette DeArmitt, Matthew Pacholec, Elizabeth Sikes, Samuel Talcott, and Peter Wake. Finally, we would like to thank DePaul University's College of Liberal Arts and Sciences for its support of this work.

1. Translators' Note: As Derrida will develop later, *là-bas* (over there) sounds like *Labat*, the name of the street in Paris where Sarah Kofman lived as a young girl.

2. "La mort conjurée: Remarques sur *La leçon d'anatomie du docteur Nicolas Tulp*, 1632 Mauritshuis, La Haye," in *La part de l'oeil* 11 (1995): 41–46. Editors' Note: An English translation appears as Chapter 10 of the present volume.

3. *Pourquoi rit-on? Freud et le mot d'esprit* (Paris: Galilée, 1986), hereafter abbreviated *PR*.

4. Maurice Blanchot, "The Two Versions of the Imaginary," in *The Space of Literature*, trans. Ann Smock (Lincoln: University of Nebraska Press, 1982), 254–63.

5. *Mélancolie de l'art* (Paris: Galilée, 1985), back cover.

6. Blanchot, "The Two Versions of the Imaginary," 255. The following quotations are from pages 256, 258, and 259, translations modified.

7. *The Childhood of Art: An Interpretation of Freud's Aesthetics*, trans. Winifred Woodhull (New York: Columbia University Press, 1988), hereafter abbreviated *CA*. Editors' Note: The first chapter of this book appears as Chapter 1 of the present volume.

8. *Smothered Words*, trans. Madeleine Dobie (Evanston, IL: Northwestern University Press, 1998).

9. *Rue Ordener, Rue Labat*, trans. Smock (Lincoln: University of Nebraska Press, 1996).

10. *The Childhood of Art*, 80. Translators' Note: In the quotations from Freud's writings, Kofman's translator gives references to *The Standard Edition of the Complete Psychological Works of Sigmund Freud*, eds. and trans. James Strachey et al., 24 vols. (London: Hogarth Press, 1953–74).

11. Kofman and Jean-Yves Masson, *Don Juan ou le refus de la dette* (Paris: Galilée, 1991), 104.

12. *Rue Ordener, Rue Labat*, 3, 9.

13. "Damned Food," trans. Frances Bartkowski, in *Substance* 49 (1986): 8. Editors' Note: This text is included in chapter 12 of the present volume.

14. Jacques Derrida, *Memoires for Paul de Man*, trans. Cecile Lindsay, Jonathan Culler, Eduardo Cadava, and Peggy Kamuf (New York: Columbia University Press, 1986), 150.

15. Emmanuel Levinas, *Totality and Infinity*, trans. Alphonso Lingis (Pittsburgh: Duquesne University Press, 1969), 283, 285.

16. *Genesis* 12:1, 15:13, in *The New Oxford Annotated Bible*, eds. Bruce M. Metzger and Roland E. Murphy (New York: Oxford University Press, 1991). For *Genesis* 12:1, the Dhormes translation reads, "Va-t-en de ton pays, de ta patrie et de la maison de ton père," or "Go away from your country, your homeland and your father's house"; and the Chouraqui translation reads, "Va pour toi, de ta terre, de ton enfantement, de la maison de ton père," or "Go away for yourself,

from your land, your birthplace, your father's house." For *Genesis* 15:13, Dhormes reads: "ceux de ta race seront des hôtes dans un pays qui n'est pas à eux," or "those of your race will be guests in a country that is not theirs"; and Chouraqui reads, "oui, ta semence résidera sur une terre non-leur," or "yes, your seed will reside on a land that is not theirs."

17. When told about the coming of Isaac (*yiskhak*: he laughs), Sarah laughs and then pretends not to have done so. But God becomes indignant that she might be doubting his omnipotence and contradicts her denial: "Oh yes, you did laugh." (*Genesis* 18:15). Later (21:3, 6), at Isaac's birth, "Abraham gave the name Isaac to his son whom Sarah bore him: *Is'hac*—he will laugh!" Sarah says, "God has brought laughter for me; everyone who hears will laugh with me." The Chouraqui translation reads, "Elohim m'a fait un rire! tout entendeur rira de moi!," or "Elohim made me a laugh! Everyone who hears will laugh at me"; the Dhormes translation reads, "Elohim m'a donné occasion de rire: quiconque l'apprendra rira à mon sujet," or "Elohim gave me an occasion to laugh: anyone who finds out will laugh at me."

18. *Genesis* 23:4. The Chouraqui translation is as follows: "Je suis moi-même un métèque, un habitant avec vous; / donnez-moi propriété de sépulcre avec vous / et j'ensevelirai ma morte en face de moi," meaning "I am myself a metic, an inhabitant with you; / give me a place for a burial site with you / and I will bury my dead one in front of me"; the Dhormes translation reads, "Je suis un hôte et résidant parmi vous. Donnez-moi la propriété d'un tombeau parmi vous, pour que je mette mon mort au tombeau hors de ma vue," which means "I am a guest and resident among you. Give me a place for a grave among you, so that I might put my dead in the grave, out of my sight."

19. *Genesis* 17:15, 17.

20. *Comment s'en sortir?* (Paris: Galilée, 1983). [Translators' Note: Parts of this book have been translated under the title "Beyond Aporia?" by David Macey, in *Post-Structuralist Classics*, ed. Andrew Benjamin (New York: Routledge, 1988), 7–44.] This text, a short treatise on the aporia, opens and closes with a quote from Blanchot's *Madness of the Day*, trans. George Quasha (Barrytown, NY: Station Hill Press, 1981): "Men want to escape death, strange beings that they are. And some of them cry out 'Die, die' because they want to escape from life. 'What a life. I'll kill myself. I'll give in.' This is lamentable and strange; it is a mistake. Yet I have met people who have never said to life, 'Quiet!', who have never said to death, 'Go away!' Almost always women, beautiful creatures" (7).

Chapter 1

"The Double Reading" is the introduction of *The Childhood of Art: An Interpretation of Freud's Aesthetics*, trans. Winifred Woodhull (New York: Columbia

University Press, 1988), 1–22. The original French text, "La double lecture," appears in *L'enfance de l'art: Une interprétation de l'esthétique freudienne* (Paris: Payot, 1970), 7–37.

1. See "The Claims of Psycho-Analysis to Scientific Interest," in *The Standard Edition of the Complete Works of Sigmund Freud*, eds. and trans. James Strachey et al., 24 vols. (London: Hogarth Press, 1953–74), 13:165–90, esp. section F, "The Interest of Psycho-Analysis from the Point of View of the Science of Aesthetics," 13:187–88. [Translator's Note: Volume and page numbers following quotations from and references to the works of Freud refer to this edition. Where necessary, I have modified the translation.]

2. See "On the History of the Psycho-Analytic Movement," 14:3–66, and "Resistances to Psycho-Analysis," 19:213–22, esp. 218.

3. Though I am not unacquainted with the copious literature on the subject I am attempting to treat in this book, I have decided, barring some exceptions, to use only Freud's texts, with the intention of making them known to the French public, which, because translations are lacking or inadequate, is unacquainted with most of his works.

4. Here Freud refers to Otto Rank and his work (*The Incest Motif in Poetry and Legend*).

5. See the beginning of the text "The Moses of Michelangelo," 13:211ff.

6. We know from Freud's correspondence that he preferred literature to the other arts and particularly appreciated it. From a letter to Fliess on August 18, 1897, we know that it was on the latter's suggestion that Freud went to Florence, where he took pleasure in visiting the museums, but found religious art dull, especially Christian art. In Milan, he liked only Leonardo da Vinci's *Last Supper*. From a letter of October 5, 1883, we can measure the extent of Freud's literary and philosophical knowledge. The two works that made the greatest impression on him at this time were *Don Quixote* and *The Temptation of Saint Anthony*. [Translator's Note: The Fliess letter appears in *The Origins of Psycho-Analysis*, eds. Marie Bonaparte, Anna Freud, and Ernst Kris (New York: Basic Books, 1977), 214–15. Passages of Freud's October 5 and July 26, 1883, correspondence with his wife concerning Dickens, *Don Quixote*, and *The Temptation of St. Anthony* are quoted by Ernest Jones in *The Life and Work of Sigmund Freud*, 3 vols. (New York: Basic Books, 1981), 1:174–75.] But Freud's literary tastes and knowledge are especially evident in the examples taken from the field of literature that adorn the entire body of his work. The authors that appear most often are Shakespeare, Goethe, Sophocles, Heine, Ibsen, Flaubert, Rabelais, Zola, Diderot, Boccaccio, Oscar Wilde, George Bernard Shaw, Dostoevsky, Molière, Swift, Homer, Horace, Tasso, Hoffmann, Schiller, Mark Twain, Aristophanes, Thomas Mann, Stefan Zweig, Hebbel, Galsworthy, Cervantes, Hesiod, Macaulay, and many others of lesser renown. His knowledge of tales, legends, and folklore is equally remarkable. In order to become

acquainted with Freud's tastes and the various criteria he uses to assess literary works, it is interesting to refer to his "Contribution to a Questionnaire on Reading" (9:245–47), in which he distinguishes between the most magnificent books (those of Homer and Sophocles, Goethe's *Faust*, Shakespeare's *Hamlet* and *Macbeth*), the most significant books (those of Copernicus, Johann Weier, and Darwin), and his favorite books (Milton's *Paradise Lost* and Heine's *Lazarus*).

Among the good books he cites are the following:
- Multatuli (who replaced the Μοῖρα, Fate, of the Greeks with Λόγος, reason, and ἀνάγλη, necessity, as does Freud himself), *Letters and Works*
- Rudyard Kipling, *The Jungle Book*
- Anatole France, *The White Stone*
- Emile Zola, *Fruitfulness*
- Dmitry Merezhkovsky, *Leonardo da Vinci*
- Gottfried Keller, *The People of Seldwyla*
- C. F. Meyer, *Huttens letzte Tage*
- Thomas Babington Macaulay, *Essays*
- Theodor Gomperz, *Greek Thinkers*
- Mark Twain, *Sketches*

He ends this questionnaire by saying that he wishes above all to be able to throw light on the relation between the author and his work.

7. See the last chapter of *Leonardo da Vinci and a Memory of His Childhood*, 11:59–137; "Dostoevsky and Parricide," 21:175–94; and "Address Delivered in the Goethe House at Frankfurt," 21:208–12.

8. See *Totem and Taboo*: "Anyone approaching the problem of taboo from the angle of psycho-analysis, that is to say, of the investigation of the unconscious portion of the individual mind, will recognize, after a moment's reflection, that these phenomena are far from unfamiliar to him" (13:26).

9. See also "On Psycho-Analysis," 12:207–11, esp. 210: "The psycho-analytic method of investigation can accordingly be applied equally to the explanation of normal psychical phenomena, and has made it possible to discover the close relationship between pathological psychical products and normal structures such as dreams, the small blunders of everyday life, and such valuable phenomena as jokes, myths and imaginative works." See also "Two Encyclopaedia Articles" ("Psycho-Analysis" and "The Libido Theory"), 18:235–59, in which Freud also indicates the link between the history of religions, culture, mythology, literature, and psychoanalysis, expressing surprise, since originally psychoanalysis had the sole aim of understanding neurotic symptoms. The bridge linking these phenomena to one another is dream analysis; it shows that the mechanisms that produce pathological symptoms are also at work in the normal man:

> Thus psycho-analysis became a *depth-psychology* and capable as such of being applied to the mental sciences, and it was able to answer a good number of questions with

which the academic psychology of consciousness was helpless to deal.... The significance of the Oedipus complex began to grow to gigantic proportions and it looked as though social order, morals, justice and religion had arisen together in the primaeval ages of mankind as reaction-formations against the Oedipus complex. (18:253)

10. I have analyzed this text in "The Double is/and the Devil," in *Freud and Fiction*, trans. Sarah Wykes (Boston: Northeastern University Press, 1991), 119–62.

11. See "On Psycho-Analysis," 12:207–11.

12. This does not mean that psychoanalysis is an art rather than a science, as it has been reproached for being.

13. Translator's Note: Here, Kofman is using the term "writing" (*écriture*) in the strong sense it has acquired in recent critical theory, especially in France. As Leon S. Roudiez says in his introduction to Julia Kristeva's *Desire in Language*, trans. Thomas Gora, Alice Jardine, and Roudiez (New York: Columbia University Press, 1980), "*Ecriture* is what produces 'poetic language' or 'text' (in the strong sense of *that* word ...)" (19). Roudiez defines "text" as "a body of words in a state of ferment and *working*, like 'beer when the barm is put in' (Bacon, as quoted in *Webster* 2)" (12).

14. It is interesting to note the religious vocabulary here, which is symptomatic of art's sacrosanct status.

15. Freud makes this distinction, for example, in "Moses, His People, and Monotheistic Religion," in *Moses and Monotheism: Three Essays*, 23:129.

16. See "Dostoevsky and Parricide," 21:175–94. Freud distinguishes three aspects of Dostoevsky's personality: the neurotic, the moralist, and the creative artist. Just as he is beginning to address the last and speak of the success of Dostoevsky's works, Freud abruptly drops the subject and moves on to the study of a work by Stefan Zweig, "Four-and-Twenty Hours in a Woman's Life." Although, as I shall show, this shift can be justified on methodological grounds, one cannot help but see in it the mark of Freud's ambivalent feelings toward Dostoevsky.

Regarding Freud's ambivalence toward Dostoevsky, see also M. Th. Neyraut-Sutterman, "Parricide et épilepsie," *Revue française de psychanalyse* (July 1970).

17. See "On the History of the Psycho-Analytic Movement": "These problems ... are among the most fascinating in the whole application of psychoanalysis" (14:37).

18. See "Repression": "Repressions that have failed will of course have more claim on our interest than any that may have been successful; for the latter will for the most part escape our examination" (14:153).

19. I am transposing onto the realm of art what Freud says about religion.

20. In a letter of September 25, 1913, he tells his wife that he goes to see the *Moses* every day. [Translator's Note: In fact the date of the letter is September 25, 1912; see Jones, *The Life and Work of Sigmund Freud*, 2:365.]

21. Letter to Weiss, April 12, 1933, in *Letters of Sigmund Freud*, ed. Ernst L. Freud, trans. Tania Stern and James Stern (New York: Basic Books, 1960), 416. [Translator's Note: The editor notes that Freud has actually mistaken the date, which was 1912.]

22. Freud himself explains this anonymity in a reply of April 6, 1914, to a letter from Abraham, who thought that readers would nonetheless surely recognize Freud's stamp: "The 'Moses' piece is anonymous on the one hand for fun, and on the other, because I am ashamed of its obviously dilettantish character which, at all events, is difficult to avoid in works for *Imago*, and finally because, even more than usual, I have doubts about the results and published it only because the editors pressed me to do so." [Translator's Note: My translation of Kofman; in *The Life and Work of Sigmund Freud*, 2:366, Jones excerpts and paraphrases similar remarks of Freud's to Abraham, but gives January 6, 1914, as the date of the letter.] Here, again, we cannot stop at Freud's declarations. The reasons he gives seem weak to me—all the more so because he himself showed the importance of the name for the unconscious, and specifically of the proper name. The counterproof is the taboo on proper names so common in primitive societies. For the unconscious, the name represents the person. Certain names must not be uttered, for to do so is to come into contact with the person himself, to risk committing a murder or incest, or to run the risk of death oneself. To bring words into relation with each other is, for the unconscious, a union analogous to the one between the sexes. It is for this reason that Jewish ritual forbade the utterance of the name of the divinity. Instead of "Jehovah," one was supposed to say "Adonai." Even theophoric proper names retained a taboo quality.

Cf. "The Significance of the Vowel Sequences," 12:341; "Group Psychology and the Analysis of the Ego," 18:69–143; and especially *Totem and Taboo*: "Even a civilized adult may be able to infer from certain peculiarities in his own behaviour that he is not so far removed as he may have thought from attributing importance to proper names, and that his own name has become to a very remarkable extent bound up with his personality" (13:56).

See also the "Dream of the Three Fates" in *The Interpretation of Dreams*, 4:207, in which Freud reports that the slightest play on his name was intolerable to him. See as well *Jokes and Their Relation to the Unconscious*, and the way aggressive *Witz* exploits proper names.

23. Anne Berman's French translation deletes "least of all by someone who is himself one of them." I am lifting this remarkable instance of censorship, which dates—and this is no accident—from the 1940s.

24. See *Totem and Taboo*, 13:90.

25. See "Group Psychology and the Analysis of the Ego":

> It was then, perhaps, that some individual, in the exigency of his longing, may have been moved to free himself from the group and take over the father's part. He who did

this was the first epic poet; and the advance was achieved in his imagination. This poet disguised the truth with lies in accordance with his longing. He invented the heroic myth. The hero was a man who by himself had slain the father—the father who still appeared in the myth as a totemic monster. Just as the father had been the boy's first ideal, so in the hero who aspires to the father's place the poet now created the first ego ideal. . . . The myth, then, is the step by which the individual emerges from group psychology. . . . The poet who had taken this step and had in this way set himself free from the group in his imagination, is nevertheless able (as Rank has further observed) to find his way back to it in reality. For he goes and relates to the group his hero's deeds which he has invented. At bottom this hero is no one but himself. Thus he lowers himself to the level of reality, and raises his hearers to the level of imagination. But his hearers understand the poet, and, in virtue of their having the same relation of longing towards the primal father, they can identify themselves with the hero. (18:136–37)

26. In *Totem and Taboo*, Freud shows that all touching, except voluntary touching, is taboo and dangerous. So it is that kings, who are also substitutes for the paternal imago, cured scrofula by mere contact. As we shall see, the artist, too, has a kind of magic power.

27. Freud also vacillates on the status of the hero in tragedy.

28. See *Totem and Taboo*, 13:90. It would be interesting to compare what Freud says here with Auguste Comte's "law of the three states."

29. See "Group Psychology and the Analysis of the Ego":

But it is precisely the *sight* of the chieftain that is dangerous and unbearable for primitive people, just as later that of the Godhead is for mortals. Even Moses had to act as an intermediary between his people and Jehovah, since the people could not support the sight of God; and when he returned from the presence of God his face shone—some of the *mana* had been transferred on to him, just as happens with the intermediary among primitive people. (18:125)

30. The other two wounds were inflicted by Copernicus and Darwin. See "A Difficulty in the Path of Psychoanalysis," 17:139ff.

31. See Derrida's distinction between concept and discourse. [Translator's Note: For example, in "Differance," in *Speech and Phenomena*, trans. David B. Allison (Evanston, IL: Northwestern University Press, 1973), 129–60.]

32. Translator's Note: One translator of Freud, Katherine Jones, makes this remark in *Moses and Monotheism* (New York: Vintage Books, 1967) about the phrase "*instinctual renunciation*," which appears in the *Standard Edition* as well: "I use this phrase (*Triebversicht*) as an abbreviation for 'renouncing the satisfaction of an urge derived from an instinct'" (144).

33. At the end of this chapter, I can protest against all the hasty criticisms leveled against Freud's conception of art, which is deemed to be a prisoner of bourgeois ideology. I am thinking, for example, of a note in Philippe Sollers's article on Lautréamont, "La Science de Lautréamont," in *Logiques* (Paris: Seuil, 1968). Here, I am quoting this text and note 1, which accompanies it:

Freudian theory's inability to approach "literature" arises precisely from this limited orality (the metaphysical space of speech).

For Freud, the "creative writer" is an "exceptional personality" who stirs others without knowing why himself, but with the aim of obtaining "honor, money, and women." He is like "the child at play," play being defined as the opposite of reality; the "poet" creates for himself "an imaginary, unreal world" and thus discloses—but with an "incentive bonus"—the mechanism of fantasy, fantasy which is present in everyone and is revealed by the neurotic. It is true that Freud intends to treat only "the less pretentious writers of romances, novels, and stories who are read all the same by the widest circles of men and women" ("Creative Writers and Daydreaming," 9:143–53). It is hardly necessary to stress the astounding naiveté of such a conception. Yet most analytical researches on the so-called literary text are still oriented toward the signified alone. On this problem, cf. Derrida's "Freud and the Scene of Writing" [Translator's Note: in *Writing and Difference*, trans. Alan Bass (Chicago: University of Chicago Press, 1978), 196–231]. Not a single one of Freud's individualist and petit bourgeois prejudices has been dislodged. (254)

In his text "Freud et la création littéraire," Jean-Louis Baudry makes approximately the same criticisms:

> Freud's conception or, one might say, his "representation" of "literary creation" (which is hinted at in his use of the words "creation," "creator," "work," etc.) thus seems to be dominated and guided by the idea, the ideologeme of representation. This ideologeme, marking Freud's tie to his time and a class, at once impregnates the bourgeoisie's conception of "art" and is diffracted in the texts themselves in such a way that their very textuality is hidden by it. In Freud's wake—but departing from the paths that he had broken elsewhere—the psychoanalytic movement and the thought inspired by it have displayed the same incomprehension, a remarkable impotence with regard to the written word, undoubtedly because of its representatives' attachment to a metaphysics, an ideology, and the interests of a class to which they belong in spite of everything. (*Tel quel* 32 [1968]: 83)

The accusation of naive reading could be turned back against Philippe Sollers. It is regrettable to see pejorative epithets or ready-made categories such as "petit bourgeois" and "individualist" substituted for arguments. Baudry's text appears to be better argued, but does not take account of the totality of the Freudian corpus, nor of the distinction I have introduced between what Freud says and what he does. The reference our two critics make to Derrida therefore requires considerable qualification.

Chapter 2

"Ce n'est pas un métier," translated here as "The Impossible Profession," is the introduction to *Un métier impossible: Lecture de "Constructions en analyse"* (Paris: Galilée, 1983), 9–29.

1. Freud seems to be thinking of Kant here, without citing him: "There are two human inventions which may be considered more difficult than any others—the art of government, and the art of education; and people still contend as to their very meaning" (*Education*, trans. Annette Churton [Ann Arbor: University of Michigan Press, 1960], 12).

2. Translator's Note: As much as possible, the word *end* has been used to translate the multivalent French term *fin*, since *end* most successfully captures the various senses of *fin* as temporal termination, as death or ruin, and as aim or purpose. When Kofman seems to be focusing on just one of these senses of *fin* in the course of developing her argument, more narrow terms have been used for the sake of clarity.

3. "Analysis Terminable and Interminable," in *The Standard Edition of the Complete Psychological Works of Sigmund Freud*, eds. and trans. James Strachey et al., 24 vols. (London: Hogarth Press, 1953–74), 23:219. All further references to Freud's writings will be to the *Standard Edition* and given parenthetically, by volume and page number, in the body of the text.

4. Translator's Note: Kofman attributes this latter phrase to "The Future Prospects of Psychoanalytic Therapy." In fact, it is located in the essay "Observations on Transference-Love (Further Recommendations on the Technique of Psychoanalysis, III)," 12:161.

5. Cf. "Constructions in Analysis," 23:255–69, and my commentary below. [Translator's Note: Kofman's commentary on "Constructions in Analysis" begins in chapter 1 of *Un métier impossible: Lecture de "Constructions en analyse."*]

6. Cf. "Analysis Terminable and Interminable," 23:248.

7. Cf. "Recommendations to Physicians."

8. D. W. Winnicott, "The Capacity to Be Alone," *The Maturational Processes and the Facilitating Environment: Studies in the Theory of Emotional Development* (New York: International Universities Press, 1965), 30, 32.

9. Translator's Note: The French title of this section is *La relève du mysticisme*. *La relève* is the term proposed by Jacques Derrida as an equivalent for the Hegelian *Aufhebung*, an equivalent that would also pronounce the effects of *différance* implicit in the doubled Hegelian operation of surpassing and preserving. The verb *relever* "can combine to relieve, to displace, to elevate, to replace and to promote, in one and the same movement" (Jacques Derrida, *Margins of Philosophy*, trans. Alan Bass [Chicago: University of Chicago Press, 1982], 121). The noun *la relève* can also be translated simply as "relief," as in the guards, athletes, or troops who come to relieve the preceding shift. Although this is not the place to enter the discussion about the relation between *relever* and *aufheben*, it is worth noting how this entire section of Kofman's essay can be read as an implicit contribution to it. In translating *la relève*, I have opted either for *sublation* (the traditional English translation of Hegelian *Aufhebung*) or for other more

specific phrasings, as seemed warranted by the context. In each case, I have used brackets to call attention to the French term.

10. Cf., for example, "On Psychotherapy," 1905, 7:255–68.

11. Translator's Note: Kofman attributes this quotation to the 1914 essay "Remembering, Repeating and Working-Through." In fact, it is found in the essay "Observations on Transference-Love," 12:169.

12. Cf. "Recommendations to Physicians."

13. Cf. "On Beginning the Treatment (Further Recommendations on the Technique of Psychoanalysis, I)," 12:121–44.

14. Cf. "On Beginning the Treatment." In "Thoughts for the Times on War and Death," Freud compares life itself to the game of chess, in which one false move can lose the game, with the further aggravation that in life, we cannot even count on a rematch. In analysis, too, "a lion only springs once," so every misstep proves costly. However, one later reads in "Constructions in Analysis" that in the case of analysis, a "rematch" is possible. The "moves," in particular the wrong ones, can in a way be set right, and error can even turn out to be beneficial. The moves of analysis can be done over, as it were, so that none are truly irreversible.

Although Freud does not take the chess metaphor in this direction, one could ask whether it does not imply a relation of aggression and competition between the two partners in the analytic game and whether analysis is not always a matter of "checkmating" the other. This would mean that there can be no such thing as analysis without tactics, strategy, and calculations made for surprising and trapping.

15. Cf. "On Dreams," 5:636–39.

16. Translator's Note: In both this sentence and in the citation in the last sentence of this paragraph, the word *Taktum* is inserted into the discussion by Kofman. In Freud's original German text, the actual word is *Takt* (literally, tact), which does have a musical connotation: it can mean a rythmic measure, marked, for example, by the movement of a conductor's baton (*Taktstock*). *Taktum* is not a German word and would seem to allude to the Latin *tactus*, which means touch, influence, or feeling, but which has no specifically musical meaning.

Kofman's introduction of a musical connotation into Freud's discussion of medical tact helps to turn the argument toward the specific problem of timing the end of an analysis. It also sets up a transition from the implicit image of the (tactful) analyst as musical conductor to the following discussion of the analyst as a genie or magician who cures patients with a wave of his wand. Finally, it prepares for the discussion in the essay's last section of the psyche as musical instrument and for the concluding allusion there to the analyst's musical tact [*tact musical*].

17. Translator's Note: The insertion of the word *Taktum* into the quotation is Kofman's and is not found in the original German text.

18. Translator's Note: *Flairer* means to smell, sniff, or scent, in the way that hunting dogs track their prey. In this sense, one can smell something fishy [*flairer quelque chose de louche*] about a situation or sniff out danger [*flairer le danger*]. Likewise, the noun *flair* can refer to a dog's sense of smell or to a more general "sixth sense" or intuition, so that one can speak of those individuals with a keen intuition or who have *du flair*.

19. This comparison is found in *Studies on Hysteria*.

20. On the anticipatory science of the poet, cf. Sarah Kofman, *The Childhood of Art: An Interpretation of Freud's Aesthetics*, trans. Winifred Woodhull (New York: Columbia University Press, 1988). Editors' Note: The first chapter of this book appears in the present volume.

21. Cf. "Psychoanalysis and the Establishment of the Facts in Legal Proceedings," 9:97–114.

22. For this entire analysis of Hamlet, cf. "On Psychotherapy."

23. Another of Freud's texts takes up the metaphor of the psychic instrument, this time in relation to the analyst's unconscious. The analyst must be able to make use of his unconscious as though it were an instrument, an ability that implies the work of a prior purification. He must submit himself to an analysis in order to eliminate the resistances that otherwise would prevent his unconscious perceptions from reaching his consciousness. Such resistances introduce a process of selection and deformation more harmful than any deformations resulting from an effort of conscious attention. Any repressed material not eliminated from the analyst's psyche constitutes a blind spot in the faculties of analytic perception. The unconscious has to function like a telephone receiver: "Just as the receiver converts back into soundwaves the electric oscillations in the telephone line which were set up by soundwaves, so the doctor's unconscious is able, from the derivates of the unconscious which are communicated to him, to reconstruct that unconscious, which has determined the patient's free associations" ("Recommendations to Physicians," 12:116).

Chapter 3

"Ça cloche" was originally a lecture delivered at "Les fins de l'homme" [The Ends of Man], the 1980 Cerisy colloquium dedicated to the work of Jacques Derrida. It was first published along with a transcript of a subsequent discussion in the colloquium's proceedings, *Les fins de l'home: A partir du travail de Jacques Derrida*, eds. Philippe Lacoue-Labarthe and Jean-Luc Nancy (Paris: Galilée, 1981), 89–116, and was later republished without the discussion in Kofman's *Lectures de Derrida* (Paris: Galilée, 1984), 115–51. This translation is based on the somewhat modified latter version. A previous English translation by Caren Kaplan has been published under the title " '*Ça cloche*' " in *Continental Philosophy II: Derrida and Deconstruction*, ed. Hugh Silverman (New York: Routledge, 1989), 108–38.

1. Translator's Note: The title "Ça cloche" has been left untranslated, because no single translation could render the multiple associations evoked by the original French. Among other things, *clocher* means to be defective, and *ça cloche* is a colloquial expression meaning "something's not quite right" or "something doesn't quite fit." *Clocher* also means to limp, and Kofman plays on associations with teetering, hobbling, and faltering at several places in the essay. Finally, *cloche* means bell and thus makes reference to the title of Jacques Derrida's *Glas* (literally, knell or death knell). In the latter sense, *ça cloche* could also be translated colloquially as "something doesn't ring true." *Ça* means *it* or *that*, and like *cloche* is a reference to *Glas*, where it designates, among other things, the Hegelian concept of absolute knowledge (*savoir absolu*, abbreviated as *Sa*) and the Freudian Id (*Ça* in French).

2. Derrida, "The Ends of Man," *Margins of Philosophy*, trans. Alan Bass (Chicago: University of Chicago Press, 1982), 116.

3. Derrida, *Glas*, trans. John Leavy, Jr., and Richard Rand (Lincoln: University of Nebraska Press, 1986), 113. [Translator's Note: All subsequent reference to the English translation of *Glas* will be given parenthetically by page number in the body of the essay. In some instances, the qualification "text modified" will be inserted into the parenthesis, to indicate either a modification of Derrida's original text (in accordance with Kofman's informal and imprecise quotations) or a modified translation (in accordance with Kofman's meaning).]

4. Immanuel Kant, *Anthropology from a Pragmatic Point of View*, trans. Mary J. Gregor (The Hague: Martinus Nijhoff, 1974), 169.

5. Kant, *The Conflict of the Faculties*, trans. Gregor (New York: Abaris Books, 1979), 185.

6. On the ends of Freud, cf. Kofman, *The Enigma of Woman: Woman in Freud's Writings*, trans. Catherine Porter (Ithaca: Cornell University Press, 1985). Editors' Note: An excerpt from this book appears in the present volume.

7. Derrida has sufficiently marked this step by step in his "To Speculate—on 'Freud,'" in *The Postcard: From Socrates to Freud and Beyond*, trans. Bass (Chicago: University of Chicago Press, 1987), 257–409.

8. *Three Essays on the Theory of Sexuality*, in *The Standard Edition of the Complete Psychological Works of Sigmund Freud*, eds. and trans. James Strachey et al., 24 vols. (London: Hogarth Press, 1953–74), 7:200. All further references to Freud's writings will be to the *Standard Edition* and given parenthetically, by volume and page number, directly in the text.

9. And following, in doing so, an entirely Nietzschean method.

10. Cf. Derrida, "The Law of Genre," trans. Avital Ronell, in *Acts of Literature*, ed. Derek Attridge (New York: Routledge, 1992), 221–52.

11. Cf. Derrida, "Living On," trans. James Hulbert, in Harold Bloom et al., *Deconstruction and Criticism* (New York: Continuum, 1979), 75–176.

12. Translator's Note: Among other things, *bander* means to bind up, to wrap, or to bandage, as well as to have an erection, and Kofman plays on both associations throughout this section, including in the section's French title, *La double bande*. The words *bander* and *bande* (which means band as well as erection or hard-on) allow for a play on two overlapping figurative strands in Kofman's essay: the figure of bandaging, wrapping, and binding, and the figure of erecting, of having an erection, and of raising up.

13. Cf. Kofman, "Un philosophe 'unheimlich,'" in *Lectures de Derrida*, 11–114.

14. "The *glas* also has to do with a war for the signature, a war to the death—the only one possible—in view of the text, then, that finally, obsequently, remains no one's. *Glas* is written neither from one side nor from the other. . . . [It] strikes between the two. The place of the clapper will, necessarily, have taken up, let us name it *colpos*. In Greek, *colpos* is the mother's [*de la mère*], but also the nurse's, breast [*sein*], as well as the fold [*pli*] of a garment, the trough of the sea [*repli de la mer*] between two waves, the valley pushing down into the breast [*sein*] of the earth" (*Glas*, 71, text modified).

15. Cf. Maurice Blanchot: "all considerations of influence, of causality, of model, of makes and counterfeits are rendered vain—except in that 'plagiarism' [that] . . . could not come after a text given as initial, even to initiate it to itself, but would repeat it as unwritten or would repeat the text about which there is no way to know if it had been produced before, since it is always and in advance reproduced" (*The Step Not Beyond*, trans. Lycette Nelson [Albany: State University of New York Press, 1992], 32–33).

16. Cf. Derrida, "Living On," and Blanchot: "in a single language always to make the double speech heard." *Awaiting Oblivion*, trans. John Gregg (Lincoln: University of Nebraska Press, 1997), 5.

17. Blanchot, *The Last Man*, trans. Lydia Davis (New York: Columbia University Press, 1987), 26.

Chapter 4

"Le mauvais œil" was originally published in *Nietzsche et la scène philosophique* (Paris: Union Général d'Éditions, 1979) and republished in a second edition (Paris: Galilée, 1986), 89–120.

1. Friedrich Nietzsche, *The Will to Power*, trans. Walter Kaufmann and

R. J. Hollingdale (New York: Vintage, 1968), 449. All further references to this work are abbreviated *WP* followed by page number directly in the text.

2. Nietzsche, preface to *The Gay Science*, trans. Kaufmann (New York: Vintage, 1974), 33–35.

3. Cf. *The Birth of Tragedy* §22 and posthumous fragments (Spring 1871). [Translator's Note: Nietzsche's posthumous fragments from 1871 are published in *Nachgelassene Fragmente 1869–1874*, vol. 7 of *Sämtliche Werke: Kritische Studienausgabe*, eds. Giorgio Colli and Mazzino Montinari (Berlin: de Gruyter, 1980).] Cf. also *Twilight of the Idols*, "What I Owe to the Ancients," and *Ecce Homo*, in which the text from *Twilight of the Idols* is cited.

4. Cf. *Poetics*, 1449b.

5. Aristotle, *Politics*, trans. Benjamin Jowett, in *The Basic Works of Aristotle*, ed. Richard McKeon (New York: Random House, 1941), 1315.

6. Cf. Plato, *Laws* 7, 790d–e.

7. "I am not easily touched by pity, and wish I were not at all, although there is nothing I would not do to comfort people in affliction, and indeed I believe that one should do everything even to the point of showing great compassion for their sufferings, for misery makes people so stupid that such pity does them all the good in the world. But I also hold that one should not go beyond showing pity, and take the greatest care not to feel it oneself. This passion should have no place in a noble soul, for it only makes one soft-hearted, and it should be left to the common people, for they never do anything because of reason and have to be moved to action by their emotions." La Rochefoucauld, *Maxims*, trans. Leonard Tancock (London: Penguin, 1959), 189–190.

8. Immanuel Kant, "Metaphysical First Principles of the Doctrine of Virtue" §34, in *The Metaphysics of Morals*, ed. and trans. Mary Gregor (Cambridge: Cambridge University Press, 1996), 205, translation modified.

9. Cf. preface to *The Genealogy of Morals*, §5.

10. Nietzsche, *The Anti-Christ* §7, trans. Hollingdale (New York: Penguin, 1981), 118, translation modified.

11. *The Anti-Christ*, 119, translation modified. Cf. also *Human, All Too Human* I, §50 and §103.

12. Plato, *The Republic* 10, trans. G.M.A. Grube (Indianapolis: Hackett, 1974), 277.

13. Jean-Jacques Rousseau, *Letter to D'Alembert and Writings for the Theater*, trans. Allan Bloom, in vol. 10 of *The Collected Writings of Rousseau*, eds. Roger D. Masters and Christopher Kelly (Lebanon, NH: University Press of New England, 2004), 265–66.

14. Rousseau, *Letter*, 10:268.

15. Rousseau, *Letter*, 10:269.

16. Nietzsche, *Twilight of the Idols*, trans. Hollingdale (New York: Penguin,

1968), 110. All further references to this work are abbreviated *TI* followed by page number directly in the text.

17. According to the title of André Green's book on the Oedipus complex in tragedy, *Un Œil en trop* [One eye too many]. [Translator's Note: This book has been translated into English as *The Tragic Effect: The Oedipus Complex in Tragedy*, trans. Alan Sheridan (Cambridge: Cambridge University Press, 1979).]

18. Nietzsche, *The Birth of Tragedy* §22, trans. Kaufmann (New York: Vintage, 1967), 132–33.

19. Nietzsche, "Nietzsche Contra Wagner," trans. Kaufmann, in *The Portable Nietzsche* (New York: Viking, 1960), 669–671.

20. Arthur Schopenhauer, *The World as Will and Representation*, trans. E.F.J. Payne, 2 vols. (New York: Dover, 1966), 1:197–98. All further references to this work are abbreviated *WW* followed by volume and page number directly in the text.

21. "I mistrust all systematizers and avoid them. The will to a system is a lack of loyalty" (*TI*, 25, translation modified).

22. Cf. *Ecce Homo*.

23. Cf. in particular "Philosophy in the Tragic Age of the Greeks."

24. Nietzsche, "Third Essay," *The Genealogy of Morals* §12, trans. Kaufmann (New York: Vintage, 1989), 119.

25. *The Anti-Christ*, 159.

Chapter 5

This text was originally published in book form as *Le mépris des Juifs: Nietzsche, les Juifs, l'antisémitisme* (Paris: Galilée, 1994). The French edition includes an appendix entitled "Métamorphose de la volonté de puissance du judaïsme au christianisme d'après *L'Antéchrist* de Nietzsche," a reprint of an early essay from 1968.

1. Friedrich Nietzsche, *Daybreak: Thoughts on the Prejudices of Morality*, trans. R. J. Hollingdale, eds. Maudemarie Clark and Brian Leiter (Cambridge: Cambridge University Press, 1997), 125, translation modified. All further references to *Daybreak* are hereafter abbreviated *D* followed by section number and page number directly in the text.

2. See Sarah Kofman, *Socrates: Fictions of a Philosopher*, trans. Catherine Porter (London: Athlone Press, 1998).

3. See Kofman, "Le complot contre la philosophie," in *Nietzsche et la scène philosophique* (Paris: Galilée, 1986).

4. On this topic, see H. F. Peters, *Zarathustra's Sister: The Case of Elisabeth and Friedrich Nietzsche* (New York: Crown, 1977).

5. For the meaning of this term in Nietzsche, see, for example, *Ecce Homo*, "The Case of Wagner" §3, in "Why I Write Such Good Books": "Psychology is

almost the measure of the *cleanliness* or *uncleanliness* of a race" (*Ecce Homo*, ed. and trans. Walter Kaufmann [New York: Vintage, 1989], 322). [Translator's Note: All further references to *Ecce Homo* hereafter are abbreviated *EH* followed by page number directly in the text.] Cf. also Kofman, "L'instinct de propreté," in *Explosion I* (Paris: Galilée, 1992), and "Dicere severum in severum," in *Explosion II* (Paris: Galilée, 1993).

6. On the Germanic *canaille*, see also "Why I Am So Clever" §3.

7. See letter to R. Bonghi, end of December 1888.

8. I have discussed this point at length in "Une généalogie fantastique," in *Explosion I*. [Translator's Note: See "A Fantastical Genealogy: Nietzsche's Family Romance," trans. Deborah Jenson, in *Nietzsche and the Feminine*, ed. Peter J. Burgard (Charlottesville: University of Virginia Press, 1994), 32–52.]

9. Cf. "A Fantastical Genealogy."

10. On the importance of translation, cf. the introduction to *Explosion I*. [Translator's Note: The introduction to *Explosion I* has been translated by Duncan Large as "Explosion I: Of Nietzsche's *Ecce Homo*," *Diacritics* 24 (1994): 51–70.]

11. "In vain do I seek among them for some sign of tact, of *délicatesse* in relation to me. From Jews, yes; never yet from Germans" (*EH*, 324).

12. Posthumous fragment from *Daybreak*. [Translator's Note: To my knowledge, there is no English translation of Nietzsche's posthumous fragments, nor have I located a comprehensive French one. I believe that Kofman translates herself from *Sämtliche Werke: Kritische Studienausgabe*, eds. Giorgio Colli and Mazzino Montinari, 15 vols. (Berlin: de Gruyter, 1980), 9:80. I have simply translated Kofman's French into English, with an eye to the German and will do the same for all other quotations of the posthumous fragments. All subsequent references hereafter are abbreviated *KSA* followed by volume and page number.]

13. See posthumous fragment from *Daybreak*, *KSA*, 9:93.

14. On the difference between Jews and Romans according to Tacitus, cf. posthumous fragment from *Daybreak*: " 'Everything that for us is impious for them is sacred! and vice versa.' This paradox was disseminated by the Christians: 'they are faithful to each other without fail and support each other in distress just as they hate all other men and consider them enemies' " (*KSA*, 9:277).

15. Cf. also: "Offenbach: French music and Voltairean wit: free, capricious with a little sarcastic sneer, but clear, witty even in banality (he doesn't disguise anything) and without the mincing graces of a sickly sensibility and without any excessively Viennese blondness" (*KSA*, 12:344).

16. See posthumous fragment, *KSA*, 12:90. For Nietzsche's tastes in music, cf. Kofman, "Intermezzo," in *Explosion I*. Speaking of Mendelsohn, Nietzsche notes that the Germans deplore the absence in his music of fundamental emo-

tional force, "which is to say, let us note in passing: the gift of the Old Testament Jews." This is from a posthumous fragment of *Human, All Too Human* (*KSA*, 8:545–46).

17. *KSA*, 9:597 and 9:649.

18. In particular, this affinity can be detected in the comic genius characteristic of both peoples. Nietzsche insists on this trait in Wagner, as early as "Richard Wagner in Bayreuth." For discussion of this "genius" as typical of the Jew, see *The Gay Science* §361, "On the Problem of the Actor" (trans. Kaufmann [New York: Vintage, 1974]):

> As for the *Jews*, the people who possess the art of adaptability par excellence, this train of thought suggests immediately that one might see them virtually as a world-historical arrangement for the production of actors, a veritable breeding ground for actors. And it really is high time to ask: What good actor today is *not*—a Jew? The Jew as a born "man of letters," as the true master of the European press, also exercises his power by virtue of his histrionic gifts; for the man of letters is essentially an actor: he plays the "expert," the "specialist." Finally, women . . . [f]alseness with a good conscience; the delight in simulation exploding as a power that pushes aside one's so-called "character," flooding it and at times extinguishing it; the inner craving for a role and mask, for *appearance*; an excess of the capacity for all kinds of adaptations that can no longer be satisfied in the service of the most immediate and narrowest utility—all of this is perhaps not *only* particular to the actor? Such an instinct will have developed most easily in families of the lower classes who had to survive under changing pressures and coercions, in deep dependency, who had to cut their coat according to the cloth, always adapting themselves to new circumstances [cf. the mimicry of animals] . . . until eventually this capacity, accumulated from generation to generation, becomes domineering, unreasonable, and intractable, an instinct that learns to lord it over other instincts, and generates the actor, the "artist" (the zany, the teller of lies, the buffoon, fool, clown at first). (316–17)

[Translator's Note: All further references to *The Gay Science* will be to this translation, hereafter abbreviated *GS* followed by section number and page number.] On the anti-Semitism of Wagner and his affinity with the Jews, see also posthumous fragments from *Human, All Too Human*: "Could Wagner be a Semite? If so, we'd understand his aversion to Jews" (*KSA*, 8:500); "A terrible savagery, heart-broken annihilation, the cry of joy, the sudden extremes, in short the qualities characteristic of Jews; I believe that the Semitic races welcome the Wagnerian art with more comprehension than the Aryan race" (*KSA*, 8:549). Cf. also *KSA*, 8:502.

19. Cf. *Moses and Monotheism*.

20. See posthumous fragment from *The Gay Science*: "From a distance, when one is abroad, one doesn't actually see how black or how white the things of one's native land are in reality, nor does one see how mottled they are: one simplifies the nuances. As an example of a great simplification of nuances, I will cite

this judgment: 'The Germans are at present divided into Jews and Haters of Jews: the latter are overzealous in their wish to be true Germans'" (*KSA*, 9:649). Cf. also *KSA*, 9:597.

21. "This plant [*ressentiment*] blooms best today among anarchists and anti-Semites—where it has always bloomed, in hidden places, like the violet, though with a different odor" (*The Genealogy of Morals*, trans. Kaufmann [New York: Vintage, 1988], 73). By placing the emphasis on "the stink" of anti-Semitism, Nietzsche ironically turns back on it a characteristic that it generally attributes to Jews. Perhaps he is thinking of Schopenhauer, who in *On the Basis of Morality* denounces the theological origin of Kantian ethics and their "Jewish stink."

22. On this anarchist formula, a symptom of the modern democratic prejudices that rise up against hierarchy and against all hierarchical feeling, see *Beyond Good and Evil* §22.

23. On this entire subject, see *Daybreak* §72, "The 'After Death,'" 43. Cf. also posthumous fragment from *Daybreak*: "The resurrection of bodies is a Jewish dogma. Death preserves flesh and blood. The one and the other have a share in eternal life. A martyr expects to find his torn entrails again at the resurrection (2 Macc.)" (*KSA*, 9:141).

24. See *Sache, Leben und Feinde* (Karlsruhe and Leipzig: H. Reuther, 1882), 283.

25. Cf. *The Gay Science* §135. Cf. also *The Gay Science* §136: "The Jews, who feel that they are the chosen people among all the nations because they are the moral genius among the nations . . ." (188).

26. *Daybreak* §68, "The First Christian," 39.

27. Translator's Note: Unless otherwise indicated, the quotations in this paragraph are from *Daybreak* §68, 40. In some cases, the translation has been modified.

28. Hegel, in "The Spirit of Christianity and Its Fate," and Freud, in *Moses and Monotheism*, stress this point appropriately.

29. See posthumous fragment from *Daybreak*: "Fanaticism, a measure taken against self-disgust—which is what Saint Paul has on his conscience? The *sarx* (the flesh) led him to impurity, to idolatry and magic, to hatred and murder, to drunkenness and orgiastic feats. Anything to procure for himself a feeling of power" (*KSA*, 9:144). In another fragment from *Daybreak*, Nietzsche describes Saint Paul as a man avid to dominate, who was able to triumph over his own invincible enemy, the Law, thanks to the death of Christ (*KSA*, 9:142–43).

30. On the necessity for Saint Paul to "disseverate himself" from the flesh (*sarx*) and, as a corollary, his disbelief—which makes him unlike the Jews in this respect—in the resurrection of the flesh, cf. also posthumous fragment from *Daybreak*:

> He took on the sensual and sinful body of man: sinful human flesh. This is *hamartia*: before the appearance of the Law, it dominates the *pneuma anthropou* unbeknownst to

it. After the appearance of the Law, it dominates the *pneuma* to its knowledge and engenders the *parabasis*. But Christ is a *pneuma Théou* holding *hamartia* in chains. By killing the *sarx* of Christ—by annihilating it—God condemned *hamartia* to death; he annihilated it. (*KSA*, 9:142)

In other fragments from *Daybreak*, Nietzsche writes:

Insofar as the death of Christ satisfied the Law one can feel oneself to be emancipated with regard to the Law. The principle hostile to God is annihilated at the moment when the carnal body of Christ perishes: it is not only a wrong that is corrected, it is "wrong" itself that is banished from the world . . . [d]efeat of the *sarx* not thanks to the earthly life of Christ but thanks to his *physical death*. Through baptism what happened to Christ happens also to the baptized. The effect is immediate. Once his *sarx* is dead, he is delivered from sin. Radical extirpation of sin. One is *united with Christ*, with "the spirit that gives life," *ergo* one becomes immortal, and is resurrected as Christ is resurrected [but this is not the resurrection of the flesh, he says further on]. Man filled with the *pneuma* is just and holy. And Luther? The carnal body did not disappear—but it died. (*KSA*, 9:144; 9:142–43)

Saint Paul believes in a celestial corporal matter, which the resurrected body receives (cf. posthumous fragment from *Daybreak*, *KSA*, 9:154–56). Cf. also *KSA* 9:144, 9:158, 9:162–63, and posthumous fragment from *Human, All Too Human*, *KSA*, 8:605.

31. See posthumous fragment from *Daybreak*, *KSA*, 9:163–64. For Nietzsche, immoralism implies that one go initially by way of "morality" the better to surmount it; he shows clearly that it is not possible, as Saint Paul considered that it was, to dispense with the Law.

32. In a posthumous fragment from *Daybreak* (*KSA* 9:142–43), Nietzsche emphasizes that the difference between the Greeks and the Jews (and also the followers of Saint Paul) is that the Greeks—for example, Philon—acknowledge that sin is the conscious abandonment of the *noûs* to the bad dimension of the corporal, whereas for the Jews (and Saint Paul), there is a religious wrong inherent in man without his being aware of it or acquiescing to it. The resistance of the inner man, thanks simply to knowledge of the Law and to the joy he finds in it, does not suffice, but remains totally impotent. Saint Paul did not think, as the Greeks did, that knowledge and appreciation of values sufficed to make the will effective.

33. Nietzsche uses this term in Kant's sense, thereby stressing what the Kantian sublime owes to Judaism.

34. Freud, for his part, shows that children who are their mother's favorite are imbued with a confidence that lasts throughout life and enables them to accomplish great things. He cites Goethe as an example.

35. In *Moses and Monotheism*, Freud will also emphasize the double "Jewish specialty," election and circumcision. He shows clearly that if the first is the

object of envy on the part of all other peoples, the second is on the contrary rejected with contempt and disgust. But he does not insist explicitly on the necessary link between the two, and he sees in circumcision a symbol of castration, not of the Law's insurmountableness.

36. This is the division maintained by Hitler, who wants to liquidate the circumcised people down to the very last man and to make Germany the first among nations, above all others. He aims to steal election without circumcision and without the Law.

37. *The Gay Science* §135, 188. I refer to this text for the following analysis in its entirety.

38. This is a quotation from Goethe in *Dichtung und Wahrheit*. In *The Case of Wagner*, the same quotation is attributed to Benjamin Constant.

39. "In their desire to invent some dignity for sacrilege and to incorporate nobility into it, they invented tragedy—an art form and a pleasure that have remained essentially and profoundly foreign to the Jew, in spite of all his poetic gifts and his sense for the sublime" (*GS* §135, 188).

40. See posthumous fragment from *Daybreak* (*KSA*, 9:330).

41. Though Nietzsche does not do so, one could obviously cite Shylock in *The Merchant of Venice* as an illustration. On this subject, cf. Kofman, "Conversions: *The Merchant of Venice* under the Sign of Saturn," trans. Shaun Whiteside, in *Literary Theory Today*, eds. Peter Collier and Helga Geyer-Ryan (Cambridge: Polity, 1990), 142–66.

42. For the meaning that Nietzsche gives to Jewish "uncleanness," I have explained my view in *Explosion I*, and I refer readers here to that work, especially to the chapter entitled "L'instinct de propreté," (p. 263 and following), and, in "*Ecce Homo* et l'écriture," to the notes on pages 46, 47, and 48. The "uncleanness" of a "race" (the uncleanness characteristic of the Germans and of the Jews, of the Jews and of the Christians [inasmuch as they are themselves Jews, and indeed, as Nietzsche says in *The Anti-Christ* §44, "Jews, always Jews, still Jews, triply Jews"]) is not to be taken as anti-Semites and Nazis mean it, in a literal sense, a racial and racist sense—even if Nietzsche does declare in the same text that "breeding is necessary" for possessing such a genius for lying—and it does not refer, in Nietzsche, to the idea of an impurity of the blood. I have already stressed this: "uncleanliness" is idealism's lack of "psychological" probity; this reevaluated notion designates the lies and denials of the real whereby idealism protects itself, as with a layer of varnish, against instinctive reality, considered "dirty, all too dirty." Nietzsche's texts on this subject are very numerous: for example, in *The Anti-Christ* §46, §47 and following; in *Ecce Homo*, "Why I Write Such Good Books," "The Case of Wagner" §3; "Why I Am a Destiny" §6.

In *Ecce Homo*, "The Case of Wagner" §3, he writes: "Psychology is almost the measure of the *cleanliness* or *uncleanliness* of a race" (322); and in "Why I Am a

Destiny" §6: "Who before me climbed into the caverns from which the poisonous fumes of this type of ideal—slander of the world—are rising? Who even dared to suspect that they are caverns? Who among philosophers was a psychologist at all before me, and not rather the opposite, a 'higher swindler' and 'idealist'? There was no psychology at all before me" (331).

43. See "Second Essay" §14, in the *Genealogy of Morals*.

44. This expression is Bernard de Clairvaux's. It is quoted by Goethe in *Italienische Reise*, in *Werke: Kommentare und Register* (Hamburg: Christian Wegner Verlag, 1948), 11:461.

45. See *The Nicomachean Ethics*.

46. See the first five paragraphs of the "Second Essay" in *The Genealogy of Morals*, and Kofman, "Wagner's Ascetic Ideal According to Nietzsche," trans. David Blacker et al., in *Nietzsche, Genealogy, Morality: Essays on Nietzsche's Genealogy of Morals*, ed. Richard Schacht (Berkeley: University of California Press, 1994), 193–213.

47. Cf. *Daybreak* §38:

> The Jews felt differently about anger from the way we do, and called it holy: thus they saw the gloomy majesty of the man with whom it showed itself associated at an elevation which a European is incapable of imagining; they modeled their angry holy Jehovah on their angry prophets. Measured against these, the great men of wrath among Europeans are as it were creations at second hand. (27)

See also posthumous fragment from *Daybreak*:

> Never has anger been developed to such a somber majesty or to such a wealth of sublime nuances as among the Jews. What is an angry Jupiter next to an angry Jehovah! They transferred that fury from their prophets to their God. Thereby anger became holy and good. And from time to time a ray of paternal kindness pierced through those storm clouds. It is in such a landscape that Christ dreamed of his rainbow, his heavenly ladder from God to man: no place else would that have been possible, if not among the people of the prophets. (*KSA*, 9:403)

Let us note that in "The Moses of Michelangelo," Freud, too, will read divine anger as a projection of the anger of Moses. Let us also remember that Nietzsche ranks Moses among his identificatory figures.

48. On the relation of Judaism and Christianity, especially in *The Anti-Christ*, see Kofman, "Métamorphose de la volonté de puissance du judaïsme au christianisme," *Revue de l'enseigement philosophique* 18 (1968): 15–19, a first sketch, very old now, of current work. [Translator's Note: This essay is the appendix of the French edition of *Le mépris des Juifs*.]

49. See posthumous fragment from *Daybreak* (*KSA*, 9:88–89).

50. "The Jews know scorn for themselves and for man in general" (*KSA*, 9:371). Cf. also posthumous fragment from *Human, All Too Human*: "That the Jews are the worst people on earth agrees perfectly with the fact that it is precisely

among them that the doctrine of the sinfulness and total abjection of man was born and that they later rejected it" (*KSA*, 8:299). And cf. also *Daybreak*: "The Jews, the best haters there have ever been" (§377, 170). In the same text, entitled "What Fantastic Ideals Seem to Indicate," Nietzsche adds that the fanciful principle "love thine enemies" must have been invented by Jews, for "it is where our deficiencies lie that we indulge in our enthusiasms" (170).

Cf. also posthumous fragment from *Daybreak*: "The fury of hatred finally made Jews (Christians) interesting" (*KSA*, 9:271). In a fragment from *Human, All Too Human*, Nietzsche remarks that were Wagner a Semite, one of the proofs of it would be precisely his tyrannical hatred of Jews. "Could Wagner be a Semite? If so, we'd understand his aversion to Jews" (*KSA*, 8:500). Cf. also *KSA*, 8:502.

51. *Twilight of the Idols and The Anti-Christ*, trans. Hollingdale (New York: Penguin, 1968), 135, translation modified.

52. *The Anti-Christ* §42, 155, translation modified.

53. I recall here the text in *Daybreak* §72, "The 'After Death,' " which I analyzed earlier:

> The Jews, *as a people firmly attached to life—like the Greeks and more than the Greeks—* had paid little attention to these ideas: definitive death as the punishment for the sinner, and never to rise again as the severest threat—that was sufficient admonition for these strange (*sonderbaren*) people, who *did not desire to get rid of their bodies* but, with their *refined Egyptianism*, hoped to retain them for all eternity. (A Jewish martyr, whose fate is recorded in the Second Book of the Maccabees, has no thought of renouncing possession of his torn-out intestines, he wants to *have* them at the resurrection—such is the Jewish way!) (43, my emphasis)

54. See *The Twilight of the Idols*, "The Problem of Socrates."

55. Cf. *The Gay Science* §137:

> *Speaking in a parable.*—A Jesus Christ was possible only in a Jewish landscape—I mean one over which the gloomy and sublime thunder cloud of the wrathful Jehovah was brooding continually. Only here was the rare and sudden piercing of the gruesome and perpetual general day-night by a single ray of the sun experienced as if it were a miracle of "love" and the ray of unmerited "grace." Only here could Jesus dream of his rainbow and his ladder to heaven on which God descended to man. Everywhere else good weather and sunshine were considered the rule and everyday occurrences. (189)

Cf. also *The Gay Science* §140: "*Too Jewish*: If God had wished to become an object of love, he should have given up judging and justice first of all; a judge, even a merciful judge, is no object of love. The founder of Christianity was not refined enough in his feelings at this point—being a Jew" (190).

56. See posthumous fragment from *Daybreak*:

> The Jews felt, with the "humblest submission," that everything earthly was weak and ephemeral, compared to the sublime enthroned in heaven. The purely spiritual being

is a Greek invention and *not* a Jewish one. But the celestial world and the terrestrial world, that is Jewish. The Jews do not believe in *unrealizable* ideals, the heavenly Tablets (said to be related to Platonic Ideas) are fully realized; the heavenly wisdom appears adequately in the Law. Very different in Plato. (*KSA*, 9:141)

57. "What is un-Greek in Christianity," §114, in *Human, All Too Human*, trans. Marion Faber, with Stephen Lehmann (Lincoln: University of Nebraska Press, 1986), 85.

58. Posthumous fragment from *Daybreak*, *KSA*, 9:353. For other points of confrontation, cf., for example, the following posthumous fragments from *Daybreak*:

> Hellenistic: accessible to revelation thanks to abstinence from meat and wine. Such conditions are not necessary in the Jewish world. (*KSA*, 9:141)
>
> The impersonal spirituality of God is something Greek. The Jews preserve the god of their people—the god of the covenant, a person. The Christians oscillate but are rather on the side of the Jews. (*KSA*, 9:147)

59. On the notion of the "heart" among the Jews according to Nietzsche, cf. posthumous fragments from *Daybreak*:

> The heart as a Jewish concept is uncomprehending, blinded, hardened, apt to be taken in by flattery. Its functions are the emotions. The Old Testament attributes the properties of the *noûs* to the heart. Only God can see into hearts. The carnal heart: with emotions, the entrails play a role. The heart corresponds more or less to the Schopenhauerian will. (*KSA*, 9:154)
>
> We have been led to understand the essential of Schopenhauer's notion of will through the Jewish concept of the 'heart' as Luther's Bible has made it familiar to us. (*KSA*, 9:172)

It seems that the "heart's genius" (of which Nietzsche speaks in *Ecce Homo*, "Why I Write Such Good Books" §6, referring back to *Beyond Good and Evil*, and which would be the Dionysian genius par excellence) is a parodic reevaluation of the "Jewish heart."

60. See *The Gay Science* §135, a text mobilized earlier in these pages.
61. See posthumous fragment from *Daybreak* (*KSA*, 9:88–89).
62. Cf. also posthumous fragment from *Daybreak*: "Only those who are in anguish claim to be civilized" (*KSA* 9:392).
63. See *The Gay Science* §135.
64. See posthumous fragment from *Daybreak*:

> What the Romans hated in the Jews is not a race but a type of superstition which they found suspicious. What repelled them in the Jews is also what repelled them in the Christians: the absence of divine representations, the so-called spirituality of their religion. A religion which fears the light, a god who cannot let himself be seen—the ritual of eating the body and the blood. Cultivated people thought then that the Jews and the Christians were secretly cannibals. . . . They imagined Jews and Christians

were capable of believing sincerely in absurdities.... In Jesus-Christ it was the Jew that demanded faith above all else... Inadmissible demand for faith. 'Credat Judaeus Apella' (Horace). (*KSA*, 9:75–76)

65. See *Daybreak* §84, "The Philology of Christianity."

66. See in this regard "A Fantastical Genealogy."

67. Nietzsche never ceases to oppose nationalism (the German variety, among others) as well as racial hatred. See, for example, *The Gay Science* §377:

> We do not love humanity; but on the other hand we are not nearly "German" enough, in the sense in which the word "German" is constantly being used nowadays, to advocate nationalism and race hatred and to be able to take pleasure in the national scabies of the heart and blood poisoning that now leads the nations of Europe to delimit and barricade themselves against each other as if it were a matter of quarantine. For that we are too open-minded, too malicious, too spoiled, also too well-informed, too "traveled." (339)

Cf. also posthumous fragment: "I know of nothing more deeply opposed to the *sublime* meaning of my duty than that abominable exasperation of sickly egoism in nations and races, which is trying at the present time to pass itself off as a 'great politics'" (*KSA*, 13:640).

68. Cf. Arnold Toynbee, "Militarism and the Military Virtues," in *War and Civilization*, which cites Saint Paul and his *militia christi*: "We are living, it is true, in the flesh. Our weapons are not of flesh. They have, with God's help, the power to overturn fortresses: we will overturn arguments that rise up like a rampart against the knowledge of God, and taking thought prisoner, we will make it obey Christ." (I thank my student Pierre Tévanian for having provided me with this reference.)

69. Cf. also *The Gay Science* §283, where Nietzsche again announces a "war to come" in the domain of thought: "I welcome all signs that a more virile, warlike age is about to begin, which will restore honor to courage above all. For this age shall prepare the way for one yet higher, and it shall gather the strength that this higher age will require someday—the age that will carry heroism into the search for knowledge and that will *wage wars* for the sake of ideas and their consequences" (228).

Cf. also *Zarathustra*, "Of Wars and Warriors," where Zarathustra speaks of a war for "warriors of knowledge."

70. Draft of a letter to Brandès of December 1888.

71. See Kofman, *Explosion II*, the chapters devoted to *Zarathustra*.

72. Cf. "Homer's Contest," where Nietzsche shows that the Greeks knew that to any one genius a second must always be opposed, so that struggle and rivalry, which engender emulation and an impulse to outdo oneself, may continue. I have developed this point in *Explosion II*, at different junctures. See notably my "Conclusion."

73. See, in particular, the "Third Essay" of the *Genealogy* §14.

74. In the name of an acute sense of cleanliness, which he did not take metaphorically, Hitler, as everyone knows, recommended in *Mein Kampf*—not limiting himself to half-measures—the isolation of the sick, a politics of eugenics, and the complete extermination of certain races judged to be too dirty and impure. Nietzsche answers him in advance by showing that he locates himself on an altogether different plane than that of "blood" and of race, when he affirms ironically that the ascetic ideal was a much more dangerous agent than syphilis in provoking the decadence and the corruption of humankind.

If Nietzsche uses the terms "impure blood," "filth," and "uncleanness," it is always to describe the "canaille" from whom the aristocracy must be separated in a precautionary and prophylactic manner in order to be spared the great "disgust" for man, which could lead it into nihilism or even into contamination by pity, which would prevent it from accomplishing its task: to overcome current "man" for the benefit of the man to come.

See "L'instinct de propreté," *Explosion I*.

75. On this subject, see "Des vendanges à la Claude Lorrain," *Explosion I*.

76. *Human, All Too Human* §224, 144. [Translator's Note: I have retranslated this sentence in accordance with Kofman's version of it.]

77. See *Explosion I* and *Explosion II*.

78. See *Explosion I* and *Explosion II*.

79. See the first five paragraphs of the "Third Essay" and Kofman, "Wagner's Ascetic Ideal According to Nietzsche."

80. My position on this is explained at length in *Explosion I* and in *Explosion II*.

81. Translator's Note: In this citation and in the citations that follow, I have compared Kofman's French translations of Nietzsche's correspondence to the original German texts published in *Briefwechsel: Kritische Gesamtausgabe*, eds. Colli and Montinari (Berlin: de Gruyter, 1975), and, in the few cases where it was possible, to Christopher Middleton's English translations in *Selected Letters of Friedrich Nietzsche*, ed. and trans. Middleton (Chicago: University of Chicago Press, 1969).

82. In a note to volume 2 of *La Correspondance de jeunesse de Nietzsche* (Paris: Gallimard, 1986), Maurice de Gandillac, to whom we owe the fine French translation of the correspondence in the Colli-Montinari edition, also takes note of what he calls a "broadening of the notion of Jewishness" in this letter to Gersdorff (581). He especially emphasizes that Nietzsche's metaphorical use of the epithet "Jew" or "Jewish" is akin to that of a large part of patristic and scholastic literature, where "Jewish" was a metaphor for servile attachment to tangible "signs" and to mere literalness. This does not seem so clear to me in the letter, where "Jewish" is associated above all with plebeian politics. In other later texts,

there are allusions to an attachment to the literal and to tangible signs, though not in a pejorative sense, but rather in order to stress the Jews' attachment to the body, to the flesh, and to life, which for Nietzsche is by no means servile, and which he contrasts with Saint Paul, whom he holds responsible for the denigration of the flesh. I have shown above that the figure of Saint Paul was decoded by Nietzsche as an ambitious epileptic who invents the Christian as a type opposed to the Jew principally in order to settle a personal problem of his own with the Law of the Jews and with the torments of the flesh.

Chapter 6

This text is excerpted from *The Enigma of Woman: Woman in Freud's Writings*, trans. Catherine Porter (Ithaca: Cornell University Press, 1985), a translation of *L'énigme de la femme: La femme dans les textes de Freud* (Paris: Galilée, 1980).

1. Translator's Note: In *New Introductory Lectures on Psycho-Analysis*, in *The Standard Edition of the Complete Psychological Works of Sigmund Freud*, eds. and trans. James Strachey et al., 24 vols. (London: Hogarth Press, 1953–74), 22:112–35 (1933a [1932]; hereafter cited as "Femininity"). Unless otherwise noted, all excerpts from Freud's works are quoted from the *Standard Edition*; the volume number is followed by inclusive page numbers except when the text in question occupies the entire volume. The publication date indicated in the *Standard Edition* is shown in parentheses, with the letter assigned to the corresponding entry in the Freud bibliography (24:47–82); the date of composition (when it differs) appears in brackets. Whenever possible, works identified in a previous note will be cited within the body of the text, identified by short titles as appropriate.

2. Luce Irigaray, *Speculum of the Other Woman*, trans. Gillian C. Gill (Ithaca: Cornell University Press, 1985).

3. Cf. "Female Sexuality," 21:223–43 (1931b; hereafter cited as "Female Sexuality"), in which a comparison is made with Dostoevsky's "knife that cuts both ways" in *The Brothers Karamazov*. (Freud's English translator points out that "the actual simile used by Freud and in the Russian original is 'a stick with two ends'" [230, n. 1]).

4. "Some Psychical Consequences of the Anatomical Distinction Between the Sexes," 19:243–58 (1925j; hereafter cited as "Consequences"), 257–58.

5. "The Dissolution of the Oedipus Complex," 19:173–79 (1924d; hereafter cited as "Dissolution"), 178.

6. The French text here is retranslated directly from the German of *Gesammelte Werke*, 18 vols. (Frankfurt: S. Fischer; London: Imago, 1952–68) (hereafter cited as *GW*), 15:124, as are most of the other excerpts from "Femininity": the existing French translation is quite dreadful, and it omits many passages. Indeed, in my view, it is no accident that most of the criticisms leveled against Freud are

based on this French "translation." Luce Irigaray claims that even the most meticulous translation would not have made much difference to the meaning of this discourse on "femininity" (*Speculum*, 13, n. 1). One may at least have one's doubts about this and wonder why, under the circumstances, Luce Irigaray almost always persists in using a translation that she knows is faulty—unless it is to further "the cause." That of Femininity? Going back to the German text is not a matter of trying to "save" Freud at all costs (I am no more likely to "save" him than she is) but only of manifesting the minimal intellectual honesty that consists in criticizing an author in terms of what he has said rather than what someone has managed to have him say: the critique will be all the stronger for it. When we turn to Freud's text, we note further that it is much more complex, more heterogeneous, than the French translation allows one to imagine. I shall return to this point. [Translator's Note: As indicated in note 1 above, English translations given here follow the *Standard Edition* except as otherwise noted. For a critique of the Strachey translations, however, and an analysis of their impact on Anglo-Saxon psychoanalytic thinking, see Bruno Bettelheim, *Freud and Man's Soul* (New York: Vintage, 1982).]

7. 18:147–72 (1920a; hereafter cited as "Psychogenesis"), 169.

8. 14:69–102 (1914c; hereafter cited as "On Narcissism").

9. See also "Three Essays on the Theory of Sexuality," 7:125–243 (1905d; hereafter cited as "Three Essays"): "For the present, therefore, no further development of the libido theory is possible, except upon speculative lines. It would, however, be sacrificing all that we have gained hitherto from psychoanalytic observation, if we were to follow the example of C. G. Jung and water down the meaning of the concept of libido itself by equating it with psychical instinctual force in general" (218; paragraph added in 1920).

10. Cf., later, the assertion of an unsublatable dualism at the level of the third topic: the opposition between Eros and the death drives.

11. Cf. the end of the lecture: "If you reject this idea as a fantastic and regard my belief in the influence of lack of a penis on the configuration of femininity as an *idée fixe*, I am of course defenceless" (132).

12. 18:3–64 (1920g).

13. See Sarah Kofman, "Freud and Empedocles," in *Freud and Fiction*, trans. Sarah Wykes (Boston: Northeastern University Press, 1991), 21–52.

14. Cf. the beginning of "Female Sexuality."

15. See Kofman, *The Childhood of Art: An Interpretation of Freud's Aesthetics* trans. Winifred Woodhull (New York: Columbia University Press, 1988). Editors' Note: The first chapter of this book appears as Chapter 1 of the present volume.

16. Cf. "Fragment of an Analysis of a Case of Hysteria," 7:3–122 (1905e [1901: the Dora case]; hereafter cited as "Fragment").

17. Translator's Note: The French text reads "coupable (en tous les sens de ce terme)." Kofman thus underlines the fact that *coupable*—guilty, susceptible to being blamed—can also be construed as meaning cuttable, susceptible to being cut (from *couper*, to cut).

18. *Standard Edition*, vols. 4–5 (1900a; hereafter cited as *Dreams*). As vols. 4–5 are paginated consecutively, page references alone are provided here.

19. See also the dream in which Freud sees his son dead, a dream that he interprets as wish fulfillment:

> Deeper analysis at last enabled me to discover what the concealed impulse was which might have found satisfaction in the dreaded accident to my son: it was the envy which is felt for the young by those who have grown old, but which they believe they have completely stifled. And there can be no question that it was precisely the *strength* of the painful emotion which would have arisen if such a misfortune had really happened that caused the emotion to seek out a repressed wish-fulfillment of this kind in order to find some consolation. (*Dreams*, 560)

20. H. Rider Haggard, *She* (London: Longmans, Green, 1887), 78.

21. Sophocles, *Oedipus Rex*, cited in *Dreams*, 263 (Lewis Campbell's translation, lines 1524–25).

22. Concerning *The Interpretation of Dreams* and "Fragment of an Analysis of a Case of Hysteria," Freud wrote in 1925 that they "were suppressed by me—if not for the nine years enjoined by Horace—at all events for four or five years before I allowed them to be published" ("Consequences," 248–49).

23. 13: 211–36 (1914b).

24. Marie Balmary, in *Psychoanalyzing Psychoanalysis: Freud and the Hidden Fault of the Father*, trans. Ned Lukacher (Baltimore: Johns Hopkins University Press, 1982), might well have referred to this dream in support of her thesis.

25. *Dreams*, 453; cf. *Dreams*, 142, n. 1: "Mephistopheles, in Goethe's *Faust*, Part I (Scene 4): 'After all, the best of what you know may not be told to boys.'"

26. 18:67–143 (1921c).

27. Earlier, in *The Childhood of Art*, I stressed the way in which the artistic space that substitutes for the totemic feast, repeating it in different ways, is opened up by this assumption of the collective murder of the father on the part of the first poet-hero. The fact that this assumption was possible only through maternal preference, thus through identification with the mother, has more recently been noted by Philippe Lacoue-Labarthe, particularly in *The Subject of Philosophy*, trans. Thomas Trezise (Minneapolis: University of Minnesota Press, 1993), and in *Portrait de l'artiste, en général* (Paris: Christian Bourgois, 1979).

28. See "Medusa's Head," 18:273–74 (1940c [1922]): "the horrifying decapitated head of Medusa" (*das abgeschnittene, Grauen erweckende Haupt der Meduse* [*GW*, 17:47]).

29. See, for example, "Leonardo de Vinci and a Memory of His Childhood,"

11:59–137 (1910c), chap. 3: "Under the influence of this threat of castration he now sees the notion he has gained of the female genitals in a new light; henceforth he will tremble for his masculinity, but at the same time he will despise the unhappy creatures on whom the cruel punishment has, as he supposes, already fallen" (95). And in a note: "The conclusion strikes me as inescapable that here we may also trace one of the roots of anti-semitism which appears with such elemental force and finds such irrational expression among the nations of the West. Circumcision is unconsciously equated with castration" (95–96, n. 3).

30. Ariadne is a maternal figure for Freud: "The legend of the Labyrinth can be recognized as a representation of anal birth: the twisting paths are the bowels and Ariadne's thread is the umbilical cord" ("Revision of Dream-Theory," 22:7–30, in *New Introductory Lectures on Psycho-Analysis* [1933a (1932)], 25).

31. Cf. "Analysis Terminable and Interminable" (1937c), 23:211–53, esp. 252.

32. Translator's Note: *Human being* is the term used in the *Standard Edition* to translate *menschliches Wesen*. Kofman prefers the French equivalent, *être humain*, to the term *créatures*, found in the 1936 translation by Anne Berman and used by Luce Irigaray.

33. My *The Childhood of Art* demonstrates this with respect to Freudian assertions on art.

34. Cf., for example, "Some Psychical Consequences of the Anatomical Distinction Between the Sexes": "In examining the earliest mental shapes assumed by the sexual life of children we have been in the habit of taking as the subject of our investigations the male child, the little boy. With little girls, so we have supposed, things must be similar, though in some way or other they must nevertheless be different. The point in development at which this difference lay could not be clearly determined" (249).

35. 19:157–70 (1924c), 161. We shall see later on how the privileged status accorded to the masculine model can also be interpreted quite differently. [Editor's Note: Kofman refers here to a section of *The Enigma of Woman* not included in the present excerpt.]

36. Cf. also "On the Sexual Theories of Children" (1908c), 9:207–26: "In consequence of unfavourable circumstances, both of an external and an internal nature, the following observations apply chiefly to the sexual development of one sex only—that is, of males" (211).

37. Cf. "Three Essays on the Theory of Sexuality."

38. "The Infantile Genital Organization," 19:141–45 (1923e), 142.

39. Cf., for example, "The Sexual Theories of Children." This text shows how parents respond evasively to the questions children ask about their own origin, scolding them (especially in the case of girls) for their desire to know, shunting aside their curiosity by giving mythological information. Children then suspect that grown-ups are keeping something forbidden for themselves, and so

they keep their own further research secret. For that reason, too, they are led to produce false theories that will contradict older and more accurate knowledge that has become unconscious and repressed.

40. "'Civilized' Sexual Morality and Modern Nervous Illness," 9:179–204 (1908d), 198–99.

41. On this problem, see Jacques Derrida, *Spurs: Nietzsche's Styles*, trans. Barbara Harlow (Chicago: University of Chicago Press, 1979); and Kofman, "Baubô: Theological Perversion and Fetishism," trans. Tracy B. Strong, in *Nietzsche's New Seas: Explorations in Philosophy, Aesthetics, and Politics*, eds. Michael Allen Gillespie and Strong (Chicago: University of Chicago Press, 1988), 175–202.

42. *The Joyful Wisdom* §71, trans. Thomas Common, in *The Complete Works of Friedrich Nietzsche*, ed. Oscar Levy (London: T. N. Foulis, 1910), 10:104–5.

43. *Studies in Hysteria*, in *Standard Edition*, vol. 2 (1895d [1893–95]; hereafter cited as *Studies*), 283, 293.

44. "'Her mask reveals a hidden sense.' Adapted from Goethe's *Faust*, Part I (Scene 1)" (*Studies*, 139, n. 1).

45. Cf. the passage from "Three Essays" quoted above.

46. "I call a cat a cat" ("Fragment," 48; in French in Freud's text).

47. "To make an omelette, you have to break some eggs" (Ibid., 49; in French in Freud's text).

48. Cf. "Psycho-Analysis and the Establishment of the Facts in Legal Proceedings," 9:99–114 (1906c).

49. "I have often in my own mind compared cathartic psychotherapy with surgical intervention. I have described my treatments as psychotherapeutic operations; and I have brought out their analogy with the opening up of a cavity filled with pus, the scraping out of a carious region, etc." (*Studies*, 305).

50. Freud knew full well, however, that with this comparison he could not help deeply humiliating the female sex:

> The pride taken by women in the appearance of their genitals is quite a special feature of their vanity; and disorders of the genitals which they think calculated to inspire feelings of repugnance or even disgust have an incredible power of humiliating them, of lowering their self-esteem, and of making them irritable, sensitive, and distrustful. An abnormal secretion of the mucous membrane of the vagina is looked upon as a source of disgust. ("Fragment," 84)

51. For the interpretation of the Irma dream, see also Monique Schneider, "Oedipe et la solution-dissolution," *Critique* 384 (1979): 461–76, concerning the reading of this dream proposed by Jacques Lacan, *The Seminar of Jacques Lacan Book II: The Ego in Freud's Theory and in the Technique of Psychoanalysis 1954–55*, ed. Jacques-Alain Miller, trans. Sylvana Tomaselli (New York: Norton, 1991), 163–64; and Conrad Stein, *La mort d'Oedipe: la psychanalyse et sa pratique* (Paris: Denoël-Gonthier, 1977).

52. See, for example, the discussion of fascination in Maurice Blanchot, *The Space of Literature*, trans. Ann Smock (Lincoln: University of Nebraska Press, 1982), 32–33.

53. Cf. "Fetishism," 21:149–57 (1927e).

Chapter 7

This essay was originally published as "L'économie du respect: Kant" in *Le respect des femmes (Kant et Rousseau)* (Paris: Galilée, 1982), 21–56. The translation first appeared in *Social Research* 49 (1982): 383–404.

1. Immanuel Kant, *The Metaphysical Principles of Virtue*, Part II, §25.
2. Ibid. §44.
3. Ibid. §45.
4. Cf. *The Anthropology* ("The Mania of Domination").
5. Ibid. ("The Character of Sex").
6. Kant, *The Metaphysical Principles of Virtue*, Part I, §7 ("On Self-Defilement by Sensual Pleasure").
7. Ibid.
8. Cf. *Conjectures on the Origins of Human History*:

> Man found . . . that sexual excitation, which in animals is founded on a passing and for the most part periodic impulse, was susceptible in himself of being prolonged or even increased by the effects of the imagination which makes its action felt in a greater measure no doubt, but also in a manner more lasting and uniform, as the object of the excitation is removed from the senses; which avoids the satiety that the satisfaction of a purely animal desire would bring.

Cf. also *The Anthropology* ("Pragmatic Consequences").

9. Cf. also *The Metaphysical Principles of Virtue* §46, where tenderness and virtue are submitted to principles and fixed rules, which prevent too great a familiarity and give as limits to reciprocal love the requirements of respect on pain of being constantly menaced by such interruption as that which takes place among men without education. "When a woman shows her love too forcefully, does she not lose by doing so something of the respect of the other, and respect once corrupted is irremediably lost internally, even if the exterior marks which belong to it (the ceremonial) resume their time-honored way."

10. *The Anthropology* ("Pragmatic Consequences").
11. Ibid.
12. "Progress is . . . bound up with the emancipation which exiled man from nature's maternal bosom. . . . In the future the difficulties of life will wrest from him more than once the wish for a paradise, his imaginary creation, where he would be able, in an undisturbed indolence and perpetual peace, to pass his existence in dreaming and frolic. Yet between man and the imaginary abode of

delights stands inexorable reason which irresistibly impels him to develop his faculties and does not permit his return to the state of natural simplicity whence it brought to him. . . . This departure of man from paradise which reason represents as the first abode of the species was only the transition of a purely animal creature from natural simplicity to humanity, from the leading strings of instinct to the government of reason, in a word, from the guardianship of nature to the state of freedom."

13. Sarah Kofman, "Ça cloche," in *Les Fins de l'homme: A partir du travail de Jacques Derrida*, eds. Philippe Lacoue-Labarthe and Jean-Luc Nancy (Paris: Galilée, 1981), 89–116. Editors' Note: An English translation appears as chapter 3 of the present volume.

14. *The Anthropology.*

15. Ibid. ("Extended Remarks").

16. Cf. n. 12.

17. Cf. §27.

18. Cf. Maurice Blanchot, *The Space of Literature*, trans. Ann Smock (Lincoln: University of Nebraska Press, 1982), 32.

19. Cf. *Critique of Practical Reason.*

20. *The Critique of Judgment* §27.

21. Cf. "On the Universal Tendency to Debasement in the Sphere of Love," in vol. 11 of *The Standard Edition of the Complete Psychological Works of Sigmund Freud*, eds. and trans. James Strachey et al. (London: Hogarth Press, 1957), 177–90.

22. "The word *respect* is found where one would expect the word *submission*. Thus in the note (p. 16 R. 20) one reads: '*Respect* simply signifies the subordination of my will in deference to a law. The direct determination produced by the law, accompanied by conscience, is called *respect*.' In what language? What is described to us there is called submission in good German. Yet the word *respect* would not have been so unfittingly used in the place of the word *submission* without some reason, there is some intention behind it, and this intention is evidently the following: it is to conceal the origin of the imperative form and the notion of duty, and how they are born from theological morals" (*Foundations of the Metaphysics of Morals*).

23. Cf. *The Metaphysical Principles of Virtue.*

24. Cf. *The Critique of Judgment* §25.

25. Cf. the long "General Remark Concerning the Explanation of Reflective Aesthetic Judgments."

26. On this text, cf. the analysis of Jacques Derrida in "On a Newly Arisen Apocalyptic Tone in Philosophy," trans. John Leavey, Jr., in *Raising the Tone of Philosophy: Late Essays by Immanuel Kant, Transformative Critique by Jacques Derrida*, ed. Peter Fenves (Baltimore: Johns Hopkins University Press, 1993), 117–71.

27. Introduction to *The Metaphysical Principles of Virtue.*

28. "On a Recently Assumed Aristocratic Tone in Philosophy."

29. Cf. Freud, for example, *New Introductory Lectures on Psycho-Analysis*, on feminine sexuality. Cf. also Kofman, *The Enigma of Woman: Woman in Freud's Writings*, trans. Catherine Porter (Ithaca: Cornell University Press, 1985). Editors' Note: An excerpt of this book appears as chapter 6 of the present volume.

30. Cf. Sándor Ferenczi, "Introjection and Transference":

> I have been able to demonstrate that many cases of impotence of a psychic origin were conditioned by a fearful respect toward women, corresponding to the resistance sometimes opposed to the incestuous object choice (mother or sister) then to an extension of this mode of defence to all women. The passionate pleasure which a certain painter exhibited in the contemplation of things and his consequent choice of career, must have compensated him for all the usual prohibitions of childhood.

This text is quoted by Michael Thevoz in *L'Académisme et ses fantasmes* (Paris: Minuit, 1980). The academic painter Gleyhe is a privileged example of those men for whom the consecration of woman, her placement at a respectful distance, her petrifying idealization, is the reversal of their misogyny.

31. This text was given in a first version in the seminar of Jacques Derrida at the École Normale Superieure, Rue d'Ulm, concerning respect in the works of Kant. It is an extract from a longer work, *Le respect des femmes*.

Chapter 8

"La mélancolie de l'art" was originally published in *Mélancolie de l'art* (Paris: Galilée, 1985), 9–33. A first version of the essay appeared in *Philosopher: Les interrogations contemporaines*, eds. Christian Delacampagne and Robert Maggiori (Paris: Fayard, 1980), 415–27. All English translations are those of the translator unless otherwise noted; citations from existing translations have been silently modified throughout.

1. This is Jacques Derrida's now well-recognized translation of the Hegelian *Aufhebung*.

2. Hegel, "Introduction," *Aesthetics*, trans. T. M. Knox (Oxford: Clarendon, 1979), 38.

3. This term is borrowed from Freud. It is usually translated as *l'inquiétante étrangeté* [the "uncanny"]. See "The 'Uncanny,'" in vol. 17 of *The Standard Edition of the Complete Psychological Works of Sigmund Freud*, eds. and trans. James Strachey et al., 24 vols. (London: Hogarth Press, 1955), 217–56.

4. I refer here to the wonderful text by Georges Bataille on *Manet*, trans. Austryn Wainhouse and James Emmons (New York: Skira, 1955), 103.

5. Jean-Pierre Vernant, "The Representation of the Invisible and the Psychological Category of the Double: The Colossus," *Myth and Thought Among the Greeks* (London: Routledge, 1983), 307.

6. Ibid., 310.

7. See E.T.A. Hoffman's "The Sandman" and Sarah Kofman, "The Double is/and the Devil: The Uncanniness of The Sandman (Der Sandmann)," in *Freud and Fiction*, trans. Sarah Wykes (Boston: Northeastern University Press, 1991), 119–62.

8. Hoffman, *The Life and Opinions of Kater Murr*, trans. Leonard J. Kent and Elizabeth C. Knight (Chicago: University of Chicago Press, 1969), 132. See also Kofman, "Vautour rouge (Le double dans *Les élixirs du diable* d'Hoffmann)," in *Mimésis: Des articulations*, eds. Sylviane Agacinski et al. (Paris: Aubier-Flammarion, 1975), 95–163.

9. Maurice Blanchot, *L'Espace littéraire* (Paris: Gallimard, 1955), 23.

10. Ibid., 268–71. Quoted by Philippe Lacoue-Labarthe in *Portrait de l'artiste, en général* (Paris: Christian Bourgois, 1979), 38–39.

11. Here I refer the reader to the work of Lacoue-Labarthe, in particular to the work just cited and to "Typologie," in *Mimésis: Des articulations*.

12. See Kofman, *Nietzsche et la scène philosophique* (Paris: Union Générale d'Éditions, 1979).

13. Exhibited at the Salon of 1763, the painting is now part of the Wallace Collection in London.

14. Denis Diderot, *Oeuvres esthétiques* (Paris: Garnier, 1965), 536. I am indebted here to Jean-Jacques Rosat and to Derrida for their readings of this text, which was discussed in a seminar on art at the École Normale Superieure, Rue d'Ulm. With respect to the "work of mourning" in art, I would also refer the reader to *The Truth in Painting*, trans. Geoff Bennington and Ian McLeod (Chicago: University of Chicago Press, 1987), the text by Derrida to which I am constantly referring here. Indeed, this is in order to "restore" [*restituer*] the thing to its rightful owner.

15. See Freud, "Mourning and Melancholia," *Standard Edition*, 14:237–58.

16. Freud, *The Interpretation of Dreams*, in *Standard Edition*, 4:312.

17. Hegel, *Aesthetics*, 42.

18. Are reason and knowledge capable of combating the magic of art and the paradoxical pathos it elicits? Plato never stops declaring as much, wishing it. But he nonetheless shows that even the rational man who is capable of mastering his passions in real life engages in mad conduct at the theater, cries or laughs out loud in public. (See *Republic* 10, 603c and following.) He recognizes in this respect the overwhelming power of the simulacrum, its terrifying efficacy for the philosopher who cannot—for this is his dream—reinscribe what belongs to an entirely different order in the trial of truth, and simply says that the simulacrum is removed from truth by "three degrees" (*tòn tõu tritou apô tès phuseôs*; *Republic* 10, 597e), even by an "infinity" of degrees (*Toû de alêthous porro panu aphestôta*; *Republic* 10, 605c).

19. Diderot, *Oeuvres esthétiques*, 483–85.

20. See Plato's *Theaetetus*, in which a Thracian servant laughs at Thales for falling into a well while looking at the stars. See also Kofman, *Comment s'en sortir?* (Paris: Galilée, 1983).

21. Michel Foucault, *This Is Not a Pipe*, trans. James Harkness (Berkeley and Los Angeles: University of California Press, 1983), 44–45.

22. See "Cartouches," Derrida's reading of the series of coffins by Titus-Carmel, in *The Truth in Painting*.

23. See Kofman, *The Childhood of Art: An Interpretation of Freud's Aesthetics*, trans. Winifred Woodhull (New York: Columbia University Press, 1988). Editors' Note: The first chapter of this book appears in the present volume.

Chapter 9

"La ressemblance des portraits: l'imitation selon Diderot" was originally published in *Mélancolie de l'art* (Paris: Galilée, 1985), 37–70. A first version of the essay appeared in *L'esprit créateur* 24 (1984): 13–32. All English translations are those of the translator unless otherwise noted; citations from existing translations have been silently modified throughout.

1. Denis Diderot's *Oeuvres esthétiques* (Paris: Garnier, 1965), 483. All references to the *Oeuvres esthétiques* will be given parenthetically as *OE* followed by page number directly in the body of the text.

2. See the *Republic* 10, 598c. Zeuxis's birds are a philosophical commonplace meant to illustrate the power of illusion of the work of art. In the introduction to his *Aesthetics*, Hegel will add Büttner's ape in an effort to rebuke and ridicule, in this appeal to animality, the proponents of a rigorous imitation of nature. On the motif of artistic illusion in the eighteenth century more generally, see Marian Hobson, *The Object of Art: The Theory of Illusion in Eighteenth-Century France* (Cambridge: Cambridge University Press, 1982).

3. See Diderot, "De la poésie dramatique," *OE*, 284.

4. On the *Unheimlichkeit* of the work of art, see Sarah Kofman, "La mélancolie de l'art," in *Mélancolie de l'art* (Paris: Galilée, 1985), 9–33. [Editor's Note: This essay appears as chapter 8 of the present volume.]

5. See *Physics* 2, 194a–b and 199a–b. The distinction between these two kinds of mimesis has been very well analyzed by Philippe Lacoue-Labarthe in "Diderot: Paradox and Mimesis," trans. Jane Popp, in *Typography: Mimesis, Philosophy, Politics*, ed. Christopher Fynsk (Cambridge: Harvard University Press, 1989), 248–66.

6. See Hobson, *The Object of Art*.

7. For this description of the genius, see the *Encyclopedia* article "Genius."

8. Hegel will reproach painting for the same reason.

9. Leonardo da Vinci, *La peinture*, ed. and trans. André Chastel, in collaboration with Robert Klein (Paris: Hermann, 1964), 185.

10. See Hegel's introduction to the *Aesthetics*, trans. T. M. Knox (Oxford: Clarendon Press, 1979), 43.

11. See, for example, *Beyond Good and Evil*, aphorism 5.

12. "The itinerary around the table at the house of the wealthy Bertin, where the Abbé de la Porte, the editor of *L'Observateur littéraire*, is stationed at the least desirable end, will be described in almost the same terms in *Rameau's Nephew*" (editorial note from the Garnier edition, *OE*, 507 n. 1).

13. Painting men as they should be is one of the three ways of imitating that Aristotle discusses in his *Poetics*. For the general opposition between the genres of the still life and the portrait in the eighteenth century, see Hobson, *The Object of Art*. See in particular La Font de Saint-Yenne, *Sentiments sur quelques ouvrages de peinture, sculpture et gravure, écrits à un particulier en province* (Geneva: Slatkine Reprints, 1970 [1754]).

> I admire all those imitations of nature carried to a certain degree of virtuosity and illusion . . . the representation of the simplest and most familiar human actions. . . . All these objects, when presented with artifice and picturesque magic, will necessarily please our gaze and find a place in our collections. But the same is not true of history paintings. . . . Besides entertaining us with pleasure and illusion, painting should still be a study of morals. (74–75)

14. See also the *Encyclopedia* article entitled "Encyclopedia": "Those who came after the first inventors were for the most part nothing but their slaves."

15. For a comparison with Nietzsche, see aphorism 7, "Reconnaissance Raids of an Untimely Man," in *Twilight of the Idols*, trans. Duncan Large (New York: Oxford University Press, 1998), 46.

16. See Lacoue-Labarthe, "Diderot: Paradox and Mimesis."

17. See the *Paradox* and "L'éloge de Térence."

18. "Naïveté is a great resemblance between the imitation and the thing, accompanied by a great facility of execution. It is water taken from the brook and splashed on the canvas" (*OE*, 825).

19. "There would be no manner, neither in drawing nor in color, were we to imitate nature scrupulously. Manner comes from the master, from the Academy, from the School, even from antiquity" (*OE*, 673).

20. See Diderot, "Essais sur la peinture," *OE*, 674.

21. On the role of posterity in the *Encyclopedia*, see James Creech's excellent article, " 'Chasing After Advances': Diderot's Article 'Encyclopedia,' " in *Yale French Studies* 63 (1982): 183–97.

22. See Aristotle, *Rhetoric* I and *On the Parts of Animals* I, 5.

23. On "La raie dépouillée [*The Gutted Skate*]," see Jean-Claude Bonne et al., "La raie," *Critique* 315–316 (1973): 679–90.

24. For Nietzsche, in addition to the preface to the second edition of *The Gay Science*, see posthumous fragment from *The Gay Science*:

What is aesthetically offensive inside the man without skin are bloody masses, excrement-filled intestines, entrails, all those monsters that suck and breathe and pump, formless or ugly or grotesque, and that smell terrible moreover. Let us therefore *abstract from all that!* That part of all this that nonetheless appears on the outside elicits shame (excrement, urine, saliva, sperm).... This body *veiled* by skin that seems to be ashamed!... Man, to the extent that he is not physiognomy, structure, is an object of repugnance to himself; he does everything he can not to think about it. (*Nachgelassene Fragmente 1880–1882*, vol. 9 of *Sämtliche Werke: Kritische Studienausgabe*, eds. Giorgio Colli and Mazzino Montinari [Berlin: de Gruyter, 1980], 460)

25. Freud, "On Transience," in vol. 14 of *The Standard Edition of the Complete Psychological Works of Sigmund Freud*, eds. and trans. James Strachey et al. (London: Hogarth Press, 1957), 303–8.

26. Ibid., 14:305.

Chapter 10

This essay was originally published in *La part de l'oeil* 11 (1995): 41–46.

Note from the editors of *La part de l'oeil*: "Sarah Kofman kept her word, as she always did. She had agreed to contribute to this issue of *La part de l'oeil* and had suggested analyzing the relationship between the body and the book in a painting by Rembrandt. Her friend Alexandre Kyritsos was kind enough to look for the manuscript and send it to us. Here it is, then, just as Sarah left it to us. From his conversations with Sarah Kofman, Alexandre Kyritsos relates a few details that deserve to be recalled here because they are part of the history of this text and thus part of its reading and interpretation: 'Sarah emphasized that this pairing of the cadaver and the book, both of them open and offered to the gazes of the doctors surrounded by objects situated in a play of light, offered, quite beyond the conventions of the genre, a representation of the scientific method. The book, a sum and source of knowledge, at once confronted and supported by the test of materiality in experimentation, gives a new impetus to the discourse of science, its texts and its commentaries.'"

The translator would like to thank the College of Liberal Arts and Sciences at DePaul University for its generous support of this work through a Faculty Research and Development Grant.

1. Claude Frontisi, *Klee, l'anatomie d'Aphrodite: le polyptique démembré* (Paris: Adam Biro, 1995): "The term anatomy can refer to several different things. First, dissection: one thus speaks of an anatomy room, of an amphitheater, of anatomical drawings, or of artistic anatomy. By metonymy, the term designates nudity (to show one's anatomy) and even the sex (one's private anatomy). Finally, beginning in the seventeenth century, the word is used in a figurative sense to refer to analytical discourse (the anatomy of a work)" (46–47).

2. See Friedrich Nietzsche's *The Gay Science*, posthumous fragment:

> What is aesthetically offensive inside a man with no skin, bloody masses, intestines full of excrement, innards, all these monsters that suck and swell and pump, shapeless, ugly, or grotesque, and moreover awful to smell.... This body hidden beneath the skin seems to be ashamed!... When he is no longer a physiognomy or structure, man is but an object of repugnance for himself, and man does his utmost not to think of this. (*Nachgelassene Fragmente 1880–1882*, vol. 9 of *Sämtliche Werke: Kritische Studienausgabe*, eds. Giorgio Colli and Mazzino Montinari [Berlin: de Gruyter, 1980], 460)

One should also read the chilling story by Georg Heym, "The Autopsy," in *The Thief and Other Stories*, trans. Susan Bennett (London: Libris, 1994), 65–67. After emphasizing the contrast between the dead person lying on a table, who has begun to give off putrefying odors and is turning completely white, and the doctors who come in ("friendly men in white coats with duelling scars and golden pince-nez"), the story goes on to describe the dissection or autopsy as a veritable butchery, sparing the reader nothing, making it difficult, in fact, to go on reading:

> They approached the dead man, and looked him over with interest, talking in scientific terms. They took their dissecting equipment out of the white cupboards, white boxes full of hammers, bone-saws with strong teeth, files, gruesome batteries of forceps, small sets of giant needles like crooked vultures' beaks forever screaming for flesh. They began their ghastly handiwork, looking like fearsome torturers, with blood streaming over their hands. They delved ever deeper into the cold corpse, and brought forth its inside like white cooks disemboweling a goose. The intestines wound around their arms, greenish-yellow snakes, and the excrement dripped onto their coats, a warm, foul fluid. They punctured the bladder; the cold urine shimmered inside like yellow wine. They poured it into large bowls; it had a sharp, biting stench like ammonia.... His skin began to fall apart. His belly grew as white as that of an eel under the greedy fingers of the doctors who dipped their arms elbow-deep in his wet flesh. (65–66)

A text like this forces us to see the intolerable and so breaks with classical aesthetics and their pharmaceutical function, with Apollonian art.

3. The tradition was that the doctors would be painted at the same time as their students so that the painting would depict the home of the corporation. In 1603, Pieter Isaacz painted the first *Anatomy Lesson*, four years after Aert Pietersz had inaugurated the practice of painting the portraits of directors and their associations. After the *Lesson of Doctor Van der Meire*, there came *The Anatomy Lesson* painted by Miereveld of Delft (1667), the *Lesson of Doctor Sebastiaen Egbertsz de Vry* by Thomas De Keyser, and, of course, the two *Anatomy Lessons* by Rembrandt, painted some twenty years apart. [Translator's Note: See Rembrandt's *The Anatomy Lesson of Dr. Joan Deijman* (1656), at the Rijksmuseum in Amsterdam.] Cf. Marcel Brion *L'âge d'or de la peinture* (Brussels: Meddens, 1964), 99ff.

4. The ruff collars here seem to play the same role that haloes around the heads of saints once did.

5. According to the account, the cadaver is that of a recently hanged man, identified by name and nickname as Abrian Adriaenz, called the kid, *Het Kind*.

6. Paul Claudel, *La peinture hollandaise* (Paris: Gallimard, 1967).

7. These attentive men, bent on scientific knowledge, are contemporaries of Van Helmont, who was teaching at that time in Brussels and had asked his confreres to give up the two pillars of all science, theology and logic, and to replace them with observation and deduction through the manipulation of natural objects rather than through discourse.

8. See the section of the "Salon of 1763" devoted to Chardin. [Translator's Note: Cf. Denis Diderot, *Selected Writings*, trans. Derek Coltman (New York: MacMillan, 1966), 150.]

9. *Pensées détachées sur la peinture*, in *Oeuvres esthétiques* (Paris: Garnier, 1994), 741–840.

10. *Diderot on Art*, ed. and trans. John Goodman, 2 vols. (New Haven: Yale University Press, 1995):

> [I]s it not to be feared that this *écorché* [flayed figure] might remain in the imagination forever; that this might encourage the artist to become enamored of his knowledge and show it off; that his vision might be corrupted, precluding attentive scrutiny of surfaces; that despite the presence of skin and fat, he might come to perceive nothing but muscles, their beginnings, attachments, and insertions; that he might overemphasize them, that he might become hard and dry, and that I might encounter this accursed *écorché* even in his figures of women? Since only the exterior is exposed to view, I'd prefer to be trained to see it fully, and spared treacherous knowledge I'd only have to forget. (1:193)

11. Cf. Frontisi, who shows how the painter Fontana, on the contrary, exhibits in the painting itself its material infrastructure, its "anatomy" (*Klee, l'anatomie d'Aphrodite*, 57).

12. Maurice Blanchot, *The Space of Literature*, trans. Ann Smock (Lincoln: University of Nebraska Press, 1982), 32–33.

Chapter 11

This text was originally published as "Shoah (ou la Dis-Grâce)" in *Les Nouveaux Cahiers* 95 (1988–89): 67.

1. Translator's Note: Translation modified from *The Philosophy of Hegel*, ed. Carl J. Friedrich (New York: Random House, 1953), 302.

2. Translator's Note: Robert Faurisson is perhaps the best known of the French "revisionists."

Chapter 12

"Damned Food" was originally published as "Sacrée nourriture" in *Manger*, eds. Christian Besson and Catherine Weinzaepflen (Liège: Yellow Now, 1980), 71–74. "Tomb for a Proper Name" was originally published as "Tombeau pour un nom propre" in *Première Livraison* 5 (1976). "Post-scriptum—1992" was originally published, along with a reprint of "Tombeau pour un nom propre," in *La part de l'oeil* 9 (1993): 84. " 'My Life' and Psychoanalysis" was originally published as " 'Ma vie' et la psychanalyse" in *Première Livraison* 4 (1976). "Nightmare: At the Margins of Medieval Studies" was originally published as "Cauchemar: En marge des études médiévales" in *Comment s'en sortir?* (Paris: Galilée, 1983), 101–12. The three translations by Frances Bartkowski ("Damned Food," "Tomb for a Proper Name," and "Nightmare") were first published under the heading "Autobiographical Writings" in *SubStance* 49 (1986): 6–13.

1. Translator's Note: *Chat-rat* verges on the French pronunciation of the name Sarah.

2. Bernard Cerquiglini, *La parole médiévale* (Paris: Minuit, 1981). [Translator's Note: The first French phrase is spoken to the hero in the *Song of Roland*, the second by the heroine Enide in Chrétien de Troyes, *Erec and Enide*.]

3. And hence its literary resonance. Cerquiglini's whole study begins with the inscription of *mar* in literary texts.

4. Jaques Bril, *Lilith ou la mère obscure* (Paris: Payot, 1981).

5. A distinction that Freud takes up from Charcot in *Studies on Hysteria*.

Contributors

Sarah Kofman (1934–1994) taught philosophy at the Université Paris I and was coeditor, with Jacques Derrida, Philippe Lacoue-Labarthe, and Jean-Luc Nancy, of the series "La philosophie en effet," put out by Éditions Galilée. She is the author of over twenty books, among them *Nietzsche and Metaphor* (1993), published by Stanford University Press.

Thomas Albrecht is an Assistant Professor of English at Tulane University. He is the author of a forthcoming book on the figure of Medusa in nineteenth-century literature and aesthetics, to be published by SUNY Press.

Georgia Albert is a lawyer based in Washington, DC. She is the translator of Giorgio Agamben's *The Man Without Content* (Stanford University Press, 1999) and Hans-Jost Frey's *Interruptions* (SUNY Press, 1996).

Jacques Derrida (1930–2004) was Director of Studies at the École des Hautes Études en Sciences Sociales and Professor of Humanities at the University of California, Irvine. He is the author, among many books, of *Paper Machine* (2005), *Rogues: Two Essays on Reason* (2005), *On Touching—Jean-Luc Nancy* (2005), and *H. C. for Life, That Is to Say . . .* (2006), all published by Stanford University Press.

Elizabeth Rottenberg is an Assistant Professor of Philosophy at DePaul University. She is the author of *Inheriting the Future: Legacies of Kant, Freud, and Flaubert* (Stanford University Press, 2005) and has translated works by Jacques Derrida, Maurice Blanchot, and Jean-François Lyotard for Stanford University Press.

MERIDIAN

Crossing Aesthetics

Susannah Young-ah Gottlieb, ed. *Hannah Arendt: Reflections on Literature and Culture*

Alan Bass, *Interpretation and Difference: The Strangeness of Care*

Jacques Derrida, *H.C. for Life, That Is to Say . . .*

Ernst Bloch, *Traces*

Elizabeth Rottenberg, *Inheriting the Future: Legacies of Kant, Freud, and Flaubert*

David Michael Kleinberg-Levin, *Gestures of Ethical Life*

Jacques Derrida, *On Touching—Jean-Luc Nancy*

Jacques Derrida, *Rogues: Two Essays on Reason*

Peggy Kamuf, *Book of Addresses*

Giorgio Agamben, *The Time That Remains: A Commentary on the Letter to the Romans*

Jean-Luc Nancy, *Multiple Arts: The Muses II*

Alain Badiou, *Handbook of Inaesthetics*

Jacques Derrida, *Eyes of the University: Right to Philosophy 2*

Maurice Blanchot, *Lautréamont and Sade*

Giorgio Agamben, *The Open: Man and Animal*

Jean Genet, *The Declared Enemy*

Shoshana Felman, *Writing and Madness: (Literature/Philosophy/Psychoanalysis)*

Jean Genet, *Fragments of the Artwork*

Shoshana Felman, *The Scandal of the Speaking Body: Don Juan with J. L. Austin, or Seduction in Two Languages*

Peter Szondi, *Celan Studies*

Neil Hertz, *George Eliot's Pulse*

Maurice Blanchot, *The Book to Come*

Susannah Young-ah Gottlieb, *Regions of Sorrow: Anxiety and Messianism in Hannah Arendt and W. H. Auden*

Jacques Derrida, *Without Alibi*, edited by Peggy Kamuf

Cornelius Castoriadis, *On Plato's 'Statesman'*

Jacques Derrida, *Who's Afraid of Philosophy? Right to Philosophy 1*

Peter Szondi, *An Essay on the Tragic*

Peter Fenves, *Arresting Language: From Leibniz to Benjamin*

Jill Robbins, ed. *Is It Righteous to Be?: Interviews with Emmanuel Levinas*

Louis Marin, *Of Representation*

J. Hillis Miller, *Speech Acts in Literature*

Maurice Blanchot, *Faux pas*

Jean-Luc Nancy, *Being Singular Plural*

Maurice Blanchot / Jacques Derrida, *The Instant of My Death / Demeure: Fiction and Testimony*

Niklas Luhmann, *Art as a Social System*

Emmanual Levinas, *God, Death, and Time*

Ernst Bloch, *The Spirit of Utopia*

Giorgio Agamben, *Potentialities: Collected Essays in Philosophy*

Ellen S. Burt, *Poetry's Appeal: French Nineteenth-Century Lyric and the Political Space*

Jacques Derrida, *Adieu to Emmanuel Levinas*

Werner Hamacher, *Premises: Essays on Philosophy and Literature from Kant to Celan*

Aris Fioretos, *The Gray Book*

Deborah Esch, *In the Event: Reading Journalism, Reading Theory*

Winfried Menninghaus, *In Praise of Nonsense: Kant and Bluebeard*

Giorgio Agamben, *The Man Without Content*

Giorgio Agamben, *The End of the Poem: Studies in Poetics*

Theodor W. Adorno, *Sound Figures*

Louis Marin, *Sublime Poussin*

Philippe Lacoue-Labarthe, *Poetry as Experience*

Ernst Bloch, *Literary Essays*

Jacques Derrida, *Resistances of Psychoanalysis*

Marc Froment-Meurice, *That Is to Say: Heidegger's Poetics*

Francis Ponge, *Soap*

Philippe Lacoue-Labarthe, *Typography: Mimesis, Philosophy, Politics*

Giorgio Agamben, *Homo Sacer: Sovereign Power and Bare Life*

Emmanuel Levinas, *Of God Who Comes to Mind*

Bernard Stiegler, *Technics and Time, 1: The Fault of Epimetheus*

Werner Hamacher, *Pleroma—Reading in Hegel*

Serge Leclaire, *Psychoanalyzing: On the Order of the Unconscious and the Practice of the Letter*

Serge Leclaire, *A Child Is Being Killed: On Primary Narcissism and the Death Drive*

Sigmund Freud, *Writings on Art and Literature*

Cornelius Castoriadis, *World in Fragments: Writings on Politics, Society, Psychoanalysis, and the Imagination*

Thomas Keenan, *Fables of Responsibility: Aberrations and Predicaments in Ethics and Politics*

Emmanuel Levinas, *Proper Names*

Alexander García Düttmann, *At Odds with AIDS: Thinking and Talking About a Virus*

Maurice Blanchot, *Friendship*

Jean-Luc Nancy, *The Muses*

Massimo Cacciari, *Posthumous People: Vienna at the Turning Point*

David E. Wellbery, *The Specular Moment: Goethe's Early Lyric and the Beginnings of Romanticism*

Edmond Jabès, *The Little Book of Unsuspected Subversion*

Hans-Jost Frey, *Studies in Poetic Discourse: Mallarmé, Baudelaire, Rimbaud, Hölderlin*

Pierre Bourdieu, *The Rules of Art: Genesis and Structure of the Literary Field*

Nicolas Abraham, *Rhythms: On the Work, Translation, and Psychoanalysis*

Jacques Derrida, *On the Name*

David Wills, *Prosthesis*

Maurice Blanchot, *The Work of Fire*

Jacques Derrida, *Points . . . : Interviews, 1974–1994*

J. Hillis Miller, *Topographies*

Philippe Lacoue-Labarthe, *Musica Ficta (Figures of Wagner)*

Jacques Derrida, *Aporias*

Emmanuel Levinas, *Outside the Subject*

Jean-François Lyotard, *Lessons on the Analytic of the Sublime*

Peter Fenves, *"Chatter": Language and History in Kierkegaard*

Jean-Luc Nancy, *The Experience of Freedom*

Jean-Joseph Goux, *Oedipus, Philosopher*

Haun Saussy, *The Problem of a Chinese Aesthetic*

Jean-Luc Nancy, *The Birth to Presence*

The authorized representative in the EU for product safety and compliance is:
Mare Nostrum Group
B.V Doelen 72
4831 GR Breda
The Netherlands

www.ingramcontent.com/pod-product-compliance
Lightning Source LLC
Chambersburg PA
CBHW021803220426
43662CB00006B/163